A Short History of
the Yugoslav Peoples

For my wife, Elizabeth

A Short History of the Yugoslav Peoples

FRED SINGLETON

PUBLISHED BY THE PRESS SYNDICATE OF THE UNIVERSITY OF CAMBRIDGE
The Pitt Building, Trumpington Street, Cambridge, United Kingdom

CAMBRIDGE UNIVERSITY PRESS
The Edinburgh Building, Cambridge CB2 2RU, UK   www.cup.cam.ac.uk
40 West 20th Street, New York, NY 10011-4211, USA   www.cup.org
10 Stamford Road, Oakleigh, Melbourne 3166, Australia
Ruiz de Alarcón 13, 28014 Madrid, Spain

First published 1985
Reprinted 1988, 1989, 1991, 1993
1994, 1995, 1996, 1999

Printed in the United States of America

British Library Cataloging in Publication data
Singleton, Fred
A short history of the Yugoslav peoples.
1. Yugoslavia – History
I. Title
949.7   DR1246

Library of Congress Catalog Card number: 84–17625

ISBN 0 521 25478 7 hardback
ISBN 0 521 27485 0 paperback

Contents

Contents

Tables

Maps

Preface

Any author who is either bold enough or foolhardy enough to attempt to write a short history of Yugoslavia must be aware from the outset that he or she is taking on an almost impossible task. First, there is the problem of the title. Yugoslavia did not exist until 1918, except as an idea in the minds of liberal-minded scholars and politicians amongst the South Slav peoples during the nineteenth century. However, although the term Yugoslav (or South Slav) peoples is the closest approximation to the subject matter of this book, linguists might point out that the Bulgarians also speak a South Slav language. What I have attempted to do is to trace the history of the South Slavs who came together at the end of the First World War to form a Yugoslav state, and who now live in the Socialist Federal Republic of Yugoslavia.

The long centuries of separation have produced cultural differences which make modern Yugoslavia a fascinating field of study for the scholar who is not directly involved in the life of the country, and provide an exciting and almost unmanageable challenge for those who attempt to govern it. The peoples of Yugoslavia cannot forget their own historical roots, and folk memories of their colourful past play an important part in shaping their attitudes to current problems. It is impossible to understand contemporary Yugoslavia without some knowledge of the historical experiences which are so deeply embedded in the consciousness of the people.

There is no such thing as objective history, and there is no consensus amongst Yugoslavs as to the interpretation of the events which have brought them to their present situation. This gives rise to the second problem which a student of Yugoslav history must face. Every sentence which one writes will be examined in fine detail, in order to discover whether the writer displays a bias towards one or other of the national groups which live within the state of Yugoslavia. In recounting the story of the medieval kingdoms which collapsed before the Turkish onslaught, or which were incorporated into the Habsburg empire, has due weight been given to the sensitivities of those who trace their ancestry back to the formative years of their national culture?

Looking at more recent times, the kingdom founded in 1918 was unable, during its brief and unhappy existence, to resolve either the national differences among its various peoples or the social and economic differences among the classes. The Kingdom collapsed when foreign invaders entered in 1941, but the task of the occupying forces was made easier by the internal dissensions which set Croat against Serb, Catholic against Orthodox Christian, class against class. The sufferings endured by the Yugoslavs during the Second World War are beyond the comprehension of those of us whose homelands were never occupied and who faced the enemy united in a common sense of national purpose. The physical and psychological torments which the Yugoslavs endured in their struggle for survival have left deep scars which will take generations to heal.

It is almost impossible for Yugoslav historians to forget their national origins and to lose their sense of identity with the group to which their loyalties are attached. The justification for a non-Yugoslav attempting to write about Yugoslavia is that he or she is not caught up in the inherited cultural and political differences which affect the judgement of the native-born, and may therefore look with a degree of detachment on issues which arouse fierce emotions amongst those who are steeped in the traditions of their people.

I must confess to a deep and abiding affection for Yugoslavia and an admiration for the people and their achievements, but I hope that the ensuing pages indicate that my affection is not uncritical and that the portrait I have painted bears some resemblance to reality.

In a book which covers so wide a compass, from Roman times to the death of Tito, there is bound to be much oversimplification, but I hope that what I have written will help the reader to understand better this fascinating country.

It has been said that Yugoslavia is the despair of tidy minds. I am sure that I have left many loose ends, and have omitted many aspects of Yugoslav life which some may think to be of vital importance. If I have offered an intelligible pattern which will provide a framework in which the interested reader may embark on further investigations, I shall be satisfied.

I must acknowledge my debt to many friends who have patiently read parts of the manuscript and have made their comments. These include my colleagues in the Postgraduate School of Yugoslav Studies in Bradford, Mr John Allcock and Mr Charles Bartlett. Dr Muriel Heppell of the School of Slavonic Studies, University of London, who collaborated with me on my first book on Yugoslavia, has kindly read the chapters on medieval history and made helpful suggestions. The late Sir Cecil Parrott, formerly of Lancaster University, who was tutor to the young King Peter, gave me the benefit of his knowledge of Yugoslavia during the regency of Prince Paul. The unfailing help of John J. Horton, Social Sciences Librarian in Bradford University Library, whose wide knowledge of Yugoslav sources was at my disposal at all times, is much appreciated. Mrs Elizabeth Wetton of Cambridge University Press has been a patient editor, and Mr M. Lear, cartographer at Bradford University, has drawn the excellent maps.

There are many more whose help should be acknowledged, but none more than my wife, Elizabeth, who has typed the manuscript, corrected various inelegancies of style, and kept me to the mark, in complete disregard for her own comfort and convenience.

None of the above bear any responsibility for any shortcomings or errors which I may have perpetrated.

Guide to pronunciation

Serbo-Croat spelling is phonetic, that is each letter of the alphabet always represents the same sound. The following guide to pronunciation is based on the Croatian alphabet, which uses the Latin script. Diacritic marks are used with certain consonants to indicate sounds which have a separate sign in the Cyrillic alphabet, used in Serbia, Macedonia and Montenegro.

The spelling of personal names and place names has been anglicised in some cases where a commonly accepted form is in general use, although the Serbo-Croat version is given in parenthesis on its first appearance – Alexander (Aleksandar), Belgrade (Beograd) – but in most cases the original form is used.

A	as in English	a in *father*
B		b in *bed*
C		ts in *cats*
Č		ch in *reach*
Ć	a sound between	ch in *reach* and t in *tune*
D	as in English	d in *dog*
Dž		j in *John*
Đ (Dj)	a sound between	d in *duke* and dg in *bridge*
E	as in English	e in *let*
F		f in *full*
G		g in *good*
H	as in Scottish	ch in *loch*
I	as in English	i in *machine*
J		y in *yet*
K		k in *kite*
L		l in *look*
Lj		ll in *million*
M		m in *man*
N		n in *net*
Nj		n in *new*

O	o in *not*
P	p in *pet*
R	r in *run* (slightly rolled)
S	ss in *glass*
Š	sh in *she*
T	t in *tap*
U	u in *rule*
V	v in *veil*
Z	z in *zebra*
Ž	s in *pleasure*

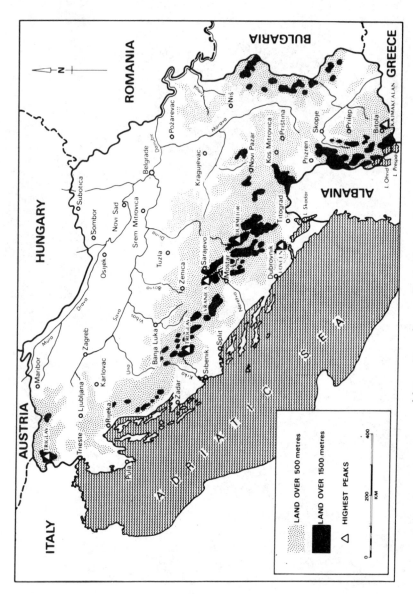

Map 1. Yugoslavia: physical geography.

1

The lands of the South Slavs

The lands which the South Slav tribes first entered, in the middle of the first millennium AD, were geographically very different from their earlier homelands north of the Carpathians, in the Vistula basin and the Ukraine.

South-east Europe is a region of great geographical diversity, in which several major physiographic and climatic zones converge. The topography and drainage patterns suggest certain routes by which invaders have penetrated from all directions into the Balkan heartland. In the north, the Pannonian lowlands, drained by the Danube and its tributaries, the Drava and the Tisa, extend across the great Hungarian Alföld to the foothills of the Carpathians and to the southern entrance of the Moravian gate near Bratislava on the Danube. It is well established that the prehistoric amber trade, from Samland on the Baltic coast, used this route, and it was probably also used by German pastoralists and barbarian invaders.

The Danube itself provides an opening into Wallachia, via the Iron Gate at the south-eastern corner of the Pannonian plain. Trajan's arch at the entrance to the Gate commemorates the Roman conquest of Dacia in AD 102. The same passage, despite the narrow constriction of the valley at Djerdap, as the Danube forces its way between the Transylvanian Alps to the north and the Stara Planina to the south, may also have been a route for invaders into the Roman province of Pannonia, although the Iron Gate Pass, some 130 km (80 miles) further north, afforded a better route for the Goths who descended on Pannonia from Transylvania in the middle of the fourth century AD.

Belgrade stands at the meeting place of these Danubian routes and of two other historic highways. Southward the Morava–Vardar corridor leads to the Aegean at Salonika (Thessaloniki). This, too, was an element in the amber route. Archaeologists have been able to follow this trade route across Europe from the Baltic to the Mediterranean by analysing pieces of amber with unique chemical properties which identify the source area in Samland. As in some majestic paperchase, they have traced the amber carriers back from the Greek islands to the pine forests and sandy heaths of the Baltic littoral. The Vardar–Morava corridor not only carried traders, it carried cultural influences from the Byzantine Greek world into the Danube basin, most notably the Christian faith as practised by the apostles of the Slavs, Kiril and Metodije. It was also used by the armies of the eastern emperor, Theodosius, when he marched through the Balkans in AD 394 to overthrow Eugenius and make himself master of both eastern and western empires. The army of Theodosius followed the Sava valley from Pannonia to confront the Romans in the Vipava valley (then known as the Frigidus), which is on the line of another historic routeway. This leads from the neighbourhood of modern Ljubljana (Roman Emona) by way of the Pear Tree Pass (Hrušica) to the Vipava and thence to the head of the Adriatic at Aquileia near present-day Trieste. Gibbon records that on the day of the decisive battle a 'violent tempest' blowing in the faces of the defending Romans 'disordered their ranks, wrested their weapons from their hands, and diverted or repelled their ineffectual javelins'. This was a *bura* (Italian *bora*), the wind which originates when an area of low pressure over the Adriatic attracts cold air from the continental interior. The funnelling effect of such gaps in the mountains as the Pear Tree Pass or the adjacent Gate of Postojna increases the ferocity of the wind, which in local gusts can reach velocities of over 160 km per hour (100 mph) and cause falls in temperature of 22 °C (40 °F) within a few hours.

A major route between the eastern and western empires, the Via Egnatia, involved a ferry crossing of the Adriatic from Brindisi to Durazzo. From Durazzo the way ran across Albania to Ohrid and Bitola (Heraclea Lincestis) in Macedonia, and then via Salonika to Byzantium (Constantinople). Further north, another route later used by Ragusan merchants followed the Neretva valley, across the Ivan Pass, to Sarajevo.

The historic importance of these routeways owes much to the fact that they connect the contrasting environments of Alpine, Mediterranean and continental Europe. The movement of goods, the interaction of cultures and the clash of empires have, by the accident of geography, been channelled through a relatively small area of south-eastern Europe, imposing an indelible imprint on its peoples.

The range of natural environments contained within Yugoslavia itself is far greater than one might expect in an area only 5 per cent larger than the United Kingdom.

Alpine Yugoslavia

Alpine fold mountains make its northern and western land frontiers. Near the meeting place of the Austrian, Italian and Yugoslav borders in north-east Slovenia the Carnic, the Karawanken and the Julian Alps come together. Triglav, 2,864 m (9,400 ft) in the Julian Alps, the highest point in Yugoslavia, no longer, as in pre-war days, marks the frontier with Italy. The post-war frontier changes have brought the Alpine valley of the Isonzo (Soča) within the confines of Yugoslavia, and the present frontier follows the ridges to the west of the Soča to the point where the river enters Italy at Gorizia (Gorica) and flows across the Friulian plain to enter the Adriatic near Monfalcone (Tržič). Another Alpine valley, that of the Sava Dolinka, occupies a deep trench between the Karawanken ranges which separate Slovenia from Austrian Carinthia and the majestic limestone peaks of the Julian Alps to the south. Another branch of the Sava, the Sava Bohinjka, rises on the southern flanks of Triglav, flowing through subterranean passages under the valley of the Seven Lakes to emerge from a cave halfway up the sheer wall of Komarča as the waterfall of Slap Savica. After passing through the 45-metre-deep (150 ft) glacial basin of Lake Bohinj, it flows northward to join its sister stream near Lake Bled, and then through Slovenia and Croatia to join the Danube 940 km (587 miles) away at Belgrade.

Other Alpine ranges, following the east–west trend line of the main European Alpine complex, occupy the area between the Sava valley and the Austrian frontier. These include the Savinjski and Kamniški Alps, which attain heights of over 2,000 m (6,560 ft), and the high plateau of Pohorje, near Maribor, which rises to over 1,300 m (4,260 ft).

Notrajnsko

South of the Julian Alps lies an area of limestone plateaus which extend southward towards Trieste and the Istrian peninsula and eastward towards the Kupa river. The Slovene name for this area is Notrajnsko (Interior). The area behind Trieste carries the Slovene name Kras. This is more widely known to geomorphologists by its Germanic corruption, *Karst*. It displays the classic erosional features of limestone areas, and because of the pioneer work of the Serbian geographer Jovan Cvijić (1865–1927), the Slavonic terminology which he devised is still used by geomorphologists throughout the world to describe limestone scenery. *Polje*, the Serbo-Croat word used for a field, bears the special connotation of a large, flat-floored depression. *Dolina* (literally a valley) is a shallow, saucer-shaped depression, often leading to a sink-hole or *ponor*. Many of the larger depressions are filled with the characteristic Mediterranean soil, *terra rossa*, and are cultivated, mainly for fodder crops and vegetables. Others are subject to flooding when underground streams, swollen by winter rains and melt waters, emerge from *sources vaclusiennes* (Slovene *vrelo*). The celebrated intermittent lake of Cerknica covers an area of 28.4 sq km (11 sq miles) and persists for several months. On the open surface of the plateau, soils are thin and in many areas almost devoid of cover, the bare rock surfaces displaying the appearance of a limestone pavement, dissected by a rectangular grid of fissures.

Intermittent drainage, underground watercourses and vast cave systems are features of the karst. The caves of Postojna and Škocjan are notable tourist attractions, and there is even a castle, Predjamski Grad, built into the mouth of a cave halfway up a sheer limestone cliff, to which access can be gained by way of a labyrinth of underground passages.

The nature of the underground drainage can give rise to international problems when streams cross under frontiers. This is the case with the Reka (Timavo) river, which disappears underground at Škocjan and emerges to enter the Gulf of Trieste, near Monfalcone, 40 km (25 miles) away.

Before the invention of refrigeration, peasants on the Slovene Karst stored blocks of ice in the depths of the caves, whence they could be transported in spring and summer to the fish market of Trieste, to be exchanged for the copper sulphate needed to treat the vines in order to control the ravages of the deadly aphid *Phylloxera*.

Although parts of the karst are barren and treeless, there are other areas where a covering of marls and sandstones known as *flysch*, derived from the deposits of the bed of an Eocene sea, provides the basis for surface drainage and soils. Tree growth is possible and, until the depredations of humans and goats destroyed much of the forest cover, timber cutting provided a much-needed additional source of income to supplement the meagre subsistence of the peasants. The forests of the Trnovski Gozd, above the Vipava valley, supplied timber to the shipyards of Trieste during the nineteenth century.

The Dinaric region

In the plateau lands of Notranjsko the north-west to south-east trend line of the Dinaric system may be discerned, in contrast to the east–west line of the main Alpine system. The western Dinaric system consists of a series of parallel limestone ranges which run behind the Adriatic coast for 720 km (450 miles) from Slovenia to the Albanian border and continue through Albania to the Pindos mountains of Greece. The predominant rocks are Cretaceous limestones, although in the Velebit mountains of northern

Dalmatia the rocks are of Jurassic age. The narrow coastal plain between the mountain rampart and the sea is covered by Eocene *flysch*, and in the largest area of flat land in Dalmatia, the plain between Zadar and Šibenik, the underlying limestone is almost entirely masked by *flysch*. This is of great importance in providing a basis for the cultivation of cereals and the grazing of animals in an area where opportunities for agriculture are severely restricted.

The scores of islands which lie off the Adriatic coast are the crests of mountain ranges which foundered during periods of tectonic disturbances. Their alignment follows the same direction as the adjacent mainland ranges, to which they are structurally related. The same process of foundering has created along the shore a number of deep-water natural harbours by the inundation of the lower courses of streams. Where a breach has been made in the outer coastal ranges, the sea has penetrated into the depressions which run behind them parallel to the main Dinaric trend. Such features are found at Bakar, Šibenik, Split and Kotor.

Unfortunately the commercial value of these natural harbours is some-what vitiated by the difficulty of communication inland across the Dinaric ranges to the centres of population in the interior of Yugoslavia. There are few rivers which are able to maintain a course across the grain of the land to penetrate from the interior to the sea. The most important are the Cetina, which enters the sea at Omiš; and the Neretva, between Dubrovnik and Split. The lower Cetina flows in a narrow, steep-sided gorge between bare mountains rising to heights of over 1,000 m (3,280 ft) which render it useless as a line of communication into the interior. The best access from this area of central Dalmatia to the upper course of the Cetina in Sinjsko Polje is from the coast at Split via Solin (Salona) and the steep defile at Klis.

The Neretva offers a better line of communication from its delta on the shores of the Neretvanski Kanal, a sheltered stretch of water lying between the coast and the Pelješac peninsula. The route inland, now followed by a railway and a modern road, leads to Mostar and then over the Ivan Pass to Sarajevo, the capital of Bosnia.

All the features of karstic topography found in Slovenia are displayed on a grand scale in the Dinaric system. Between the parallel ranges lie a series of *polja* extending for over 640 km (400 miles) and reaching inland in a belt 100 km (64 miles) wide. The individual *polja* can be over 65 km (40 miles) long, but are seldom more than a few kilometres across, their long axes conforming to the north-west to south-east direction of the Dinaric trend lines.

Life in these karstic *polja* is an unremitting struggle against a cruel environment. In pre-war times the Croatian economist Rudolf Bićanić undertook a survey of life on the Dinaric karst for the Croat Peasant Party, which he published under the title *Kako živi narod* (How the People Live). It describes the life of peasants in some of the poorest *polja* – Livno, Lika, Imotski and Sinjsko. To the natural hazards of intermittent drainage, alternate floods and droughts, and infertile, stony soil were added the human obstacles of antiquated systems of land tenure, primitive methods of farming, neglect of welfare services, poor communication and exploitation by moneylenders and merchants. The situation has improved in many ways, but it is not easy to overcome the problems created by natural obstacles and compounded by the legacy of centuries of neglect. These regions are still amongst the poorest and least developed in Yugoslavia. Visitors to the resorts on the Dalmatian coast do not always realise the poverty and backwardness which lie over the mountains only a few kilometres away from the bright lights of Split, Zadar and Šibenik.

The Adriatic coastlands

Relatively isolated from the interior of Yugoslavia by the mountain barrier which rises above them, the Adriatic coastlands and islands belong geographically to the Mediterranean world. The way of life of the Dalmatian peasants and fisherfolk, and of the citizens of the former Venetian colonies of Split, Šibenik and Zadar has for centuries resembled that of the Italians on the western shore of the Adriatic rather than that of their Slav cousins who inhabit the Balkan interior. The sea was a link not only with Italy but also with a wider world beyond the Mediterranean. Merchants from Ragusa (Dubrovnik) traded with the Levant and with northern Europe. Dalmatian sailors served in many fleets – with the Spanish Armada, with the Dutch, the English and the French during the period of their colonial rivalries in the sixteenth and seventeenth centuries, with the Venetians during the heyday of the maritime republic, and even with the Americans during the War of Independence. When Trieste became the major outlet for the trade of central Europe, Dalmatians were found in ships of the Lloyd Triestino line.

E. A. Freeman's description of Dalmatia as 'a Slavonic land with an Italian fringe' refers to the cultural geography of the Adriatic coastlands, but it might also be applied to the physical geography (as 'a Dinaric land with a Mediterranean fringe'). The regime of the vine and olive is restricted to a zone varying in width from a few hundred metres under Velebit to 30 km (18 miles) near Zadar. Just as the coastal cities were subjected throughout the centuries to incursions from the interior by the forces of whichever power held sway beyond the mountains – Byzantines, Hungarians, Serbs and Turks – so the tranquillity of the Mediterranean climate is brutally violated from time to time by the icy blasts of the *bura*. The islands present a bare and inhospitable face to the mainland, as their landward slopes receive the full force of the wind. The sheltered, seaward-facing slopes support a typically Mediterranean vegetation, composed of aromatic shrubs (the maquis) and evergreen woods of Aleppo pine. The cultivated plants include figs, olives and vines. This vegetation pattern is also found on the sheltered lowland strips which lie in the shadow of the coastal mountain ranges.

The Dinaric ranges

There is an abrupt change in climate and vegetation once the coastal ranges are crossed. The height of the *polja* floors varies between 1,000 m (3,280 ft) in Glamočko Polje in the north and 400 m (1,300 ft) in Sinjsko Polje in central Dalmatia, descending to under 50 m (165 ft) at Titograd. In a few places, as in the lower Neretva valley, a breach in the mountain wall permits a gulf of Mediterranean air to penetrate inland, but more commonly the unbroken barrier shuts out the ameliorating influences from the sea. The contrast between the conditions on the coast and in the interior is illustrated by the climatic statistics for two stations less than 30 km (18.5 miles) apart. Ostra Point (Rt. Ostra) at the mouth of the Bay of Kotor enjoys a hot, dry summer, with average July temperatures of 25 °C (77 °F), and has warm, moist winters, with average January temperatures of 9 °C (48 °F). Of the annual rainfall of 975 mm (38.4 in), more than two-thirds occurs between October and March. In July and August the average number of rain days is only four per month. Cetinje, 720 m (2,205 ft) above sea level, the old capital of the kingdom of Montenegro, lies only 30 km away, on the landward side of the Lovčen range. Here January temperatures are below freezing point (−0.5 °C, 31 °F) and only in the three summer months does the average temperature rise above 15.5 °C (60 °F), July attaining 21 °C (70 °F). Total rainfall is 3,550 mm (139.7 in), over three times the amount received at Ostra.

Further inland, from the Dalmatian hinterland, in Bosnia and the Sandžak, strong continental influences are apparent, with a marked rainfall maximum in early summer – Sarajevo's wettest month is June – and much colder winters.

The Pannonian region

The full rigours of the continental climate are experienced in the Sava–Danube lowlands. Winters are cold, with biting winds sweeping in from the Hungarian plain. Summers are hot, with monthly averages of over 22 °C (70 °F). Total rainfall is low – Belgrade has only 609 mm (24 in) – and the wettest period is March–June. Summer thunderstorms are common, but the torrential downpours which they often bring are soon evaporated in the hot sun and are of limited value to agriculture. Irrigation is necessary to sustain the crops which grow on the fertile, loess-covered lowlands of one of Europe's richest grain-growing regions. Paradoxically, large-scale drainage and flood-control measures are also needed at other times of the year. The Danube and its principal tributaries, the Sava, Drava and Tisa, rise in areas where heavy rainfall is supplemented by melt water from Alpine glaciers, causing frequent inundation on the low-lying ground further downstream.

The Vardar region

The Vardar river, which flows through the centre of the Macedonian republic, reaches the Aegean Sea near Salonika. It provides the corridor through which the cold *Vardarac* wind – a cousin of the Dalmatian *bura* – brings continental influences from the Danubian lowlands in winter. Average January temperatures are below freezing point, even as far south as Bitola, which lies in the same latitude as Naples. By contrast, summers are very hot, with monthly averages above 22 °C (70 °F). Mediterranean influences penetrate northwards into the Vardar valley and the lowlands of Pelagonija. In these inland basins, separated from each other by rugged mountain ranges of crystalline rocks, sub-tropical crops such as rice, tobacco, cotton and opium poppies are grown. Total rainfall is low, with many places receiving under 500 mm (20 in) a year, but irrigation is possible, the water being provided by the Vardar and its tributary the Crna Reka, which rises in areas of higher rainfall. The Vardar region contains some of Yugoslavia's largest natural lakes – Ohrid, Prespa and Dojran, which occupy tectonic basins. Ohrid, the deepest lake in Yugoslavia (286 m (935 ft) at its greatest depth) is of great scientific interest, as it contains a species of trout which, like the omul in Lake Baikal, has survived from before the last Ice Age, the lake having being formed during the Tertiary period.

The rich variety of geographical environments provides a background to the diversity of ways of life and traditions of the Yugoslav peoples. Each region offers different opportunities and imposes different kinds of restriction on its inhabitants. Although certain routeways of international importance cross through their territory, many Yugoslav communities have lived in isolation from each other, developing unique cultural characteristics. The problem which faced the rulers of royal Yugoslavia and now faces the present communist-led society, is to create a sense of common loyalty amongst peoples whose geographical circumstances and historical experiences have tended towards diversity.

2

The early Slav settlers

The Roman occupation

When the Romans first began to expand into the Balkans in the third century BC, the area was inhabited by Thracian, Illyrian and Celtic tribes. The Thracians and Illyrians had been to a great extent Hellenised during the fourth century BC, when the Macedonian empire of Philip and Alexander flourished. Greek colonies had been established along the Adriatic coastlands even earlier. The Celts, who migrated into the Balkans in the fourth century BC and settled mainly in the northern lowlands, became assimilated into the Illyrian community, the chief legacy of their presence being numerous Celtic elements in place names. For a time before the Roman invasions several powerful Illyrian or Graeco-Illyrian kingdoms existed in places as far apart as modern Albania and Macedonia in the south and the upper Sava basin in the north. Remarkable examples of the wealth, power and high cultural attainments of the Illyrians have been found in the excavations of royal tombs. The friezes which decorate the situla discovered at Vače, near present-day Ljubljana, depict scenes of ritual sacrifices, feasts, battles, sport and pastimes which suggest that a highly organised, metal-using society existed in this area in the fifth century BC. There are signs of both Greek and Etruscan influences.

The Illyrians were the first to feel the power of Rome. During the third century BC Roman attacks began on Illyrian tribes settled in the Neretva valley, followed by raids on the Greek cities on the Albanian coast. Most of the coastlands were brought under Roman rule during the Illyrian wars of Octavian in 35–33 BC. Further advances were made following a rising of the Illyrians in 9 BC, and the final subjugation of the Illyrians in the western Balkans was achieved under Tiberius in AD 9. At the same time, Rome extended its rule over Celtic tribes in Serbia and Bulgaria, and by AD 14 the whole of the Balkans south of the Danube was in Roman hands.

The logic of imperialism forced the Romans to extend their frontiers continually, invading territories from which their 'barbarian' enemies launched attacks on the frontiers of the empire. Trajan, in AD 101, crossed the Danube and incorporated the province of Dacia (modern Wallachia and the Banat) into the empire in AD 105. Although this extension of the frontiers beyond the Danube, even to the banks of the Dniester, gave Rome access to the rich grain-growing areas of Wallachia and the mineral wealth of Transylvania, it also stretched the imperial lines of communication and made central control from Rome more difficult.

It was Gibbon's opinion that Trajan's conquest of Dacia was maintained for reasons of prestige, and that it contributed to the weakening of the empire. Dacia was not strong enough to beat off the barbarians, and not rich enough to satisfy them once they had conquered it. In AD 272 the Romans were forced out of Dacia by Goths invading from across the Dniester. The frontier was again placed on the Danube, but the loss of the buffer zone of Dacia threatened the security of Moesia, the province which covered modern Serbia and Macedonia. The defences on the Danube had been neglected, for as long as the frontier lay on the Dniester the inhabitants of Moesia believed themselves to be secure.

In AD 285, shortly after the withdrawal from Dacia, Trajan's successor, Diocletian, himself a native of Dalmatia, divided the empire into two administrative areas, a western half governed from Rome and an eastern half based on Constantinople. Constantine effected a reunion, but, on the death of Theodosius in AD 395, a second division was made, between the emperor's two sons. The 'great and martial praefecture of Illyricum' was divided between Arcadius and Honorius. The dividing line ran north–south from the Sava near Sirmium (Sremska Mitrovica) to Lake Scutari (Skadar) on the present Montenegrin–Albanian border. This line became a permanent feature on the cultural map of Europe, separating Byzantium from Rome, the Greek from the Roman cultural heritage, the Eastern Orthodox from the Roman Catholic Church and the users of the Cyrillic script from those of the Latin.

The legacy of Rome

Roman culture absorbed that of the Illyrians. Those Illyrians who did not assimilate probably moved to the less hospitable mountainous areas, but little is known of their fate. They are as mysterious as the Etruscans, the pre-Roman occupants of the Italian peninsula. Albanian historians believe that the modern Albanians developed from the ancient Illyrians and that there is a continuity of Illyrian settlement in their country from the Bronze Age to the present time.

Under Roman rule the Illyrians were drawn into the mainstream of European culture. Those who were assimilated adopted Latin speech, enrolled in the Roman army and became citizens of Roman towns such as Salona, the capital of Roman Dalmatia and birthplace of the emperor Diocletian.

Diocletian (reigned 284–305) was one of five sons of Illyrian peasants who were to wear the imperial purple. He retired from the imperial throne in AD 305 and spent the last nine years of his life in cultivating the soil of his native Dalmatia, constructing the city which still forms the heart of modern Split and, according to Gibbon, enjoying the 'most exquisite trout' which were bred in 'the little stream of the Hyader' (now the Jadro). The city, the aqueduct and the trout are still there.

The Romans found an existing road pattern which went back to Neolithic times and which followed the natural corridors of movement suggested by the topography. In many cases the Romans merely paved the existing roadways, but their needs were not always those of their predecessors, and they were obliged to pioneer new routes. There were two overriding needs which had to be met by the Roman road network – military and economic. The Via Militaris ran from Singidunum (Belgrade) to Byzantium (Constantinople) via Naissus (Niš) and Serdica (Sofia), following the Morava valley for the first 200 km (125 miles) of its 924 km (575 mile) length. As its name implies, the Via Militaris was a major line of communication for the Roman armies defending the eastern frontier, and as a stage in one of the links between Italy and Byzantium it already had an important role to play in the vital intercourse between the eastern and western halves of the empire. More important in this connection, however, was the Via Egnatia, which was in effect a continuation of the Via Apiae (Appian Way). This led from Rome to the ferry port of Egnatia, between Bari and Brindisi. From there travellers took ship to Dyrrachium (Durrës) and then followed the road across Albania and Macedonia to Salonika. This was the most direct route from Rome to Byzantium. Roman roads ran the whole length of Dalmatia, linking Salona with the main seaports. Where the terrain demanded, as under Velebit, the roads left the coast to follow the interior *polja* behind the coastal ranges. Branch roads linked the main mining centres, enabling the lead, silver, iron and copper products of the interior to be brought to the coast for export across the Adriatic or, in the case of the Serbian and north Bosnian mines, to be transported to the Danube.

Abundant archaeological evidence – milestones, cobbled surfaces, artefacts related to mining – bears witness to the existence of a network of main roads linking the coast with the main Sava–Danube–Morava–Vardar axis. It is only in recent decades that anything resembling this framework has been re-established.

Along the roads urban settlements grew up. Those along the coast and in the north-west were primarily civilian and commercial establishments. Further inland, and especially in the Pannonian lowlands and along the Vardar–Morava corridor, the military character of the Roman settlements became more pronounced. Most of Yugoslavia's main cities can trace their origins back to Roman foundation or, where earlier settlements can be identified, to a revival of activity in Roman times. Ljubljana (Emona), Sremska Mitrovica (Sirmium), Belgrade (Singidunum), Niš (Naissus), Skopje (Scupi), Osijek (Mursa), Mostar (Andetrium) and Bitola (Heraclea) are some of the principal Roman settlements which are still important urban centres in modern Yugoslavia. Most of the coastal towns, from Pula in Istria, with its magnificent amphitheatre, to Stari Bar in Montenegro were Roman ports, some, like Epidaurus (Cavtat), being built on Greek foundations.

The arrival of the Slavs

The Slavs first appeared in the Balkans in the late fourth century AD as marauders who raided the Romanised settlements south of the Danube from their temporary resting place in Hungary. They had moved south-wards from their previous homeland in the area between the Pripet marshes and the Carpathians, in what is now Poland and the Ukraine, during the third and fourth centuries. The impetus which drove them to expand in all directions from this base is not fully explained. It may be that the same forces impelled the Slavs which affected the Asiatic peoples who moved into Europe from the east during the period of folk migrations which accompanied and contributed to the fall of the Roman empire. It was during this period of what used to be called the Dark Ages that the ethnic map of Europe began to assume a character which in the main survives today. The nations of modern Europe can be discerned in embryo by the end of the first millennium, after the upheavals which accompanied the disintegration of the Pax Romana. The Slavs were one of a score of peoples who ravaged the Roman world, but they are one of the few whose cultural identity has remained intact. The Goths, the Avars, the Lombards, the Huns, the Franks became absorbed in the Romanised populations they dominated. This happened to some extent to the Slavs who invaded Greece in the sixth century, but in the Balkans three distinct Slav groups may be identified by the tenth century – the ancestors of the present-day Serbs, Croats, and Slovenes. These South Slavs became separated from related groups in Poland, Czechoslovakia, Russia and the Ukraine by a wedge of non-Slavs – the Germans of Austria, the Romanians of Wallachia and the Magyars of Hungary. Once they had settled in the Balkans they also became separated from each other, partly because of the geographical obstacles to easy movement within the peninsula, and partly because of the historical circumstances of foreign occupations.

The term South Slav (or Yugoslav) is primarily a linguistic category which came into use in the eighteenth century. It gained currency during the period of national reawakening in the nineteenth century. It is probable that the linguistic differentiation which separates the South Slavs from the Western Slavs (Poles, Czechs, Slovaks) and the Eastern Slavs (Russians, Bielorussians, Ukrainians) had not become apparent at the time of the migration. It is equally probable that the separation of the South Slav languages into Serb, Croat, Slovene, Macedonian and Bulgarian was then in an early stage of development, if it had occurred at all.

The first records of Slav incursions into the Balkans refer to plundering raids on the Byzantine settlements and fortresses of the Danubian lowlands and the Vardar–Morava corridor. In 517 a major invasion occurred when Slav horsemen advanced as far as Thermopylae and Epirus. The attacks increased in intensity and duration in the reign of Emperor Justinian I (527–65). One ancient chronicler, Prokopie Kesarinski, refers to the Slavs and Antii crossing the Danube almost every year and attacking Illyria, Thrace and 'all the regions of the Ionian Gulf as far as the outlying districts of Constantinople'. In 548 they stayed in the Balkans for a whole year and destroyed many towns and fortresses, including the Byzantine centre of Lychnidus (Ohrid). Gradually groups of Slavs moved in to colonise areas which they had occupied during their raids. Around AD 570 the Slavs of the Pannonian basin were subjugated by an invading Turkic people, the Avars. Slavs accompanied the Avar hordes who invaded the Byzantine empire in the late sixth century, laying waste cities as far south as Tiveropolis (Strumica in south-east Macedonia) and enslaving or slaughtering the indigenous population.

The Avars also raided westward into Italy, following the routes taken in previous centuries by Theodosius and his Gothic allies in 394; by Alaric the Goth advancing towards Rome, which he sacked in 410; by Attila the Hun in 452; and by Alboin and the Lombards in 568. Unlike the earlier horders who crossed the Julian region to descend upon the rich plains of Venetia, the Lombards settled, and fortified the passes through which they had invaded, to secure their eastern boundary against the infiltration of further invaders. They remained long enough to give their name to the region of Italy where they settled, and to create the marcher duchy of Friuli as a buffer zone against attacks on their kingdom by the occupiers of the Sava–Danube lowlands – the Slavs and their overlords, the Avars. In 610 a combined Avar–Slav army thrust across the karst, following the route of Theodosius over the Pear Tree Pass (Hrušica) and the Vipava valley. Although the Avar army withdrew after sacking towns in Friuli and killing the Duke of Friuli, the raid of 610 appears to mark the beginning of Slav colonisation of the upper Sava valley. In 627 a Slav prince, Samo, appears as ruler of a Slav empire which endured until after his death in 658. Samo's empire, about which little is known, held sway over the Sava valley from Zagreb to the Julian Alps, and northward from Ljubljana across Austria, Bohemia and Moravia into Saxony. This was the first occasion on which the ancestors of the modern Slovenes found themselves included in a political unit which extended into central Europe. A century later, when Charlemagne, the Frankish Christian king, accepted a papal commission to subdue the rebellious Lombards, he included the remnants of Samo's kingdom in his new state, from which the Holy Roman Empire developed.

Charlemagne proceeded to the conversion of his new subjects to Christianity. The old Roman city of Aquileia, the seat of a patriarchate under the archbishopric of Salzburg, was the religious centre for the conversion of the Slovenes. Thus the Slovenes were drawn into the cultural and religious life of western Europe under German princes and within the spiritual jurisdiction of the Roman Church. The imprint of these deep-rooted influences still stamps the national character of the Slovenes. The only attempt to revive the Slav kingdom of Samo, which Ottokar of Bohemia made in the thirteenth century, was decisively crushed by the Holy Roman Emperor at the battle of Marchfeld (1278). Thenceforward, until the Slovenes broke with the Habsburg empire and joined the newly formed Serb–Croat–Slovene state in 1918, the fortunes of this small Slav community were linked to those of Austria.

At the end of the eighth century most of the area of present-day Yugoslavia south of the Sava–Danube line was colonised by Slav tribes, whose influence also extended into Albania and central Greece. Byzantine writers referred to this area as Sclavonia, the land of the Slavs. This should not be confused with the later usage of Slavonia, which, in a geographical sense, refers to a region of south-east Croatia centred on Slavonski Brod, but in a wider context is used to cover the historic Habsburg province of Slavonia, which lay between the valleys of the Sava and the Drava. In the north, Charlemagne's empire covered Slovenia – the land of the Slovenes – the mid-Sava valley and the northern Adriatic coast from Istria to the neighbourhood of Šibenik. The Byzantine empire controlled enclaves on the coast around Split and Dubrovnik and the whole of the Albanian and Greek coasts, the Aegean islands, southern Macedonia and Bulgaria south of the Stara Planina. To the east and north of Sclavonia, in modern Hungary, Romania and northern Bulgaria, the Bulgars, the Avars and the Magyars were to be found.

Within the territory occupied by the Slavs were many non-Slavs. Some were survivors of the Illyrians, others were Vlahs, a people of Romance speech whose name is related to Wallachia. The Vlahs were sufficiently numerous in south-west Serbia for their name to survive in the Stari Vlah region, south of Titovo Užice. Some Vlah communities survive today in the mountainous regions of Macedonia and in northern Greece. In Pannonia, beyond the limits of Slavonia, there were many Slav subjects of the Avars. The coastal cities of Dalmatia, whether under Byzantine or Slav rule, still contained many Romanised Illyrians who retained their Latin culture.

During the ninth century a struggle developed for the souls of the Slavs between the two Christian confessions, the Eastern Church based in Byzantium and the Western Church based in Rome. The Slovenes and some Croats had been converted during the time of Charlemagne, and the Croats of Dalmatia were converted by missionaries from Rome during the early seventh century. Although Byzantium made some inroads in Dalmatia during the next two centuries, the issue was finally settled in favour of Rome at the end of the ninth century by the Croatian prince Branimir (879–92).

Christianity came to the Macedonians and Serbs from the east, under the influence of the Byzantine emperors, who were the nominal overlords – and in some cases the real rulers – of the Slavs in the southern Balkans. There may have been a formal recognition of Christianity by the leaders of some Serbian tribes as early as the seventh century, but the real beginnings of Christianity in this area date from the last decades of the ninth century and are associated with the 'Apostles of the Slavs', the brothers Constantine-Cyril (Kiril) and Methodius (Metodije). In 863 the ruler of Moravia, Prince Rastislav, sent to the Byzantine emperor, Michael III, a request that missionaries should be sent to instruct his people in the Christian faith, through the medium of the Slavonic tongue. Michael, although reputedly a licentious and irreligious man, sent Cyril and Methodius on a mission which had far-reaching consequences for the future of Christianity, although their mission to Moravia achieved only a temporary victory for the

Byzantine cause. After the death of Methodius in AD 885 the other members of his mission, including Clement and Naum, who were later canonised for their work amongst the Macedonians, were driven out of Moravia.

Cyril's great contribution was to devise an alphabet, the glagolitic (*glagol* = verb), in which the Gospels could be written in Slavonic. The glagolitic alphabet was probably an adaptation from the old Greek cursive script. It was a phonetic alphabet, in which each sound in the spoken language of south-east Macedonia was represented by a symbol. This language, which formed the basis of Old Church Slavonic, was diffused throughout the Balkans and into central Europe, as far as Moravia and southern Poland, through the missionary activities of Constantine-Cyril and Methodius. Its use in the liturgy was at first opposed by the papacy, but, following the Council of Split in 1079, both the Old Church Slavonic language and the glagolitic script were permitted to exist in central Dalmatia. In the mid thirteenth century Pope Innocent IV reaffirmed the right of the diocese of Senj and the island of Krk to retain their traditional usages.

A slow process of diffusion then took place and glagolitic spread into Istria, Slovenia and Slavonia. In the fourteenth century it even penetrated as far as Prague and Krakow. Meanwhile, in its home area of Macedonia it had been replaced by the Cyrillic alphabet, named after Cyril, even though he probably played no direct part in its development. Cyrillic, which was also a phonetic alphabet, was based on the Greek uncial script. It appeared at the end of the ninth century and spread during the next two centuries throughout the Eastern (Byzantine) Church. Adaptations were made in order to incorporate the idiosyncrasies of the evolving Slavonic languages – Bulgarian, Serbian, Macedonian and Russian – within the domain of the Orthodox Church. The Old Church Slavonic became ossified and bore a relationship to the vernacular tongue of the people similar to that which church Latin bore towards Spanish, Italian and French. At the time of its first dispersal, however, the languages had sufficient in common for Cyril and his followers to be understood by the Moravians, who were subjects of Prince Rastislav.

The fate of glagolitic became involved with the ecclesiastical politics of Dalmatia, where Byzantine and Latin religious influences overlapped. In some areas of Dalmatia and Croatia the use of glagolitic was encouraged by Benedictine and Franciscan monks as a weapon in the battle against Greek Orthodox influences. Thus glagolitic became known as a Croatian script, although its origins were in Macedonia. A 'Glagolitic' Seminary existed until 1820 in Priko, in the district of Poljica, which lies between the lower Cetina valley and the coast between Split and Omiš. In fact, it was no longer a glagolitic institution, as Cyrillic had replaced glagolitic in most of Dalmatia south of Split by the fifteenth century, and Cyrillic was in its turn replaced by the Latin script during the next few centuries. The statute of the independent principality of Poljica, the earliest parts of which date from 1444, is written in a form of Cyrillic known as Bosančica. Poljica's independence was suppressed by Napoleon in 1806, and its incorporation first into the Illyrian Provinces and later into the Austrian province of Dalmatia assisted the spread of the Latin script, which by this time had become common throughout Dalmatia. Nevertheless, the last documents from the seminary at Priko, before its dissolution in 1820, were written in a form of Cyrillic. The exact relationship between glagolitic and Cyrillic is a matter of dispute amongst scholars. According to Blaže Koneski, the foremost authority on the evolution of the Macedonian language, the existence of the glagolitic script was a precondition for the development of Cyrillic.

One of the most devoted of the pupils of Cyril and Methodius, Clement (Sveti Kliment) of Ohrid, built a monastery on the shores of Lake Ohrid, which was to be a centre of Christian learning for the last thirty years of his long life (he died in 916). In 893, Tsar Simeon appointed Clement to be the first Slav bishop of the diocese of Velika (Titov Veles), but he still maintained regular contact with the Ohrid School. Clement and his successor Naum established the Slav tongue then spoken in Macedonia instead of the Greek of the Byzantine Church as the language of worship.

The great days of the Macedonian Church culminated in the creation of the patriarchate of Ohrid in 976, during the reign of Tsar Samuel (Samuilo), but the whole picture changed after the defeat of Samuel by the Byzantine emperor, Basil II, in 1014. The patriarchate was reduced to an archbishopric, Greek replaced Slavonic in the liturgy and a process of Hellenisation began.

Eastern influences also dominated the Serbs in the ninth century. They were officially placed under the jurisdiction of Byzantium by the *župan* (ruling prince) of the Serbian principality of Raška in 891. Although during the next three centuries the Serbs were victims of a struggle between Rome and Byzantium, the Eastern Church finally triumphed during the reign of Stephen Nemanja in the late twelfth century. In 1196 Stephen retired to become a monk, and in 1199 he and his younger son, Rastko (St Sava), founded a Serbian monastery on Mount Athos. Although Stephen's older son, who succeeded him, was crowned as the first Serbian king by a representative of Pope Honorius III in 1217, the allegiance of the Serbs to the Eastern Church was not affected. Two years later St Sava was created the first Bishop of the autocephalous Serbian Church by the Patriarch of Byzantium. In the next century, during the reign of Tsar Dušan, a Serbian patriarchate was established at Peć. Although the patriarchate was annulled and restored again on several occasions during the Turkish occupation it was not finally abolished until 1766. Peć is still the spiritual centre of the Serbian Orthodox Church, but it lies in a remote corner of Yugoslavia, close to the Albanian border, in the Albanian-speaking province of Kosovo.

The Bogomils

The Bogomil heresy, which first appeared in Macedonia during the tenth century, was a disruptive force not only to the Byzantine Church but also to those rulers – Bulgar, Serb or Byzantine – whose authority was derived from the spiritual sanction of the Patriarch of Constantinople. In the last two centuries it has also been a source of scholarly controversy amongst historians, theologians and philosophers. The view of Dmitri Obolensky, a leading authority on the Bogomils, is that they are the first European manifestation of a tradition which extends for over a thousand years from the teachings of Mani in third-century Mesopotamia to the Albigensian heresy, which appeared in southern France in the thirteenth century. Manichaeism is a dualistic faith which believes in the existence, from the time of creation, of two opposed and independent principles – God and Matter, Light and Darkness, Soul and Body. The liberation of the soul from the body, the separation of the light from the darkness, is the basis of Manichaean ethics. It involves an attitude of extreme asceticism and a hatred of all worldly things – especially the pleasures of the flesh.

The first wave of Manichaeism swept over the Levant and Asia Minor in the third and fourth centuries – Bogomilism was the first manifestation of a neo-Manichaean movement which penetrated into southern and western Europe between the ninth and thirteenth centuries. Some modern Macedonian historians see Bogomilism as a reaction by oppressed Macedonian serfs against the imposition of feudalism by the Bulgarian emperors Simeon and Peter. Taken from this viewpoint, the priest Bogomil who roused the people of the village of Bogomila on the slopes of the Babuna mountain above Prilep was a revolutionary who found a ready response from the oppressed peasantry when he denounced the system. There were, certainly, revolutionary implications in the Bogomil heresy, implications which both Church and state authorities recognised as the heresy spread into Serbia, Bosnia–Hercegovina and even Dalmatia during the eleventh and twelfth centuries. Both Byzantium and Rome felt themselves threatened and attempted to suppress the Bogomils. Hungarian kings, with papal blessing, attempted to conquer Bosnia and Hercegovina, in order to destroy the Bogomils, at the same time winning territory for themselves and souls for Rome. Hungarian pressure was particularly strong during the reign of Kálmán (1095–1116), who in 1102 became King of Croatia and Dalmatia. At that time Croatia extended southward to the Neretva and covered most of Bosnia. A century later, a Bosnian state emerged under the legendary Ban Kulin (1180–1204). Kulin abandoned Rome and embraced the Bogomil heresy, but was forced to recant a year before his death, under pressure from Hungary. Bogomilism in Bosnia revived in the fourteenth century during the reigns of the Kotromanić rulers, Stephen II and his son, Tvrtko, who was crowned King of 'Serbia, Bosnia, the Primorje and the western lands' in 1377. Stephen owed his election as ban in 1322 to the Bogomils, but after he had been persuaded by the Hungarian king to submit to Rome, the Bogomils looked to Tsar Dušan of Serbia for help. In the fifteenth century, when Christian Europe was threatened by the Turk, the Bogomils turned to the Crescent rather than the Cross, and many eventually accepted Islam.

The absorption of the heretic Bosnian (Bogomil) Church into the Islamic world did not come about as a result of a dramatic act of mass conversion, but, if Ottoman statistics are to be believed, it was a relatively rapid process. According to a census of 1489, only 18.4 per cent of the population of Bosnia practised the Islamic faith. The census of 1520–30 records 46 per cent in the whole of Bosnia, and 100 per cent in the newly built city of Sarajevo. It has been suggested that the rapid increase in the Muslim population during this period cannot be attributed to the mass conversion of Bogomils, as the greatest increases were recorded in the areas where Bogomils were fewer in number, especially in the towns. Nevertheless, the Bosnian Church gradually disappeared and a native-born, Slav-speaking Muslim aristocracy came into existence. The 1.5 million Muslims in modern Bosnia, who are listed in the Yugoslav census as 'Muslims of ethnic origin', are the descendants of those early converts.

Islam and Christianity

During the heyday of the Ottoman rule in Europe the Bosnian Muslims played an important part in the administration of the empire, one of them, Mehmet Sokolović, rising to be grand vizier to the sultan, Suleiman the

Magnificent, in the sixteenth century. Bosnian Muslims also provided the Ottoman bureaucracy in Hungary after the battle of Mohács in 1526. At lower levels of administration, the Orthodox and Roman Catholic Christian peasants of the *raya* were governed by Slav Muslim landowners, who, whilst retaining their Slavonic speech, adopted the manners and dress of the Turkish court. Like many converts, they often 'out-Ottomaned the Ottomans in their religious zeal'.

Outside Bosnia, in the Ottoman-occupied territories of Serbia, Macedonia and Albania, the Muslims were a thin stratum of Turkish immigrants, landowners and administrators, ruling over a mass of Christian peasants. Although there were some examples of forcible conversion, the Ottomans on the whole left their Christian subjects alone, recognising their right to practise their faith, although subjecting them to social and economic disabilities. Perhaps the harshest imposition was the forcible enlistment of young Christian boys into the corps of janissaries (*yeni çeri* = new troops). This system, known as *devşirme*, began in the fifteenth century and died out in the late seventeenth century. It was an extension of the old Ottoman practice of enslaving prisoners of war. In the Balkans the burden fell most heavily on the Slavs of the Orthodox community. The conversion of the Albanians was achieved during the seventeenth century largely through a discriminatory taxation system, the *djize*, which imposed severe burdens upon those who remained Christians.

Systematic persecution of non-Muslim religious minorities was not, however, a part of Islamic religious teaching nor, for the most part, of Ottoman state practice. The Ottomans took over and extended the old Byzantine practice of placing religious communities (for example the Jews) under the supervision of their religious leaders, who were responsible for maintaining order, administering justice and collecting taxes within their community. The religious communities – or *millets* – occasionally petitioned the sultan for redress if their religious leaders behaved in an oppressive manner, but on the whole they were left alone, provided they paid their taxes and caused no trouble. The Balkan Christians were placed within the *millet-i-Rum*, no distinction being made between Orthodox and Roman Catholic believers – most were in fact Orthodox. The system enabled the Orthodox Church to survive amongst the Serbs, Macedonians and Bulgarians throughout 'the long Turkish night'.

The close involvement of religious leaders with the civil affairs of their followers had fateful consequences during the nineteenth century when the declining Ottoman empire faced the rising tide of Slav nationalism. Orthodoxy and national identity were inextricably intertwined, and religious leaders became the spokesmen of national revolt. It was during this period that savage Turkish reprisals against Balkan nationalist movements gave the last of the sultans an unsavoury reputation for religious persecution which has coloured the writings of some western historians in their assessment of the whole record of the Ottoman empire.

The Ottoman conquests of the fourteenth and fifteenth centuries brought the Turks to the line of the Sava and the Danube, a line which held for almost five hundred years. In the great days of Suleiman the Magnificent the sultan's armies reached the gates of Vienna in 1529, having already subdued Hungary at the battle of Mohács three years earlier. They again reached, but did not capture, Vienna under Mehemet IV, in 1683, but by 1791 the border was back to the Sava–Danube line.

As the Ottoman threat advanced northward through Bosnia and Serbia during the fifteenth century, Christian Europe prepared to resist. The standard bearer of Christendom was the Austro-German House of Habsburg. The Habsburgs acquired Styria after the defeat of Ottokar of Bohemia by the Holy Roman Empire at the battle of Marchfeld in 1278. A few years later the duchy of Austria was awarded to one of the sons of Rudolph of Habsburg. Carinthia and Carniola were acquired in 1335, and during the next half-century the Tyrol, Istria, part of the Voralberg and the city of Trieste were added. In the early fifteenth century Albrecht II became Holy Roman Emperor and the title remained with the House of Habsburg from 1437 until 1806, when Napoleon abolished the institution which by that time was, in Voltaire's words of 1756, 'neither Holy, nor Roman, nor an empire'.

Whilst the Habsburgs were consolidating their power in central Europe they were confronted on the east by Hungary and in the south by the Venetian republic. The Hungarians acceded to the throne of Croatia in 1102 and the link remained through many vicissitudes until the collapse of the Austro-Hungarian empire in 1918. The death of the Hungarian king, Lajos (Louis) II, at the battle of Mohács created a vacancy. A dynastic struggle conducted under the hovering threat of Turkish occupation eventually led to Ferdinand of Habsburg gaining the throne, but his effective authority existed over only a fragment of Hungary and Croatia–Slavonia. In 1522 the first attempts were made to establish a border defence zone – the military frontier – to protect the Habsburg lands against the Turks in Bosnia and Serbia. This zone, which at its greatest extent ran from Transylvania to the Adriatic, following the line of the Danube and Sava rivers, was not finally abolished until 1881.

By this time the Ottoman empire had long since ceased to be a threat to Christian Europe. The threat to European peace arose from the consequences of the slow decline of 'the sick man of Europe' and to the rivalries of the Christian powers over the disposal of the Ottoman patrimony. The awakening of national consciousness amongst the subject peoples was a major factor in undermining the power of the sultans. Serbia became an independent kingdom in 1882, after a struggle which began with Karadjordje's revolt in 1804. Montenegro trebled its area at Turkey's expense by the Treaty of San Stefano in 1878, but the treaty was never ratified, and the Congress of Berlin a few months later forced Montenegro to surrender some of its gains. At the same time Bosnia–Hercegovina came under Austro-Hungarian occupation, and Turkey's waning power in the lands of the South Slavs was confined to Macedonia.

In the Habsburg lands Slav nationalism assumed different forms from those it displayed in the Ottoman empire, but it eventually had the same disruptive force in challenging the five-hundred-year-old supremacy of the imperial institutions. A potent infuence in shaping national consciousness arises from the perception of their history which the subject peoples nurture, and which is fed by folk traditions, by the preservation of the vernacular language and by the influence of traditional religious beliefs.

Throughout the nineteenth century the national movements which developed within the great multinational empires which dominated eastern and central Europe were inspired by the sense of deep historical roots which went back into an imaginary golden age before the Ottomans, the Habsburgs, the Romanovs and the Hohenzollerns enslaved the ancient nations of medieval Europe. The Poles looked back to two periods of greatness – the kingdom of the Piasts, which disintegrated in the twelfth century, and that of the Jagiellonians under whose rule Poland's frontiers were extended from the Baltic to the Black Sea. The Magyars drew inspiration from the history of the kingdom established by St Stephen (István) in AD 1000. The South Slav nationalists of the nineteenth century could also boast of medieval greatness under Slav rulers. For them, however, there was no single champion who had forged a South Slav empire which flourished before the arrival of the alien invaders, for until 1918 the Yugoslav peoples had never been united in a single state. Each national group had its own glorious epoch which it did not share with its neighbours; in fact, the glories of one medieval kingdom were often achieved at the expense of its neighbours. The cynical definition of a nation as 'a group of people united by a common error as to their origins and a common dislike of their neighbours' has a tragic relevance in the history of the Yugoslav peoples.

3

The early Slav kingdoms

Serbia

The Serbs are first referred to as a distinct group in the Balkans in the writings of the Byzantine emperor Constantine VII (Porphyrogenitus, nominally emperor from 913 to 959 but effectively so from 945). His massive work *De administrando imperio*, written in the tenth century, refers to Serbs who were subjects of his predecessors and who were converted to Christianity in the ninth century. They appear to have been settled in the seventh century in areas now known as Kosovo, Montenegro and Bosnia. Their early attempts to create some kind of political unity from the scores of minor clans, each under its own chieftain or *župan*, were continually beset by difficulties arising from the attempts of both the Byzantines and Bulgars to dominate them. In the middle of the ninth century one of the Serbian chieftains, Vlastimir, became grand *župan* (*veliki župan*) of a Serbian principality which owed allegiance to Byzantium. Vlastimir enlarged his domain by marrying the daughter of the neighbouring *župan* of Travunija, which gave him access to the Adriatic coast in the Kotor region. After Vlastimir's death internal quarrels and invasions by both Bulgarian and Byzantine forces seriously weakened the Serbs, but in the eleventh century a revived Serbian kingdom emerged, centred on the old Roman town of Doclea, near the present-day site of Titograd. This is known to historians both as Duklija (after Roman Doclea) and Zeta, after the river which flows between Nikšić and Titograd. After a brief period of independence in the second half of the eleventh century – an independence recognised by Pope Gregory VII in 1077 – Zeta was eclipsed by a new Serbian principality, known as Raška, situated in the wild mountainous districts of southern Serbia, which later became known as the Sandžak of Novi Pazar. Raška, whose name survives in a small town at the confluence of the Raška and Ibar rivers, was the nucleus from which grew the great medieval Serbian empire. In 1169 Stephen Nemanja became Grand Župan of Raška. For the next twenty years of his reign he fought against the Byzantines to establish Serbia's independence. He added Zeta to his realm in 1186, and forged a strong alliance between his state and the Church. In 1196 he retired in order to become a monk, first at Studenica and later at the Serbian monastery of Hilendar on Mount Athos, both of which religious houses had been founded by him. The tradition of piety was followed by his sons, Sava and Stephen. The former became the first Serbian archbishop of the autocephalous Church established at Žiča in 1219, and later moved to Peć. The latter succeeded his father as grand župan and in 1202 received the symbols of royalty from Pope Innocent III. Stephen the First Crowned (Prvovenčani) was a worthy successor of his father, both in piety and in organising ability. He consolidated the economic and political base of the Nemanjić dynasty, and when he died in 1227 he left behind a secure and well-organised state which was able to survive both the external pressures from the rising power of the revived Bulgarian empire and the internal quarrels of the subordinate Serbian županates.

Medieval Serbia reached its zenith in the fourteenth century during the reign of Dušan (1331–55), who was crowned Tsar (Emperor) of 'the Serbs and Greeks' in Skopje in 1346. He later moved his capital to Ohrid. He extended the boundaries of his empire in the north at the expense of the Hungarians and to the south by wresting territory from the Byzantines. At its greatest extent Dušan's power reached from Belgrade to the Aegean, taking in Albania, Epirus, Thessaly, Macedonia and most of the Adriatic and Ionian coasts from the mouth of the Neretva to the Gulf of Corinth.

Dušan built on the foundations laid by his predecessors during the previous century. The Serbian Church, founded by his pious ancestor St Sava, was given an enhanced status and Peć became the centre of a patriarchate. The economy was strengthened and German miners were brought in from Transylvania to develop the copper, tin, gold, silver and lead mines of the interior. Merchants from Ragusa and Venice transported the produce of Serbia throughout Europe and the Near East. Agriculture flourished on the fertile soils of Kosovo and Metohija.

Dušan the Mighty (Sihi) is known to history as the Lawgiver because of his introduction of a legal code between 1349 and 1354. This combined elements of Byzantine law with the traditions and customary practices of the Serbs. Although it included the Byzantine penalties of blinding and mutilation for certain offences, it was far in advance of the legal practices of many medieval states, and it was the first comprehensive legal code amongst the South Slavs.

Dušan's ambition led him to aspire to the throne of Byzantium. The empire was in a state of decline which had begun with the havoc wrought in 1204 by the Fourth Crusade and was made worse by internal conflicts. Between 1341 and 1343 Dušan gave his support to a claimant to the Byzantine throne, John Cantacuzenus, whose daughter married the Ottoman ruler Orhan. After Dušan's agreement with Cantacuzenus broke down, the Byzantines called on the Ottoman Turks to assist them in holding the Serbs at bay. It was a tragic irony for the Byzantines, and for Christian Europe, that the first Ottoman incursion into Europe, in 1345, should have been at the invitation of one of the rulers of Constantinople. Dušan withstood the eastern invaders both in 1345 and 1349, but within thirty years of his death in 1355 most of his empire had been overrun by the Turks and Serbia awaited the *coup de grâce*, which came in 1389 with the defeat of Prince Lazar at Kosovo Polje.

Dušan never achieved his ambition to take over Byzantium. After his death his empire quickly disintegrated. His son, Stephen Uroš (1355–71), was unable to hold the Serbs together despite the growing Turkish threat. His authority was disputed by two brothers, Vukašin and John Ugleš, great feudal landowners who controlled Macedonia. Both brothers perished at the battle of Marica in 1371, and a few months later, with the death of Stephen Uroš, the last Serbian tsar, the Nemanjić dynasty came to an end.

Many of the Serbian nobles accepted the Turkish yoke and became vassals of the sultan. One of the most famous was Vukašin's son, Marko, the ruler of Prilep. As the legendary Kraljević Marko, he became the hero of a cycle of popular ballads, embodying all the heroic and tragic characteristics of the Serbian people. Marko served with the sultan's army, as did other Serbs who accepted the status of tributary princes, including Prince Lazar's son, Stephen Lazarević.

The ruler of the much reduced Serbian state was Prince Lazar Hrebeljanović. Aware of the danger from the Turks, he attempted to create alliances with his northern and western neighbours, the Bosnians, the Hungarians, the Croats, the Ragusans, the Venetians and the Albanians. He won an initial victory in 1386, but his cosmopolitan army was no match for Sultan Murad I when battle was joined at Kosovo Polje on Vidovdan (St Vitus' Day), 1389. Murad himself was murdered by a Serb on the eve of the battle, and Lazar also perished.

The Turks were not able to follow up their victory immediately. Murad's successor, Bayezid I, was forced to turn his attention to the threat to his base in Asia Minor posed by the advance of the Mongol hordes of Timur the Lame (Tamerlane).

Although it was almost a century before the Ottomans eradicated the last traces of the medieval Serbian empire by taking the Serbian fortress of Smederovo on the Danube in 1459, the battle of Kosovo sounded the death knell for independent Serbia.

The Serbian rulers who followed Lazar were forced to accept the Turks as overlords and to supply soldiers to the sultan's army. Stephen Lazarević, Lazar's successor, actually fought for Bayezid's Turkish army at the battle of Ankara in 1402 when Timur defeated the Turks and so gave the Byzantines a half-century respite before the conquest of Constantinople by Sultan Mehmed II in 1453. One consequence of Timur's victory was a temporary revival of Byzantine power. On his way home from Asia Minor Stephen Lazarević called on the Byzantine emperor, Manuel II Paleologus, who conferred on the Serbian leader the title of despot. Under Stephen and his successor, Đurad Branković (1427–56), Serbia enjoyed a 'silver age', in which Serbian national culture displayed a vigour and intensity which seem like a brave defiance in the face of the overwhelming pressures from all sides which led in 1459 to the extinction of the Serbian state.

The Turks made a swift recovery after their defeat at Ankara and by 1413 Stephen Lazarević was again compelled to submit to Turkish suzerainty. His nephew, Đurad (George) Branković, sought help from his Christian neighbours, the Ragusans, Albanians, Hungarians and Venetians. The attempts of the Serbs to form a Christian coalition against the advancing Turks were as ineffective as those of the great Albanian leader, Skanderbeg, who, like Đurad Branković, found that the would-be allies often exacted a heavy price for their help and were quite capable of deserting the cause when it suited them.

Thus in 1428 it suited the Hungarians to make a pact with the Turks, who were then fighting the Venetians in Greece. Part of this settlement was to create a Servian buffer state, and both Sigismund and Murad agreed to recognise Đurad Branković as the legitimate ruler of an independent Serbia. The Serbs were forced to accept Hungarian occupation of Belgrade and the capital was shifted to Smederovo, where an impressive fortress was built on the banks of the Danube, 50 km downstream from Belgrade. A few years later the Turks attacked Hungary in sporadic raids which culminated, after the death of Sigismund in 1437, in a full-scale expedition. Serbia was occupied in 1439 and became a Turkish province, but Murad's siege of Belgrade in 1440 was repulsed by the Hungarians. In 1443 a Hungarian army under János Hunyadi advanced into Serbia. The Turks were forced to retreat, and agreed to the re-establishment of the independent Serbian buffer state as a condition of peace with Hungary. The young king, Ulászló, Hunyadi's master, was persuaded by the papal legate that treaties made with non-Christians could be broken, and Hunyadi was ordered in 1444 to attack the Turks once more. This time, something like a Christian front emerged, albeit temporarily, and the campaign took on the character of a crusade, the so-called Crusade of Varna, under the blessing of Pope Eugenius IV. The Christian army which crossed the Danube in 1444 included Hungarians and Wallachians under Hunyadi's command, Albanians under Skanderbeg, and Serbs led by Đurađ Branković. They were joined by Byzantines and by the Venetian fleet when they reached the Dardanelles. Murad II came out of retirement to inflict a severe defeat on this motley force when he confronted them at Varna. The Hungarian king was killed in the battle, and Hunyadi fled back into Hungary with the remnant of his army. In 1448 Murad's army routed Hunyadi once more, this time on the historic field of Kosovo Polje. These Turkish victories at Varna and the second battle of Kosovo sealed the fate of the Serbs and the Byzantines. Constantinople fell in 1453. In 1456 Đurađ Branković died, and his squabbling successors were pushed across the Danube when the Turks took Smederovo in 1459. The Serbian state ceased to exist.

Croatia

The Croats first settled in their present homeland in the seventh century and were converted to Christianity in the first half of the ninth century, shortly after they accepted the suzerainty of the Holy Roman Emperor, Charlemagne, in 803. The early history of the Croats is obscure. References in the work of Constantine Porphyrogenitus, written in the tenth century, indicate that they were settled in Dalmatia in his time and had probably been there for two hundred years. An inscription on a stone at Nin, dating from the end of the tenth century, refers to a Slav prince ('Slavenski Knez'). Nin, which lies on a sheltered bay 20 km north of Zadar, was the seat of the first Croatian bishopric and was under the authority of the Patriarch of Aquileia, which indicates that Christianity came to the Croats from the west. The patriarchate of Aquileia was under the protection of Charlemagne, and the influence of the Frankish kings was felt both in Dalmatia and in the Pannonian region, where Croat tribes were established to the east of the Slovenes, in the middle Sava valley.

In the late ninth century the Byzantines temporarily reasserted their control over the Croats, but in 924 Tomislav, *župan* of Nin, declared himself King of the Croats and established a kingdom free from both Frankish and Byzantine rule. The exact extent of the Croatian kingdom, which flourished during the tenth and eleventh centuries, is a matter of dispute. For a time it probably controlled the Adriatic coast from Rijeka to the Neretva and extended inland to the Hungarian border north of Zagreb and to the Drina valley in the south, where it faced the Byzantine empire and the Serbian principality of Rǎska. In 1089 the death of the ruling Croat prince, Zvonimir, was followed by a dynastic dispute which was finally settled in 1102, when Prince Kálmán of Hungary, a nephew of Zvonimir's widow, succeeded to the crown of Croatia. In 1106 Kálmán acceded to the Hungarian throne, and so began the long and often troubled relationship between Croatia and Hungary which lasted for over eight centuries. The Croats have always maintained that they were never legally part of Hungary. In their eyes Croatia was a separate state which happened to share a ruler with the Hungarians. The degree of Croatian autonomy fluctuated from time to time, as did its borders. At times Slavonia in the north and parts of Bosnia in the south were detached, and in the sixteenth century the whole inland area south of the Sava fell to the Turks. Croatia was confined to a small area round Zagreb and a stretch of the northern Adriatic coast.

Hungary was overrun by the Ottomans and in 1527 the Croatian Sabor elected Ferdinand of Habsburg as its king. Ferdinand also acquired the throne of Hungary, although after 1526 most of that country was under Ottoman occupation. The claims of the Hungarians that the personal union of crowns did not imply the loss of separate Hungarian sovereignty are similar to those which the Croats asserted and the Hungarians denied with respect to Croatia. These claims became burning issues in the nineteenth century, when Magyar nationalism asserted its right to equal status with Austria within the Habsburg empire, and when Croat nationalists fought a bitter struggle against Hungarian domination.

Montenegro

During the two centuries before the Turkish invasions the territory of present-day Montenegro comprised the Serbian principality of Zeta. The inhabitants were culturally indistinguishable from Serbs elsewhere in the Balkans. They spoke the Serbian language and, as members of the Eastern Church, they used the Slavonic liturgy. The development of a separate Montenegrin political and cultural entity came about as a result of the forcible separation of Zeta from the main body of the Serbs after the death of Tsar Dušan in 1355. As the Ottoman tide swept across Macedonia, Serbia, Bosnia, Hercegovina and Albania during the fourteenth and fifteenth centuries, Zeta remained an island which was never completely submerged.

Zeta's administrative separation from Serbia began with the break-up of

Tsar Dušan's empire, some thirty years before the battle of Kosovo. A local feudal family, the Balšići, seized their opportunity and established themselves as rulers of Zeta. By playing off the rival ambitions of the Venetians, the Turks and the Serbs, the Balšići managed to retain their power until the death of Balsa III, the last of the male line, in 1422. Although Zeta was then formally incorporated into the Serbian despotate, the chieftains of Zeta resented Serbian overlordship, and in 1455 a number of them, led by Stevan Crnojević, placed themselves under Venetian suzerainty. The death of the Serbian despot, Đurađ Branković, in 1456, followed by confusion in Serbia as the Turks advanced towards the Danube, created a new situation in Zeta. The Crnojevići attempted to win Venetian support for a determined stand against the Turks, but the astute Italians, with an eye on their future prospects, chose not to offend the increasingly powerful Muslims in the interests of a tiny Christian principality. The Venetians had already gained control of the Montenegrin coast and were developing the trade between the Adriatic ports and their Ottoman-held hinterland which was to bring them so much wealth during the ensuing centuries. Stevan's son, Ivan Crnojević, known as Ivan the Black, was forced to leave his country in 1475, but he returned in 1481 to recover territory lost to the Turks. His success was short-lived and within a few years Ivan had to accept Turkish suzerainty. He remained in Zeta, however, as a subordinate prince to the sultan and had *de facto* control of the inner heartland of Zeta, centred on Ivan's capital, Cetinje. Although the coast was lost to Venice and the eastern territories of Zeta to the Ottomans, the forebears of the modern Montenegrins were able to maintain their traditional culture in their remote redoubt inland from the coastal ranges of Lovčen and Paštrovići.

The Crnojević dynasty lasted for less than a century, but during this period the foundations of a separate Montenegrin nation, with its own forms of government and its own culture, began to crystallise. Ivan founded a monastery at Cetinje, and it was from the monks who lived there that the orthodox bishops were chosen. During periods when the ruler was absent from Cetinje – often trying to persuade the Venetians to help him to resist Turkish pressure – the bishop took charge of the government. After the expiry of the Crnojević line in 1516, the bishops acquired a permanent hold on the machinery of government, electing one of their number as ruler. These prince–bishops were known as Vladikas.

Ivan's son Đurađ is honoured as the first man to introduce a printing press into the Balkans. This invention came to Obod, near Cetinje, from Italy in 1493, only twenty-five years after the death of Gutenberg and within the lifetime of Caxton. It was used to print religious texts in Cyrillic characters and was able to function even during the period of Turkish overlordship after 1499, when Cetinje was incorporated into the sandžak of Skadar.

Bosnia–Hercegovina

The inhabitants of this area of the interior of modern Yugoslavia never had the same clearly defined national identity in the Middle Ages as the Serbs and Croats. This may partly be explained by the geographical circumstances. On the west the present-day boundary between Bosnia and the Dalmatian region of Croatia corresponds roughly to the historic boundaries of Roman Dalmatia, and later of the Venetian and Ottoman empires. Bosnia is a landlocked area, shut off from the Adriatic by the parallel ranges of the Dinaric Alps. On the landward side, however, there is no clear geographical divide. The valleys of the rivers which drain northward to the Sava, following the trend lines of the Dinaric system, afford access into the heart of Bosnia. Hercegovina looks to the Adriatic, with the valley of the Neretva providing a route from the capital, Mostar, to the sea.

The relative openness of Bosnia to influences from Croatia in the north and from Serbia in the south and east facilitated invasion and conquest from Croats, Hungarians, Serbs, Macedonians, Byzantines and Turks. Much of Bosnia belonged to the medieval Croatian kingdom between the ninth and eleventh centuries, at a time when Hercegovina was largely incorporated into the contemporary Serbian kingdoms. For a time the Macedonian ruler Samuilo held power over parts of Bosnia–Hercegovina until he was defeated by the Byzantine emperor Basil in 1014. The Hungarians acquired the mastery of Bosnia when they acceded to the Croatian crown in the early twelfth century. The first distinctly Bosnian state emerged in the late twelfth century under the legendary Ban Kulin (1180–1204). Kulin's adherence to the Bogomil heresy provoked the papacy to interfere. During the half-century after Kulin's death his successors, who either sympathised with or were unable to control the heretic Bosnian Church, were the object of crusades led by the Hungarian kings with the blessing of the pope. For over a century the Bosnian chieftains (bans) were forced to accept Hungarian overlordship. In an attempt to win the people over from Bogomilism, the Hungarians introduced the Franciscans into Bosnia, and their influence continued into the twentieth century.

Internal dynastic disputes in Hungary in the fourteenth century, and the advance of the Turks into Serbia following the fall of Dušan's empire, weakened Bosnia's opponents and provided an opportunity for the revival of the spirit of independence. In 1322 a Bogomil, Stevan Kotromanić, was elected ban. Stevan's son, Tvrtko (1353–91), assumed the title 'King of Serbia, Bosnia and Primorje' in 1377. During the next decade he expanded his kingdom to include central Dalmatia, Hercegovina and part of the old Serbian kingdom of Zeta. After Tvrtko's death the Bosnian nobles quarrelled and, although the Kotromanić family continued to reign for the next seventy years, their power rapidly declined. Squeezed between the conflicting pressures from their own nobles and from the Hungarians and Venetians, and with the ever present menace of the Turks threatening them from the south, they gradually sank into oblivion. Venice reasserted its power in Dalmatia. Hercegovina achieved a degree of autonomy under Stevan Vukšić, who gave himself the title Duke ('Herceg') of St Sava (1448) in honour of the Serbian royal saint of the thirteenth century. When the Turks finally overthrew the last of the Kotromanić rulers in 1463, Vukšić continued to resist for another twenty years. The Hungarians attempted to create a marcher zone to protect their frontier against the Turks by supporting Bosnian resistance in the area between Jajce and the Sava, but after the battle of Mohács in 1526 these pockets of resistance soon collapsed and virtually all Bosnia and Hercegovina lay under the rule of the sultans until the late nineteenth century.

Many Serbs and Croats who had lived in Bosnia fled to the Venetian-occupied coastal areas of Dalmatia or to Habsburg territory north of the Sava. The former, known as the *uskoks*, continued their resistance to the Turks by border raids and guerrilla attacks from fortresses such as those at Klis near Solin and at Senj in northern Dalmatia. The latter were organised by the Habsburgs into *graničari* (frontiersmen), who were given special privileges in return for military duties. The *militär grenze* (military frontier zone) established in 1578 was largely settled by refugees from Turkish-occupied Bosnia and Serbia. The existence today of a large Serbian minority in southern Croatia goes back to this period.

Many of those who stayed behind, especially the adherents of the Bogomil faith, accepted Islam, and their descendants form the nucleus of the Islamic community which embraced 37 per cent of the population of the republic of Bosnia–Hercegovina at the time of the 1981 census.

Macedonia

Macedonia, lying across the southern end of the Vardar–Morava corridor which connects the central Danubian lowlands to the Aegean coasts, has always been fought over by rival powers. In the classical world of ancient Hellas, the strategic importance of this area which controlled the neck of the Greek peninsula was turned to advantage by Alexander the Great in his bid to conquer the known world. From the time of the first Slav settlements in the seventh century until the Second World War Macedonia has always been a meeting place of contrasting cultures and a cockpit of rival political ambitions.

Greeks, Romans, Byzantines, Bulgars, Turks, Albanians and Vlahs all at different times during the medieval period made their cultural, political and ethnic contributions to the Macedonian melting pot. The original Slav settlers came under Byzantine influence until, under the emperor Simeon (893–927), they were forced to submit to Bulgarian rule. The Byzantines struggled to reassert their authority and succeeded in subduing the eastern half of Simeon's former realm, but the western half passed to the control of a Macedonian empire under Samuilo (Samuel) (976–1014). In a brief period of energetic expansion, Samuilo enlarged his empire, from its centre in the Prespa/Ohrid area, so that by the end of the century it extended from the Black Sea to the Adriatic and into Greece, even as far as the Peleponnesus, although the Aegean port of Salonika successfully resisted his attempts to occupy it.

Whilst Samuilo was extending his power at the expense of Byzantium, the emperor Basil II was preoccupied with internal problems and with the advance of the Fatimids into his possessions in Asia Minor and the Levant. He overcame the challenge to his authority at home by enlisting the support of the Kievan ruler, Vladimir, who sent a band of 6,000 Varangian mercenaries from Sweden to the emperor's assistance. They stayed on in Constantinople and became the nucleus of the Varangian Guard, which lasted for many centuries. Having subdued the Fatimids and re-established his authority in Antioch, Basil then returned to deal with the challenge in the Balkans. After over a decade of fighting, Basil defeated Samuilo at the battle of Kleidon in 1014. The cruel vengeance which Basil exacted from the thousands of prisoners taken at Kleidon – he blinded all save one in every hundred, and compelled the sighted ones to lead their blind comrades back to Prilep, where Samuilo died of shock at the piteous sight – earned him the name of Bulgaroctonos (Slayer of the Bulgars). In 1018 Basil entered in triumph Samuilo's castle at Ohrid and Macedonia came once more under the Byzantines. Despite several revolts during the eleventh century, Macedonia remained under Byzantine rule until this was challenged by the rising power of Serbia in the late thirteenth century, in the reign of Milutin (1282–1321), and eclipsed by Dušan in the mid fourteenth century.

Macedonian religious and cultural life continued to flourish under the

Byzantines, with Greek and Bulgarian influences fusing with the original Slav elements to produce a rich tradition in literature, wall paintings and wood carving. No separate Macedonian political unit emerged, however. Byzantine rule was followed by Serbian and then by Turkish occupation. Macedonia did not re-emerge from the shadows until the twentieth century. The memory of its brief period of medieval glory is still a source of inspiration to modern Macedonian nationalists, although their interpretation of its significance has been challenged by Bulgarian, Greek and Serbian historians.

In the foregoing pages the history of five medieval South Slav states has been briefly outlined. Reference has also been made to the early history of the Slovenes, who never controlled a state of their own, apart from the brief episode of Samo, the ruler of a seventh-century Slavonic empire which includes part of modern Slovenia. The Slovenes were under Austrian/German rule for most of their long history, from the Middle Ages until the twentieth century, yet they retained their distinct Slav culture; their national revival in the nineteenth century could draw on a rich cultural heritage.

Some of the non-Slav peoples within the present Yugoslav borders can trace their ancestry back to settlers who entered their present homelands in the centuries before the area was divided between the Ottoman and Habsburg empires, but many more owed their settlement to colonisation sponsored or tolerated by the imperial rulers.

4

The South Slavs under foreign rule

The Ottoman occupation

Osman (Uthman) I, who gave his name to the Ottoman empire, inherited the crumbling Seljuk patrimony at the end of the fourteenth century. Within 150 years of Osman's death in 1324 his successors had overrun what remained of the Byzantine empire and had occupied almost all the territory of present-day Yugoslavia which lies south of the Sava–Danube line. Only Dalmatia and a tiny enclave in Montenegro remained outside Turkish control. Within the next 50 years Ottoman armies crossed the Danube and even penetrated into Hungary and Romania, laying siege to Vienna in 1529. For another 150 years after this, the Ottoman empire continued to expand northwards and westwards until a high-water mark was reached in 1683, with Ottoman forces assembled for the second time before the gates of Vienna. They were driven back and confined to the area south of the Sava–Danube–Una line, where the frontier remained for almost two centuries. The southern area, comprising present-day Serbia, Bosnia–Hercegovina, Kosovo and Macedonia, was incorporated into the Turkish system of government, whilst Slovenia and Croatia–Slavonia, north of the military frontier, were under the dominion of the Habsburgs. Vojvodina was recovered from the Turks at the end of the seventeenth century, and was reunited to a liberated Hungary, also under Habsburg rule. Vojvodina was the chief area of settlement of refugee Serbs fleeing from the Ottomans. Although the very name of the province derives from the promise of Emperor Leopold I that the immigrant Serbs would be given the right to elect their own *vojvoda*, or duke, the Habsburgs did not honour this pledge, and the area was incorporated into the military frontier under direct Habsburg control. Nevertheless, Vojvodina became the cradle of the Serbian renaissance.

Thus, for hundreds of years before the formation of the first Yugoslav state in 1918, the South Slav peoples were subjected to different forms of political and cultural pressure. There were four main elements – the two multinational empires, divided by the Sava–Danube line; the coastlands, including the independent state of Ragusa, under strong Venetian influence; and the tiny independent principality of Montenegro. The legacy of the different cultures which evolved within these four areas still influences the attitudes and ways of life of Yugoslav people today.

The 'millet' system

The incorporation of the occupied lands into the Turkish system of government involved two important features which made a deep imprint on the social life of the Balkans. They were the *millet* system and the *devşirme*.

Islam teaches its adherents that the prophet Mohammed was the last of a long line of prophets who proclaimed the one true God. These included the Jewish prophets of the Old Testament and also Christ himself. Thus, although non-Muslim monotheists, like the Christians and the Jews, had not travelled as far along the road to truth as the Muslims, they were travelling in the same direction. There was, therefore, no sanction in Islam for the persecution of the religious minorities within the Turkish empire. Each religious community – or *millet* – was placed under the supervision of its own leaders, who acted as agents for the imperial government in collecting taxes and maintaining order amongst their people. The Christians belonging to the millet-i-Rum were under the authority of the Patriarch of Constantinople at the top level, and locally under their own bishops. When Mehmed the Conqueror took the city of Byzantium in 1453 he personally invested the new patriarch, Gennadios II. The Jewish community continued to be led by the Chief Rabbi, as it had been under the Byzantine emperors.

On the whole, the system worked as well as any of the administrative systems which functioned in contemporary Christian Europe. The Ottomans depended upon their non-Muslim subjects to conduct the trade of the empire and to provide most of the leading medical practitioners and other specialists. In return, the non-Muslims, although officially regarded as second-class citizens, were free to practise their religion and most were not conscripted for military service. There are many cases recorded in which Christian subjects petitioned the sultan to redress grievances which they suffered at the hands of overbearing church leaders, and where the sultan acted in the interests of the petitioners.

Until the Ottoman empire began to decline in the late eighteenth century, Christian subjects in the Balkans were probably treated no worse than were the peasants of central Europe by their Christian feudal overlords. The unsavoury reputation which the last of the sultans acquired during the late nineteenth century – especially Abdülaziz (1861–76) and Abdülhamid II (1876–1909) – has coloured the view which many western historians have taken of the Ottoman empire as a whole, but to many Christian subjects the Ottoman empire in its heyday was far from the horrific picture conjured up by the use of the phrase 'the long Turkish night'.

'Devşirme'

One of the least attractive features of Ottoman rule was the compulsory enrolment of Christian boys into the military and administrative service of the empire. They were not only pressed into service, but were forced to become Muslims and to learn Turkish, and they were not allowed to marry. A system of military service had been introduced for Turkish Muslims in Anatolia in the early days of the House of Osman. Land was provided to maintain the families in peacetime, and the males were required in turn to rally to the colours in time of war. During wartime a money payment was made from the sultan's coffers to supplement the spoils of war. In addition it was permitted to enslave prisoners of war in order to provide ancillary troops and labourers for the Turkish small-holder/soldiers. These slaves could be admitted into the ranks of the sultan's 'New Troops' – the *yeniçeri* or janissaries.

In the fifteenth century these methods of raising an army proved insufficient and a new method of collecting men was introduced – the *devşirme*. At intervals of a few years recruiting officers were sent out with powers to conscript young Christian boys between the ages of eight and twenty. There were strict rules which the recruiting officers were required to follow. For example, they were not to recruit Muslims, Jews, members of certain skilled trades, orphans, only children and married men. In practice most of the *devşirme* boys came from Orthodox Christian families of Slav, Greek and Albanian origin. Even if the rules were obeyed, the system was clearly oppressive both to the families whose best sons were torn from them and to the young boys who would never see their parents again. But, as with the press-gang system for recruiting sailors in eighteenth-century England, the rules were often not obeyed. Bribery and the corrupt use of power by unscrupulous recruiting officers were all too common.

There are, however, cases which suggest that the Christian communities

who were potential victims of the system did not always look upon
devşirme as being wholly evil. It was possible for *yeniçeri* to rise to the
highest offices in the state. Several grand viziers entered the Sultan's service
via the *devşirme*, including Ibrahim, the Greek who served Suleiman the
Magnificent from 1523 to 1536; the Macedonian Koçu Bey, adviser to
Murad IV in the seventeenth century, who has been called the Turkish
Montesquieu; and Mehmed Sokolović (Sokollu), the Bosnian who held the
post from 1564 to 1579, serving Suleiman, Selim II and Murad III.
Sokolović is well remembered in his native Bosnia and in Serbia. He was
instrumental in persuading the sultan to allow the revival of the see of Peć,
and had his brother installed as metropolitan. Some Christian families saw
the advantage of having a son who was a power at court, and attempted to
bribe the recruiting officers – the *yaya-başis* – to take one of their own.
Although many of the *yeniçeri* forgot all about their origins and became
fanatical Muslims, behaving oppressively to their former compatriots
when they were posted back into the Balkans, others, like Sokolović, kept
in contact with their people and tried to help them. In addition to the forced
conversions of Christian boys through the *devşirme* system, there were also
voluntary conversions which took place gradually between the fifteenth
and seventeenth centuries and which help to explain the presence in
modern Bosnia of a large Slav-speaking Muslim community.

The administrative system of the Ottoman-occupied areas

The rural areas
Estimates based on contemporary data suggest that about 90 per cent of the
population of the Balkans in the sixteenth century lived in rural areas. A
form of feudal tenure governed the relations of the Christian peasantry to
their Ottoman overlords. As elsewhere in Europe, the feudal order was
based on the principle that landholding was tied to certain duties. At the
pinnacle of power the sultan owned all the lands in 'the domain of the
House of Osman' and was the absolute master of all who dwelt therein,
whether Muslim or Christian. They were his flock (or *raya*) and could be
shorn by him at will. The sultan was expected to be a good Muslim and to
act justly in accordance with Islamic teaching. He was served by a
professional class of Ottoman civil servants and soldiers. Between these
officials and the mass of the peasantry were the mainly urban-dwelling
traders, merchants and manufacturers, on whom the feudal obligations
(which bore heavily on the country folk) were somewhat lightened. The

sultan's army was supplied with troops by the *timarli* – the holders of fiefs known as *timars*. In the early days of the system, the majority of *timarli* were cavalrymen – the *spahis* – but during the seventeenth century the janissaries (*yeniçeri*) began to replace the *spahis* and the *timar* system was allowed to decay, being replaced by *iltizam*, a form of leasing under which the obligation to raise troops was replaced by a monetary payment.

An important source of revenue to the sultan's exchequer was the poll tax, or *cizye*. Although Muslims in some areas paid *cizye*, the burden of this tax bore most heavily on the Christians, who were required to pay for every male of twelve years of age on a sliding scale, according to his assessed wealth. The justification for the discrimination between Muslim and non-Muslim was that the latter were not usually drafted into the army and were therefore required to contribute in cash towards their defence.

In addition to the poll tax, there was a complex system of taxes based on land and on crops, some paid in kind, which could amount to as much as 25 per cent of the harvest. For example, a tax was levied in fodder crops, to pay for the upkeep of the *spahis'* horses. Certain lands were set aside for the upkeep of religious and charitable foundations – the *vakifs*. The element 'vakuf' in place names in Bosnia and Serbia (e.g. Skender Vakuf, Gornji Vakuf) is derived from the Ottoman *vakif*.

At first, the Ottoman taxation system, although it bore more heavily on the Christian peasantry than on other inhabitants of the *raya*, was not as oppressive as were the arbitrary and often extortionate levies made by the medieval Christian rulers in western and central Europe. There was an orderly system of collection, monitored by the Christian bishops, and it was possible to appeal to the sultan's court in cases of abuse. Later, however, the system became corrupt and capricious. A particular form of abuse which was greatly resented was the levying of extra taxes to pay for imperial ceremonies – for example the assumption of power by a new sultan – and for the increasing costs of the wars which the empire was forced to fight as its power was challenged by its enemies, notably the Habsburgs during the eighteenth and nineteenth centuries. The consolidation of these extra taxes into a regular additional impost (the *bedel*) was a cause of peasant revolts, which increasingly provoked savage reprisals from the threatened Turkish authorities.

In rural Serbia a form of local self-government, based on the *zadruga*, the extended family often comprising all members of a village, kept alive the traditions of Serbian culture and religion. Groupings of villages, under a *knez* of local origin, formed the next tier of local administration, the *knežina*. By the eighteenth century the heartland of Serbia, the district known alternately as the sandžak of Smederovo and the pašalik of Belgrade, contained between forty and fifty *knezine*, each subject to control by a council of village elders, drawn from the heads of the *zadrugas*, who influenced the actions of the *knez*.

Urban life

The self-government of the *knežina* was limited to internal matters concerned with the Serbian peasantry. Any issues affecting the relations of the Serbs with the imperial authorities or with their Muslim landlords and neighbours had to be dealt with by the Muslim authorities, most of whom operated from the cosmopolitan cities. As well as containing the Muslim legal, military and administrative officials, the cities were the homes of craftsmen, organised in guilds whose members could be either Muslim or *zimmi* (non-Muslim citizens under the protection of the sultan). There were also large colonies of traders of Greek, Jewish, Turkish and, especially, Ragusan origin. The last group were important not only for their commercial activities but also because of their different religious and cultural background, which influenced those with whom they came into contact. A well-known Serbian–American historian, Michael Boro Petrovich, considers that the most far-reaching effect of the Ottoman occupation was the isolation of Serbia from the main currents of western thought and western social development. This included the Renaissance and the Reformation, the development of science and the beginnings of capitalism and modern industrialisation.

There is much truth in this bleak picture of Serbia under Ottoman rule and, to varying extents, of Macedonia, Bosnia, Hercegovina and Montenegro during the same period. The harsh outline is modified, however, when one considers the cities. The Dalmatians from Ragusa represented the most important of the outside influences which penetrated into the heart of the Balkans. They were Roman Catholics and they brought their own priests, their own life style and a cultural heritage which owed much to Italy. Ottoman law required them to live separately in their own quarter of the town, and forbade their priests to proselytise. Nevertheless, it is because of their influence that Roman Catholic adherents were found in the seventeenth century as far east as Bulgaria. The Ragusans represented a way of life which was completely different from that imposed upon the Balkan peoples by the Ottoman occupation, and their influence on life in the cities was of great historic significance.

The proportion of Christians and Jews in the urban population varied from city to city. According to a census in the sixteenth century, Sarajevo was 100 per cent Muslim, but in Bitola (Monastir) in Macedonia 20.2 per cent were Christian and 4.8 per cent Jewish, and in Skopje the proportion was 23.7 per cent Christian and 1.5 per cent Jewish. In the countryside, however, apart from the special case of Bosnia, the overwhelming majority of the sultan's European subjects were Christians, Slavs and peasants.

The economy under the Ottomans

The Ottoman empire has been described as 'a cosmopolitan military feudal theocracy'. For most of the period, from the first conquests in the fourteenth century until the rise of the South Slav nationalist movements in the nineteenth century, the empire was either preparing for a war against its Christian neighbours, fighting a war or recovering from a war. The whole administrative machine was geared to raising taxes and levies of men to fight to defend the Islamic realm against the encircling infidels. Little regard was given to the economy.

When the Turks occupied the old Serbian and Bosnian kingdoms they acquired rich natural resources. Under Dušan the Serbs had encouraged German miners (known as Saxons) from Transylvania to develop the mines of Kosovo, some of which had been worked in Roman times. Copper, lead, zinc and silver were the chief minerals extracted, although in places iron was also worked. Bosnia and Serbia possessed rich forest resources, which were used to provide charcoal for the metal workers' furnaces as well as timber for the construction of houses. A fifteenth-century French traveller refers to the wealth and sophistication of Serbian life, comparing the life style of the upper classes to that enjoyed in France.

After the Turkish conquest the non-agricultural economy withered. The Turks despised trade and commerce and left it to the Christian *zimmi* to conduct such activities. Many of the urban craftsmen were also *zimmi*. Some Turkish administrators, such as the grand vizier Sokollo, encouraged public works, building bridges, mosques, *medreses* and aqueducts, but little was done to encourage industry. Writing of Bosnia in the late nineteenth century, that intrepid English educator Adelina Pauline Irby noted the neglect of the province's economy under Turkish rule, and the sufferings of the poor, burdened by heavy taxation from their Turkish masters and by the exactions of their own Christian clergy.

Thus, according to the British consul, writing in 1873, after four centuries of Turkish rule the commercial life was contemptible, 'plums being the most valuable article of trade in the province'. This sorry state of affairs existed despite the fact that, in Miss Irby's words, 'The soil of

Bosnia teems with various and valuable minerals; her hills abound in splendid forests; her well-watered plains are fertile and productive.' The same picture could be painted of Serbia and Macedonia under Turkish rule. The modern paradox, that the areas of Yugoslavia which are most richly endowed with mineral resources and other industrial raw materials are the least economically developed, can only be understood in the context of the long centuries of neglect from which Yugoslavia south of the Danube–Sava line suffered during the Ottoman period.

The 'çiftlik' system

During the seventeenth and eighteenth centuries there was a rapid growth of large privately owned estates known as *çiftliks*. Strictly speaking they were contrary to Islamic law, as private land ownership was not allowed. In its original meaning *çift* referred to the smallest unit of land which could support a family, and in the early days of the *timar* system the *çift* was the core holding which the *timarli* farmed himself for the benefit of his own family. The *timarli* did not own the *çift*, but he could pass on to his eldest son the right to cultivate it. The size of a *çift* varied from place to place, according to the fertility of the soil, and ranged between four and thirty-five acres.

The growth of *çiftliks* undermined the *timar* system and eventually replaced it. Subsistence agriculture, based on a feudal system of land tenure, gave way to large private estates owned by Muslim lords and worked by Christian tied labourers. This major social and economic change can be attributed to two main causes. First, the old system of raising funds for maintaining the sultan's war machine proved inadequate when the technology of war changed and the *spahi* cavalry ceased to be the indispensable core of the army. Infantrymen bearing firearms and artillerymen became more important than horsemen. The sixteenth century saw the Ottoman conquest of Hungary, the surrender of the Morea and Cyprus by Venice, the sieges of Malta and Vienna and the battle of Lepanto. During this period of rapid territorial expansion the empire was almost continually at war. The cost of these wars put an intolerable strain on the economy, and was mainly responsible for the inflation which afflicted the empire during the second half of the sixteenth century.

A second impulse which prompted economic change came from outside the empire. Despite the fact that the sultans were more often at war than at peace with their Christian neighbours north of the Danube–Sava line, trade with Christendom flourished. The intermediaries in this trade were often merchants from Ragusa, Venice and the city states of northern Italy. The growth of population and the urbanisation of western and central Europe, which occurred during the Age of Discovery and throughout the sixteenth and seventeenth centuries, created a growing demand for the importation of basic foodstuffs and agriculturally derived raw materials such as cotton, wool and hides. Ragusa became an important entrepôt, which, in the words of Sir Paul Rycant, a shrewd English observer, writing in 1668, was 'the port for transmitting the manufactures of Venice, and all Italy, into Turkey', and in return received the necessities of life for distribution to the rest of Europe, often in its own ships. Rycant's book *The Present State of the Ottoman Empire* was published a year after the earthquake of 1667, which marked a downturn in the fortunes of Ragusa. Thereafter the Ragusans began to lose their control of the carrying trade to British, French and Dutch merchantmen.

Concerning the goods carried, records of the Ragusan Lazarette for 1626 show that 120 ships left the port, carrying insured cargoes of 400,000 kg of assorted wool and 70,000 kg of cattle and buffalo hides.

The demand for primary products from Austria–Hungary and western Europe encouraged the change from subsistence agriculture to market-oriented farming, and this was best achieved under the *çiftlik* system rather than under the medieval *timar* or prebendary system. Large estates, often based on virtual monoculture, provided grain, wool, hides and, later, cotton and silk to Christian Europe. The high cost of transport meant that areas with access to the sea or to navigable rivers such as the Danube were better placed than inland areas. For example, in southern Macedonia, within easy reach of the port of Salonika, the *çiftlik* system was more fully developed than in Bosnia and Serbia.

The growth of private estates increased the burdens for the Christian peasants of the *raya* and, increasingly during the eighteenth and nineteenth centuries, protests against the extortion and virtual peonage which the *çiftlik* system imposed on them provided fuel for the fires of peasant revolts.

The culture of the South Slavs under Ottoman rule

The *millet* system enabled the Christian Slavs to maintain their churches and monasteries. Their religious leaders even had a defined role to play within the Ottoman system. During the first century after the fall of the Serbian despotate in 1459, the Serbian Church was placed under the authority of the Greek archbishop of Ohrid, although the local parish clergy remained Slav. The autonomy which the Serbian Church had enjoyed since the creation of the patriarchate in 1346 was replaced by centralised control from Constantinople by the compliant Greek Phanariot clergy, who were considered by the Turkish administration to be the proper representatives of their Christian subjects. The Serbs resented the imposition of alien bishops. The struggle between the Greek and the native Slav influences within the Byzantine Church goes back to the time of Cyril and Methodius, and it continued into the nineteenth century in both the Serbian and Bulgarian churches. The identification of the Serbian Ortho- dox Church with the Serbian nation is deeply rooted in the national consciousness. The medieval rulers of the Serbs were closely identified with the struggle for the autonomy of the Serbian Church. Several members of the Nemanjić dynasty founded monasteries, some became monks, and the pious St Sava, son of Stephen Nemanja, in 1219 became the first archbishop of an autocephalous church, freed from the jurisdiction of the Greek-led archbishopric of Ohrid. This autonomy was extinguished in 1459. The national Church re-emerged from its subjection to Greek influences in 1557, thanks to the intervention of the Bosnian-born grand vizier, Mehmet Sokolović. The first four heads of the newly created patriarchate were members of the Sokolović family. The area of the patriarchate was much greater than its medieval forerunner. It bordered the much reduced archbishopric of Ohrid on the south, but Tetovo and Skopje were within its jurisdiction. To the north it extended beyond the Sava and Danube, to take in the sultan's newly conquered lands in Hungary and Transylvania. Virtually all the Serbian nation came under its authority. Although later boundary changes occasioned by the fortunes of war effectively restricted its jurisdiction, the patriarchate remained until 1766, when, together with the archbishopric of Ohrid, it was placed under the Greek Patriarch of Constantinople.

The importance of the Serbian Church as a rallying point for Serbs, both within and outside the Ottoman empire, cannot be too strongly emphasised. It was the only institution which was able to keep alive the sense of national identity during three and a half centuries of subjugation to foreign rule, which stretched between the fall of Smederovo in 1459 and the revolt of Karadjordje in 1804.

Many Serbs fled from the advancing Turks and settled north of the Sava in the Hungarian-held lands which came to be known as Vojvodina. Some of the Serbian nobles, like Đurađ Branković, their ruler, actually owned land in southern Hungary and were able to move to their estates across the river. Others became refugees and provided the Habsburgs with some of their frontiersmen. With them came priests and bishops, and Serbian monasteries and churches were established, especially in the hills of Fruška Gora, near Novi Sad (Ujvidék). The Turkish occupation of this area, which lasted from the sixteenth century to the eighteenth, did not cause these Serbian communities to be dissolved. They received an influx of new blood in 1691, during one of the many episodes in the interminable struggle between Austria and Turkey for control of the Balkans. The patriarch Arsen III, fearful of Turkish reprisals following an abortive Austrian advance into Serbia, organised a mass migration of Serbs – probably over 30,000 families – to follow the retreating Austrians back across the Danube, where they joined their compatriots in Vojvodina. The flowering of Serbian national culture which occurred in the late eighteenth century and which led to the national awakening and later re-establishment of a Serbian state, owes much to the Orthodox monasteries in Fruška Gora.

The oral folk traditions

If the Church provided the institutional framework within which Serbian national culture could be nurtured, the oral folk traditions of the peasants provided a rich source of inspiration to those who needed reassurance that the nation would eventually rise against its oppressors. This reassurance came from the epic poems (the *pesme*) which celebrated the heroes of the struggle against the Turks after the tragedy of Kosovo. The singing of the *pesme* was accompanied by the music of the *gusle*, a one-stringed fiddle, or a *tambura*, a two-stringed mandoline. The best-known of the folk heroes was Kraljević Marko, son of 'King' Vukašin (Mrnjavčević), who ruled at Prilep until his death in 1371.

Marko in real life succeeded his father as ruler of Prilep, but after 1385 became a Turkish vassal, served in the Turkish army during the battle of Kosovo, and was probably killed fighting for the Turks at Rovine in 1395. This may seem an odd background for a Serbian national hero, although it was part of Marko's obligation as a Turkish vassal (see above, p. 26). In any case, the Marko of the epic poems bears little resemblance to what is known of the historical character whose name he bears. The legendary Marko is an embodiment of all that the Serbs wanted to believe of themselves – his heroism, his gentleness, his respect for the religious and social customs of his people, his 'machismo', even his cruelty, but above all his fierce opposition to the Turks and his intense national pride.

The poems reflect the life and times of the people who created them, their moral values, their understanding of their own history, their hopes and fears for themselves as individuals, and, above all, their consciousness of belonging to a community under threat from alien forces. The thread that runs through the epics, from the medieval roots to the nineteenth century, is of the struggle for survival of the Christian Slavs against the Turks. Svetozar Koljević, in his study *The Epic in the Making*, has also drawn attention to the importance of the oral tradition in a peasant society, most of whose members had no access to the written word. 'In a largely illiterate society this oral epic singing also had the function roughly corresponding to the modern mass media – it spread the political news, much more slowly but perhaps not less reliably than the modern press, radio and television.'

The process of oral transmission across many centuries led to modifications and even radical changes in the themes and in the characteristics of the main actors. Kraljević Marko's exploits, for example, span more than two centuries after Kosovo, and different attributes of this many-sided hero appealed to different generations of singers. Most of the songs originated with the Serbs, but they also influenced the other Slav peoples of the Balkans, including the cultivated literati of Ragusa and the Dalmatian cities. The songs can be conveniently classified into four main groups – those originating in pre-Turkish times; the cycles relating to Kosovo and the adventures of Kraljević Marko; the struggles of the *hajduks* and *uskoks* against the Ottoman occupation; and the wars of independence of the Serbs and Montenegrins during the eighteenth and nineteenth centuries. Some of the poems were written down and became known to the outside world before the end of the eighteenth century. Richard Knolles, writing in 1603, refers to the 'country songs' of the Serbs which tell of the alleged duplicity of the faithless George Branković who betrayed Christendom to the Turks. The translations by Alberto Fortis, an Italian traveller and scholar, of fragments of epic poems which he had collected in Dalmatia and published in 1771, brought the rich oral tradition to the notice of men like Herder and the western European scholars of the Romantic movement. Vuk Karadžić's systematic compilations in the early nineteenth century brought them into the mainstream of European culture.

The chief figures in the Kosovo cycle are the Serbian prince Lazar and his sons-in-law Miloš Obilić and Vuk Branković. Obilić is depicted as a hero who sacrificed his life to murder the Turkish sultan after Vuk had taunted him with treachery and cowardice. The Turkish version of the battle of Kosovo Polje differs from that which is presented in the epic songs and is probably closer to the historical truth. According to a *firman* sent by Sultan Bayezid, the murdered Murad's son, to the Kadi of Brusa, Murad's murder by Obilić took place after the battle. The victorious Murad was supervising the execution of the Serbian nobles, including Lazar, who had been captured in battle. Bayezid writes, 'We enjoyed the greatest pleasure in seeing how the severed heads of the Christian dukes rolled under the horses' hooves, and how many of them with tied hands, and others with broken legs, stood by.' In the midst of this appalling scene, Obilić appeared and approached the sultan to declare his conversion to Islam. As he stooped to kiss Murad's feet he drew a poisoned dagger and stabbed the Turkish leader, causing 'the illustrious sultan to drink the sherbet of martyrdom'.

It is, perhaps, of minor importance whether Lazar was slain in battle or ignominiously beheaded in the presence of the dying sultan, or whether Obilić and Vuk Branković were traitors. It is of far greater historical significance that the legends of Kosovo helped to keep alive for centuries the spark of Serbian national consciousness which burst into flame with the Karadjordje revolt of 1804, and which led ultimately to the founding of an independent Serbian kingdom.

The Kosovo legends are peculiar to the Serbs. The anniversary of the battle, 28 June, is still commemorated as Serbia's national day. It was also the day of Serbia's national saint, St Vitus (Vidovdan). It was on this symbolic day in 1914 that Gavrilo Princip shot the heir to the Habsburg throne, during a state visit to occupied Sarajevo. It was also chosen in 1921 by the rulers of the kingdom of Serbs, Croats and Slovenes as the day on which to promulgate the Vidovdan constitution, a fact which emphasised the primacy of the Serbs within the Triune Kingdom.

The Kraljević Marko legends have had wider currency amongst the Yugoslav peoples, appealing to Croats, Slovenes, Macedonians and Bulgars, and even Turks and Albanians. They formed a strand in the cultural tradition which drew the different peoples together in the formation of the Yugoslav Movement of the early nineteenth century.

The oral tradition lived on into the nineteenth and twentieth centuries. An Englishwoman married to a Serb (Mrs Lawton-Mijatović) wrote of a visit to the old Serbian royal capital, Kragujevac, in 1873. The Skupština (Assembly) was in session, and each day a deputy of peasant origin came into the square outside the building, to deliver to a large audience a blank-verse poem, giving a highly coloured account of the debates on a bill to reform the currency! Epic poems were sung to commemorate such events as the battles against the Turks during the Balkan wars of 1912–13 and (shades of Kosovo) the defeat of the Serbs in 1915 at the hands of the Habsburgs and their allies. The Slav Muslims also had their oral traditions, the most celebrated of their ballads being the *Hasanaginica*, which was first written down in the eighteenth century. English versions of this tragic tale affected the writers of the Romantic period, and amongst the English translations are those which appear under the names of Lord Byron, Sir Walter Scott and Lord Lytton (Owen Meredith).

'Hajduks' and 'uskoks'

Resistance to the Turks did not end with the overthrow of Đurađ Branković's Serbian kingdom and the occupation of Bosnia and Hercegovina. Many of those who fled across the Danube became *graničari* (frontiersmen) in the military frontier zone set up by the Habsburgs; others manned fortresses in Dalmatia, combining defence against the Turks in the interior with piracy in the Adriatic. These were known as *uskoks*. From amongst those who stayed behind, bands of outlaws, known as *hajduks*, took to the woods and hills in order to harass the Turkish officials and landowners. When Austrian raids were made into Turkish-occupied Serbia and Bosnia, *hajduks* joined forces with the raiders. As with the resistance movements of occupied Europe during the Second World War, many *hajduks* outwardly collaborated with the occupying administration, whilst clandestinely supporting the resistance. The *hajduks* of popular legend were Robin Hood figures, robbing the rich Turks in order to give to the poor Serbs. In real life the distinction between sheer brigandage and patriotic guerrilla activities was often blurred. In most cases the *pesme* sing of tragic heroes who met violent deaths, martyrs to the national cause. Such were the Bosnian *hajduks* of the seventeenth century and Serbian hero Banović Strahinja. Not all the theses of the *pesme* were concerned with large national issues. The heroes come across as people who lived their lives to the full and knew how to love and laugh as well as how to fight. Although Serbian society was patriarchal, there are some impressive female characters, like the tragic mother of the nine Jugovići sons in the Kosovo cycle and Banović Strahinja's spirited wife. The stories about Strahinja tell of a classic conflict between love and duty when the hero's wife falls in love with the Turk who has abducted her from the family home whilst her husband is away in Kruševac visiting his wife's relatives, the powerful Jugovići family. This legend forms the basis of a compelling play by the modern Serbian writer Borislav Mihajlović, which achieved a notable success when first produced in Novi Sad in the early 1960s. A film on the same theme has also been made.

The rich oral tradition of the *pesme* made a great impression on writers and folklorists during the Romantic revival of the nineteenth century. Jakob Grimm called them Homeric in their epic majesty and Goethe compared the Kosovo *pesme* to the Song of Songs. Their importance to the history of the Yugoslav peoples is that they kept alive the spirit and culture of a downtrodden nation during the centuries of foreign occupation.

Slovenes, Croats and Serbs under Habsburg rule

The link between the Habsburg dynasty and the South Slav peoples began in the late thirteenth century, following the defeat of Ottokar, the Przemysl king of Austria–Bohemia by the German prince Rudolf of Habsburg at the battle of the Marchfeld near Vienna in 1278. Within fifty years Habsburg rule had penetrated southward from Inner Austria and Styria to the Adriatic, incorporating Carinthia and Carniola in 1335. Istria was added in 1374 and Trieste in 1382. The Slovenes of these newly acquired territories were no strangers to German rule, which they had first experienced under Charlemagne. Hungary first came under Habsburg rule in 1437, when Albrecht II of Austria was nominated by the Holy Roman Emperor, Sigismund, to succeed him. From then until the dissolution of the Empire by Napoleon in 1806 the Imperial crown was effectively the hereditary possession of the Habsburg family. With Hungary went also the crown of Croatia. Dynastic disputes followed the death of Albrecht, who died from dysentery in 1439, whilst preparing an army to keep the Turks at bay, and the Habsburgs were temporarily eclipsed as incumbents of both the Imperial and Hungarian thrones. The succession to the Empire was soon re-established in the Habsburg line and the link with Hungary came again after the battle of Mohács in 1526, when Ferdinand I of Austria succeeded the last Jagellonian King of Hungary and Bohemia, Ludovic, who was drowned while fleeing from the battlefield. In 1527 the Croat Diet also elected Ferdinand as King of Croatia.

Although Ferdinand's domain was much reduced by the advance of the Turks into Hungary and Croatia, the association of the Hungarians and Croats with the Habsburgs remained until 1918. Hungary also included the Vojvodina, with its considerable population of Serbs, many of whom had crossed the Danube in front of the advancing Ottoman armies. During the next 150 years most of Hungary lay under Turkish rule, but the Habsburgs held on to Slovenia and parts of Croatia and Slavonia, including the Zagreb region. In 1578 the military frontier (*Militärgrenze*) was established as a defensive zone protecting the Habsburg lands from the Turks. As the Habsburgs were the standard bearers of the Holy Roman Empire, they saw this frontier as the protective wall which shielded Christendom from the infidel Islamic hordes.

The geographical position of the frontier fluctuated with the fortunes of war. At its greatest extent it stretched from the Adriatic coast below the Velebit mountains, across the northern Dinaric ranges to the Sava, along the Sava to the Danube and along the Danube to the western margins of Transylvania and Wallachia. The western end of the line held firm for most of the three centuries of the frontier zone's history, although there were frequent Turkish raids into Carinthia, Carniola, Styria and Croatia. The eastern end was not fully established until the early eighteenth century, when the Turks were driven from Hungary, Transylvania and the Banat.

The lands which formed the military frontier had suffered greatly from the passage of armies in both directions during the fierce fighting of the fifteenth and sixteenth centuries, and when the defensive zone was established many of the villages had been depopulated. One of the first tasks of the Habsburgs was to induce settlers to occupy the empty lands. Amongst those who took advantage of the privileges offered, the majority were Serbs, but others also moved in, notably Germans, Hungarians and Slavs from other parts of the multinational Empire. They were offered lands, homes and a relaxation of feudal obligations in return for military service in defence of the frontier. The eighteenth-century historian and topographer Freiherr Johann von Valvasor describes the life of the frontiersmen: 'Whenever a man was working in the fields he always carried his arms with him and kept a horse saddled near his plough. When the Turks appeared he immediately mounted, either to give battle, or, if they were too numerous, to ride off and raise the alarm.'

The descendants of those who occupied the military frontier form a large element of the 550,000 Serbs who still live in Croatia. There are villages in Lika, Kordun, Banija and Gorski Kotor, between Zagreb and the northern Adriatic coast, where over 70 per cent of the present-day inhabitants are Serbs. Other old-established Serbian communities are found in the Dalmatian hinterland. The place name Srpsko Polje, on the route across the Velebit mountains from the old *uskok* castle of Senj, is one example.

The Slovenes

During the Habsburg period the territory inhabited by the Slovenes was divided into six administrative areas, all of which formed part of Austria. These were Styria (Steiermark), acquired by the Habsburgs in 1278; Carniola (Krain) and Carinthia (Kärnten), which came to the Habsburgs in

1335; and Trieste, Görz–Gradisca and Istria, which were absorbed into the expanding Austrian realm later in the fourteenth century. With Habsburg rule came a strengthening of German cultural influences. Austro-German barons acquired lands in the newly won territories and built their castles on their estates. German-speaking bishops appointed by the Archbishop of Salzburg administered large tracts of Church lands; other areas belonged to the bishoprics of Brixen and Freising. German-speaking settlers moved into Slovene-speaking districts as landowners, merchants and craftsmen. In 1360 Rudolf IV organised a mass settlement of thousands of German colonists in the Gottschee (Kočevje) area of Lower Carniola. Their descendants remained until they were expelled to Austria at the end of the Second World War. Many Slovenes were absorbed into the dominant German culture and into the Austro-German nobility. Yet, with remarkable tenacity, the mass of the Slovene peasants retained their Slav culture and language.

The Reformation

In the early sixteenth century the Reformation made considerable progress amongst the Slovenes, and Protestant schools and churches were established in Laibach (Ljubljana) and other Slovene towns. Although the Habsburg-led Counter-Reformation eventually extinguished this movement, it bore fruits which were of enduring significance in the cultural history of the Slovenes. In 1555 Primož Trubar made the first translation of the New Testament into Slovene and in 1584 a Slovene grammar was produced. The works of Trubar and his collaborators were printed in Germany and circulated not only amongst Slovenes but also amongst Croats and Serbs. This early manifestation of a Yugoslav cultural movement lay dormant until the late eighteenth century, when, during the reign of Joseph II (1780–90), the apostle of the Enlightenment, there was the reawakening of the national cultures of the Slavs within the Empire. The works of Trubar and his contemporaries were rediscovered and had an influence on such figures in the Yugoslav renaissance as Kopitar and Vuk Karadžić.

As elsewhere in Europe, the Reformation in Slovenia coincided with a period of social unrest which was characterised by a number of peasant revolts. In Slovenia and Croatia a serious peasant rising, led by Matija Gubec, threatened the city of Agram (Zagreb) in 1573. The rallying cry of the rebels, '*za stare pravice*' (for the old rights), does not suggest that the peasants were inspired by Protestant ideas. In fact, in so far as religion was involved, the contrary was probably the case, as the ideas of the Reformation affected the nobles and the town dwellers more than the peasants. There is some evidence of an organised conspiracy to spread the revolt throughout the Slovene-speaking areas of Styria, Carniola and Istria, and evidence that Gubec was only one of a number of local leaders in different areas. In fact, the rising was limited to the Zagorje region of north-western Croatia and the adjoining Slovene areas. The centre of the revolt was the village of Donja Stubica, some 24 km (15 miles) north of Zagreb. The first encounter took place there on 29 January 1573. Within a few days the Slovene peasants of the Krka valley between Novo Mesto and the Croatian border had also risen. In all, some 8,000 to 10,000 peasants were involved in both Slovenia and Croatia. Gubec was executed on 15 February. The revolt was suppressed with abominable cruelty. Gubec was taken to the cathedral in Agram (Zagreb), where he was crowned 'King of the Peasants' in the presence of a jeering congregation. The iron circle which was placed on his head was first raised to white heat, and the peasant leader expired to the taunts of 'Ave rex rusticorum' (*Živio seljački kralj*). His remains were then hung on a gibbet as a warning to others. Although the revolt lasted less than a month and its effects were confined to a small region, Gubec became a folk hero to the peasants. Later, Slovene and Croat historians depicted him as a martyr to the cause of Slav resistance to foreign rule, because the nobles against whom he rebelled were Germans, Hungarians or Slavs who had adopted the culture of their Habsburg masters. The great Croat writer, the late Miroslav Krleža, in his *Ballade Petrice Kerempuha*, written in the *kajkavski* dialect of the Zagreb region, was one of many who drew inspiration from the terrible events of 1573.

The Reformation came to Slovenia and Croatia at a time when the Turkish threat was at its height. The divisions amongst the Christians weakened their power of resistance and may have contributed to the Ottoman victories of the sixteenth century. At the eastern end of the Habsburg–Ottoman line there was a total collapse, leading to the occupation of Vojvodina and most of Hungary and Slavonia by the Turks. In the centre and west, in Croatia and Slovenia, the military frontier held, but throughout the sixteenth and seventeenth centuries these areas were the victims of frequent raids by marauding bands of Turks, who even penetrated as far as Graz. Slovene churches in the path of these invasions had defensive walls built around them, behind which the inhabitants of a threatened village could take refuge until the storm passed. In the more vulnerable areas there was serious depopulation as villages were abandoned. By the end of the seventeenth century the danger had receded, and the eighteenth century saw steady economic progress in an atmosphere of stability and calm.

The Slovene literary language

The Counter-Reformation crushed the spirit of Protestantism in Slovenia, but it did not completely suppress the influence of Trubar and his contemporary Slovene writers. Even the Jesuits, who were called upon in 1573 to lead the *Kulturkampf* against the Protestant heresy, were forced to provide devotional literature and hymns in Slovene. The first known secular literature in Slovene was composed of the baroque poems of an Augustinian friar, Marko Pohlin, written in the mid eighteenth century. Although modest in their poetic achievement, they helped to sustain the tenuous thread of the Slovene literary language which led back to Trubar. In the late eighteenth century the influence of the Josephine Enlightenment encouraged the pioneer Slovene industrialist Baron Žiga Zois to patronise the Slovene literary movement. Further impetus was given during the brief Napoleonic occupation of the Illyrian Provinces (1809–13), when the Slovene language was encouraged in the schools. It is significant that one of the figures to emerge from this period, the poet Valentin Vodnik (1759–1819), wrote poems in praise of Napoleon. Another was the first Slovene playwright, Anton Linhart. Vodnik was in many ways a typical figure of the European Romantic movement, drawing inspiration from the oral folk tradition of the peasants, which had a vigour and directness often lacking in the more formal literary tradition. The generations of poets who followed him, notably Prešeren (1800–49) and Stritar (1836–1923), were able to combine a familiarity with the central European literary heritage with an ear for the cadences of peasant speech. After them the literary scene in Slovenia throughout the nineteenth century resembles that of many of the small nations of Europe struggling to free themselves from the shackles of the great multinational empires which straddled the continent from Finland to the Aegean. The rediscovery of rich veins of vernacular literature, which had been kept alive in the oral traditions of the peasants during centuries of domination by alien cultures, gave a feeling of self-confidence to the national movements which were striving for independence. In many cases the touch of Napoleonic France's magic wand awoke the sleeping nations to the call of destiny. The Slovenes had the added advantage of a literary language which was three centuries old.

The Slovene economy under the Habsurgs

The Slovene lands formed part of the Austrian polity, both in an administrative and economic sense. Although the provincial assemblies of the Estates, representing the nobility, the clergy and the burghers, had at certain times some degree of local responsibility, for the most part the life of the realm was directed from the Austrian capital. This became increasingly the case under the centralising regimes of Maria Theresa and Joseph II in the second half of the eighteenth century. A description of Carniola in the late seventeenth century by the Germanised Slovene nobleman Von Valvasor depicts a vigorous economic life, based on the exploitation of local mineral and agricultural resources. A major Imperial trade route passed through Slovene territory, linking Vienna, via Graz, Marburg (Maribor) and Laibach (Ljubljana), to the Adriatic port of Trieste. Foreign trade played an important part in the Slovene economy, Italy and the German states being important trading partners. Slovenian-made goods such as iron utensils from the forges in the forested uplands which lay alongside the Laibach–Trieste artery; timber; quicksilver from the mines at Idrija; farm produce, notably wool, cattle, fruits, grain and honey, were the principal exports. Many of the ships built at Trieste used timber from the slopes of the Trnovski Gozd above the Vipava valley. The forests also supplied charcoal for the forges. As the pace of economic exploitation quickened in the nineteenth century the forests were depleted, the ravages of the woodmen being supplemented by the destructive habits of the goats kept by the peasants.

In return for these exports the Slovenes were able to import a range of goods not only from Italy and Germany but also from the Levant and the Far East, via Trieste and Venice. Silk, spices and, later, coffee were amongst these overseas imports. This provided a richer and more varied diet and a grander life style for those in the middle and upper ranks of society than would have been possible if they had been dependent only on the products of a self-contained peasant economy. Already by the end of the eighteenth century a substantial educated Slovene middle class had come into existence. They were in touch with the main currents of European political and cultural life and were able to send their sons to universities such as Göttingen, Tübingen, Vienna and the Sorbonne. They were infected by the ideas of the Enlightenment and were ready to welcome the Napoleonic soldiers and administrators who incorporated the Slovene lands into the Illyrian Provinces in 1809 for a brief, but fateful sojourn of four years.

One of the most outstanding figures was Baron Zois, who owned iron workings at Stara Fužina, on the shores of Lake Bohinj (Wocheiner See) in the Julian Alps. Mention has already been made of his influence on the Slovene literary movement. As an industrialist and landowner he was a forward-looking innovator who, like his English contemporaries, the improving landlords of the eighteenth-century agricultural revolution, introduced new farming techniques on his estates and exploited the mineral resources which he found under his lands.

The dissolution of the monasteries by Joseph II also had important economic consequences for Slovenia. It gave an opportunity for entrepreneurs to acquire the lands, workshops, fishponds and mines which the monks had worked, and to integrate them into the developing secular economy. Some of the effects of this can be seen at the Slovene technical museum housed in the old monastery buildings at Bistra, on the edge of the Ljubljansko Barje (Ljubljana Heath).

Other economic achievements of the late eighteenth century were the draining of the marshes in the old lake bed of the Ljubljansko Barje – work which had been started in Roman times and is still not completed – the introduction of maize and potatoes into the crop rotation, the expansion of viticulture and the development of the textile industry.

Although the Slovene economy developed during the nineteenth century as a satellite economy to that of Austria, at the end of the eighteenth century it had a sufficient degree of autonomy to sustain a self-reliant, Slovene-speaking middle class which could act as a spokesman for the national movement. When the ideas of the French Revolution concerning the rights of nations to self-government reached the Slovenes, they already had many of the attributes of a modern nation, but it was to take them over a century to achieve a form of self-determination within the wider Yugoslav state. The peculiar circumstances of the Slovene nation's historical experience help to explain why Slovenia today enjoys a higher standard of living, a higher level of industrial and educational achievement, and a greater degree of 'westernization' than do the other Yugoslav republics.

The Croats

The personal union of the crowns of Croatia and Hungary which began in 1102 did not, according to Croatian historians, subordinate the Croats to the Magyars. They resist the Hungarian claim that the three regions of Slavonia, Croatia and Dalmatia were annexed to Hungary. The Croats point to the fact that they retained their own chief executive – the ban; their own assembly, the Sabor; and their own judicial system. They even had some control over their own finances and their own armed forces. It would seem, however, that real power rested in the hands of the feudal nobility which acknowledged the suzerainty of the Hungarian king, but held considerable power independently. The dominant families did not display any strong national feelings, Croat or Hungarian. They were more concerned with the consolidation of their estates and with the expansion of their personal power. Two of the leading families, the Zrinski and the

Frankopani, held land in both countries and moved freely between their lands.

The power of the crown was severely restricted, and the magnates usually elected weak rulers in order to safeguard their own privileges. In 1458, however, fear of the Turkish menace overcame their fear of a strong king, and they elected the ruthless and able Matthias Corvinus (Mátyás Hunyadi). Matthias, for the first time, summoned Croat nobles to the Hungarian Diet and reorganised the defences against the Turks, building fortresses along the Sava and Kupa in what later became the military frontier zone. The Croatian nobles were forced to supply troops and funds for the defence of the frontier, although the Sabor was permitted to appoint the supreme army commander.

The death of Matthias in 1490 left the succession in dispute, as he had no legitimate offspring. A dynastic struggle between Jagellonians and Habsburgs drew in the Croat magnates, who generally supported the Habsburg cause. This was despite the fact that one of the claimants, John Zápolya, who was crowned King of Hungary in 1514, was of Slavonian origin and was known to the Magyars as the Slav King. A period of anarchy followed, in which the Turks were able to take advantage of the divisions amongst their Christian enemies to raid into both Croatia and the Slovene lands of Carniola. In 1493 a battle between the Croats under Ban Mirko Derenčin and a force of 8,000 Turkish cavalry occurred near the town of Udbina in the Lika region. Ten thousand Croats fell to 'the red wind of the Moslem scimitars' and, with them, the flower of the Croat nobility. Stanko Guldescu, the historian of medival Croatia, has described this disaster as having 'more significance for the subsequent fate of Europe than the more publicised Serbian debacle' at Kosovo Polje in 1389. A contemporary writer from Lika compared it to the Mongol invasions and the depredations of the Goths and Attila the Hun. Even today the district between Udbina and Titova Korenica is known as Krbava (*krv* = blood) and the valley between Udbina and Bunić, where the battle occurred, is called Krbavsko Polje, the Field of Blood.

The dynastic struggle was eventually resolved in favour of the Habsburgs, but not before the death of Zápolya in 1540. Ferdinand of Habsburg secured the votes of the Croatian Sabor on 1 January 1527, three months after Suleiman's victory at Mohács, but Zápolya, referred to by the sultan as his vassal, continued to dispute the throne of Hungary and refused to recognise the vote of a section of the Hungarian Diet in favour of Ferdinand. Zápolya had, after all, been crowned with the iron crown of St Stephen, the sacred symbol of Hungarian sovereignty. In practice, however, the real power in Hungary and much of Slavonia and Croatia lay in Turkish hands.

The Habsburgs took the Turkish threat more seriously than Matthias had done. In 1522 the emperor Charles V, head of the House of Habsburg, and since 1520 Holy Roman Emperor, entrusted to his younger brother, Archduke Ferdinand, the government of the Austrian province, which included the Slovene areas of Styria, Carinthia and Carniola, and the march lands along the Croatia–Slavonia border. In return Ferdinand renounced his claims to the Spanish and Burgundian lands held by the Habsburgs, but he later acquired the crowns of Bohemia and Hungary and ascended the Imperial throne on the abdication of Charles in 1558. Ferdinand gave high priority to the defence of his realm, and of Christendom itself, against the Turks, and he intervened directly in Croatian affairs to ensure that adequate preparations were made. He created a chain of fortified villages and strongpoints and established a corps of mercenary troops to guard them. These villages were settled by colonists who were given exemption from feudal obligations to the local Croatian nobility in return for their willingness to take up arms against the Turks. This was the beginning of the *Militärgrenze* system, which was not finally abolished until 1881. This system suited Ferdinand in several ways: it was relatively cheap: it gave defence against small border raids and a trip-wire to provide early warning against major invasions; it also broke the power of the remaining Croatian noble houses, which had survived the massacre of Krbavsko Polje; and it might provide a corps of *Kaisertreu* troops in case of trouble from rebellious Hungarian magnates. This last point was still valid two centuries later, as referred to in a report by the governor of the Varaždin district in 1737: 'diese granitz nicht allein als ein antemurale contra Turcam, sed etiam contra Hungarum in casu rebellionis anzusehen ist' ('this frontier is not only a defensive outwork against the Turk, but can also be seen as protection in case of rebellion in Hungary').

The ideal settlers for the zone, which was directly administered by the Austrians, were refugees from Serbia, the so-called *uskoks*. They had reason to hate the Turks, who had driven them from their homes; they were grateful for the grants of land which enabled them to settle down in their new homes, and they owed no allegiance to the Croatian and Hungarian nobles. It is not surprising, therefore, that the frontiersmen (*graničari*) were regarded as being amongst the most loyal of the Emperor's troops. This tradition persisted even after the dissolution of the military frontier in 1881. During the First World War, General Boroević's *graničari*, serving on the Isonzo front, were responsible for the defeat of the Italians at Caporetto in 1917.

The existence of the military frontier, which was eventually extended eastward to Transylvania, did not save Croatia–Slavonia and Hungary from Turkish occupation. From the mid sixteenth century until the Treaty of Karlovci (Carlowitz) in 1699, only a small portion of western Croatia, extending along the borders of Styria and Carniola from Zagreb to the Gulf of Kvarner (Quarnero), remained effectively under Habsburg control. The year 1699 marked the turn of the tide. As the Habsburgs advanced step by step, with occasional setbacks, the Turks were gradually pushed back south of the Sava and Danube, and the military frontier was re-established along the full length of the line from Transylvania to the Adriatic. As more of Croatia–Slavonia came under Habsburg control, the old links between the Croat and Hungarian nobility were re-established. Whilst they no longer had need to make common cause against the Turks, they now had a new common enemy in the Austro-German Habsburgs, whose centralising tendencies during the reigns of Maria Theresa and Joseph II stimulated resistance from the non-German nobility.

The Croat nation had taken a severe battering between 1526 and 1699, but that portion which flourished in Dalmatia kept alive the spirit and culture of the people.

Dalmatia and the Adriatic littoral

The Adriatic coast and the offshore islands form a distinct geographical zone, separated from the interior of the Balkan peninsula by the formidable barrier of the Dinaric Alps. The Mediterranean climatic zone, and the mode of life associated with it, is restricted to a thin fringe extending only a few miles inland. Communications by sea across the enclosed waters of the Adriatic has always been easier than by land routes across the mountains or along the narrow coastal strip. Even until after the Second World War, the cities of Dalmatia could more easily maintain contact with each other by sea than along the tortuous roads and tracks which were the only means of land transport. It is not surprising, therefore, that cultural influences from Italy have, until comparatively recently, had a greater effect than have those emanating from the Balkans. The Romans found the Dalmatian environment congenial, and the traces of their colonisation are still to be found in coastal cities such as Zadar, Šibenik and, above all, Split. The Byzantines inherited Dalmatia from the Latins, and their sovereignty, although often disputed, was recognised, however nominally in later centuries, for as long as five hundred years. The two chief rivals for Dalmatia from the ninth century to the twelfth were the Croats and the

Venetians. The medieval Croatian kingdom which emerged in the early tenth century under Tomislav (AD 910–30) had its base first of all at Nin, 15 km north of Zadar, and later at Biograd-na-Moru, 25 km to the south. Both of these early Croatian capitals occupied sheltered sites on the coast. Behind them lay the fertile, *flysch*-covered lowlands of the Ravni Kotari region, the largest area of flat land in Dalmatia. Although requiring constant attention to water management, it provided a geographical base for the infant kingdom superior to that offered by the bleak, intermontane valleys inland, across the high limestone ranges of the Velebit mountains.

Tomislav's contemporary, Bishop Gregory of Nin (Grgur Ninski), is regarded by modern Croat historians as being one of the early heroes of the Croatian nation. He fought a vigorous battle for the right of the Croat Church – at this time under the patriarchate of Aquilaea, which owed allegiance to Byzantium – to use the Slavonic liturgy and the glagolitic alphabet, in opposition to the Roman influences of the neighbouring bishopric of Split. Although the bishopric of Nin was abolished and the Latin rite eventually triumphed in Croatia, Grgur Ninski's assertion of the individuality of the Croat nation provided a spiritual sanction to Tomislav's claims to kingship.

At its greatest extent in the late eleventh century the Croatian kingdom reached down to the Neretva, where its frontier met that of medieval Serbia. For most of the two centuries after Tomislav's accession in AD 900, the effective authority of Croatia lay in the coastal region north of Šibenik. Inland it extended into Slavonia, where it came into contact with Hungary. In 1102 the crown of Croatia passed to Hungary, and this land-locked power achieved its long-held ambition, to possess an outlet to the sea.

For the next three centuries the history of Dalmatia was dominated by the rivalry between Hungary and Venice. For Venice, the freedom of navigation along the Adriatic was vital to the maintenance of its seaborne trade with the Levant. The possibility of a potentially hostile power occupying bases in Dalmatia was a matter of life and death to the republic. Even if the Hungarians or the Turks could be kept at bay, there was also the threat of piracy to be met. Venice, therefore, had an imperative need to extend its influence over the Dalmatian coastal cities. The first decisive blow struck by the Venetians was in AD 1000, when the doge, Pietro Orseolo II, defeated the Croats and advanced to the mouth of the Neretva, where his fleet destroyed the nest of pirates, the Neretljani, who menaced the shipping routes in the southern Adriatic. Orseolo stopped short at Pelješac, and did not attempt to attack the independent city state of Ragusa (Dubrovnik). The Croatian cities conquered in this expedition retained a degree of local autonomy by playing off Venice against Hungary as the fortunes of Dalmatia oscillated between the two rival powers. In 1202 the Venetians persuaded the armies of Christendom to divert their attention from the Fourth Crusade to assist in the subjugation of Zadar, whose citizens had risen against Venice. During the thirteenth and fourteenth centuries the Dalmatian cities changed hands many times, but despite these upheavals they enjoyed long periods of prosperity and their commerce and their arts flourished.

A complication was introduced in the fourteenth century by the rise of the Serbian and Bosnian kingdoms, which briefly controlled parts of the coast, the Serbs during the reign of Dušan in the middle of the century, and the Bosnians under Stevan Tvrtko after 1390. The Turkish occupation of the Balkans created a new situation. Hungarian power was broken, the Slav kingdoms were crushed, and a single, powerful occupying power threatened the coastal cities from beyond the mountains. For the next three centuries Dalmatia's fortunes were determined by the struggles between the sea power of Venice and the land-based might of the Ottoman empire. The northern area from Rijeka to Zadar was incorporated into the military frontier, which was under the control of the Habsburgs. Dalmatia proper extended from Zadar to Ragusa.

The Turkish conquest of the Balkans impelled large numbers of Serbs and Bosnian Croats to flee into the neighbouring lands of Croatia, Slavonia and Dalmatia. Many of those who settled in Dalmatia mixed with the existing Croat population. Thus the Slav element in Dalmatia increased at the expense of the Italians. The presence of a mixed Serb and Croat population who had lived and worked together for centuries was a factor of some importance in the nineteenth and early twentieth centuries, when Serb and Croat deputies in the Austrian parliament worked together, first for the reunion of Dalmatia and Croatia, and later for the creation of a South Slav state. Between 1468 and 1718 Turkey and Venice were officially at war seven times, the period of hostilities totalling forty-two years. Between the wars there were periods of comparative peace, but the Turkish occupation of the hinterland was an ever present menace. In the face of a common enemy, Serbs, Croats, Italians and Vlahs were able to unite in defence of the Dalmatian city states which owed allegiance to Venice.

An important defensive position against the Turks was the fortress of Klis, which stands on an isolated pinnacle of rock overlooking the route which leads from Solin (Salona) to Sinj, in a gap between the Kozjak and Mosor mountains. It was the route by which the Turks could penetrate the mountain barrier separating the coastal lowlands around Split from

Turkish-held Bosnia. The Croat feudal lord Petar Kružić gathered together a garrison composed of Croat refugees, who used the base at Klis both to hold the Turks at bay and to engage in marauding and piracy against coastal shipping. Although nominally accepting the sovereignty of the Habsburg emperor Ferdinand I, who obtained the Croatian crown in 1527, Kružić and his freebooting *uskoks* were a law unto themselves. When a large Turkish force invested the castle at Klis in 1536, Kružić appealed to Ferdinand for help, but the Emperor's attention was diverted by a Turkish invasion into Slavonia and he was unable to prevent the surrender of the garrison. With Kružić dead and the sultan in possession of Klis, the Turks were soon able to overrun most of Dalmatia between Split and the Ragusan border. Split, under Venetian control, was not taken, and the northern coastlands and islands between Zadar and Rijeka remained under Austria or Venice. The surviving *uskoks* were able to settle in the fortified town of Senj, on the rugged Velebit coast, opposite the southern tip of Krk island.

War between Venice and Turkey broke out in 1571, following the participation of Venetian ships in the Christian fleet which defeated the Turks at Lepanto, but it resulted in a stalemate in which neither side gained territory. For the next seventy years an uneasy truce prevailed, until hostilities were resumed in 1644. The peace which ended this episode was not concluded until 1669. Although Venice lost territory elsewhere, including the island of Crete, there was little change in Dalmatia. Turkish fortunes began to decline after the raising of the second siege of Vienna (1683), and the Treaty of Karlovci (Carlowitz) in 1699 recorded the first major Ottoman defeat and the beginning of the slow retreat of the Turks from Europe. The Venetians gained a large area inland from the coast, including the Neretva valley below Mostar and the towns of Sinj and Knin in the central Dalmatian hinterland. The frontier settlement agreed to in 1699 included an arrangement whereby the Turks were given two tiny footholds on the coast. One, at Neum near the root of the Pelješac peninsula, separated the Venetian settlements at the mouth of the Neretva from the northern boundary of the Ragusan republic. The other, at the southern end of Ragusan territory, gave the Turks an even smaller strip of the shoreline at Sutorina on the Gulf of Kotor, again with the object of keeping the Ragusans and Venetians apart. The Sutorina strip was abolished in 1918, but the traveller heading southward to Dubrovnik may still wonder why a 5 km strip of the Magistrala motor road passes through Bosnia. After the seventh war with the Turks (1714–18) the Venetians were able to advance up to the present Bosnian border, taking in the whole of Sinjsko Polje and Imotski. Thereafter the Turkish menace was laid to rest and Venice had no serious challenge to its authority in Dalmatia until Napoleon extinguished the republic itself in 1797.

Social and cultural life in Dalmatia

Whilst Croatia and Slavonia were being laid waste during the centuries-long struggle between the Habsburgs and the Ottomans, Dalmatia, although not entirely at peace, enjoyed relative prosperity and order. In the Venetian cities and in the republic of Ragusa there was a unique flowering of the arts, blending the spirit of the Italian Renaissance with the native culture of the Slavs.

The genius of the Dalmatians showed itself particularly in architecture, sculpture and literature, and their artistic output was sustained over many centuries from the builders of the early Christian churches of the seventh and eighth centuries to the eighteenth-century cathedral of Dubrovnik, and from *Historia Salonitana*, by the thirteenth-century Thomas, Archdeacon of Split, to the black comedies of Vlaho Stulli-Stulić, written in the closing years of the Ragusan republic and still performed today. There is an even older architectural tradition, going back to Roman times. The magnificent palace of Diocletian at Split, which inspired Robert Adam, the English designer of the eighteenth century, and also influenced the contemporary Georgian styles, still forms the outer shell, a square mile in area, which surrounds the vibrant city which has grown up over the centuries within and around its protective walls.

The greatest creative period was between the thirteenth century and the seventeenth. The debt to Italy, and particularly to Venice, is apparent in many of the finest buildings in Šibenik, Trogir, Split and Dubrovnik, and one does not need the constant reminders of their origins which are provided by the many replicas of the winged lion of St Mark's which adorn them.

Architecture and sculpture

Dalmatian architects and sculptors developed a style which built on the Romanesque tradition but which blended elements from the later Gothic and Renaissance styles.

The cathedral of Split, which dominates the Roman peristyle in the heart of Diocletian's city, is built on the site of the emperor's mausoleum. A church was first consecrated there in AD 649, but the present cathedral dates from the thirteenth century and is a monument to the Split school of architects who gave new life to the Romanesque style in Dalmatia.

One of the great sculptors of the period was Andrija Buvina. The reliefs on the walnut folding door which Buvina decorated in 1214 represented a fusion of the classical inheritance and the realities of the contemporary Slav environment of the fifteenth century. As Milan Prelog, the Croatian art historian, has written in *Enciklopedija Jugoslavije*, 'Buvina's masterpiece is a proof of the progress achieved in a local sculptor's workshop at the beginning of the thirteenth century. It relates to the Byzantine tradition and also to contemporary trends in art; towards the Graeco-Roman heritage and towards the immediate reality.'

Following Buvina came the Trogir-born sculptor Radovan, whose most famous work is the Romanesque doorway of the cathedral at Trogir. The humanity and realism expressed in the faces and attitudes of the figures which decorate the doorway are in contrast to the stylised figures of the earlier Romanesque carvings. Zvane Črnja has written of Radovan's Adam and Eve that they 'are not Biblical personages at all. They are simple, honest Dalmatian labourers, humanly ashamed because surprised in a proscribed, yet human, act.' The Latin inscription engraved on the doorway states, 'This doorway was made by Radovan, the best of all the masters of this art, as witnessed by his sculptures and reliefs, in the year one thousand two hundred and fifty.' Radovan may not have completed the work on the doorway, but his pupils continued in his style. They were also responsible for the reliefs decorating the campanile of the cathedral in Split.

Two centuries after Radovan, the cathedral at Šibenik, 50 km up the coast from Trogir, was being built under the guidance of Juraj Dalmatinac (Georgius Mattei Dalmaticus), who was born in Zadar in the early fifteenth century. In 1441 he took over the work from two Venetian architects and supervised the work for the next three decades. Dalmatinac, like many of the Dalmatian artists of the time, had worked in Italy. There was a relatively easy interchange between the city states of Dalmatia and Renaissance Italy, and the work of Italian artists, especially from Venice, can be found throughout Dalmatia.

Evidence of Dalmatians (whom the Italians called Schiavone or Slavs) working in Italy goes back at least to the time of Radovan. One thirteenth-century artist was Simun Dubrovčanin (Simon of Ragusa), who carved the main door of the cathedral of Santa Maria Maggiore at Barletta on the western shore of the Adriatic, opposite Dubrovnik. One of Juraj Dalmatinac's early works was the Loggia dei Mercanti at Ancona.

Painters
Although the art of painting was not as well developed as architecture and sculpture, there were, nevertheless, a number of Slav artists from the

Adriatic coastlands who displayed considerable talent and whose works are to be found in church frescoes and other paintings on both the Italian and eastern shores. Nikola Schiavone from Bar, whose work was described by the Italians as 'fantasticus et barbarus'; Andrija Meldol-Medulić Schiavone, who achieved a European reputation; Stjepan Crnota from Rab, who was celebrated in Venice; and Juraj Klović (Don Guilio Clovio), a miniaturist, who was heralded as 'a small and new Michelangelo', are a few of the Dalmatian painters who settled in Italy between the fourteenth and sixteenth centuries. An interesting fifteenth-century painter was Vincent of Kastar (Vincent iz Kastva), who was born near Rijeka. His frescoes in the central Istrian church of Sv. Marija na Škriljna, near Beram, painted in 1471, display a naive vitality and a medieval peasant's sense of the harsh realities of life which are in contrast to the more cultivated products of the Italian Renaissance painters. The whole interior walls of the church in this little Istrian village are covered with paintings on such themes as the Dance of Death *(Mrtvački ples)*, the Adoration of the Magi *(Poklonstvo kraljeva)* and *Christ on the Mount of Olives (Krist na maslinovoj gori)* in which the poetic idealism of the painter shines through the simple techniques employed to convey his vision of spiritual truth.

Literature

The fusion of cultural influences from Italy – both the original Latin and the Renaissance elements – with those of Slavonic origin, which was a feature of the plastic arts, also characterised the literature of Dalmatia. It is epitomised in the use of three different alphabets – Latin, Cyrillic and glagolitic – in early Croatian literature.

One of the earliest literary works emanating from Dalmatia is the *Historia Salonitana*, written in Latin by Thomas the Archdeacon (1200–68), a native of Split, who was partly educated in Bologna. In Italy he was impressed by the preaching of St Francis of Assisi on the virtues of poverty. When he returned to Split, however, he joined the Latinised clergy of the Metropolitan Church and became a fierce opponent of the poor Slavs and their culture.

During the fourteenth and fifteenth centuries a school of Dalmatian humanists, still writing mainly in Latin or Italian prose and poetry, broke away from the narrow ecclesiastical concerns of men like Thomas and became part of the mainstream of the European Renaissance. They wrote on such subjects as education, art, philosophy and science. Juraj Sizgorić (Georgius Sisgoreus) of Šibenik was the first Croatian to publish a volume of Latin verse, which appeared in Venice in 1477. In his wide-ranging survey of the cultural history of his native land, *De situ Illyriae et civitate Sibenici*, he described the Illyrians (meaning Croats) as possessing superior intellectual gifts, especially those of Dalmatia. This was not simply a boastful assertion of the worth of his own cultural background, for there is no doubt that at this time the Dalmatians included theologians, philosophers, poets and lawyers whose 'minds were admired by Italy itself'. Sizgorić, even though he wrote in Latin, was aware of the rich vernacular folk poetry of the Slav peoples and himself translated a volume of folk sayings and proverbs into Latin.

In the late fifteenth century and throughout the sixteenth a number of Slav scholars from Dalmatia achieved European fame in a wide range of intellectual and artistic fields. Ilija Crijević from Ragusa (Aelius Lampridius Cervinus) became a member of the Quirinal Academy in Rome in 1484 at the age of twenty-one years, and was crowned poet laureate for a treatise on Virgil. He was also renowned for his unconventional, erotic poetry. Autun Vrančić (1504–73, Antonius Verancius) of Šibenik, a truly Renaissance man, travelled widely as a diplomat, had love poems published in Krakow and became Primate of Hungary. He also made translations from Turkish to Latin. His nephew, Faust Vrančić (1551–1617), invented machines, wrote texts on logic and ethics and compiled a dictionary in Latin, Italian, German, Croatian and Magyar.

The development of a specifically Croatian literature in Dalmatia is normally attributed to the high-born, Italian-educated Marko Marulić (1450–1524) from Split, although many of his predecessors and contemporaries spoke Croatian and were aware of the vernacular tradition. Antun Vrančić, for example, always regarded the 'Illyrian' language as his mother tongue, but, following the customs of civilised Europe at that time, he wrote in Latin. Marulić also wrote in Latin, as might be expected from a man who had studied in Padua. Some of his Latin works were translated into the major European languages. He is remembered with particular pride in Yugoslavia, however, for his epic poem *Judita* (Judith), written in the *čakavski* dialect in 1501 and published in Venice in 1521.

At about the same time several young Ragusan aristocrats were writing love poems in Croatian, in the manner of Petrarch's *Canzoniero* and of the troubadours who followed the Tuscan tradition. These included Šiško Menčetić and Djore Držić. A powerful figure in Ragusa was the Benedictine friar Mavro Vetranović, who was born in 1482 and who lived for over eighty years. His output included fierce denunciations of the secular character of the erotic poetry of the troubadours, but his fierce inner struggle against the pleasures of the flesh, which found expression in his moral sermons, concealed a passion which he could not always contain. As an ascetic he was in the mould of the medieval Christians, but when his heart overruled his intellect he would write warm, sensuous love poetry under the cloak of religion. He also wrote Biblical dramas which display a deep love of nature.

Djore Držić's nephew, Marin Držić (1508–67), was a poor scholar who was sent to the University of Siena on a stipend from the Ragusan Senate. When he returned home he was given employment as a personal companion to an Austrian count, who took him to Vienna and Constantinople. The count found Držić a witty and entertaining companion, and Držić, a poor cleric, benefited greatly from sharing in the cosmopolitan life of his master. His first poems followed the Petrarchan tradition of his uncle, but he soon established himself as a versatile playwright, capable of producing dramas, pastorals, masques and, above all, comedies. His *Skup* (The Miser) was, like Molière's *L'Avare* a century later, based on Plautus. This may explain why Držić was known as 'the Croatian Molière'.

Ragusan literature reached its highest point in the early seventeenth century. The greatest figure of that period was Ivan Gundulić (1588–1638), who became Rector of the Republic. He is best known for his epic poem *Osman*, which, although running to 11,000 lines, was unfinished at his death. It was inspired by the victory of the Poles over the Turks in Bessarabia in 1621 and sings of the heroism of the Slavs in their long fight against the infidels. Gundulić also wrote dramas, masques and pastorals.

A contemporary of Gundulić was Junije Palmotić (1606–57), a Ragusan noble who lived for a time in Bosnia, and who drew upon the Slav folk tales as well as on contemporary Italian and ancient classical traditions for the abundant outpouring of songs, satires, verse epics and dramas which he composed. His near contemporary and namesake, Jaketa Palmotić (Dionović), is best known for his long epic poem *Ragusa Restored*, which describes the tragedy of the 1667 earthquake, in which the author's wife and children perished, and the efforts of the republic to rebuild the city.

It is interesting to note that neither of the Palmotićs receives even a passing mention in Zvane Črnja's standard *Kulturna historija Hrvatske*, although Jakita is described by Sir Arthur Evans as one of 'the most celebrated names in the long annals of Ragusan literature' and Junije is referred to by one English historian as 'the creator of the national drama'.

The golden age of Ragusan literature was not the only manifestation of Dalmatian literary energy in the seventeenth century. In Hvar, Zadar and the other cities, poems and dramas continued to appear. Works produced at the theatre in Hvar, rebuilt in 1612 after its destruction in 1571, five years before London's first theatre was built, carried on the literary traditions of the Hvar literary school established in the previous century. Nor was Dalmatian writing confined to poetry and drama. There was a remarkable output of scientific and philosophical writing, which culminated in the renowned Rudjer Bošković (1711–87), an all-round scientist who had a European reputation for his writings on optics, physics, mechanics, astronomy, mathematics and philosophy. He held the chair of mathematics at Pavia, taught in Paris, was director of optics in Louis XV's ministry of marine, ran an observatory in Milan, and was elected to the Royal Society in London and the French Academy of Science in Paris. Despite this cosmopolitan background he never forgot his humble origins in Ragusa, and proudly affirmed his Slav language and culture when mistakenly referred to as an Italian.

The creative activity went on to the end of the Venetian and Ragusan republics at the turn of the nineteenth century and even beyond. By then the Turkish menace had receded. The revival of Croatia–Slavonia and the development of the Croat national movement in the nineteenth century saw a merging of the distinct Dalmatian tradition with the invigorated culture of the northern Croatian region to form the modern Croatian mainstream.

The city state of Ragusa (Dubrovnik)

Both names – the Latin Ragusa and the Slavonic Dubrovnik – have been used since the end of the first millennium to designate the settlement which was established on a rocky site below the limestone cliffs of Mt Srđ (412 m), facing the island of Lokrum. Although there may have been a settlement of Illyrian-Greeks there before the second century BC when the Roman occupation of Dalmatia began, there is little evidence of continuous use of the site until the seventh century AD. The destruction of nearby Epidauros (Cavtat) by the Avars in the mid seventh century, and of Salona, near Split, some thirty-five years earlier, may have contributed an influx of Romanised refugees who swelled the population of a pre-existing community of Slav fisherfolk. The fact that Cavtat was later known as Ragusavecchia (Old Ragusa) supports the view that some of the town's early inhabitants originated in Cavtat. For the purposes of the present work, it is sufficient to know that by the end of the seventh century a town inhabited mainly by people of Latin culture existed on the site, and that the surrounding countryside was peopled by Slavs. In the early ninth century, when northern Dalmatia was brought under the influence of the Holy Roman Emperor, Charlemagne, Ragusa and southern Dalmatia were included in the Byzantine sphere. The city was fortified and was able to repel raids by pirates and a siege by the Saracens in 866–7. Already at this time Ragusa's influence as a trading centre was being felt throughout the Mediterranean. An important item in this trade was timber for the construction of ships. The wooded slopes of the mountains inland from Dalmatia supported forests of oak and pine, in contrast to the barren interior, which lay behind the southern (African) shore of the Mediterranean, where the Arab empire was established in the seventh and eighth centuries. The export of wood by merchants from Ragusa and other Dalmatian cities to the Arabs in Egypt, North Africa, Spain and Sicily contributed to the deforestation of the immediate hinterland.

As Byzantine power waned, the Venetians advanced. Ragusa was seen as a rival which had to be subdued and brought under Venetian control. In 948 an attempt by Venice to conquer Ragusa was repulsed, according to legend, with the miraculous help of St Blaise (San Biagio; Sveti Vlaho), who in England is known as the patron saint of woolcombers. As a result, the Ragusans adopted him as their patron saint and his effigy still gazes out over the Stradun. Fifty years later, however, the Venetians succeeded, and forced the Ragusans to pay tribute to them, although the local laws and customs were not interfered with. The Ragusans became adept at knowing how to bend the head to powerful rivals without losing the substance of their autonomy. During the ensuing eight centuries they recognised, at different times, the suzerainty of the Byzantine, Habsburg and Serbian emperors, the King of Hungary, the Doge of Venice and the Sultan of Turkey, but in the main they kept their own internal self-government.

The longest period of Venetian ascendancy lasted from 1204 to 1358, during which time there was constant friction because of the restriction placed on Ragusa's maritime trade by its great rival. Ragusa was able, however, to develop its overland trade with the Balkan hinterland, as this activity did not bring it into direct competition with the seaborne trade of Venice.

Territorial growth

Between the eleventh and fourteenth centuries the republic of Ragusa was able, by treaties with its neighbours and by purchase, to extend its territorial base. This growth was achieved mainly by diplomacy and by playing off, at the appropriate times, the contending powers of the Slav kingdoms – the Byzantines, the Venetians and the Turks. In 1050, for example, Stephen, who claimed the title of ruler of Bosnia and Dalmatia, made a grant of land along the coast which extended the boundaries of Ragusa to Zaton, 16 km north of the original city, giving the republic control of the abundant supply of fresh water which emerges from a *source vauclusienne* at the head of the Ombla inlet. The driver who enters modern Dubrovnik by the Magistrala road from the north follows the shores of this inlet, 5 km long and in places only 400 m wide. The shore is lined with the majestic warehouses (factories) and residences of Ragusan merchants. Stephen's grant also included the harbour of Gruž, which is now the commercial port for Dubrovnik.

Two further important acquisitions were in 1333 and 1419. The first allowed Ragusa to take control of the Pelješac peninsula on payment of an annual tribute to Tsar Dušan, ruler of the Serbian empire. In 1419 Stephen Ostojić, King of Bosnia, made a grant of land to the south, which took in the fertile Konavli valley, which runs parallel to the coast from Cavtat to the Gulf of Kotor. The islands of Mljet (1345) and Lastovo (1252) and the string of smaller islands between Pelješac and Ombla had already been acquired. Thus, by the early fifteenth century Ragusa's authority extended from the delta of the Neretva in the north to the Gulf of Kotor in the south, a distance of 190 km (120 miles) as the crow flies. The Pelješac peninsula provided an easily defended rampart to the north, and the screen of islands protected the central zone in which the city itself lay. These frontiers held with minor changes until the republic was abolished by Napoleon in 1808. For a few years after 1413 a lease on the islands of Korčula, Hvar and Brač was obtained with the agreement of the Habsburg Emperor, Sigismund, but the Ragusans failed to maintain their position in face of the hostility of the islanders and the rivalries of their Venetian, Hungarian and Slav neighbours. In 1700 minor frontier adjustments created two Turkish corridors to the sea which separated the Ragusan republic from Venetian territory.

Hungary and Venice

A turning point in the history of the republic came in 1358, when Ludovic of Hungary forced the Venetians to cede to him the whole of Dalmatia, except for Ragusa. Nevertheless, the Ragusans thought it prudent to accept the nominal suzerainty of the Hungarian king. In reality the change of allegiance brought almost total autonomy in return for an annual payment of 500 ducats and the support of the Ragusan fleet in time of war.

The position changed again in the early fifteenth century, when Ladislas of Naples, who aspired to the throne of Hungary, sold his claims over

Dalmatia, Zeta and Albania to the Venetians. It took the Venetians until 1420 to win control of all the territory promised to them by Ladislas, who in fact never realised his ambition to wear the crown of Hungary. Although Venice was again in a position to dominate the Adriatic, Ragusa never reverted to the degree of subordination which had existed before 1358.

Trade

The Ragusan Senate became the elected council of an independent trading city state. It had the foresight to see the possibilities of trade with the newly arrived Ottoman power which had moved into the Bosnian hinterland, and, armed with a papal dispensation from Urban V, Ragusa became the first Christian power to enter into treaty relations with the infidels. It also had the acumen to remain neutral in most of the wars fought between Venice and Turkey and between Austria and Turkey between 1420 and the Austro-Turkish war of 1737–40. Later, in the eighteenth century, it also kept aloof from the War of the Austrian Succession (1741–48) and the Seven Years' War (1756–63). Ragusa's heyday as a trading city was between the mid fourteenth and early sixteenth centuries. Its principal function was as an intermediary between the Ottoman provinces in Europe and the shores of the Mediterranean. Silver, lead, copper, iron and mercury were the most important metals which were brought in from the mines – some of which were owned by Ragusan merchants – in Bosnia, Serbia and Kosovo. They were exported by sea to Italy, Greece, Turkey, Egypt and the Levant. Another important item which followed the same route was white slaves, who were more highly prized in Italy than the Africans who were supplied by the Arabs. Many of the slaves were Bosnian children from Bogomil families, whose human rights were disregarded because of the heretical beliefs of their parents. This trade came to an end during the fifteenth century. Other Balkan products distributed around the Mediterranean in Ragusan ships were hides, timber, wax and wool.

Commodities which travelled in the opposite direction were salt, which came by sea from Cyprus, the Greek islands and Albania, and which was distributed by means of pack animals to Bosnia and Serbia; and cereals brought in from the Aegean, Cyprus, Asia Minor and Sicily, and used mainly for local consumption. Ragusa, in common with Venice and Genoa, played an important part in the transportation of spices from the Middle and Far East to southern and western Europe.

The city's trading connections extended outside the Mediterranean to Antwerp, London, Southampton and the Hanseatic towns of Germany. Cloth – mainly wool and linen – was the mainstay of this trade. In the sixteenth century it was found more convenient and safer for these goods to be transported overland to the ports of northern Italy, where they were picked up by Ragusan merchants.

A change in the character of Ragusan trade came in the century following the Age of Discovery. Once the route round Africa to the Far East was established and the Muslims who controlled the land across the Middle East had been outflanked, the spice and silk trade of the Mediterranean began slowly to decline. The opening up of colonies in the West and East Indies and America shifted the focus of world trade to the maritime nations of western Europe – Portugal, the Low Countries, England and France. Economic changes within the Balkans, following the consolidation of Ottoman power, led to a decline in the trade in minerals, but the exports of raw wool and hides increased, as did the imports of textiles from northern Europe.

During the seventeenth and eighteenth centuries the pace of Mediterranean commercial life slackened and the inland sea, which had once been the major artery of European trade, became a cul-de-sac. Venice and Ragusa, Genoa and Leghorn all suffered from this change in the patterns of world trade. When the Mediterranean again became an important routeway after the opening of the Suez Canal, the city states around its shores had all disappeared. The Ragusan republic fell to Napoleon in 1806 and was incorporated into the Illyrian Provinces between 1808 and 1814. Following the Congress of Vienna in 1815 all Dalmatia, including Dubrovnik, was placed under Austrian administration, where it remained until 1918.

5

The development of independence

The Serbian revolts

The century following the Peace of Carlowitz (Karlovci) between the Habsburgs and the Turks in 1699 saw many changes in the relations among the European powers, some of which directly affected the South Slav peoples, and others which had delayed and indirect effects on them, the significance of which did not become apparent until well into the nineteenth century.

The most obvious direct result of the treaty was the repossession by the Habsburgs of Hungary, Transylvania and the Turkish occupied areas of Slavonia and Croatia. In 1718, by the Treaty of Passarowitz (Požarevac), the Banat, Little Wallachia, Belgrade and the Serbian regions of Šumadija, Posavina and Mačva were ceded by Turkey. These last three territories lay south of the Sava–Danube line and represented the first Habsburg advance across that symbolic divide since the catastrophe of Mohács in 1526. A Turkish recovery twenty years later re-established Ottoman control south of the line (Treaty of Belgrade, 1739), but the Habsburgs remained in the Vojvodina, Croatia and Slavonia. The Turks never again crossed the Danube–Sava line. In 1791, by the Treaty of Sistova, Belgrade was restored to Turkey, briefly reoccupied by Austria in 1789–92, and was not formally surrendered until the last Turkish garrison withdrew in 1867, although effective Turkish control had ceased some fifty years earlier.

The expulsion of the Turks from Vojvodina gave an opportunity for the Serbs of that area, many of whom were descendants of the refugees who had fled across the Danube in front of the advancing Ottomans during the previous two or three centuries, to develop their national culture in a freer atmosphere than had existed under Islamic rule. The Orthodox monasteries of the Fruška Gora were the cultural centres of the Serbian renaissance which culminated in the Serbian revolts of the early nineteenth century and, eventually, in the establishment of a Serbian state. The reforms of Joseph II (1780–90), which were carried through in the spirit of the Age of Enlightenment, included a secularisation of education and the recognition of the rights of the Slav subjects of the Empire to instruct in their own language. In 1791, during the brief reign of Joseph's successor, Leopold II (1790–2), the first Serbian secondary school was opened in Sremski Karlovci (Karlowitz). One of its pupils in 1805 and 1806 was the philologist Vuk Stefanović Karadžić, the father of the modern Serbian language.

During the eighteenth century there were signs of the first rumblings of the tectonic upheaval which shattered the old order in Europe, and from its ruins created a group of nation states out of the submerged nations which lay under the surface of the great multinational empires. It was not until the First World War that the last vestiges of the Habsburg, Ottoman and Romanov empires finally crumbled, making way for a tier of nation states which lay across the map of Europe from the Baltic to the Aegean. The process began with the Serbian revolt of 1804 and culminated in the rebirth of Poland and the creation of the new Czechoslovak and Yugoslav states in 1918.

The changes in the constellation of European powers which occurred during the eighteenth century had an indirect bearing on the destiny of the South Slav peoples. Russia under Peter the Great and Catherine began to take a major part in the affairs of Europe. Peter's initiative in opening Russia to western influences, his modernisation of the administration and his development of industries were in sharp contrast to the Muscovite traditions of the sixteenth and seventeenth centuries. The territorial expansion of Russia during Peter's reign led to the incorporation of Karelia, Estonia and Latvia. His successors, during the seventy-five years after his death in 1725, added Lithuania, parts of Poland and the Ukraine, Bessarabia, the Crimea and the Kuban region. The expansion of Russia to the south gave control of the north shore of the Black Sea from the mouth of the Danube to the Caucasus. This was achieved at the expense of Turkey, following a series of wars. That which ended in 1774 resulted in the Treaty of Kutchuk Kainardji (Kücük Kaynarca), which wrested the Khanate of Crimea from the Turks and gave the Russians the right to protect the Christian subjects of the sultan. The involvement with Turkey raised the question of Russian access to the straits connecting the Black Sea to the Mediterranean. It also raised the question of the Christian Slav subjects of the sultan. Peter had already made contact with the Montenegrins early in the century. The Slavs were mainly adherents of the Orthodox Church, and many of the Slav clergy saw in the Russian Church an ally in the struggle against the Phanariot Greek clergy, backed by the sultan, who wished to remove Slav influences both from the liturgy and from the administration of the Church. In 1727 the Synod of Moscow sent a mission which spent ten years amongst the Serbs of Vojvodina and Srem, forging strong links with the Serbian Orthodox clergy and their flocks. As Russia advanced westward and began to play a role alongside the major European powers in the determination of the affairs of the continent, the Slavs of the Balkans turned to St Petersburg for diplomatic and military support, which was usually forthcoming.

The industrial revolution of the eighteenth century brought England into the ranks of major European powers, and although the English were somewhat detached from the affairs of the continent, and more concerned with imperial expansion overseas, the events of the French Revolution and the wars with Napoleonic France forced them to play an ever increasing role in Europe.

The movement of Napoleonic France into central and south-eastern Europe had a dramatic impact on the South Slavs. The direct occupation by French troops of Slovenia, Istria and Dalmatia, followed by the creation of the Illyrian Provinces, was welcomed by the leaders of Slav opinion within both the Habsburg and Ottoman empires. The effect was greatest, however, amongst the liberal-minded Slovene and Croat intellectuals. The poet Vodnik, once a Franciscan friar, even held office in the administration of the Illyrian Provinces in Carinthia between 1809 and 1813. The Illyrian Movement which developed during the early nineteenth century adopted the idealistic stance that all Slavs were one people, with four dialects – Russian, Czech, Polish and Illyrian. The 'Illyrian language' which they advocated was the *štokavski* dialect used by the great writers of Dubrovnik. It happened that this was also the form advocated by Vuk Karadžić in Serbia, and for a time Ljudevit Gaj (1809–72), the leader of the Illyrian Movement in Croatia, warmed to the idea that Serbs and Croats shared a common language and culture. Vuk, however, was less enthusiastic, and wrote of his own people, 'It is hard to induce them to acknowledge that they are Serbs, and we would be crazy if we agreed to abandon our famous name and to adopt another one [Illyrian], which is dead and today has no meaning in itself.'

The ideas which influenced the liberal-minded intellectuals and the small but growing commercial middle classes amongst the Slovenes, the Croats and, to a lesser extent, the Serbs, were those of the eighteenth-century Enlightenment, which developed into the democratic liberalism of the French Revolution. Many of the leading scholars amongst the South Slavs during the late eighteenth and early nineteenth centuries were widely travelled and had studied in France, Germany, Austria and Italy, where they were caught up in the intellectual ferment which was abroad at that time. An essential element in the movement was the discovery of the rich vernacular traditions of the submerged nations, and the assertion of the right of people to use their own language instead of the German, Magyar or Latin – or even Old Church Slavonic in Serbia – which were the languages of the cultured classes and the church leaders in the respective occupied territories. With recognition of the language came the assertion of separate national identity. It was the remarkable achievement of Napoleon to carry the principle of nationhood throughout Europe, including the lands of South Slavs.

The first Serbian revolt

There were, of course, other forces at work which were driving the subject peoples to oppose their alien overlords. Romantic nationalism based on the demand for recognition of cultural identity was a sentiment which moved the educated middle classes. The peasants, who still constituted the majority of the population, were more affected by their feelings of material oppression and their opposition to the arbitrary rule of their masters. The dam broke in Serbia in 1804 and at first took the form of a protest by Serbian peasants against the janissaries.

The janissaries, who were once the elite corps of the sultan's army, had degenerated by the end of the eighteenth century into an unruly and lawless rabble, who were at best an embarrassment and at worst a threat to their rulers. The system of *devşirme* (see above, pp. 37–8), by which Christian boys were forcibly enlisted, was abandoned in the seventeenth century. Sultan Mahmud I (1730–54) attempted to disband the janissaries and to put in their place a modern force, modelled on the standing armies of his European enemies. Unfortunately for the Serbs, he was only partly successful. In an attempt to remove the influence of the janissaries from Istanbul, where they naturally formed a powerful opposition to his reforms, Mahmud tried to buy them off by offering them a virtually free hand in garrisoning the remote provinces of the empire. There they could plunder and abuse the local Christian peasantry with impunity, even dispossessing them from their lands. The pashalik of Belgrade was one such province to which the janissaries were dispersed. Mahmud may have bought time for himself, but he stored up trouble for his successors. Matters came to a head during the reign of Selim III (1789–1807), the reforming sultan, described by Geoffrey Lewis as 'one of the most enlightened members of the House of

Osman'. Selim was the first Turkish ruler to attempt to understand the currents of thought in western Europe and to come to terms with the contemporary world. Even as heir-apparent, he had been in correspondence with Louis XVI of France concerning his plans for reorganising the army, and the overthrow of the French monarchy in the year of his accession, 1789, did not diminish his enthusiasm for learning from the west. In fact, for a time he saw in the New Order in France a possible source of ideas which he could implement in the construction of his New Order (*Nizam-i Cedit*) in Turkey. France was the main foreign influence: French military advisers came to establish military training schools, the French language was made compulsory for all students, and libraries of mainly French books were opened. In 1793 the first Republican French ambassador received a rapturous welcome when he arrived off Seraglio Point, his ship flying the Ottoman, Republican French and American colours, 'and those of a few other powers that had not sullied their arms in the impious league of tyrants'. Selim had formidable obstacles to overcome, however, in modernising the archaic structure of the Ottoman empire. The chief centres of resistance were the *ulema* (learned religious functionaries who were custodians of the *Şeriat* or Islamic holy laws) and the janissaries. Eventually they defeated him. In 1806 the *ulema* roused the people of Istanbul against him, and his untried, partly reformed army was defeated by the janissaries. To prevent him from making a comeback after his deposition, his successor, Mustapha IV, had him strangled in 1808. Lewis referred to him as 'a man martyred for his belief in the destiny of his country, a man whose worst fault was that his courage outran his prudence'. He was, perhaps, the nearest approximation which the Ottoman empire could produce to the eighteenth-century enlightened despots of the stamp of Joseph II and Frederick the Great.

Selim became sultan during the disastrous war with Russia and Austria, into which his predecessor, Abdülhamid I (1773–89), had been precipitated by Potemkin's seizure of the Crimea in 1783. The war between Russia and Turkey broke out in 1787. Austria joined in 1788, taking advantage of Turkey's weakness to seize the pashalik of Belgrade. The Austrians armed a corps of Serbian volunteers under an Austrian major of Serbian origin, Mihailo Mihaljević, to fight the Turks. One of the many Serbs who gained their first military experience during the brief Austrian interlude was Djordje Petrović (Karadjordje) (*kara* in Turkish = black), a pig dealer from the Šumadija, who was later to lead the Serbian revolt of 1804 and to be the founding father of one of the Serbian royal houses. The war of 1788–91 is known to Serbian historians as 'Koča's War', after Koča Andjelković, the military leader of the Serbian bands which joined in the insurrection against the Turks in Šumadija. Unfortunately for the Serbs, the Austrians abandoned them when they settled their differences with the Turks at the Treaty of Sistova (1791). Belgrade was returned to the Turks in exchange for minor territorial concessions to the Austrians in northern Bosnia.

Selim, aware of the strength of feeling amongst the Serbs against the janissaries, attempted to prevent the return of these unruly troops to the pashalik. The janissaries defied the sultan's order and were soon involved in a struggle for power with the Turkish governor of Belgrade. They enlisted the help of a rebellious warlord from Vidin, in Ottoman-occupied Bulgaria, Osman Pazvant-oglu, and the governor was able to maintain his position only by arming the Serbs to defend themselves against the invaders. Selim did not have the power to punish the rebels, and in 1798 he made peace with Pazvant-oglu and a year later permitted the janissaries to return to Belgrade. The hapless governor, who had vainly tried to uphold the sultan's authority, was beheaded by the janissaries in 1801.

The forced retreat of Selim III indicated the extent to which the authority of the Sublime Porte had declined since the glorious days of Suleiman in the sixteenth century. In the first decade of his reign Selim had attempted to appease the Serbs by granting them a degree of self-government. The local *oborknezovi* were given greater authority, the rights of the Orthodox Churches were respected, and a local Serbian militia was permitted. The tax system was reformed and the peasantry was given greater protection against the arbitrary actions of some of the local Moslem *spahis*. By 1799 the position was entirely reversed. The lawless janissaries and their local Turkish supporters were now appeased at the expense of the Christian peasants. The Serbs, however, had learned something from their experiments, and the taste of self-government, however limited, had given them a self-confidence which could not be crushed by the cruelty of their new masters. In fact, the behaviour of the janissaries bred a smouldering resentment which erupted from time to time into acts of armed resistance. The mistrust which their recent sufferings had engendered against all Turks made it impossible for the Serbs to collaborate with the more reasonable *spahis*, who were themselves the victims of the janissaries, whose leaders were known as *dayis*. Thus in 1802 when a group of *spahis* called on the Serbs to join them in resisting the *dayis* very few Serbs responded. They were already planning the Serbian revolt, which broke out in 1804. Their plans included an attempt to enlist the support of the Vladika (Prince–Bishop) of Montenegro and of the Austrian military command in Vojvodina. The event which prompted the revolt was the brutal murder, on the orders of the *dayis*, of scores of prominent Serbs. This 'slaughter of the *knezes*' in January and February of 1804 was met by a spontaneous rising of the Christian peasant (the *raya*), who joined forces with the *hajduk* bands in the hills. At first they were leaderless. Many of the *knezovi* who had survived the massacre were unwilling to risk further reprisals, should the revolt fail. The occasion produced the man. At a meeting of local Serbian leaders in Orašac, in mid February, the thirty-six-year-old Djordje Petrović (Karadjordje) was asked to lead the rebellion, although legend has it that he twice refused, excusing himself on the ground that his violent temper would make him an unsuitable leader. He had an impeccable record of anti-Turkish activity, from the time he had enlisted in Major Mihaljević's forces at the age of twenty, fighting with the *hajduks* after the Austrian desertion in 1791, and serving as an officer in the Serbian militia which fought off Pazvant-oglu's attack in 1797. In the intervals between his military activities Karadjordje had carried on a successful business as a livestock trader, selling pigs across the border into Austria, and he had acquired a modest level of prosperity. He had also made contacts amongst the Austrian administrators and the Serbian exiles over the river.

At first the rebels appealed to the sultan, whose authority they claimed to be upholding against the janissaries. Both the Austrians and the Russians responded to Karadjordje's appeals for help. The latter sent material aid, the former attempted to mediate between the Serbs and the Turks in order to win by negotiation the reforms which the Serbs desired – a degree of autonomy and the restoration of Selim's reforms of 1783. In May 1804 a meeting was arranged in the presence of an Austrian field-marshal in Zemun (Semlin), the Austrian-occupied town across the Sava from Belgrade. Appeals were sent to the sultan, and also a Serbian delegation went to Tsar Alexander I in St Petersburg. The sultan responded by sending an army of 7,000 men under Bekir Pasha, the Vizier of Bosnia, to discipline the *dayis*. The Serbs welcomed them as liberators and the *dayis* fled, pursued by Karadjordje's men. The most prominent of the *dayis* were captured and beheaded, their heads being sent to the sultan (except for one which was carried away by the Danube whilst being washed by a gypsy in preparation for the journey to Istanbul). By the end of August it seemed that the revolt was over. The *dayis* had gone. Belgrade was in the hands of Bekir Pasha, a man whom the Serbs trusted and who had promised to implement the sultan's reforms.

Karadjordje himself was less sanguine than the Serbian *knezovi* in their expectations that the Porte would, or even could, carry out the promised reforms. He still dreamt of avenging the shame of Kosovo and of ending for all time the 'long Turkish night'. He had encouraging pledges of support from Petar I of Montenegro and from sympathetic Serbs in Bosnia and Hercegovina. He also expected support from Russia, but the tsar was too preoccupied with the affairs of Europe, where Napoleon was at the height of his powers, and Adam Czartoryski, the Russian foreign minister, advised negotiations with the Turks, rather than war. Napoleon was at this time trying to push the Russians into war with Turkey, and Czartoryski, aware of this, had no wish to see Russia involved on Serbia's side in a conflict with the sultan. Napoleon himself, despite his general blessing on movements of national independence, gave no encouragement to the Serbs.

The sultan suspected that Karadjordje's demand that Serbia should be accorded a status similar to that of the other semi-autonomous tributary provinces within the Ottoman empire – Wallachia, for example – was but the first step towards a declaration of complete independence. In August 1805 he ordered Hafiz Pasha to advance from Niš and to crush the Serbs, but his plan misfired when the Serbs withstood the attack. The Serbs followed their victory with the establishment of an elected government, composed of representatives from each district, chosen by an assembly of 'elders, officers, monks, priests, village heads and the common people'. Karadjordje had previously received support from local assemblies which had been convened at his request, but this was the first time that an embryonic, partly elected government of Serbia had come into existence.

In the winter of 1805–6 the Serbs went on the offensive and soon gained control of the whole of the pashalik, including the city of Belgrade. The sultan, afraid of Russian support for the Serbs, and shaken by Karadjordje's military victories, agreed to terms laid down by Serbia in September 1806.

There was no consensus amongst the Serbs as to the form of government they wanted if they were to be able to force recognition of Serbian autonomy from the sultan. Karadjordje, as a man of action and a mighty leader, was impatient with the idea that he should submit his unbridled power to the arbitration of assemblies, courts and councils. In the early days of the insurrection he made his position clear when Božo Grujović (formerly known as Filipović) lectured an assembly of Serbian leaders on the rule of law at Borak in September 1805. Grujović, an Austrian Serb, had been professor of law at Kharkov, and had acted as secretary to the Serbian delegation which had been sent to St Petersburg to enlist the support of the Russians. The delegation, headed by Karadjordje's rival, Prota (Dean) Matija Nenadović, returned with a proposal that the Serbs should establish a central council (soviet) and a constitution based on the rule of law. Karadjordje's response was to declare: 'It is easy for the Sovereign Law of yours to rule in a warm room, behind a table, but let us see tomorrow, when the Turks strike, who will meet them and beat them. A hobbled horse cannot run a race.' A soviet (or governing council) representing each of the twelve *nahijes* (districts) within the pashalik was established, but its powers were vaguely defined and it became an instrument which Karadjordje could use or ignore as he felt fit.

Karadjordje's dictatorial tendencies came into conflict with the older tradition of peasant democracy, which was itself in conflict with the patriarchal structure of Serbian village life. Karadjordje had to contend with a group of strong-willed oligarchs who enjoyed considerable power within their own territories and who jealously guarded the various perquisites which they had acquired, such as the levying of ferry tolls and local taxes. In a clan society based on the extended family, or *zadruga*, the elements of patriarchal oligarchy and crude democracy were inextricably interwoven. Karadjordje's attempt to impose himself on this structure by having himself declared 'Supreme Leader' created tensions which were never resolved during the nine years of his rebel regime. In 1811 the Assembly (Skupština) not only confirmed him as supreme leader, but also recognised the hereditary principle by pledging loyalty to 'his lawful heirs'.

Another complicating factor in the situation was the growing interest of the European powers, and especially of Austria and Russia, in the position of Serbia within the declining Turkish empire. The eventual collapse of Turkey would raise the question of the disposal of the assets of the corpse. The prospective legatees even produced schemes for the partitioning of the Ottoman lands in Europe amongst themselves. When Napoleon wrested the Slovene lands and Dalmatia from Austria, and established the Illyrian Provinces in 1809, France began to take major interest in Balkan affairs. A year earlier, at Erfurt, Napoleon had agreed with the tsar to accept the right of Russia to Wallachia and Moldavia, but to leave Serbia within the Ottoman empire. After the Treaty of Schönbrunn in 1809, the hope of the Serbs was that France, now firmly established on the Adriatic shore of the Balkan peninsula, would be sympathetic to their claims.

Karadjordje wrote to Napoleon, praising him for his treatment of 'our compatriots' in Illyria, and in 1810 he sent his emissary, Rade Vučinić, to Trieste and Paris to request French support. The French, like the Austrians and the Russians, were quite ready to consider the exclusion of the Turks from Serbia and, indeed, from all their European provinces, if they could see an advantage for themselves, but they also saw the danger of a disastrous confrontation if any of them moved before the time was ripe. It might be better for them to prop up the Ottoman empire for a while longer, but at the same time to keep their options open by maintaining contact with the various factions amongst the Serbs. The British, having no territorial ambitions in the Balkans, and being anxious to preserve the balance of power in Europe, tended to favour the continued existence of the Turkish empire in Europe.

The Serbs were aware that the powers were not genuinely interested in Serbian independence, and tried to play one off against the other. On the whole, however, they had greater hopes of Russia than of Austria. In 1807 the tsar sent a representative, Constantine Rodofinikin, to assist the Serbs in drafting a constitution. Rodofinikin had a hopeless task, as his instructions were drafted in the light of a Russo-Serbian agreement which presupposed a Russian victory over the Turks. The convention included the following plea to the tsar: 'The Serbian people humbly beg His Imperial Majesty to appoint a capable governor who will bring order to the people, administer the Serbian land, and devise a constitution in consonance with the customs of the people.' Even before Rodofinikin arrived in Belgrade, Russia had concluded the Peace of Tilsit with Napoleon, which required, *inter alia*, Russia to make peace with Turkey.

In 1810 Russia, again at war with Turkey, sent troops up the Danube and helped the Serbs to clear the Turks out of the pashalik of Belgrade. The Serbs even gained territory in Bosnia and advanced towards Niš. Again the Serbs were disappointed, for in 1812 at the Treaty of Bucharest the Russians again made peace with the Turks and agreed that Serbia should remain within the Ottoman empire. Tsar Alexander I ratified this treaty on the day that Napoleon began his Russian campaign.

The Serbs were not consulted about the terms of Article VIII of the Treaty, which stated:

It has been deemed just, in consideration of the share borne by the Servians in this war, to come to a solemn agreement respecting their security. Their peace must not in any way be disturbed. The Sublime Porte will grant the Servians, on their petition, the same privileges which her subjects in the Islands of the Archipelago, and in other parts, enjoy; and will moreover confer upon them a mark of her generosity, by leaving the administration of their internal affairs to themselves – by imposing upon them moderate taxes, and receiving them only direct from them – and by making the regulation requisite to this end in an understanding with the Servian nation themselves.

The Turks took advantage of the situation to reoccupy Serbia and they exacted a terrible vengeance on the helpless Serbs. Karadjordje, the

Metropolitan of Belgrade, Leontius, and many of the Serbian leaders fled across the Danube to Zemun, and some found refuge in the Orthodox monasteries in the Fruška Gora, where the *prečani* (= across the river) Serbs kept alive the culture and traditions of Serbdom. At Bucharest the Turks had promised an amnesty for the Serbian rebels, but before the sultan's authority could be established, the Turkish, Albanian and Bosnian Muslims who formed the occupying army pillaged and looted in a reign of terror which included the killing of all males over the age of fifteen in some areas, the enslavement of women and children, and the brutal torture of any Serbian leaders who fell into their hands. One account describes the impalement of scores of men on wooden stakes, where they were left to die along the side of the roads leading to Belgrade. Some lived for several days in this pitiful condition, their feet gnawed by dogs, until they died in agony.

The Grand Vizier Hursid Pasha, who entered Belgrade in late October 1813, was powerless to stop this holocaust, but once he was able to assert his authority he attempted to conciliate the Serbs. He declared an amnesty for those leaders who had survived, even those who had fled across the river, although the metropolitan and Karadjordje himself were specifically excluded.

One of those who took advantage of the amnesty was Miloš Obrenović, who was made *oborknez* of his home district of Rudnik, and was later made the chief (*bašiknez*) of the neighbouring *nahijes* of Čačak and Kragujevac.

The second Serbian rising

The second Serbian rising broke out in 1815 in the Valjevo district, and soon spread throughout the Šumadija. Its leader was Miloš Obrenović, a man who had played a part in the Karadjordje revolt, but who had remained in Serbia when many of the leaders of the first rising had fled across the river to Austrian territory. As the most prominent Serb who served in the administration after the restoration of Turkish rule in 1813, he might be thought to have compromised too far with the enemy to be considered as the leader of a national revolt. This would be a misreading of the situation in Serbia between 1813 and 1815. After the initial excesses which followed the reoccupation of Belgrade, the grand vizier declared an amnesty, and many Serbs who had fled into the hills and the impenetrable oak forests of Šumadija returned to their homes. Others returned from exile in Austrian-held Vojvodina. Miloš was not the only one of the former rebels who was given a post in the new administration. Even the *hajduk* leader, Stanoje Glavaš, was given command of the troops guarding the main road along the Morava valley which formed part of the imperial highway between Belgrade and Istanbul. The Turkish garrison in Belgrade remained, but the army of occupation was withdrawn by the end of 1813. The Serbian *oborknezovi* and *bašiknezovi* who ran the local administration were left very much on their own by the Turks as long as they maintained order and collected the taxes required of them. Given the primitive road system connecting Belgrade with the interior, it was impossible for a garrison of 5,000 troops in Belgrade to maintain order without the support of the Serbian *knezovi*. The 130-km journey from Belgrade to Kragujevac took three days on horseback and five by horse-drawn carriage, but in 1814 only Miloš, the metropolitan and the Turkish governor had such vehicles. Thus, the local Serbian chiefs had considerable freedom of action, and most, like Miloš, used it arbitrarily and grew rich and powerful by the exercise of their power.

Miloš, like Karadjordje before him, was not an attractive personality. Although he was more in control of his temper than had been his predecessor, Miloš was cruel, greedy, corrupt, devious and also illiterate. He did, however, have one quality which proved to be an asset to his country – he knew how to win by craft and diplomacy what he could not gain by force.

Before the successful insurrection of 1815 there had been several isolated incidents in which bands of Serbs attacked and murdered Turkish officials. One of Karadjordje's former commanders, Hadži-Prodan of Požega, attempted to lead a national rising. He appealed to Miloš to join him, but Miloš judged that the time was inopportune and promptly told the Turkish governor in Belgrade of the plot. Süleiman Pasha accepted Miloš's offer to suppress the revolt, which he did without difficulty. He had hoped by this gesture to spare his people the customary vengeance which the Turks exacted indiscriminately against the population when Serbs defied them. In this he was disappointed. Several Serbian leaders who had remained loyal to their Turkish masters were savagely butchered, including Glavaš, whose head was on display in the Kalemegdan fortress when Miloš went to a conference of the *knezovi* called by Süleiman Pasha.

Rumours spread amongst the Serbs that a massive punitive expedition against them was being prepared. At a meeting in the church at Takovo, near his home town of Rudnik, on Palm Sunday 1815, Miloš accepted the leadership of a new insurrection. The Serbs took the Turks by surprise, and the local garrison troops were soon isolated in Belgrade, whilst the rest of the pashalik was firmly in Miloš's grip. He also beat off attacks from

Turkish forces who moved in from Bosnia in the west and Rumelia in the south-east. After six months Miloš made a ceremonial entry into Belgrade to parley with the newly appointed Turkish governor, Marasli, who had been given a mandate by the sultan to make concessions in order to pacify the Serbs.

Throughout 1815 Miloš maintained that his quarrel was with the oppressive regime of Süleiman Pasha and not with the sultan. He did not ask for independence and never attempted to repudiate the suzerainty of the sultan. He did not, however, rely solely on the strong right arm of the Serbian forces. Through the intercession of the Serbs in Vojvodina he made contact with the representative of the European powers, and especially with the Austrians and Russians. At first the powers showed little interest, as they were preoccupied with the post-Napoleonic settlement, following the Emperor's final abdication on 22 June after his defeat at Waterloo four days earlier. By the autumn, however, the Russians, through their ambassador in Istanbul, Andrei Italinskii, began to threaten the sultan that if he did not make concessions to the Serbs they would intervene to enforce the disputed Article VIII of the Treaty of Bucharest (see above, p. 81). Neither the Austrians nor the Russians, and still less the British, wanted to see a complete dismemberment of the Turkish empire, but they were prepared for *de facto* autonomy for Serbia. Miloš and Marasli negotiated a settlement which provided for a Serbian administration, based on a national council of the *knezovi* of each of the twelve *nahijes*, who in their own districts would work alongside a Turkish administrator (*müsellim*). The *müsellim* would have no power to interfere with the right of the Serbs to collect taxes and, in cases where Christian subjects were being judged in the courts, the *müsellim* would have to sit with a Serbian *knez*.

The national council at its first meeting on 21 November 1815 proclaimed Miloš as 'supreme *knez* and leader of the Serbian people'. During the following twelve months the sultan issued a series of decrees which gave formal recognition to the Miloš–Marasli agreement. During the next few years Miloš gradually increased his influence within the administration of the pashalik, using the considerable wealth at his disposal to bribe Turkish officials. Miloš was himself a rich man, with large estates in Wallachia as well as his Serbian lands. He also found it possible to direct public funds to his own use. Marasli wanted nothing but a quiet life, and turned a blind eye to Miloš's encroachments. When he died in 1821 the Serbs had acquired in practice, if not in law, the right to appoint the local Turkish officials, to collect customs and ferry duties and to levy special taxes. Miloš used these funds to buy estates from the Turks, and then he transferred them either into his own hands or into those of his Serbian friends. Thus he began to erode the Turkish feudal system.

Miloš did not have the support of all the Serbian chiefs, especially those, like Dean Matija Nenadović and Petar Moler, who had crossed into Austrian territory with Karadjordje in 1813 to return later to share in Miloš's success. In 1817 Miloš discovered that Karadjordje himself was back in Serbian territory. Miloš ordered the murder of his rival, which was carried out on 25 July 1817 by Karadjordje's host and *kum* (godfather), Vujica Vuličević, who axed him to death whilst he slept. Miloš had his victim's head stuffed and sent to Istanbul as a present to the sultan. This savage act was not simply an act of mindless brutality against a rival for power. Miloš knew that Karadjordje had been in contact with the representatives of the Greek nationalist organisation Philike Hetairia (Society of Friends), which was planning a general rising of all the sultan's Christian subjects. Miloš feared that this would fail and that the reprisals which the Turks might take would result in the loss of all the gains which the Serbs had made since 1815.

In 1821 revolts broke out in Moldavia and Wallachia, Turkish provinces ruled by a Greek aristocracy under Constantine Ypsilanti. In this case, however, the Romanian peasantry under Tudor Vladimirescu took arms against their Greek masters. The start of the Greek war of independence shortly afterwards was a more serious affair for the sultan. Its immediate effect was to harden the Turkish attitude to the demands of the Serbs.

The Greek revolt focussed the attention of the European powers on the plight of the Christians under Ottoman rule. The newly enthroned Tsar Nicholas I moved troops up to the Turkish frontier and forced the sultan to sign the Convention of Akkerman (October 1826), by which the Turks agreed to implement the clauses of the Treaty of Bucharest which recognised the rights of the Romanians and Serbs. Britain and Austria gave diplomatic backing to this move.

By Article V of the Convention, the sultan promised to negotiate with the Serbs on their demands for freedom of worship; the right to establish their own schools and printing presses; the return of areas won during the first revolt and forcibly returned to Turkish rule in 1813; the right of Serbian merchants to trade freely throughout the Ottoman empire; a prohibition on any new Turkish settlement outside the major towns; and an increase in the powers of Serbian government.

Serbian delegates were in Istanbul discussing the implementation of the Convention when British, French and Russian ships blasted the Turkish fleet out of the water as it lay at anchor in the enclosed natural harbour at Navarino (Pylos) in the southern Morea on 20 October 1827. The first reaction of the sultan was to order the arrest of the Serbian delegates and to repudiate the Convention. He changed his mind, however, when Russia declared war in 1828 and advanced through Bulgaria to take Adrianople the following year. The Treaty of Adrianople, signed in September 1829, required the sultan to implement the Convention within a month. A *hatti şerif* (edict) of October 1829 implemented most of the terms demanded by the Russians, and on 6 February 1830 Miloš read out its terms at a ceremony in Kragujevac and Serbian autonomy was officially proclaimed. It required a further *hatti şerif* a year later which recognised Miloš as hereditary Prince of Serbia, established a commission to settle the boundaries, and regularised the payment of the annual Serbian tribute to the Sultan. By 1830 Miloš was the internationally accepted ruler of a virtually independent state.

During the years between 1813 and 1830 Serbia, under Miloš, had experienced a social, cultural and economic transformation which brought it from the medieval obscurity of a declining oriental despotism to the threshold of modern European statehood. Miloš was a man nurtured in the old society, and his regime and life style still bore the marks of his origins. In 1830 in his house – or *konak* – there were no tables, chairs or beds. Visitors squatted on the floor or sat on low, Turkish-style divans. Miloš dressed in Turkish clothing. He was unable to read or write and books in Serbian were almost unknown. The main streets of the towns were rough mud tracks. Window glass was not used even in the ruler's *konak*. There were no street lights and at night the streets were deserted.

Modernisation came mainly through the activities of foreigners or Serbs who returned from exile. As the Turks moved out, their estates in the rural areas were bought by Serbs and their houses in the towns were occupied by diverse groups of immigrants, who also took over their occupations. One such group were the Cincars, descendants of a people of Romanian origin who moved into the Balkans during the early days of Turkish rule. Their alternative name, Vlah (Wallachian), suggests their origin but by the nineteenth century most had become Hellenised, speaking and acting as intermediaries between the Greek clergy and their Serbian parish priests. The Cincars were also prominent in commerce, as also were native-born Greek immigrants and Jews. Most of the Balkan Jews were of Iberian origin and were thus of the Sephardic branch of Jewry. They found refuge in the Ottoman empire from Morocco to Moldavia when the Catholic monarchs of Spain and Portugal drove them out. The Sephardic community in Belgrade dates back to the early sixteenth century and was well established in the commercial life of the city. They lived in the Turkish quarter and in outward appearance resembled the Turks, although their religious and cultural life was very different from that of their neighbours. Another group whose origins and way of life marked them out from the Serbs were the gypsies (*cigani* or *romi*) who are still to be found throughout Serbia and Macedonia. Their total number at the 1981 census was about 168,000, 90 per cent of whom are found in Serbia proper, Kosovo and Macedonia. Their rate of natural increase is more than twice the national average, and their numbers increased by 214 per cent between 1971 and 1981.

The most important elements in the new Serbia, however, were those Serbs who lived within the Habsburg empire, especially those on the opposite banks of the Danube and Sava rivers, in the province known as Vojvodina. Some were descended from refugees who had fled before the advancing Turks in the fifteenth century; others had forebears who were led out by the Patriarch Arsenije of Peć in a mass migration of an estimated 100,000 Serbs in 1691. A third group were followers of Karadjordje, who fled in 1813 when the first revolt was crushed. Some of the early settlers had been integrated into the life of the Habsburg empire – like Metropolitan Stefan Stratimirović of Karlovci, who was a privy councillor of the Austrian court. Two figures who have been described respectively as the grandfather and father of Serbian literature were Dositej Obradović (1743–1811) and Vuk Karadžić (1787–1864). Both also played an active part in the national movement. Dositej was minister of education in Karadjordje's administration and Vuk was involved with both Karadjordje and Miloš.

Dositej entered the Hopovo monastery in the Fruška Gora at the age of sixteen, but he soon became disillusioned with the restricted life of a monk and two years later he escaped. He travelled widely throughout the Balkans, then went to Vienna in 1771, where he was employed as a language teacher. After five years in Vienna he taught in Trieste, Greece and Moldavia before studying philosophy in Halle. He also spent a year in England and became fluent in English. He read widely in all spheres of learning and became inspired with the idea that he had a mission to introduce the learning of western Europe to his countrymen in Serbia. He wrote works of philosophy in Serbian, which were published in Germany and Austria and circulated amongst the scholars in the Serbian gymnasium at Karlovci and amongst literate Serbs in the pashalik. He also translated English, French and German classics into Serbian. Despite his cosmopolitan background and his great linguistic ability, he never forgot that he was a Serb. His advocacy of the ideas of the Enlightenment aroused the suspicion of the Orthodox Church leaders in Karlovci when he returned there after the Karadjordje revolt. Not only was 'Dositejism' denounced by Metropolitan Stratimirović because of its anticlericalism, its suspected 'Protestantism' and its attachment to an alien western culture, but it was also seen as a threat to the language. Until the mid eighteenth century the language of the Church was based on Old Church Slavonic, but after the Suvorov mission sent by the Synod of Moscow in 1727 (see above, p. 74) a form of Russian was adopted, known as 'Serb–Slavonic'. Dositej wrote in a language which was closer to the everyday speech of the Serbian people.

The Orthodox Church had played a more important role in keeping alive the culture of the exiled Serbs in Catholic Austria than had the Greek-speaking hierarchy of the Orthodox communities in the Ottoman empire. This was particularly the case after the extinction of the patriarchate of Peć in 1766. In those latter areas it was left to the Serb-speaking parish priests, many of whom were illiterate, to act as upholders of Serbian culture. By the time of Dositej, the Austro-Serbian Church was led by narrow conservatives whose attitudes were a hindrance to the development of a popular Serbian culture appropriate to the needs of the nation struggling to be born.

Vuk Karadžić continued the work of Dositej, whose writings had influenced the younger man during his formative years. They both worked in the administration of the Karadjordje regime, Dositej as a minister and Vuk as a more humble clerk and customs official. Despite his lame leg, he also served with the *hajduk* leader Veljko in the last months of the Karadjordje revolt, and fled across the Danube when the Turks recaptured Belgrade in 1813.

Vuk had not completed his education when he crossed the river in 1807 to join Karadjordje, although he felt he had learned all he could from his teachers in Karlovci. When he left Serbia in 1813 he joined the South Slav community in Vienna, where he came to the notice of the imperial censor for Slavonic languages as a result of an article he wrote for the newspaper *Srpske Novine* (Serbian News). The censor, Jernej Kopitar, a Slovene who had worked in the household of Baron Žiga Zois, the patron of the Slovene literary revival (see above, pp. 53–4), became a close friend of Vuk. They shared many intellectual attitudes: both were anticlerical, both believed in the encouragement of a Slavonic culture within the Habsburg lands, and both had an interest in the development of a South Slav language based on the everyday speech of the common people.

In 1814, inspired by Herder's *Stimmen der Völker*, Vuk produced a volume of Serbian national songs, in the preface to which he drew attention to the need for standardisation of the language, for 'no two people approve of each other's ways and write alike, but also no single man writes consistently . . . so it will be without cease, until our learned men . . . can agree amongst themselves, and in cooperation write a Serbian grammar and a single dictionary'.

Vuk himself took up the task, and his first effort appeared in October 1814. It was badly received by the Church authorities, although it was enthusiastically reviewed by Kopitar. In 1815 he returned to Karlovici to collect material for a second song book, which later inspired a glowing review from Jakob Grimm, in which he compared the Serbian love songs to Solomon's Song of Songs and wrote that the 'Serbs are by virtue of their language . . . the most blessed with poems, songs and stories, and it looks as if the good God had, by this rich gift of popular poetry, wished to make up to them for their lack of books.'

Vuk's next project was a Serbian dictionary, and to help him in collecting words to include in it he made a journey to Serbia in 1816 on his way back to Vienna, calling on his old friend the archimandrite Lukian Mušicki in the monastery at Šišatovac in the Fruška Gora. The archimandrite was rebuked by Metropolitan Stratimirović for keeping 'that blasphemer amongst your priests'. Stratimirović tried to prevent Vuk from publishing his grammar by invoking an order of Leopold II giving a monopoly to the publishing of books in Serbian to the Serbian press in Buda, which, unlike that in Vienna, was under the influence of the Church. Eventually Vuk and Kopitar found a way to get the book published and it appeared in 1818 as a Serbian–Latin–German dictionary.

In his efforts to secure funds to finance the publication of his dictionary Vuk wrote to Miloš, but received a derisory offer in return. In the summer of 1820, after a visit to Russia the previous year to promote his recently translated New Testament, which eventually saw the light of day in 1847, Vuk again approached Miloš, this time offering to teach the ruler to read and write. He had hopes of following in the footsteps of Dositej and becoming minister of education. Whilst in Russia he had been in contact with representatives of the Russian Bible Society, and through them had learned of the monitorial system of schoolteaching pioneered by Lancaster and Bell in Britain. He hoped to introduce this method into Serbia. Miloš, however, was not interested, and after wasting Vuk's time for over a year he let the scholar return to Austria empty-handed. He returned later to Serbia, and hoped then to secure the support of Miloš by writing a biography of the ruler. However, Vuk was too honest and too independent-minded to please Miloš, and when he again crossed over to Zemun in April 1832 he wrote a frank letter, telling Miloš what he believed to be wrong with his regime and advising him to introduce a constitution. Miloš exploded with anger when the letter was read out to him. He tore it into pieces and then sent three messengers to Zemun to confront Vuk. In the presence of a large crowd in a public square the messengers shouted vulgar abuse at Vuk. The mildest of the printable epithets were that Vuk was a traitor, a 'wretched, shameless and malicious creature' and a 'lame imp of hell'. Miloš also wrote to the Austrian authorities and Metternich thought it advisable to remove Vuk from Zemun, first to Buda and then to join his Austrian wife and their two children in Vienna.

Whilst in Vienna he had the good fortune to meet Petar II Petrović-Njegoš, the Vladika of Montenegro, who was passing through on his way to St Petersburg for his consecration as bishop. The Montenegrin poet and the Serbian philologist made friends immediately, and in 1834 Vuk was invited to Cetinje to assist in the establishment of a new printing press, using Vuk's phonetic orthographic principle.

Two years after his return from Cetinje, Vuk received official confirmation of rumours and hints that Miloš was considering giving him a pension. This eventually materialised and a kind of reconciliation took place. The abdication of Miloš in 1839 temporarily interrupted the payment of the pension, but the new government eventually continued it. The deposed Miloš (from his Wallachian exile) also supported Vuk, and in 1844 he persuaded Toma Vučić, the power behind the *coup d'état* which brought Alexander Karadjordjević to the throne in 1842, to give him a pension. His financial position was secure for the first time, and for the last twenty years of his long life he was able to devote himself to his work of creating a Serbian literary language and bringing to the notice of his countrymen and the world the riches of the Serbian oral tradition.

His collaboration with the Croatian Ljudevit Gaj, and his contacts with literary figures such as Petar Petrović-Njegoš in Montenegro, helped to create a sense of Yugoslav cultural unity. The phonetic orthography of both the Cyrillic alphabet of Serbia and the Latin alphabet of Croatia and Slovenia made for easier communication and understanding among the Yugoslav peoples and led to common political action. The Literary Agreement signed in Vienna in 1850 by Vuk and a number of Serb, Croat and Slovene authors – including Miklošič, the Slovene who succeeded Kopitar as imperial censor – attempted to create a common literary language based on the South Serbian dialect, written in either Cyrillic or

Latin. Echoes of this declaration were revived over a century later with the Novi Sad Agreement of 1954.

Serbia from autonomy to independence

By 1830 Miloš had brought his country to the status of a self-governing principality, with himself as hereditary prince, but he was incapable of responding to the needs of his people for an orderly, constitutional form of government. His arbitrary habits soon alienated powerful elements in the new state and there were occasional armed revolts, the most serious of which, known as Mileta's Revolt after one of its leaders, Mileta Radojković, occurred in December 1834. Miloš was forced to grant a constitution, known as the Presentation constitution because it was promulgated on the feast day commemorating the presentation of Christ in the temple. Although the constitution guaranteed certain civil rights and promised the abolition of forced labour, which was a survival from the Turkish *kulluk* system, it did little more than establish a council of chiefs to share the prince's oligarchic powers. It is, therefore, rather odd that the European powers and especially the Austrians saw it as a dangerously – and perhaps contagiously – liberal document. They prevailed upon Miloš to go to Istanbul to discuss the matter with the sultan's ministers, and Miloš willingly shelved the constitution. The only practical result of his four months' stay in Istanbul was an agreement to permit foreign diplomatic representatives in Belgrade. An Austrian was appointed immediately, followed by an Englishman, Colonel Hodges, a Frenchman and a Russian. These foreign consuls interfered in Serbian politics – none more so than Hodges – in the interests of their own governments, taking sides in the complex intrigues of the Serbian notables.

One of Miloš's chief opponents was Toma Vučić-Perišić, who became the leader of a group of Defenders of the Constitution (Ustavobranitelji), working in exile in Wallachia to force Miloš either to accept a constitution or to abdicate. They even won the support of Miloš's brother, Jevrem, and his much wronged wife, Ljubica. Under Hodges' guidance Miloš tried to steal the Constitutionalists' thunder by promising a constitution and guaranteeing civil rights. A commission was established, whose appointment of personnel was dictated by the Russians and the Austrians. After months of fruitless argument in Belgrade, the commissioners went to Istanbul. Under pressure from the Russian ambassador, the sultan issued a *hatti şerif* on 24 December 1838, promulgating the so-called Turkish constitution. This preserved Ottoman sovereignty and gave Russia the status of a guarantor. It established a seventeen-man council (soviet), appointed by Miloš but holding office for life, which had to approve all laws and taxes. A cabinet, responsible to the soviet, was packed with Constitutionalists. The first steps were taken to set up an independent judiciary. Provision was made for the convening of a Popular Assembly (Skupština) whenever the soviet felt it desirable. The people had no automatic right to be consulted, however. If the Turkish constitution did not bring democracy to Serbia, at least it brought an end to the absolute monarchy, and it survived for thirty years. Miloš was completely demoralised by the loss of his absolute power and fled to Zemun (Semlin), whither a delegation from the council followed him and persuaded him to return. A month later he made a half-hearted attempt to rally loyal troops to his side, but Vučić acted firmly to quell the rebellion against the council, and Miloš was forced to abdicate in June 1839 and to go into exile on his Wallachian estate. He was succeeded by his nineteen-year-old son, Milan, who was dying of tuberculosis.

A regency council headed by Vučić took charge. Milan died in July and the regency invited his younger brother, Michael (Mihailo), then sixteen years old, to take the throne. The required approval from the sultan was not granted until 1840, and then only after further curbs on the ruler's powers had been forced on the young prince. He was placed under the strict supervision of the regents. Miloš continued to stir up trouble from his safe exile, and in 1840 an abortive rising on his behalf alerted the powers to the possibility of his return, and to the overthrow of the constitution. The council called an *ad hoc* Popular Assembly, which gave qualified support to the constitution and to Michael as head of state, but which also castigated the Constitutionalists as being self-seekers who had abused their powers.

In 1842 Vučić organised a *coup d'état* which overthrew the Obrenović dynasty. The supporters of the ruling family were ruthlessly hounded down and either forced into exile or thrown into jail. A Skupština was assembled in Belgrade to proclaim a new ruler. They chose Alexander Karadjordjević, the son of the first Karadjordje. He received the reluctant blessing of the sultan in 1843 after he had satisfied the Russians and Austrians that he would honour the constitution. In 1844 the two leading Constitutionalists, Vučić and Petronijević, who had been exiled on the insistence of the Russians, were allowed to return.

The Obrenović family and their supporters continued to plot the overthrow of the new regime, which had faced both internal unrest and foreign pressure. The Austrians and Russians continually interfered, their relative strengths varying with the state of European power politics. Austrian pressure kept Serbia from supporting Russia during the Crimean War, and the Treaty of Paris (1856), which brought that conflict to an end, abolished Russia's special status as protector of the Serbs. It put in its place a consortium of all the powers, who were given a watching brief on behalf of the sultan's Christian subjects.

The ageing Miloš turned Alexander's troubles to his own advantage. In 1848 he supported the Slavs in the Vojvodina and in Croatia–Slavonia, who were in revolt against the separatist regime of Lajos Kossuth. Alexander temporised, although thousands of Serb volunteers crossed the Danube to support their kinsfolk against the Magyars.

The government of Serbia during this time was dominated by a statesman who was a great champion of the 'Yugoslav Idea', Ilija Garašanin (1812–74). In 1844 he produced a memorandum (Načertanije) which advocated the creation of a Greater Serbia, reminiscent of the old medieval empire of Tsar Dušan. He saw Serbia as the rallying point for the Slavs of both the Habsburg and Ottoman empires, and he was greatly encouraged in 1848 when Serbs, Croats, Bosnians and Montenegrins rallied to the cause of the Slavs under Hungarian rule. An assembly convened in Karlovci on May Day 1848 drew in representatives of Serbs from the principality and from both empires. They demanded the addition of Vojvodina to Serbia and the restoration of the patriarchate of Peć. They sent the 'patriarch' whom they had elected, in total disregard of canon law, on a mission to Zagreb to demonstrate their solidarity with the Croats. Of course the assembly had no legal status, and its gestures bore no immediate fruit. In 1849 when the Austrians, with Russian help, crushed the Magyar revolt and sent Kossuth into exile, the Vojvodina was placed for a time under direct Austrian rule, and all manifestations of Serb irredentism were suppressed. Nevertheless, the idea of South Slav unity under Serbian leadership had been established in the minds of the Serbs and it became the *Leitmotif* of Serbian policy until 1918.

Garašanin, who became premier in 1853, was dismissed under Russian pressure in 1854, but returned to office after a few years and continued to serve in various posts until his retirement in 1868.

The suspicion that Alexander was unduly influenced by the Austrians, and the inability of his regime to give order and stability to the country, gave an added impetus to the pro-Obrenović party. In 1858 Alexander was deposed by an assembly summoned by Garašanin and Vučić, who temporarily sank their differences. The assembly was called on the feast day of St Andrew, who was, ironically, the patron saint of the Karadjordjević family. This was the first Serbian assembly which was convened under any kind of regular legal authority. Previously Popular Assemblies had been called on an *ad hoc* basis, without any set order of procedure or any uniform system of choosing those who attended. They were often held in the open air and bore as much resemblance to a constitutional assembly as a mass meeting called by shop stewards at a factory gate bears to the British Parliament. The St Andrew's Assembly of 30 November 1858 was called under a law of the previous month, passed by the Serbian Council (soviet). It consisted of 376 elected representatives and 63 *ex officio* office holders and religious leaders. It was in session for a month. Its first few days were occupied with a discussion on a proposal to establish a permanent, elected Assembly, with considerable legislative powers, but this was watered down by a compromise which required the agreement of the Council before any legislation proposed by the Assembly could become law.

Its most important act was, on 23 December, to depose Alexander and proclaim the restoration of Miloš Obrenović, then in his eightieth year but still full of energy. The sultan gave his approval three weeks later, and in February 1859 Miloš returned and attempted to put the constitutional clock back to 1838. His method was to pack the Council with ministers of his own choosing, purge the bureaucracy and ignore the protests of the Assembly. Vučić was arrested, and died whilst in custody, although the rumour that he had been poisoned was never proved.

By appealing to the people over the heads of the professional politicians and officials, Miloš struck a popular note with the Serbian peasants. He also showed himself to be a master of political intrigue, successfully setting the Conservatives under Garašanin against the Liberals under Grujić and Janković. Had he not died in the autumn of 1860 he would probably have established a paternalistic, populist absolutism, which only another *coup d'état* could have stopped.

Miloš was again succeeded by his son Michael (Mihailo), a man of thirty-five years who had spent most of his life outside Serbia. He had been given a western education and was far more polished and sophisticated than his illiterate and boorish father. Although the style of his government was different from that of Miloš, father and son both had the same autocratic ambitions.

Michael's chief aim was to develop Garašanin's Draft Programme (Načertanije) of 1844, which aimed at the creation of a Greater Serbia, as being the focal point for a South Slav state. This could only be achieved, in Michael's opinion, by launching a war of liberation against the Turks. He also realised that Austria no longer needed to worry about the Turkish threat, and that Slav nationalism was a more pressing preoccupation of the Habsburgs. Michael's first aim, therefore, was to build a strong Serbian army to prepare for the coming struggle. He brought in foreign advisers and spent a large proportion of his budget on building a standing army of some 90,000 men. It was supplied by arms smuggled in from Russia via the Romanian provinces and from Austria across the Danube. The arsenal in Kragujevac, the royal capital, also began to manufacture small arms, under the guidance of foreign advisers. Although it appeared to be a formidable fighting force, the Serbian army lacked discipline and was badly equipped and badly organised. Nevertheless it gave the Serbs a feeling of strength and self-confidence and boosted Michael's popularity.

Michael's greatest success was to secure the withdrawal of the Turkish garrisons from the Kalemegdan fortress in Belgrade and from the five other towns, including Smederovo on the Danube, Šabac on the Sava and Užice in the Šumadija. This was achieved in two stages. The first, in 1862, started with the killing of a Serbian boy by Turkish soldiers, and soon escalated into a confrontation between the Serbian army and the garrison in Kalemegdan. The consuls of the foreign powers intervened after Turkish guns had bombarded houses in Belgrade, killing tens of Serbian civilians. The sultan eventually agreed to hand over the two interior fortresses of Užice and Soko Banja, on the southern frontier, but the Turks retained the riverside positions in the north. In 1867, largely thanks to Russian diplomatic pressure, the sultan acceded to Michael's request that the remaining garrisons should be withdrawn, although Michael had to accept that the Turkish flag would still be flown over Kalemegdan as an acknowledgement that he was a Turkish vassal.

In domestic policy Michael behaved autocratically, although he made populist gestures by introducing a bill of rights and guaranteeing the independence of the judiciary. In practice, however, he flouted his own avowed principles whenever it suited him. For example, in the winter of 1863–4 an alleged plot to assassinate the prince was uncovered. The accused were acquitted by the Supreme Court. Michael ordered the trial of the judges by a rigged court composed of his own nominees, and several of the highest judicial authorities in the land were sentenced to prison terms of up to three years.

By 1868 Michael's popularity, even with the peasant masses, was waning. His private life also caused a scandal which shocked the devout and traditionally minded peasantry. His wife Julia, a Hungarian Catholic aristocrat, was unable to provide him with a son and heir. In 1865 Julia and Michael agreed to separate, and he then declared his intention to marry a sixteen-year-old Serbian girl, Katarina, who was his distant cousin. The situation bristled with difficulties. Julia, as a devout Catholic, could not agree to a divorce. The Orthodox Church regarded marriage to even so distant a cousin as the young Katarina as incest. Michael's relations with the two women aroused the deepest mistrust amongst his peasant subjects. It was bad enough that he had married a foreign, high-born Roman Catholic, whom he accompanied to Mass every Sunday. To compound the offence, he had married a barren wife. Even worse, he now proposed to break the Orthodox Church's strict rules of consanguinity in order to marry a girl of sixteen. On 9 June 1868 he was murdered in Topčider Park whilst riding in his carriage alongside his bride-to-be, her mother and grandmother and Ilija Garašanin's son, Svetozar.

The succession passed to his fourteen-year-old cousin, Milan Obrenović, who was at the time studying in Paris. Milan's election on 2 July was forced on the Skupština by the minister of war, Milivoje Blaznavac, who engineered a *coup d'état* on the day after the murders, pushing aside the premier, Garašanin. and the three provisional regents who had been legally appointed. A new three-man regency was elected to govern until Milan came of age. They were Blaznavac, the Liberal leader Jovan Ristić, and the venerable scholar and statesman Jovan Gavrilović, a relic of the early days of Miloš Obrenović's regime.

The murder of Michael took no one by surprise, as it had been common coffee house talk for some time. The actual assassin, Pavle Radovanović, may have had a personal grudge against the prince, but it is far from clear who was standing behind him. Various culprits have been suggested, including the exiled Alexander Karadjordjević. It has also been suggested that the Austrians may have lent their support to the conspiracy.

Michael bequeathed to his cousin, Prince Milan, a highly centralised state machine, with an armoury of constitutional and administrative weapons which enabled the ruler to wield considerable personal power. There were a strong state security machine and a large standing army to back up the prince's autocratic powers.

Michael's autocracy was of a more modern and efficient character than that of his father, Miloš. Under his rule Serbia began to acquire the trappings of a modern state, with a regular parliament, albeit with limited powers, in which two political parties – the Liberals and Conservatives – contended for the political favours of an electorate which included most adult male householders. The beginnings of manufacturing industry and of a free commercial life were apparent; there were a proper judicial system and a framework of educational institutions which at least provided secondary and higher education for the urban middle classes, even if the peasants, who made up over 80 per cent of the 1.25 million inhabitants, remained illiterate.

The greatest achievements of Milan's twenty-one-year reign were to enlarge the territory of Serbia by incorporating the Niš, Pirot and Vranje regions to the south; and to win international approval for Serbia's total independence from Turkey. These were achievements which resulted from the big powers' compromise at the Congress of Berlin in 1878. The final achievement was to proclaim the independent kingdom of Serbia in 1882. These successes owed less to the abilities of the prince than to the decisions of the European powers in their pursuit of the answer to the riddle of the Eastern Question. In 1876, for example, when public opinion forced him to join the Montenegrins in an attack on Turkey in order to support the revolt of the Bosnians, he was only saved from defeat by the intervention of Russia (see below, p. 103).

Milan hoped, with Austrian help, to extricate himself from internal problems, which were largely of his own making, by a resounding victory in the Balkans. In 1885 he ordered an attack on Bulgaria, hoping to gain both territory and prestige. The excuse for the Serbian attack was the Bulgarian coup of 17 September 1885 which proclaimed the union of Rumelia with Bulgaria, thus upsetting the arrangement reached at Berlin in 1878 (see below, pp. 103–4). Milan saw that a strengthened Bulgaria would be in a favourable position to wrest Macedonia from the Turks, and his ill-prepared attack was a pre-emptive strike in order to safeguard Serbian interests. It was a disastrous failure. The Bulgarians routed the Serbs at the battle of Slivnica, 17 November, and went on to invade Serbia itself. This time Austria–Hungary came to the rescue and, by the Treaty of Bucharest in March 1886, the *status quo ante bellum* was restored.

Milan became even more unpopular with the Serbian people. He was obviously in the pocket of the Habsburgs; his foreign policy was a total failure; and his scandalous private life alienated the pious Serbian peasantry.

In 1889 he abdicated in favour of his thirteen-year-old son, Alexander, and a Regency Council was formed under Jovan Ristić. Milan and his divorced wife, the pro-Russian Natalie, continued to live in Serbia until 1893, when Alexander abolished the regency and withdrew the constitution which had been adopted when he came to the throne in 1889. Alexander was a true son of his father. He continued to depend on the backing of the Austrians; his dealings with his own people were corrupt and arbitrary; and his private life was full of scandal. Milan was invited to return from his exile in Biarritz and became commander-in-chief of the army until his death in 1901. In 1897 Alexander married Draga Mašin, a widow of ill repute who was ten years his senior. This did nothing to endear him to his people. In June 1903 the Obrenović dynasty came to a bloody end when a group of young officers entered the palace and butchered the King and Queen, throwing their mutilated bodies from their bedroom window, to the cheers of the crowd assembled in the palace grounds. The premier and minister of war, together with other members of the royal entourage, were also murdered on the same night. The belief that Peter, the son of the deposed King Alexander Karadjordjević, knew of the plot was strengthened by his actions when he ascended the throne. The regicides (in particular Apis) were honoured, and several of the plotters were taken into the government. The revulsion of the other crowned heads of Europe towards the new monarch prompted Edward VII to refuse to send a representative to Peter's coronation in 1904. Several governments withdrew their diplomatic representatives in Belgrade, and relations with Britain were not resumed until 1906.

The Skupština met and invited Peter Karadjordjević to become king. The 1889 constitution was restored and Serbia embarked on a period of stable constitutional rule, during which considerable economic progress was made. The dominant figure in political life was the Serbian radical leader, Nikola Pašić, who was premier for most of the time until the declaration of the kingdom of Serbs, Croats and Slovenes in 1918.

Macedonia

One of the objectives of Serbian policy throughout the nineteenth century, which was pursued with equal enthusiasm, but with varying degrees of skill, by both the Obrenović and Karadjordjević dynasties, was the acquisition of Macedonia. The geographical area of Macedonia came within the Turkish *vilayets* of Kosovo, Monastir and Salonika, and contained a mixed population of Slavs, Greeks, Turks, Albanians and Vlahs. The largest element were the Macedonian Slavs, who were claimed as fellow nationals by both the Bulgars and the Serbs. Few accepted the idea that there might be a separate Macedonian nation, although Gladstone had raised the slogan 'Macedonia for the Macedonians' during the Midlothian campaign of 1879–80.

The inhabitants of Macedonia had the misfortune to live in a strategically important area which controlled the historic routeways leading from central Europe to the Aegean. The battle for the control of Macedonia was waged on many fronts, not least through the schools and churches. The

Turkish *raya* system permitted the Christian subjects of the sultan to practise their own religion, but in Macedonia the great question was the national identity of those who were appointed to minister to the people. Were they to be Serbs, Bulgars or Greeks? After the elimination of the Serbian patriarchates of Peć and Ohrid in the mid eighteenth century, the predominant influence was Greek, but Greek supremacy was challenged by the Bulgars in the nineteenth century, and in 1870 the Bulgarian exarchate was established. During the next twenty years Bulgarian bishops were appointed to most of the Macedonian sees. With the bishops came Bulgarian schools and pro-Bulgarian propaganda. In the 1890s revolutionary societies began to be established whose aim was to accomplish the overthrow of the Turks. Some were controlled by Bulgarians, but there were others, like IMRO (the Internal Macedonian Revolutionary Organisation), which had as their objective the establishment of an autonomous Macedonia, although sections of IMRO came under Bulgarian domination. There was also a Greek revolutionary society, Ethnike Hetairia.

Some of the secret societies organised terrorist activities against the Turks, but the autonomist wing of IMRO began to prepare a Macedonian uprising, which broke out on St Elijah's Day (Ilinden), 2 August 1903. The leaders of the Ilinden rising are regarded today as national heroes and Ilinden has become the Macedonian national day. One of the most remarkable of the Macedonian revolutionaries, Goce Delčev (1872–1903), was the spokesman of a generous, humanist philosophy, which, whilst proclaiming the right of his own people to liberation, did not deny the same right to others. He declared that it was not necessary to hate the Turkish people while fighting against Ottoman tyranny. The initial aim of the rising was to create an independent state in the *vilayet* of Monastir (Bitola), and then to extend the free area to the whole of Macedonia. The appeal was not only to the Slavs, but also to 'Turks, Albanians and Moslems' who suffered under the Ottoman yoke. A 'republic' was established in the town of Kruševo, but the revolt was ruthlessly suppressed after only eleven days. Delčev was killed in a preliminary skirmish before Ilinden. Another leader, Dame Gruev, escaped immediate retribution, but was killed later in a guerrilla action against the Turks in 1906.

The savage repression which followed the Ilinden rising prompted the powers to make another attempt to persuade the sultan to behave in a more civilised way towards his Christian subjects. The so-called Murszteg Programme involved the appointment of British, French, Italian, Austrian and Russian advisers to supervise the carrying out of reforms which the Turks promised to introduce. The Bulgarians promised to use their influence to curb the activities of IMRO. Neither side had the slightest intention of carrying out its promises. The Greeks and Serbs, who were not parties to the agreement, continued to press their causes through their various societies. In 1908 the Turks, flushed with the success of the Young Turk revolt, proclaimed the equality of all peoples within the empire, and the powers, apparently believing them, abandoned their system of control. The unfortunate people of Macedonia continued to be the victims of Turkish repression and of the conflicting intrigues of the Serbs, Bulgarians and Greeks. Macedonia for the Macedonians had to wait for another generation, two world wars and a revolution before anything resembling its fulfilment occurred.

The South Slavs and the European powers

The Eastern Question can be summarised as follows: 'Who will fill the power vacuum left by the gradual disintegration of the Ottoman empire in Europe?' There were several claimants, the chief of which were the Slav, Greek and Romanian subjects of the sultan; the Habsburgs; the Romanovs; and, in the background, the French and British and, after 1870, the Russians. The last three were more concerned with protecting their commercial and strategic interests than in annexing territory.

Because of these conflicting interests the South Slavs could not be allowed to settle their own affairs without outside interference. The ambitions of their northern neighbours, Austria and Hungary, to control the routeways from central Europe to the Adriatic and the Aegean; the German *Drang nach Südosten* during the fifty years preceding the First World War; and the Russian need for access to the Mediterranean via the straits, all coloured the attitude of the powers to the struggles of the Slavs to emancipate themselves from the dead hand of Ottoman rule. Disputes within the Balkans either between the Turks and their Christian subjects or between the subject nations could not be left to groups directly involved. Every step they took echoed through the chancelleries of Europe, where statesmen watched every move to see if it afforded them an opportunity to intervene in pursuit of their own interests.

Russia had a great advantage over the other powers in its dealings with the South Slavs, and especially the Serbs, Montenegrins and Bulgars, because of the common linguistic traditions of the Slav peoples and the confessional links through the Orthodox Churches. The Treaty of Kutchuk Kainardji (1774) forced Turkey to recognise Russia's special interest in the Orthodox Christians; and the Panslavist movement, which developed after the Slavonic Ethnographic Exhibition held in Moscow in 1867, had an important influence on Russian policy during the later nineteenth century.

The main interest of the Habsburgs was to encroach on the western half of the peninsula, especially in Bosnia–Hercegovina, which was occupied in 1878 and annexed in 1908; and in Dalmatia, which was acquired in 1815. One aspect of Habsburg policy was to prevent the spread of Slav nationalism amongst its own Slav subjects in Croatia–Slavonia, Dalmatia, Vojvodina and the Slovene lands.

At times it suited the powers to give support to the Turks and to slow down the process of disintegration of the Ottoman empire. This was a fairly consistent policy of Britain during most of the nineteenth century, motivated partly by fear of Russia. Only for a brief period during the Greek war of independence did Britain act with Russia against Turkey, until Gladstone in his Midlothian campaign of 1879 fought a successful election on a foreign policy issue. Gladstone advocated cooperation with the powers, including Russia, to force the Turks out of Europe. Macedonians today still quote with gratitude his battle cry 'Macedonia for the Macedonians!' When he became prime minister he insisted on Turkey fulfilling the territorial clauses of the Treaty of Berlin relating to Serbia and Montenegro, but was unable to overcome domestic pressure against joint action with Russia. Thereafter Britain made compassionate protests over the mistreatment by the Turks of their Christian subjects, but did little or nothing to bring about the expulsion of Turkey from Europe.

The Austrians and Russians from time to time acted to preserve the Turkish empire, especially during the period of Metternich's ascendancy between 1829 and the 1840s. Even as late as 1875, on the eve of the Bosnian revolt, which led three years later to the Austrian occupation, Andrássy, the Austro-Hungarian foreign minister, in a report to the Crown Council, stated:

Turkey possesses a utility almost providential for Austria–Hungary. For Turkey maintains the status quo of the small Balkan states and impedes their national aspirations. If it were not for Turkey all those aspirations would fall on our heads . . . if Bosnia–Hercegovina should go to Serbia or Montenegro, or if a new state should be formed there which we cannot prevent, then we should be ruined and should ourselves assume the role of 'Sick Man'.

During the period 1875–80 dramatic developments within the Balkans substantially altered the balance of forces. What A. J. P. Taylor has called the Great Eastern Crisis began in the remote Hercegovinian village of

Nevesinje, near Mostar. Revolts by the *raya* against local Turkish officials were common, and Hercegovina was one of the more turbulent areas. Usually the Turkish authorities were able to contain the rebels and matters were settled when a punitive expedition entered the village where the recalcitrants lived, burned their homes, hanged their leaders, raped their womenfolk and enslaved their children. In 1875, however, there were special circumstances which caused the revolt in Nevesinje against the tax collectors to spread. The harvest of 1874 had been a poor one over a large area of Bosnia and Hercegovina. Christian peasants saw their families starving whilst what little food was produced by the last harvest was taken to satisfy the demands of their Muslim landlords and the sultan's tax collectors. It needed only an incident like that at Nevesinje in July 1875 to turn the widespread discontent into open revolt. The successes of the Serbs in 1867 (see above, p. 95) and the Greeks in 1866–9 had shown that the Balkan peoples could, with profit, take matters into their own hands. They need not always be the pawns of the European powers, who in the past had manipulated the Slavs, the Greeks, the Bulgars and the Romanians to further their own selfish interests. In Taylor's words, 'The Balkan Slavs alone launched the crisis of 1875.'

As the revolt spread throughout Bosnia and Hercegovina the powers, for different reasons, tried to damp it down. The Austrians feared that the unrest might spread to their Slav subjects and that, if Serbia stepped in to support the rebels, there might be permanent damage to Habsburg interests in south-east Europe. Andrássy, the Austro-Hungarian foreign minister, proposed to the powers that their consuls on the spot should form a commission and attempt to mediate. This failed, and in December 1875 Andrássy, in a memorandum to the Porte, proposed a programme of reforms which the sultan must accept and which would be supervised by the powers. The elderly Abdülaziz outwardly conformed to Andrássy's demands, but did nothing. The Slav rebels were dissatisfied with the inability of the powers to enforce their wishes on the Turks. The situation was exacerbated by the savage repression which the Turks meted out to the Bulgarian peasants who had risen in revolt in 1876. In May Abdülaziz was deposed and a few days later committed suicide. His successor, Murad V, went mad a few weeks later, after an officer had run amok in a cabinet meeting and murdered several of the ministers. Before the Turks had had time to instal the new sultan, Abdülhamid II (Abdul the Damned), Serbia and Montenegro, taking advantage of the disarray in Istanbul, declared war and invaded Bosnia. The Serbs fared badly. Milan Obrenović had been pushed into war by public pressure and by the fear that if Montenegro went in alone his standing amongst the Balkan Slavs would be tarnished. The Montenegrins made a better showing and, largely due to their military successes and to Russian diplomatic intervention on behalf of Serbia, a ceasefire was agreed in November. Abdülhamid made promises which he had no intention of keeping, and in April 1877 the exasperated Russians decided to invade Turkey. Serbia and Montenegro again took up arms and a full-scale war raged throughout the Balkans. The Russian advance was held up for six months at the fortress of Plevna (Pleven) in Bulgaria, 32 km south of their crossing point on the Danubian frontier, and they were unable to penetrate south of the Stara Planina until Plevna fell in December 1877. Taylor may exaggerate in stating that 'Plevna is one of the few engagements which changed the course of history', but it certainly gave the Turks a breathing space, and enabled the powers to recover their equilibrium and organise their diplomatic counterattack to thwart Russian ambitions and control the straits. When an exhausted Russian army reached the straits in January 1878 an armistice was arranged. On 3 March the Russians and Turks signed the Treaty of San Stefano, which provided *inter alia* for the creation of an autonomous Bulgaria which included most of modern Macedonia and provided the new state with an outlet to the Aegean. It also recognised Montenegro's territorial gains and its status as an independent principality, and guaranteed Serbian independence.

The fear of predominant Russian influence in the Balkans through client Slav states, which was implied by this settlement, alarmed the powers. In July the European leaders, meeting in Berlin under Bismarck's chairmanship, forced the Russians to accept an agreement which was less favourable to the Slavs and which spared the Ottoman empire for another four decades. Bulgaria was denied Macedonia, and the Big Bulgaria of San Stefano was cut back to two separate provinces, an autonomous Bulgaria in the north, and a quasi-autonomous province of Eastern Rumelia. Macedonia was handed back to Turkey. Since 1878 the Bulgarians have made several attempts to regain the San Stefano frontiers, and have twice succeeded for short periods during the First and Second World Wars. The Macedonian question remains a bone of contention between Yugoslavia and Bulgaria. Memories of San Stefano are a powerful element in present-day Bulgarian sentiments of friendship towards Russia.

Montenegro's territorial gains were reduced at Berlin in order to prevent the possibility of a common frontier with Serbia, for which San Stefano almost provided. The buffer zone of the sandžak of Novi Pazar, under Ottoman suzerainty but with Austrian garrisons, lay between the two Slav states.

Serbia lost some of the territory granted by San Stefano, but still made considerable gains at Turkey's expense, acquiring the Niš and Pirot regions.

Austria gained most territorially from the Berlin settlement. The powers granted her the right to occupy Bosnia–Hercegovina. Nominally the occupation was to be for a temporary period, until order was restored, but no one doubted that the province would become at least an Austrian colony and at most that it would be annexed as an integral part of the Habsburg realm. By a convention signed at Novi Pazar in April 1879 between Turkey and Austria, the Austrians recognised Turkish sovereignty and promised to safeguard the rights of the Muslims, but this agreement was frequently ignored by the new administrators. Because of a disagreement between Austria and Hungary over the financing of the occupation regime, effectual control passed to the imperial civil service, which dealt, under the guidance of a joint council (the Delegation), with questions which affected the whole monarchy rather than its separate halves. The joint minister of finance became the effective ruler of Bosnia.

The Austrians showed their determination to secure their new acquisitions by embarking on a programme of railway construction to link Sarajevo with the main Zagreb–Belgrade line (completed 1884) and with the Adriatic at Metković in Hercegovina (1890). In 1906 the line through the sandžak completed the link between Sarajevo and the main Turkish line through Skopje to Salonika. These narrow-gauge lines, built primarily for military purposes, were in use until well after the Second World War.

The Austrians hoped to show by their administration of this newly acquired colony that they could be trusted to govern Slav-speaking subjects with justice and to develop the Bosnian economy. They were particularly anxious to placate the Muslims, who represented a third of the population, but who controlled key positions in local government and in economic life. The Muslims, despite some initial resistance, proved cooperative. It has been said of them that 'they early developed a "client strategy" of supporting whoever was ruling them . . . in return for favors or concessions'. However, despite a long period of tranquillity, Muslim political consciousness eventually broke through the outwardly bland surface, and by the end of the Austrian period there was a strong Muslim political organisation. The Orthodox Serbs never became reconciled to Austrian rule and looked to Belgrade for leadership. The Catholic Croats were in a weak position. Although at first they sought support from Vienna, they were affected by the rising tide of Slav nationalism as the Yugoslav movement developed in Croatia–Slavonia and Dalmatia.

The Slavs within the Habsburg monarchy 1815–1914

Mention has already been made (see above, pp. 87–8) of the assistance which the Serbs within the Habsburg monarchy gave to the struggle of their cousins in Serbia. In the early days they provided a sanctuary for rebellious Serbs fleeing from the wrath of the Ottomans and later a reservoir of talents from which the Serbian rulers could draw for their military leaders, their educators and administrators. Above all they kept alive and developed the cultural traditions of their nation.

The Croats of Croatia–Slavonia and Dalmatia had different perspectives and faced different problems. The Yugoslav movement owed much to them. Its point of departure was the Napoleonic episode of the Illyrian Provinces. For four years Serbs, Croats and Slovenes lived together under a regime which not only tolerated but actively encouraged the development of their cultures and languages. The idea of a permanent form of union, embracing all the South Slavs within the monarchy, did not die with the expulsion of the French and the reimposition of Habsburg rule in 1815. Dalmatia and Ragusa were placed under direct Austrian rule. The Slovene lands were again partitioned among the Austrian provinces of Carinthia, Carniola and Styria, and western Croatia reverted to its Hungarian allegiance.

Although both Austria and Hungary shared a common Habsburg monarch, the administrations of Vienna and Buda did not adopt identical policies towards their Slav subjects. This divergence became even more apparent after the creation of the Dual Monarchy following the *Ausgleich* of 1867. Even within the Austrian-administered areas there was a great difference between Dalmatia and the Slovene lands. There is much evidence to support the claim of the Dalmatian deputy to the Vienna parliament, Dr Josip Smodlaka, speaking in 1910, that 'the great Napoleon . . . did more for the country in five years than Austria in 105 years'.

The isolation of Dalmatia from the rest of the monarchy was the result of a deliberate policy directed against the possibility of an 'Illyrian' Party in Dalmatia joining forces with the Croat movement in Zagreb and demanding the union of Croatia–Slavonia and Dalmatia. Such a large Croat province within the Habsburg empire, with access to the sea, would seriously disrupt the balance of forces within the multinational empire and encourage the Czechs and Slovaks to demand a similar union. In 1848, in the face of Kossuth's rising in Hungary, the emperor conceded to the Croat leader, Baron Josip Jelačić, the right of the Croats to form an autonomous unit under the imperial crown, comprising Croatia–Slavonia and Dalmatia. In return for this promise Croat troops under Jelačić gave invaluable assistance in the struggle against Kossuth. The Croats were bitterly disappointed, however, when the promise was not redeemed and they were placed under Austrian control. During the rule of the authoritarian Austrian chancellor, Alexander Bach (1849–60), they were subjected to a ruthless policy of Germanisation. The defeat of Austria in the war with Prussia in 1866 gave the Hungarians an opportunity to press their claims for recognition as a separate and equal kingdom within a Dual Monarchy. The *Ausgleich* of 1867 recognised this claim and also restored Croatia to Hungary. It was then necessary for the Hungarians to come to terms with the Croats. This was achieved by the Nagoda or Agreement of 1868, which recognised the existence of a separate Croat national entity, entitled to a degree of self-government under its own assembly, the Sabor. It also promised the eventual incorporation of the military frontier and Dalmatia into Croatia. The final abolition of the military frontier in 1881 made possible the transfer of these regions, but Dalmatia, under Austrian rule, remained separated from its Croatian hinterland. When railway construction began in the mid-nineteenth century no attempt was made to link the central Dalmatian ports with the rest of Croatia. Split and Šibenik were not connected until the 1920s, although the Südbahn from Vienna to Trieste via Ljubljana (Laibach) was opened in 1857, and the Zagreb–Rijeka line a decade later. Although isolated from the rest of Croatia by deliberate policy and allowed to stagnate economically, there was a lively political movement amongst the middle classes of both Serbian and Croat origin. There were two elements within this movement. One group pressed for a greater share for the Slavs in the commercial and administrative life of the province at the expense of the Italians and Austrians, who had a predominant role in these spheres. They looked forward to a greater degree of autonomy, or even for independence for Dalmatia. The other group, with memories of the Illyrian ideal, sought union with Croatia, and beyond that to the creation of a Serb–Croat state. In both tendencies the Serbs and Croats collaborated, but especially in the Illyrian group.

The Illyrian movement was given a forward impulse by the work of Bishop Strossmayer, the Slavonian prelate who dominated the Yugoslav movement in Croatia–Slavonia during the second half of the nineteenth century. Josip Strossmayer was born in Osijek, the capital of Slavonia, in 1815. His surname suggests his Austro-German family origins, but his forebears had settled long before his birth and had become fully Croat in culture. After graduating from the University of Pest he became chaplain at Petrovaradin, the fortress overlooking the Danube near Novi Sad in

Vojvodina. From there he moved to Vienna in 1847, where he was director of a theological seminary and a chaplain to the imperial court. During his stay in Vienna he became familiar with Jelačić and many of the leading Croat figures. In 1849 he became Bishop of Djakovo in his native Slavonia, a post which he held for the next fifty-six years until his death in 1905. Strossmayer was a man of wide learning, an impressive Latin scholar; a linguist, fluent in French, German and Italian; a brilliant dialectician; and a liberal-minded patriot. His see, at the time the largest in Europe, gave him responsibility for the Roman Catholics of Bosnia, Srem and Serbia, as well as for those in Slavonia. His achievements during a long and fruitful life included the founding, in 1867, of a South Slav Academy of Arts and Sciences at Zagreb and of the University of Zagreb in 1874. He became known throughout Europe for his independence of mind when he supported Döllinger at the Vatican Council of 1870 in attacking the doctrine of papal infallibility. He also gained international recognition for his advocacy of the cause of the Slavs within the Ottoman empire, corresponding with Gladstone, Lord Acton and other European statesmen on issues such as the 'Bulgarian Horrors' and the ill treatment of Christians in Bosnia. To his own countrymen he symbolised the Yugoslav idea – the cooperation of Serbs and Croats, each respecting the uniqueness of their own culture, but recognising their common interests in resisting the pressures from their Turkish and Austro-Hungarian overlords. His broadminded pleas for mutual tolerance between Catholic and Orthodox and his advocacy of South Slav unity displeased the more dogmatic Croats. An extreme Croat nationalist party, Stranka Prava, or the Party of the Right, formed in 1881 by Ante Starčević, opposed Strossmayer's tolerance to the Serbs in Croatia, whose numbers were greatly increased by the incorporation of the military frontier in 1881. The Hungarians encouraged Serb–Croat hostility as a means of dividing the opposition and facilitating their programme of Magyarisation, which was pursued with increasing venom during the reign of Ban Khuen-Hedérváry between 1883 and 1903.

Resistance to Magyarisation had been an important element in Ljudevit Gaj's Illyrian movement of the middle years of the century. Gaj had always looked beyond Croatia to a wider alliance of South Slavs. He spoke of Illyria as 'a triangle between Scutari, Varna and Villach', implying a South Slav unit covering all of present-day Yugoslavia and Bulgaria. The revival of Magyarisation under Khuen-Hedérváry provoked a new resistance movement which saw the South Slavs as a part of the Pan-Slav movement, which embraced the Czechs and Slovaks.

Croat nationalist students who were forced to leave the University of

Zagreb after taking part in demonstrations in 1895 completed their studies in Prague, where they came under the influence of Professor Thomas Masaryk. They started a journal, *Nova Doba* (New Age), which appealed for a common front for all the Slavs within the monarchy. As the pressure built up, the Hungarian authorities, who also administered Slovakia, tightened their repressive measures. Matters came to a head in 1903, when Croat demands for financial independence from Budapest were rejected out of hand. Demonstrations and protest meetings were rigorously suppressed, the Croat press was heavily censored, and journalists and editors were arrested. These acts provoked a wave of sympathy in Dalmatia, where, under the less repressive Austrian regime, Serbs and Croats had gained control of the municipal councils' of the main towns and had a strong representation in the Austrian parliament. Meetings of solidarity with the Croats, resolutions demanding the removal of Khuen-Hedérváry, and petitions by Croat deputies to the government in Vienna followed. Rumours of massacres in Zagreb increased the excitement. A delegation of thirty Dalmatian deputies went to Budapest, where Franz Joseph was staying, but the emperor refused to see them. R. W. Seton-Watson, the British scholar, who was closely involved with the Yugoslav movement, considered that this rebuff 'was a turning point in the relations of the Habsburg dynasty and the Southern Slavs'.

Troubles with the Slavs were partly responsible for the fall of the cabinet in Budapest and the replacement of Premier Szell by Khuen-Hedérváry in June 1903. Khuen's immediate successor in Croatia was somewhat less aggressive in pursuing the Magyarisation policy, but in essentials the Croats fared no better. In 1908 a more militant enemy of the Slavs, Baron Rauch, resumed the policies of Khuen-Hedérváry. After the death of Starčević in 1896 the extreme Croat nationalists were led by Dr Joseph Frank, who, despite his Jewish origins, was even more fanatical than Starčević in his hostility to the Serbs. His new 'Party of the Pure right' broke away from the more moderate nationalists, who then formed an alliance with Strossmayer's Independent National Party.

The extreme wing of the nationalits stirred up animosity between native Croats and the Serbian minority, who in the 1910 census numbered 25 per cent of the population of Croatia–Slavonia. These divisions amongst the Slavs played into the hands of the Hungarian authorities and assisted the process of Magyarisation. In 1902 anti-Serb riots in Zagreb led to a reappraisal by the Serbs of their position within Croatia. A group of younger Serbs came to realise that Magyarisation threatened them as much as the Croats. The Independent Serb Party which they formed entered into a Serb–Croat coalition with the more moderate Croats. There was also a small Serbian Radical Party, which had links with the governing Radical Party in Serbia led by Nikola Pašić. In the Sabor elections of 1908, held a few weeks after the appointment by the Hungarians of the new ban, the uncompromising and authoritarian Baron Paul Rauch, the Serb–Croat coalition won fifty-seven of the eighty-eight seats. The extreme right Frankists lost ground and were reduced to twenty-four seats; and the pro-government candidates supported by Rauch were completely wiped out. Rauch reverted to the divide-and-rule tactics of the Khuen regime, and at first attacked the Serbs. He claimed to have discovered a Serbian plot to stage a rebellion, and a government supporter, Dr Friedjung, alleged that the leaders of the Serb–Croat coalition were in the pay of the Serbian government. The trial of fifty-three Serbs on charges of treason began in 1909, after some of the accused had been incarcerated for nine months in the most unpleasant circumstances. They were accused of conspiring to overthrow the state and to place Croatia–Slavonia under Serbian rule.

The decision to pursue this absurd treason trial was probably made at the highest level. It has been suggested that Aerenthal, the Austro-Hungarian foreign minister, who came to office in 1906, encouraged Rauch in the preparation of the indictment, as it would have suited his foreign policy objectives. He aimed at extending Habsburg influence into the Balkans in order to secure the monarchy against the disruptive possibilities inherent in a Serb–Croat coalition. Even if this meant only the upsetting of the fragile Austro-Hungarian compromise of 1867 by the creation of a third Slav partner, equal in status to the other two, it spelled trouble for the government of Vienna. Behind this Trialist solution to the monarchy's nationality problems there lay an even more horrifying prospect – the union of the South Slavs under Serbian leadership and their secession from the Habsburg crown. There were also commercial and strategic interests which Austria shared with Prussia in promoting a German *Drang nach Südosten*. The abortive Sandžak railway scheme was one element in this policy. Even more important was the successful annexation in 1908 of the already Austro-Hungarian-occupied Ottoman provinces of Bosnia–Hercegovina. It suited the Austrians in this context to strike a blow at the Serbs in Croatia, and the so-called Agram treason trials of 1908–9 were intended to further this policy. In fact they rebounded on their perpetrators.

The fifty-three accused were eventually brought to trial in March 1909, although they had been arrested at the beginning of the Bosnian crisis in July 1908. The trial, which lasted until October 1909, was a travesty of justice, the enormity of which was spelled out in great detail by a British observer, R. W. Seton-Watson. Partly through his efforts the trial became a European scandal which did the name of Habsburg justice no good in the eyes of the world.

The judgement was so severe – thirty-one defendants sentenced to periods of penal servitude of from five to twelve years – that it was quashed on appeal. Nevertheless, the wretched victims – mostly middle-class Serbian professsional and business men – remained in custody until they were released by a royal decree in September 1910.

The libel action against Dr Friedjung which began in December 1909 was entered on behalf of the fifty-two deputies who formed the Serb–Croat coalition in the Sabor. Dr Friedjung is not the first respected historian to have been deceived by forged documents! In this case the forgeries emanated from the Austrian government. Friedjung claimed, in an article in the *Reichspost*, to have evidence that the Serb–Croat deputies were in the pay of Belgrade. The documents were proved to be forgeries, and the trial ended in a compromise which left Friedjung with a battered reputation and those whom he had accused with their honour intact. The hand of Aerenthal was apparent in the background, but he was never brought to book.

One of the deputies accused by Friedjung was the Dalmatian Franjo Supilo, editor of *Novi List* of Fiume, a leading journal of the Serb–Croat movement, which circulated in both Dalmatia and Croatia–Slavonia. He was later to become one of the leaders of the Yugoslav movement in exile, which worked amongst the Allies during the First World War to lay the foundations of the first Yugoslav state.

The Bosnian crisis and its consequences

If 1908 was remembered in Croatia as the year of the treason trials and the Friedjung case, to the rest of Europe these events passed virtually unnoticed except by men like Seton-Watson and Masaryk. The annexation of Bosnia–Hercegovina by the Austrians on 7 October produced a major European crisis. It was not so much that the powers objected to the fact of the annexation as to the timing and the manner in which it was carried out. The Russians were particularly angry that they got no compensation for this breach of the Treaty of Berlin – for example by gaining control over the straits. They were induced to acquiesce only because of Germany's strong backing for Austria.

The reasons for Austria's move were partly bound up with Aerenthal's forward policy in the Balkans which naturally had German support. He was also concerned, however, with internal affairs within the occupied provinces, and with the activities of Serbian nationalists who were encouraged by an increasingly stronger and more aggressive Serbia. One of the first acts of the Young Turk revolution which overthrew Abdülhamid II was to proclaim a constitution. The Muslims of Bosnia temporarily joined forces with the Serbs in order to press for constitutional reform. In 1910 they succeeded in forcing a constitution out of the reluctant Austrians. This gave some degree of local autonomy to the elected parliament, but it fell far short of what had been demanded, and it left all important decisions in the hands of the Austrian governor.

The Bulgarians put an end to the division of their country imposed at Berlin in 1878, and declared their independence. Aerenthal was able to use as an excuse for his unilateral action Bulgaria's proposal to regularise the situation by means of an international treaty guaranteed by the powers. At the same time as he announced the annexation, he also reported Austria's intention to remove its troops from the sandžak and to hand over full control to the Turks.

Serbia reacted violently to the news, because the Serbs believed they had a reversionary interest in both the sandžak and Bosnia. As long as Austria only occupied Bosnia–Hercegovina under Turkish sovereignty, there was a chance that Serbia could acquire them when the Ottoman empire collapsed, but if Austrian sovereignty were to be recognised, the prospects for Greater Serbia were bleak. Serbia mobilised and threatened war, but the hoped-for Russian backing was not forthcoming. Turkey recognised the *fait accompli* in December, and during 1909 the rest of Europe followed suit.

The Serbs realised that there was no hope of a route to the sea across Bosnia–Hercegovina, and turned their attention southward to Macedonia and the Aegean. They saw themselves in a prison to which Austria held the key. They had already tasted the bitter consequences of their dependence on Austrian goodwill for their export trade. In 1906 the Austrians imposed prohibitive tariffs on Serbia's main export, pig meat. The Serbs were able to lessen the blow by making a deal with the Turks which enabled them to export through Salonika. The 1908 crisis only confirmed their need for an outlet to the sea. If their sworn enemy, Austria, blocked the way across Bosnia, then salvation lay southward through Macedonia.

The Montenegrins, who had supported the Serbs in 1908, and who had been humiliated by the arrest of their delegate by the Zagreb police whilst en route for a conference in Belgrade, also looked to the possibilities of territorial expansion at the expense of the waning Ottoman power in Europe. Gradually, during the two years after the crisis, the Slav peoples of the Balkans began to work out an alliance which would expel the Turks and also undo Austria's plans. Bulgaria and Serbia agreed to partition Macedonia; Montenegro and Serbia to partition the sandžak. Greece also joined the coalition, and was promised the southern part of a partitioned Albania.

The Balkan wars

The small states which banded together, with Russian encouragement, to form the Balkan League each had their own territorial and political objectives, some of which were mutually contradictory. The only unifying force was a common hatred for the Turks. It was comparatively easy for them, therefore, to act together against Turkey, but impossible for them to agree about the distribution of the spoils once victory was won.

In October 1912 the four allies became involved in a war with the Turks, the occasion being the ill treatment of Albanian and Macedonian rebels by Turkish soldiers. Montenegro attacked first on 8 October, and the others followed during the next ten days. To the amazement of Europe, the Turks were driven back within a few weeks. The Serbs advanced across Albania and reached the Adriatic, thus gaining their long-desired 'window on the sea'. The alarmed Austro-Hungarians suddenly became champions of Albanian independence and mobilised their troops in Bosnia, threatening war with Serbia if it did not abandon the outlet to the sea. Italy and Germany offered support to their Habsburg ally, and Russia cautioned the defiant Serbs to give way. A face-saving formula promised Serbia economic access to the sea by means of a railway, linking Belgrade to the Adriatic across northern Albania. The peace settlement reached in London in May 1913, under the aegis of the European powers, gave most of the fruits of victory to the Serbs and Greeks, and greatly offended the Bulgarians, who had sustained the greatest losses, by rejecting Bulgaria's claims in Macedonia. It was also agreed to establish an independent Albania under the protection of the powers, a decision which did not please the Serbs and Montenegrins.

A month after the signing of the Treaty of London the Bulgarians attacked Serbia and Greece, hoping to win by war the Macedonian areas lost at the peace conference. Romania decided to attack Bulgaria in order to annex the Dobrudja; and Turkey, still smarting from defeat in the first Balkan War, joined the Romanians.

In August 1913 Bulgaria was compelled to accept the Treaty of Bucharest, which deprived it of the Silistria district of Dobrudja and forced it to abandon its claims to Macedonia. The victorious alliance of Serbia, Romania, Greece and Montenegro faced the defeated Bulgarians and Turks – an alignment which was to appear again in the First World War.

The outlines of the larger conflict were also discernible in the attitudes of the powers to the Balkan states. Austria–Hungary was, of course, implacably anti-Serb, and there is some evidence that Conrad von Hötzendorf, the chief of staff, had hoped that Serbia's march to the Adriatic in 1912 could have been used as a *casus belli*, giving the Habsburg armies the excuse they wanted to destroy the nest of vipers in Belgrade. A second opportunity was missed in October 1913, when Serbia occupied territory in northern Albania to crush bands of Albanian irregulars who had been raiding Serbian villages. The Foreign Minister, Count Berchtold, sent an ultimatum to Belgrade and refused to discuss the matter with Pašić, the Serbian premier. The Serbs, knowing that Germany supported Berchtold's strong line, had no option but to withdraw. In early 1914 Pašić went to St Petersburg and was assured of Russian support. The battle lines were being drawn up in preparation for the next confrontation.

6

The First World War

The outcome of the Second Balkan War did much to enhance Serbia's standing in the eyes of the South Slavs within the monarchy, and especially amongst the Serbs in Bosnia–Hercegovina. They began to hope that their liberation from the Austro-Hungarian yoke would not long be delayed and that their deliverance would be achieved with the help of the Serbian army. These hopes were, however, totally unreal. Serbia's resources had been stretched almost to breaking point by the recent wars. The acquisition of Macedonia, Kosovo, Metohija and a part of the sandžak of Novi Pazar almost doubled Serbia's territory and increased its population from 2.9 million to 4.4 million. Most of the new citizens were non-Serb and many were hostile to the new administration. Albanian and pro-Bulgarian elements were receiving encouragement from abroad to continue fighting, and the depleted Serbian army was involved in a pacification campaign against groups of insurgents in the newly occupied territories. The civil administration was preoccupied with the problem of assimilating the former Turkish provinces into the Serbian system of government – a task which had not been completed when the first Yugoslav state came into existence in 1918. In addition there was internal political dissension within Serbia. When war was declared in July 1914 an election campaign was in progress, which had to be called off because of the outbreak of hostilities. In every respect the country was unprepared for war, and there is abundant evidence that the government of Premier Pašić did all it could to prevent it. However, the tide of events was running too strongly in favour of war. The 'war party' in Vienna had long sought a settling of accounts with the Serbs. They had hoped to provoke a war with Serbia over the annexation of Bosnia–Hercegovina in 1908, but Serbia's diplomatic capitulation, under pressure from the European powers, removed any excuse for military action.

In 1914 the opportunity came which General Conrad von Hötzendorf and the Austrian militarists had hoped for. It is even suspected that they had helped to create the circumstances which led to the *casus belli*, namely the assasination of the heir to the Habsburg throne. Archduke Franz Ferdinand was an advocate of the so-called Trialist solution to the nationalities problems of the monarchy. This envisaged the creation of a Slav kingdom which would share equal status with the Austrian and Hungarian lands. This concept found little favour amongst the ruling circles in either Austria or Hungary, and was also viewed with suspicion in Serbia. If the Slavs within the monarchy could be bought off with the offer of an enhanced status within the Habsburg realm, the dream of either a Greater Serbia or an independent South Slav state would vanish.

The decision to send the archduke to Sarajevo on a much publicised official visit on 28 June 1914 was a deliberate provocation to nationalist feelings in Bosnia. The choice of Serbia's national day, Vidovdan, as the date of the visit was calculated to offend the Serbs. A. J. P. Taylor has suggested that it was comparable to sending a member of the British royal family to Dublin on St Patrick's day at the height of the Troubles. Despite the obvious security risks involved, the authorities took surprisingly few precautions to protect the archduke and his wife. Count Bilinski, the civilian administrator for Bosnia–Hercegovina, was given an informal warning by the Serbian ambassador to Vienna, that trouble might arise during the visit, although the Serbian government did not disclose its knowledge that armed members of a Bosnian nationalist organisation had crossed the frontier from Serbia a short time before the archduke arrived in Sarajevo. There is no doubt, however, that the authorities in Vienna were aware of the dangerous situation in which they were placing the heir to the throne. It is not clear whether the inadequate security arrangements, which were in glaring contrast to those made during Emperor Franz Joseph's visit in 1910, were the result of monumental inefficiency or whether there is a more sinister explanation.

The conspirators who carried out the archduke's assassination were members of a revolutionary group, Mlada Bosna (Young Bosnia), one of the many nationalist organisations which flourished in the Balkans. Mlada Bosna was particularly active amongst high school students, and one of its most enthusiastic groups was in the area of Hercegovina. Gavrilo Princip and several of those involved in the Sarajevo incident were in touch with this branch. Amongst the papers seized by the Austrian police after their arrest were documents which disclosed links with other European revolutionary movements both amongst the Czechs and Poles within the monarchy and with French, German and Russian organisations. There were even pamphlets and letters indicating that they had discussed the ideas of the British Fabian Society. These idealistic young people, with their notions about Pan-Slav brotherhood and socialism, could not have organised the assassination without the help of underground groups in Serbia.

The conspirators were trained and equipped in Serbia and sent to Bosnia by a secret society known as Ujedinjenje ili smrt (Unification or Death), which was popularly known as the Black Hand (Crna Ruka). This body was formed in 1911 by a group of young Serbian army officers under the leadership of Colonel Dragutin Dimitrijević, also known as Apis, who had planned the murder of King Alexander Obrenović and Queen Draga in 1903. The aim of the Black Hand was to work amongst the Serbs within the Austrian and Turkish empires for the achievement of a Greater Serbia, and to use its influence within Serbian ruling circles to encourage a militant policy of expansionism. Its methods were symbolised by its melodramatic coat of arms, which incorporated a skull and crossbones, a dagger, a bomb and a poison bottle. Members were enrolled at a secret ceremony during which they swore to subordinate themselves absolutely to the authority of the society and to accept that death might follow any disobedience or treachery to its aims.

A more open and respectable organisation, Narodna Odbrana, was founded three years earlier than the Black Hand. It had a much wider range of support amongst army officers, civil servants and politicians who were outraged by the annexation of Bosnia–Hercegovina in 1908. Its first task was to organise Serbian volunteers to enter the annexed territories and to promote resistance to Austro-Hungarian power. The Serbian government had been forced publicly to disown Narodna Odbrana in 1909, when, under extreme pressure, it had accepted the annexation. Narodna Odbrana stood in the same relationship to the Black Hand as Haganah stood *vis-à-vis* the Jewish terrorists of the Stern Gang in Palestine in the late 1940s, or as Sinn Fein stands today in relation to the militants of the Irish underground organisations. There were secret links among the various groups, but these could always be disavowed if circumstances required it. Thus, although after the Serbian government's condemnation in 1909 Narodna Odbrana officially confined itself to cultural and political propaganda, it maintained an intelligence network in Bosnia and had an overlapping membership with the Black Hand.

When the fateful day, 28 June (15 June Old Style), arrived, several members of Mlada Bosna were amongst the crowds which lined the Appel Quay, alongside the river Miljacka, to watch the procession of cars which brought the archduke and his entourage to the town hall, where the mayor waited to greet the royal visitors. The first attempt failed, when Nedeljko Čabrinović hurled a bomb at the procession. He missed the archduke's car, but wounded one of the officers in the escort car which was travelling close behind. The procession continued after the injured officer had been removed to hospital. The archduke, who was clearly a man of great personal courage, arrived in the town hall with his uniform spattered with blood. He interrupted the mayor's formal speech of welcome with an angry denunciation of the authorities for their failure to protect their guests. On the way back to the spa hotel at Ilidža, outside Sarajevo, where the couple were staying, the archduke ordered a change of route so that he could visit the hospital where the injured man had been taken. There was some confusion, because the new orders had not been passed to the drivers, and the archduke's car stopped and began to reverse into a side street. Gavrilo Princip, a nineteen-year-old student who was one of the conspirators, having missed one opportunity, was given a second chance to aim his pistol at Franz Ferdinand. This time he succeeded in killing both the heir to the throne and the archduchess. The spot where Princip is believed to have stood is now marked by footprints set in the pavement outside the Mlada Bosna Museum, which contains souvenirs of the conspirators. One of them who survived the vengeance of the Austrian authorities, Vaso Čubrilović, became a professor in Belgrade University in the 1930s and a minister in Tito's post-war government. Princip died in prison in April 1918. The bridge over the Miljacka near the scene of the assassination was later renamed Principov Most (Princip's Bridge) and the conspirators were regarded in Serbia as national heroes. Even the Black Hand and its leader, Apis, who fell foul of the Serbian government in exile and who was executed for allegedly plotting to murder the prince regent in Salonika in 1917, were formally exonerated by the Serbian Supreme Court in 1953.

The immediate consequences of the shooting were, however, far more cataclysmic and, in a literal sense, earth-shaking. The war party in Vienna, whether or not they had hoped for such a tragic outcome to the visit, saw their opportunity to deliver the death blow to the troublesome Serbs. It is not clear whether they had thought out the consequences. Did they merely wish to teach the Serbs a lesson and put an end to the Pan-Serb agitation amongst their own subjects, or did they intend to invade as a prelude to the incorporation of Serbia into the monarchy? They could not have foreseen that their actions during the next few weeks would lead to a world war and to the eventual collapse and dismemberment of their empire.

At first there appeared to be a stunned silence, but behind the scenes Austrian diplomats were in touch with their German allies to ensure that they would receive support from that quarter for any action they might take against Serbia. On 23 July an ultimatum was presented to the Serbian government which contained the following points.

(1) To suppress any publication directed against Austria–Hungary.

(2) To dissolve the Narodna Odbrana and to suppress similar societies in future.

(3) To eliminate anti-Austrian propaganda from the public schools.

(4) To remove army officers and civil functionaries guilty of propaganda against the monarchy.

(5) To accept the collaboration of Austrian representatives for the suppression of the subversive movement.

(6) To take judicial proceedings against accessories to the Sarajevo plot, with Austrian delegates participating in the investigation.

(7) To arrest Tankošić and Ciganović. (Major Vojin Tankošić was a Serbian officer who had been involved with *četnik* organisations during the Balkan wars. Milan Ciganović was a student, six years older than Princip, who came from the same district (Bosansko Grahovo) and who had shared accommodation with him in Belgrade in 1912. Both Ciganović and Tankošić were involved in the supplying of arms to the assassins, and were in contact with Apis. At the trial of the assassins in Sarajevo it was alleged, but not proven, that Ciganović and Tankošić were Freemasons. When arrested by the Serbian authorities in fulfilment of point 7 of the ultimatum, Tankošić told the arresting officer that he had supplied the arms 'in order to spite Pašić'. This suggests that Pašić knew nothing of the conspiracy.)

(8) To prevent the illicit traffic in arms and to punish the officials who helped the conspirators to cross the frontier.

(9) To explain hostile utterances of Serbian officials.

(10) To notify the Austro-Hungarian government of the execution of these measures.

The Serbian reply, which was delivered within the forty-eight-hour deadline demanded by the Austrians, met virtually all the points in the ultimatum. The only ones which were not fully accepted were those which would have infringed Serbian sovereignty. Even on these points the government was prepared to submit the case to judgement by the Hague Court, or to accept the arbitration of 'the Great Powers which assisted in the formulation of the Serbian Government declaration' of March 1909. This was the document which was forced on the Serbs at the end of the

Bosnian crisis, in which they recognised the annexation and agreed to disown the Serbian patriotic societies.

Their reply can be summarised as follows:

(1) Yes: will suppress all anti-Austrian publications.

(2) Yes: will suppress the Narodna Odbrana and similar societies.

(3) Yes: will expel all anti-Austrian teachers and teaching as soon as evidence given.

(4) Yes: will expel all anti-Austrian officers and officials, if Austria will furnish names and acts of guilty persons.

(5) Yes: will accept collaboration of Austrian representatives in these proceedings, as far as consonant with principles of international law and criminal procedure and neighbourly relations.

(6) Yes: will take the judicial proceedings; will also keep Austria informed, but cannot admit the participation of Austrians in the judicial investigations, as this would be a violation of the constitution.

(7) Yes: have arrested Tankošić; ordered arrest of Ciganović.

(8) Yes: will suppress and punish traffic in arms and explosives.

(9) Yes: will deal with the said high officials, if Austria will supply evidence.

(10) Yes: will notify without delay.

The naming of Narodna Odbrana as the culprits suggests that the Austrians had been misinformed by their intelligence services about the relationships among the various Serbian societies. Nevertheless the Serbs agreed to suppress Narodna Odbrana and to take action against those named as accomplices in the assassination plot. They also followed Russian advice to withdraw their troops from the frontier regions, whilst at the same time mobilising their army and preparing for the attack which they feared was imminent. The Austrians ignored Kaiser Wilhelm's comment on the Serbian acceptance of the ultimatum: 'This is more than one could have expected ... With it, every reason for war disappears ... I am convinced that, on the whole, the wishes of the Dual Monarchy have been acceded to.'

Berchtold, the Austro-Hungarian foreign minister, reported that the Germans would support the monarchy if it declared war on Serbia. The Germans ignored Sir Edward Grey's attempt to persuade them to intervene in order to restrain the militarists in Vienna, and Grey's efforts at mediation were rejected by the Austrians. Conrad, Berchtold and the Hungarian premier, Tisza, who had at first resisted the war party, combined to persuade the emperor that there was no alternative to war. The Serbian note was rejected out of hand within hours of its being received, and on 28 July a telegram was sent from Vienna to the Serbian government, then meeting in Niš, informing them that war had been declared. The Austro-Hungarian armies began their bombardment of Belgrade on the same evening. On 11 August they crossed the Danube and Sava in force.

It is an interesting sidelight on the conduct of war in 1914 that the declaration should have been made by the dispatch of an ordinary open telegram, and that the Austrian authorities should have placed a special train at the disposal of the Serbian commander, General (Vojvoda) Radomir Putnik, to enable him and his mistress to return from the Austrian spa at Bad Ischl so that he could lead the Serbian army. No such courtesies were offered when the Germans bombed Belgrade twenty-seven years later as a prelude to their invasion in April 1941.

In response to the declaration of war on Serbia, the Russians ordered a general mobilisation. Germany used this as an excuse to declare war on Russia on 1 August, and on Russia's ally, France, on 3 August. Germany's decision to invade France via Belgium precipitated Britain's entry into the war on 4 August. Turkey became involved as an ally of Germany and Austria on 1 November. During 1915 Italy joined on the side of the western Allies, and Bulgaria on the side of the Central Powers. Finally Romania, on being promised Transylvania, threw in her lot with the Allies in 1916. Virtually all Europe was locked in a struggle which became known as the First World War, but which might more appropriately be called the Great European Civil War.

The offensive which the Austro-Hungarians launched on 11 August took the Serbs by surprise. They had expected a frontal attack on Belgrade, but instead the enemy struck across the Drina and Sava rivers into the plain of Mačva, taking the town of Šabac. The Serbs counterattacked and drove the invaders back into the Srem region. By 24 August there were no enemy troops on Serbian soil. The victory was short-lived, however. A second offensive forced the depleted and ill-equipped Serbian army back to Belgrade, which fell on 2 December. The only hope which the Serbs had of saving their country was to delay the enemy advance long enough to enable their allies to come to their aid. They fought with desperate heroism against overwhelming odds. The Austrians wanted a quick victory in the Balkans so that they could turn their attention to the Russian front, but they were not able to overcome the Serbs as easily as they had expected. Belgrade was retaken on 15 December and the Serbs went on to win a magnificent victory on the Kolubara river. The Austro-Hungarians suffered 50,000 casualties and were once again chased back across the Sava.

For the second time in four months Serbian soil was free of enemy troops. The respite was achieved at a heavy cost. In addition to the loss of fighting men and war material, tens of thousands of homeless civilian refugees imposed a heavy strain on Serbia's limited resources. To make matters worse, an outbreak of typhus raged throughout the winter of 1914–15, killing over 150,000. The inadequate sanitary precautions which enabled the outbreak to spread throughout the whole of Serbia, even to the Greek frontier areas in Macedonia, are vividly described by Dr Johnston Abrahams, one of the British doctors sent to Skopje as a surgeon in October 1914. He expected to be treating war wounds, but by February 1915 all medical resources were concentrated on fighting the typhus epidemic. In his diary *My Balkan Log* he writes, 'It was now the middle of February 1915. All real fighting had ceased since Christmas, and no more fresh wounded were coming down the line from the Danubian front. The country, however, was now infected with typhus fever, on an epidemic scale, and the authorities seemed powerless to do anything to check its ravages. Stories circulated of whole villages down with it, towns where two or three thousand cases were lying in the hospitals without doctors, medicines or any sort of skilled attention. Every building up the line was said to be full to overflowing. Patients were dying in the streets. The doctors were dying.'

The Serbs received only a trickle of supplies from their allies, although these included valuable medical help from the British Red Cross and the Serbian Relief Fund. The only supply route by which goods could be sent was via the Greek port of Salonika. Neutral Greece was prepared to turn a blind eye to Allied military 'advisers' in plain clothes and was willing to allow non-military stores to pass across the frontier. They were anxious not to provoke the Bulgarians, who were known to be negotiating with the Germans and Turks in preparation for entering the war. When Bulgaria did enter, in October 1915, Macedonia was annexed and Salonika was isolated.

The situation changed dramatically in 1915. Von Mackensen's victories against the Russians in Galicia in April enabled the Central Powers to turn their attention to the Balkans. Their ally, Turkey, was under threat from the Allied landing at Gallipoli in February, and it was vital that a direct link should be established between Vienna and Istanbul. This could be achieved only across the body of a defeated Serbia. Whilst the Central Powers were making their plans for an attack on Serbia, the Allies were discussing the possibility of a landing at Salonika. An Allied advance along the Vardar–Morava corridor would bring relief to Serbia and might also draw Romania into the war on the side of the Allies and deter Bulgaria from joining the Central Powers. The landing was made on 3 October. Three days later von Mackensen ordered the bombardment of Belgrade and by the middle of October the Bulgarians were moving into Macedonia, in accordance with a secret agreement with Germany. There was little hope that the Allies could bring help to the Serbs in time.

The first practical difficulties were that Salonika was only a small port and that the railway running north was only a single line of rails. At an Allied war council on 6 January 1915, it was admitted that this single line could not support a large army.

There were also political difficulties. Constantine, the pro-German King of Greece, dismissed his prime minister, Venizelos, because of the latter's support for the landing. A screen of neutral Greek troops was thrown between the Anglo-French forces in Salonika and the Bulgarians in the interior of Macedonia. For three years a large Allied force was held prisoner in Salonika, unable to make contact with the enemy. Malaria took a heavier toll of casualties than did enemy action. During the summer of 1916, for example, 35,000 French troops were admitted to hospital, of whom only 700 were suffering from war wounds. As the British official history comments, the situation 'would have been ludicrous had it been less tragic. Britain was sending troops only to help Greece to fulfil her obligations and now it was almost certain that Greece did not intend to fulfil them . . . To crown all, it was probable that the landing had in any case been made too late to save Serbia.' Whilst the British and French commanders quarrelled about the desirability of maintaining the Salonika bridgehead, an ill-equipped army of Serbian peasants fought a heroic rearguard action against overwhelming odds.

Von Mackensen's attack began with the bombardment of Belgrade. Soon he had forced a crossing of the Sava and the Danube and was advancing into northern Serbia. Belgrade fell on 9 October and the fortress of Smederovo was taken on the 11th. On 10 October Bulgarian troops had begun to move into Macedonia. By the end of October the Serbian army was concentrated around the munitions centre of Kragujevac, 96 km (60 miles) south-east of Belgrade in the Šumadija region. This position soon became untenable, and in order to avoid encirclement Putnik ordered a retreat to the south along the Ibar valley to Kosovo. For the second time in Serbian history Kosovo Polje was to witness the destruction of Serbian independence. When it became clear that there was no hope of an Allied advance northward from Salonika the Serbian high command was faced with three possibilities. They could stand and fight, with the certainty of defeat as the enemy bore down upon them from the surrounding hills; they could surrender; or they could break out to the west across the wild mountains of Montenegro and Albania, preserving as much as they could from the ruins, in the hope that, somehow, at some time, they could fight their way back to Belgrade. The last possibility was the only one which was seriously considered.

The appalling conditions of the Serbian retreat from Kosovo across the mountains of Montenegro and Albania to the Adriatic coast took a terrible toll of men, women and children. Thousands died of hunger, cold and disease as they trekked through the mountains, battered by snowstorms and bitter winds. Thousands more died within sight of the Adriatic. When they reached the Albanian shore near Shkodër, the Italians, who were in control of this area, refused either to assist them on the spot or to provide transport to convey them to British-held Corfu. They were forced to trudge southwards for a further hundred miles through the malarial coastal low-lands of Albania to Valona (Vlöre), whence the survivors were transported in French ships to Corfu, Tunisia and Corsica. The main concentration of troops, some 120,000, was on Corfu, where the Serbian government was temporarily established.

Whilst this pitiful exodus was taking place, the Austro-Hungarian forces invaded Montenegro. In January 1916 King Nikola fled to Italy, where his daughter was married to King Vittorio Emanuele, leaving his son Mirko to arrange the surrender of his country to the enemy and the demobilisation of the army. Nikola eventually settled in Paris with a scarcely credible government in exile, which was mainly ignored by the Allies, especially after it became known that he had been in secret contact with Vienna at the time of the Serbian collapse. Only Italy continued to give real support to Nikola's claims for the restoration of an independent Montenegro under the Petrović–Njegoš dynasty.

In the bitter polemics which accompanied the incorporation of Monte-negro into the new South Slav state in 1918, the behaviour of the Montenegrin government in the winter of 1915–16 in failing to assist the Serbs in their hour of need was often cited as a justification for the deposition of Nikola. There were reports that as the wretched Serbian refugees made their way through the Montenegrin mountains they were refused assistance by their so-called allies, and were even attacked and robbed by them. There is no doubt that when they passed through Albania, the local population, who had no reason to love their Slav neighbours, harassed the bedraggled and defenceless Serbs, but it is unlikely that the ordinary Montenegrin villagers behaved badly towards them. There was a strong feeling of kinship between Serbs and Montenegrins, who share a common language and religious culture. The cowardice, treachery and incompetence of the rulers, however, were in sharp contrast to the courage, tenacity and independence of spirit of their subjects.

The opening of the Salonika front by the British and French in the autumn of 1915 gave the Serbian army an opportunity to re-enter the war. Over 100,000 Serbs joined the Allied forces and participated in an offensive in 1916 which established a foothold in Macedonia. The Serbs drove back a combined German–Bulgarian force in September, storming the frontier peak of Kajmakčalan and crossing into Serbian territory. In November, Serbian and French troops entered Bitola (Monastir) and held this small bridgehead for two years until the final advance of the Allied forces in October 1918 drove the Central Powers out of the Balkans. They lost 27,000 men in capturing these few square miles of their homeland. The two-year stalemate on the Salonika front prompted Clemenceau to refer to the Franco-British and Serbian armies as 'the gardeners of Salonika', who spent their time digging trenches instead of fighting.

In 1916 the prospects for the South Slavs were bleak. Apart from the Bitola salient, all the lands which in 1918 were to be included in the new South Slav state were under foreign occupation. The Bulgarians ran a brutally oppressive regime in Macedonia; Montenegro had capitulated; and Austro-Hungarian and German troops harassed the citizens of Belgrade. In Bosnia and Hercegovina Austrian troops were told that any pro-Yugoslav manifestations were 'to be stifled in the germ with draconian severity'. There were some elements in Croatia and Slovenia who resented Serbia's leadership of the Yugoslav cause, fearing that Pašić and the prince regent, Alexander, were planning to create a Greater Serbia rather than a genuine union of the South Slavs. Slovene troops within the Austrian army fought loyally for the emperor on the Italian front, because they suspected that, in the event of a collapse of the monarchy, Italy would occupy the western Slovene lands. The rout of the Italians at Caporetto in 1917 could not have been accomplished without the tenacious fighting skills of the Slav troops under the command of General Boroević. The rumours of Italian territorial ambitions proved to be true when Trotsky opened the Tsarist archives and published the terms of the Secret Treaty of London (1915), which offered Italy Istria, large parts of Dalmatia and the Julian Region as rewards for entering the war on the Allied side.

Amongst the South Slav communities in exile there were two main groups. The strongest was that of the Serbian exiles under the authority of the government led by Pašić. Serbia had been terribly mauled by the catastrophe of 1915. King Peter, who had accompanied his people on the long trek to Corfu, told a reporter from *The Observer* in October 1917, 'My people numbered well over four million when the war began, and now barely two and a half million are living.' But, despite the losses, a Serbian army survived. The king, the prince regent, the commander-in-chief and the premier, together with most of the ministers, escaped and were able to function as a government in exile, giving a sense of legitimacy and keeping alive the concept of the continuity of the Serb nation. Pašić's government was internationally recognised and there was a profound respect and sympathy for 'gallant Servia' amongst the peoples of the Allied nations. Serbian relief committees were established in Britain, France and the USA to care for the refugees and especially for the thousands of children who found themselves homeless orphans in foreign lands. Yugoslav students are still, in the 1980s, being sent on scholarships abroad with funds originally collected in 1916 to assist these refugees.

Serbia's authority as the standard bearer for the South Slavs in the monarchy eventually came to be accepted by the Allies, but at first the Allied leaders were careful to commit themselves no further than to promises of a restoration of pre-war Serbia. Even as late as January 1918 the American diplomatic representative with Pašić's government on Corfu reported that 'there is depression among the Serbians here ... at the passages in the recent speeches of the President ... and the British Premier relating to the Austro-Hungarian Empire, which are interpreted as meaning that Serbia will not have support for the Allies in securing union with ... the Yugoslavs'.

The other main group of exiles represented the South Slavs within the monarchy. These included the Serbs and Croats of Dalmatia, Bosnia and Croatia–Slavonia and the Slovenes of Carinthia, Carniola and Styria. Their leader was the Dalmatian Croat Ante Trumbić, former Mayor of Split, who had drafted the Resolution of Fiume in 1905 calling for the union of Dalmatia and Croatia. Another important figure was Franjo Supilo, a journalist of Dalmatian origin who had long been an advocate of Serb–Croat cooperation. He had been an enthusiastic supporter of the Resolution of Zara, in which twenty-six Serbian deputies declared that 'Croats and Serbs are one nation by blood and language.'

Trumbić, Supilo and the Dalmatian sculptor Ivan Meštrović met a group of Serbian exiles from Bosnia in Florence in November 1914 and formed a Yugoslav Committee, the aim of which was to promote the idea of a Yugoslav federation. The Yugoslav Committee eventually set up its headquarters in London, where Wickham Steed, editor of *The Times*, and

R. W. Seton-Watson, the champion of all the oppressed nationalities within the monarchy, were able to give influential support in British government circles. The Committee also established an office in Paris and had close links with the Yugoslav communities in the USA.

There was undoubtedly a conflict of aims from the outset between the Serbian government and the Yugoslav Committee and, although this was concealed for tactical reasons in the face of the common enemy, it resurfaced with tragic consequences during the first years of independence after 1918. The Yugoslav Committee were genuine believers in an equal partnership between Serb and Croat in a new South Slav state. Pašić saw the new state as an enlarged Serbia.

The Slovenes at first held aloof from the movement. Monsignor Antun Korošec, the leader of the Slovene Clerical Party and a deputy in the Vienna parliament, was eventually converted to the view that the destiny of the Slovenes lay in an independent South Slav state, but initially many prominent Slovenes looked no further than the achievement of a greater degree of autonomy within the monarchy. In May 1917 a declaration of the Yugoslav Club in the Vienna parliament, of which Korošec was president, 'demanded independence of all Slovenes, Croats and Serbs and their union in one national state under the sceptre of the Habsburgs'. If this were to be taken literally, it would mean the incorporation of the Serbian kingdom into the Habsburg empire, presumably under some triune arrangement in which the Slavs shared equal status with the Austrians and Hungarians. This was clearly not a practical possibility. The obvious explanation is that the phrase 'under the sceptre of the Habsburgs' was included to prevent the Austrian police from prosecuting Korošec, as an Austrian subject, for the treasonable advocacy of the dismemberment of the empire. It was clear that Korošec, realising the probable collapse of the monarchy, and fearing the expansionist designs of the Italians, had become a supporter of the Yugoslav idea as promoted by Trumbić and Supilo. The Vienna *Reichspost* tried to sow dissension amongst the supporters of this concept by arguing that 'the Yugoslav Idea is Pan-Serbian under the mask of Yugoslavism'.

The Yugoslav Committee, led by Trumbić, held a conference in Corfu in the summer of 1917 with the representatives of the Serbian government, headed by Pašić. The meeting lasted for over a month, and much of the time was taken up with the working out of a compromise between Trumbić and Pašić on the form of government which the new state would take. Pašić wanted a highly centralised state in which the Serbs, as the most numerous element, would be dominant. Trumbić advocated an arrangement in which the constituent elements would have considerable autonomy. In the end a declaration emerged which left the issue vague, but which favoured the Serbian view. The fourteen points of the Corfu Declaration, signed on 20 July 1917, were headed by a preamble which affirmed the unity of the Serb, Croat and Slovene peoples.

The fourteen points included the establishment of the kingdom of Serbs, Croats and Slovenes as a 'constitutional, democratic and parliamentary monarchy headed by the Karadjordjević dynasty'. The equality of the three national groups named in the title was guaranteed. The Declaration also guaranteed the free exercise on an equal basis of the Orthodox, Roman Catholic and Islamic faiths and the equality of the Cyrillic and Latin alphabets. Any suggestion of 'a partial solution' to the problems of the national liberation of the three named groups was rejected. 'Our people pose as an indivisible whole the problem of their liberation from Austria–Hungary and their unification with Serbia and Montenegro in a single state'.

The declaration appeared to suggest that the Serbs, Croats and Slovenes had the same language and culture, and it ignored completely the separate existence of the Macedonian Slavs. The Montenegrins, who were not even represented at Corfu, were treated as being Serbs. Their separate historical experiences for several centuries were disregarded. It is true that the Serbs and Montenegrins shared a common language and religious tradition, and that the Montenegrin Committee for National Union, composed of exiles in Paris, telegraphed to Corfu expressing the view that Montenegro's role as an independent state was at an end 'and that, therefore, as a purely Serbian country she ought consequently to range herself by the side of and unite with the Kingdom of Serbs, Croats and Slovenes'. This view was, of course, bitterly contested by King Nikola, although some of his ministers supported the Corfu Declaration. The Allies, after some hesitation, accepted the Declaration as a basis for the post-war settlement of the former Habsburg lands. In January 1918 Lloyd George and Woodrow Wilson were still talking about the 'autonomous development' of the South Slavs within the monarchy and the restoration of Serbia and Montenegro as independent kingdoms. They had not then accepted the idea that the monarchy might disintegrate and be replaced by a group of wholly independent states, one of which would be the Yugoslav unit envisaged in the Corfu Declaration. The Italians continued to back King Nikola's resistance to the incorporation of Montenegro into an enlarged Serbia, partly because they feared that a powerful Slav state in the eastern shore of the Adriatic would frustrate their ambitions in Dalmatia. The revelation by the Bolsheviks in early 1918 of the terms of the secret Treaty of London exacerbated the already bad relations between the Yugoslavs and the Italians. The treaty, which was signed by Britain, France and Tsarist Russia in April 1915, promised Italy large stretches of the Dalmatian coast, Istria and the Julian Alps, which were to be detached from Austria–Hungary, a naval base at Valona (Vlorë) in Albania, and other territories to be taken from Turkey, in return for an Italian declaration of war on the Central Powers. Italy fulfilled her part of the bargain in May 1915 and expected to receive full payment at the end of the war. The situation in 1918, however, was quite different from that which obtained when the Treaty of London was signed. The parties to the secret treaty assumed that the monarchy would survive the war, although being forced to submit to some loss of territory. They were content to promise Italy parts of the Habsburg empire as the spoils of war. Italy was willing to pull out of the Triple Alliance and to join the Entente in the name of '*sacro egoismo*'. However, the people of the lands to be annexed were never consulted. Serbia, although being an ally, was not told about the Treaty of London, although rumours of its contents circulated amongst politicians of the Entente powers and were played upon by the Viennese press. In 1915 the promises made to Italy were thought to be at the expense of the enemy, but in 1918 when Italy presented its bill, the infant Yugoslav state was expected to settle the account.

The Pact of Corfu was concluded against a background of fears about the Italian menace. Trumbić and the Slovenes accepted the ambiguities and made concessions to Serbian views about the nature of the new state because they feared Italy more than Serbia. Pašić regarded the Yugoslav Committee as a useful tool in furthering his Greater Serbian plans, but he did not consider that the Committee had any legal status. The British friends of Yugoslavia, notably Seton-Watson and Steed, tried to bring the two sides together and to persuade the Serbs to accept representatives of the Yugoslav Committee into a coalition government, which would serve as the basis for a provisional government when the new state was consti-tuted. The autocratic Pašić, later described by Seton-Watson as being 'too old to shake off altogether the semi-Turkish traditions of his youth', knew that he held the whip hand and ignored the appeal, as he also ignored Trumbić's request to convene a conference in Paris of all the parties concerned – the Serbian government, the Yugoslav Committee, the Serbian opposition parties and the Montenegrin Committee.

One useful achievement of the two British sympathisers was to arrange a meeting between the Yugoslav Committee and a number of liberal-minded

Italian politicians, headed by Senator Torre, which, although it did not specifically renounce the secret treaty, encouraged the hope that an amicable settlement could be reached between Italy and the Yugoslavs. Sir Arthur Evans, writing in the *Manchester Guardian* in March 1918, referred to the Torre–Trumbić agreement as giving 'the *coup de grâce* to the ill-starred secret convention concluded in London on April 15, 1915 ... and lately published by M. Trotsky in full'. He also felt that 'the Pact of Corfu, though not actually named, is implicitly recognised'. As events later unfolded these liberal hopes were wildly optimistic.

Whilst the complicated political manoeuvres among Pašić, Trumbić, the Italians and the Allied powers were taking place, the Slavs within the monarchy began to organise in order to seize the reins of power as the war entered its final weeks. The Bulgarian front collapsed in September and the Allied forces began to advance along the Vardar–Morava corridor. The Italians began to push the Austro-Hungarians back on the Isonzo front in early October, avenging their humiliating defeat at Caporetto a year earlier. Events moved rapidly during October. The emperor issued a manifesto on 16 October, offering to reorganise the Austrian half of the monarchy on a federal basis, but by this time the South Slavs within the monarchy, under the leadership of Monsignor Korošec, had formed a National Council of Slovenes, Croats and Serbs (the Narodno Vijeće) in Zagreb as the nucleus of a government, and they were not interested in the emperor's offer. On 20 October Woodrow Wilson declared his support for the independence of all the subject nations within the monarchy. He had already recognised the right of the Czechoslovaks to independence and this was proclaimed in Prague on 28 October. On 29 October the Croatian Diet declared the independence of Croatia and the vesting of Croatia's destiny in the hands of the Narodno Vijeće. The German-Austrian deputies within the Austrian parliament constituted themselves as the Provisional National Assembly of the independent state of German-Austria on 28 October and appointed the Social Democrat Karl Renner as state chancellor. Hungary had proclaimed its independence ten days earlier. The Serbian army entered Belgrade on 1 November and proceeded across the Danube into Vojvodina. The empire had already disintegrated when the armistice was signed on 3 November, and on 11 November the emperor 'renounced all part in conducting the business of state'. The sudden appearance of the Narodno Vijeće took Pašić by surprise. He could ignore the claims of the Yugoslav Committee when it stood alone, but he could not dismiss those of a *de facto* provisional government under its respected president, Antun Korošec, and especially one which had mandated the Yugoslav Committee to represent it in negotiations with the Allies. Pašić was compelled by pressure from the Allies, notably from the French, to parley with the Narodno Vijeće and the Yugoslav Committee. A conference held in Geneva on 6–9 November brought the three parties together, and a reluctant Pašić was forced 'with tears in his eyes' to sign a declaration which proposed the setting up of a joint provisional government, whilst at the same time recognising the right of the Narodno Vijeće to administer the territories under its control until a Constituent Assembly could be elected to settle the form of government for the new state. The Serbian government promptly repudiated Pašić's signature. The Italians were already moving into Dalmatia, with the consent of the Allies. There was chaos in many parts of the war-torn country. The Montenegrins were quarrelling about their position within the new political order which was being shaped. On 27 November a delegation from Zagreb arrived in Belgrade to negotiate the terms for the unification of their state of Slovenes, Croats and Serbs with the kingdom of Serbia. Bosnia–Hercegovina and Vojvodina had voted for union with Serbia, and on 24 November the Montenegrin Assembly, meeting at Podgorica under the shadow of a Serbian military presence, deposed Nikola and declared for union 'with brotherly Serbia in one state under the Karadjordjević dynasty'. The delegates from Zagreb had no time to haggle about details. They agreed to the proclamation of the kingdom of Serbs, Croats and Slovenes, which was announced by the prince regent, Alexander Karadjordjević, on 1 December 1918.

7

The kingdom of Serbs, Croats and Slovenes

The proclamation of 1 December 1918 marked the beginning of a process of nation building which is not yet complete. The tensions which existed between the Yugoslav Committee, representing the Croats, Slovenes and Serbs who had been citizens of the Dual Monarchy, and the Serbs and Montenegrins who lived within their respective kingdoms could not be removed by resolutions passed by politicians who were temporarily carried away by romantic notions of South Slav unity. At no stage in the manoeuvres which accompanied the preparations for the formation of the new state were the aspirations of the Macedonian people taken into account. If they were considered at all, it was as a subordinate branch of the Serbian nation. Even less thought was given to the large number of inhabitants who had no claims to call themselves South Slavs. These included over half a million German-speakers, just under half a million each of Magyars and Albanians, a quarter of a million Romanians and 150,000 Turks. In addition there were Czechs, Slovaks, Ruthenians, Russians, Poles, Italians, Vlahs, Bulgars and Greeks. There were three main religious groups: the Serbian Orthodox and Roman Catholic Christians and the Muslims. There were also tens of thousands of Jews as well as Protestant and Uniate (Greek Catholic) Christians.

In addition to the complexities of the linguistic and religious pattern which the citizens of the new state displayed, there were also formidable administrative problems facing any government attempting to create some form of cohesion from the organisational chaos which it inherited from the collapse of the old order. There were six customs areas, five currencies, four railway networks, three banking systems and even, for a time, two governments until the Narodno Vijeće in Zagreb and the Serbian government in Belgrade were merged into a single authority. There were also the remains of four legal systems which had to be assimilated into a common code of law. It may be that the sense of Yugoslav unity had some meaning to the middle-class professional politicians, lawyers, writers, artists and

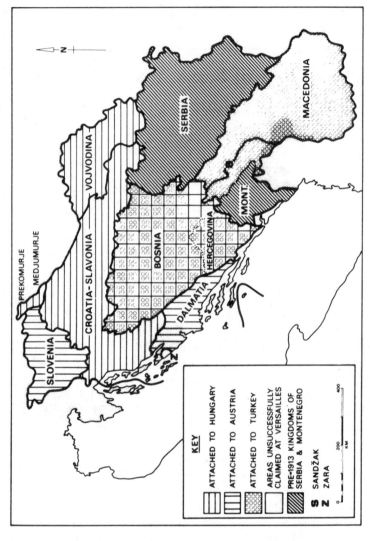

Map 2. The formation of the Yugoslav kingdom.

Note: Bosnia–Hercegovina, Turkish from the fifteenth century, was placed under Austro-Hungarian administration in 1878 and annexed to the Dual Monarchy in 1908.

Table 1. *Population of the kingdom of Serbs, Croats and Slovenes*
(according to the census of 31 January 1921)

% of total population	Linguistic groups		%	Religions	
74.4	Serbo-Croats	8,911,509	46.7	Orthodox	5,593,057
8.5	Slovenes	1,019,997	39.6	Roman Catholic	4,708,657
82.9	Total South Slavs	9,931,506	11.2	Muslim	1,345,271
			1.9	Protestant	229,517
4.2	Germans	505,790	0.5	Jewish	64,746
3.9	Magyars	467,658	0.3	Uniate	40,338
3.7	Albanians	439,657	—	Others	3,325
1.9	Romanians	231,068			
1.25	Turks	150,322			
0.96	Czechs and Slovaks	115,532			
1.2	Others (includes Ruthenes, Russians, Poles, Italians, gypsies and Vlahs)	143,378			
	Total non-South Slav	2,053,405			
	Total population	11,984,911			

teachers who promoted the idea of a South Slav state, but it had not penetrated deeply into the consciousness of the mass of the peasantry, who constituted over 80 per cent of the population. To them government was a remote and often alien force which descended upon them from time to time, usually with unpleasant consequences. Tax collectors came to take away some of their hard-earned money; recruiting officers came to conscript their sons to fight in distant wars; or policemen came to harass them for breaches of laws which they had no part in making. Their loyalties were first of all to their own kinsfolk, who belonged to the extended family which was the basis of the social organisation throughout the Balkans. If their horizon extended beyond the self-contained village community, it was to the nearest market town. Local loyalties to the immediate region which they inhabited meant more than wider national loyalties. In some areas blood feuds between rival families or clans were more real than wars between rival armies. Religion, local customs and traditions were part of the heritage which provided bonds of cultural identity far stronger than the abstract concept of a nation. Awareness of the wider world outside sometimes came to villages through the migration of their sons to seek work abroad, either temporarily or permanently. The lands of the South Slavs have long been centres of emigration. In Macedonia the practice of *pačelba*, the seasonal migration of young men to work as, for example, woodcutters in Transylvania or boatmen on the Volga, was an important feature of rural life. In Dalmatia, the sea beckoned the youth of the coastal areas to seek their fortunes overseas. A moving poem written in the local dialect of Dalmatia describes the feelings of a mother saying farewell to her son who is travelling to America. She urges him to remember the values which he absorbed with the milk he drew from her as a child. She knows that she will never see him again. The women, of course, remained in the villages and were the custodians of the traditional beliefs. These were transmitted orally, as the majority of the peasants could not read or write. The level of illiteracy varied from about 9 per cent in Slovenia to over 80 per cent in Macedonia, Bosnia and Kosovo, the national average being around 50 per cent. The resolutions, manifestoes, laws and constitutions which emanated from the cities made little impact on the mass of the peasantry. Harold Laski commented that, although it is comparatively easy to change governments, the greatest task of innovators is to change the everyday habits of thought of ordinary people. The changes which were made in 1918 had little immediate impact on the attitudes of most of the peasants. The account of life in the villages behind the Dalmatian coast which Rudolf Bićanić recorded in the 1930s in his *Kako živi narod* (How the People Live) is a vivid reminder of the persistence of the old ways. Even today, after a catastrophic war and four decades of a socialist regime, one can still find in the rural areas echoes of a way of life which owes little to the existence of a Yugoslav state, still less of a socialist society.

The leaders of the kingdom of Serbs, Croats and Slovenes attempted to impose from above, on this heterogeneous mixture of different social and cultural groups, a common set of rules and a common political and economic order. The fact that they did not succeed is partly due to the intractable nature of the problem, made worse by their own mistakes. It may be that a recognition of the nature of the different cultures and a willingness to permit a broad degree of local autonomy – as suggested by Trumbić – might have worked. The creation of a Greater Serbia, under the guise of a South Slav state, ensured that the Yugoslavia of the inter-war years was a society at war with itself. The founding fathers, in their declarations during the First World War, and in their approaches to the peacemakers at Versailles, pretended that a Yugoslav nation already existed, with a common language and a common sense of community.

They ignored even the existence of Slovene as a language separate from Serbian and Croatian, and disregarded the difference in outlook which had evolved during centuries of life under totally different regimes. Politicians cannot easily divest themselves of the illusion that the winning of votes in constituent assemblies and parliaments in some way changes reality. By ignoring the realities of life at the grass roots, the constitution makers sowed dragon's teeth, which continue to yield a bitter harvest.

The settling of the frontiers

Before they could settle the constitution, however, they had to define, first of all, the territorial limits within which it was to operate. This involved negotiation with hostile neighbours and even recourse to military action. It was not until 1926 that international agreement was finaly achieved with all the interested parties.

The most urgent task was to prevent Italy from occupying all the territories promised to it under the secret Treaty of London. The Torre–Trumbić agreement of March 1918, endorsed later by resolutions of a Congress of Oppressed Nationalities which the Italian government sponsored in Rome, gave the Yugoslavs some hope that they would be able to reach a compromise with the Italians. However, as soon as the war was over, the Italians rediscovered their *sacro egoismo* and demanded the full implementation of the promises made to them in 1915. The Italians were already in occupation of a large part of the disputed territory, and in international politics possession is usually worth more than argument or appeals to justice. The position of the Allied representatives at Versailles was complicated by Woodrow Wilson's refusal to accept the results of secret treaties and his affirmation of the right of the Yugoslavs to self-determination. This conflicted with the Italian claims, which would have placed over half a million Slavs under Italian rule. Throughout Dalmatia, Istria and the Julian region there were scarcely 50,000 Italians.

The first phase in the negotiations over the Italian frontier took place in Paris and lasted until March 1920. During this period President Wilson produced a compromise proposal which would have given Italy most of Istria, whilst reducing the Italian demands in Dalmatia, and awarding Fiume (Rijeka) to the Yugoslavs. This was accepted by the Yugoslav delegates, although it would have placed 300,000 Slovenes and Croats under Italian rule. The Italians were unable to accept Yugoslav control of Fiume, although it was pointed out to them that they could have no possible use for the port if they already had Trieste. Fiume was developed as the part for the Hungarian half of the Dual Monarchy, just as Trieste served the Austrian part. Fiume's hinterland lay in Croatia–Slavonia and the central Danube area. There is some suspicion that the Italians intended to run down the facilities at Fiume in order to build up Trieste as the port for the Danubian lands, in furtherance of an expansionist economic policy. A suggested compromise, under which Fiume would become part of a free state administered by the League of Nations, with a plebiscite held after three years to test the wishes of the inhabitants, was also rejected by the Italians. The Fiume issue was eventually settled by force. The Italian poet and nationalist adventurer Gabriele D'Annunzio seized the town with a band of armed followers and held it in defiance of the Allied Council of Ministers. The proposal for a free state was dropped and eventually Fiume was handed over to Italy.

The so-called Adriatic Question had greatly enlivened the proceedings at Versailles. In May 1919 it produced a dramatic walk-out by Signor Orlando and Baron Sonnino, the leaders of the Italian delegation, and in February 1920 a frank memorandum from President Wilson threatening to withdraw the American delegation entirely from the whole peacemaking process. 'The Adriatic issue as it now presents itself raises the fundamental question as to whether the American Government can on any terms cooperate with its European associates in the great work of maintaining the peace of the world.' Although Wilson's sharp tone shook the French and British into attempting another compromise, they were unable to break the deadlock. In March 1920 Wilson and the European leaders agreed to hand the whole Adriatic Question over to direct negotiation between the Italians and Yugoslavs. As they must have known, in such negotiations the stronger party, Italy, would win. In November 1920 the Treaty of Rapallo was signed by Italian and Yugoslav delegates. One of the Yugoslav signatories commented, '. . . we felt that the big Allies had left us to our own destiny and simultaneously put upon our shoulders the responsibility for the peace of Europe'.

The Rapallo settlement gave Italy the whole of Istria and a larger part of the Julian region than had been promised in the Treaty of London. In Dalmatia Italy received Zara (Zadar) and the islands of Cres (Cherso) and Losinj (Lussin) in the northern Adriatic, and Palagruža (Pelagosa) and Lagosta (Lastovo) further south. D'Annunzio's comic opera state of Fiume was solemnly recognised and its boundaries extended to provide it with a corridor to Italian-held Istria. This unusual situation came to an end in 1924 when the Yugoslavs reluctantly acquiesced in the incorporation of Fiume into Italy. The Yugoslavs were forced to give guarantees to the small

Italian minority in Dalmatia, but the Italians refused to give similar guarantees to their Yugoslav citizens, on the grounds that everyone took it for granted that minorities in Italy were properly treated. In fact, the Slovenes and Croats were subjected to a ruthless process of Italianisation under Mussolini's fascist regime. They were forbidden to use their own language in schools and churches, and could not baptise their children with Slav Christian names.

The Treaty of Rapallo was signed in the shadow of two events in the autumn of 1920 which had seriously undermined the morale of the Yugoslavs. The first was the withdrawal of Woodrow Wilson from public life after he collapsed on 26 September 1919 during a speech-making tour in which he was attempting to win public support for the Versailles settlement in the face of a hostile Congress. The loss of their champion came shortly before another defeat for the cause of self-determination for the South Slavs – the Klagenfurt Plebiscite.

The Austrian frontier

The linguistic boundary between Slovenes and Germans ran through the Austrian province of Carinthia. There were many Slovene villages in the area between the Karawanken mountains and the valley of the river Drava, although the cities of Klagenfurt and Villach were mainly inhabited by German-speakers. Under the terms of the Treaty of St Germain (September 1919) Austria agreed that a plebiscite should be held in the disputed area, which was divided into two zones for voting purposes. Zone A, which undoubtedly contained a large majority of Slovenes (some estimates put it at 80 per cent), was to vote first. If it opted for Yugoslavia, a vote would then be held in Zone B, which included the city of Klagenfurt. When the first vote was taken on 10 October 1920, a 60 : 40 majority for Austria was returned. This made the vote in Zone B unnecessary, and the whole area was retained by Austria. The Yugoslavs alleged that the election had been rigged. They could not accept that a majority of Slovene-speakers could have voted for Austria and, in a desperate attempt to reverse the decision, they invaded Zone A. An ultimatum from the big powers forced them to withdraw and to accept what appeared to be a humiliating defeat. The frontier was fixed along the crest line of the Karawanken range, which involved the transfer to Yugoslavia of two small enclaves on the southern slopes of the mountains. It has remained there ever since, although the Yugoslav claim was revived in 1945.

The Hungarian frontier

The region which now forms the autonomous province of Vojvodina, between the Sava and the Hungarian and Romanian borders, is one of the richest agricultural regions of Europe. There is no natural divide which separates Vojvodina from the Danubian lowlands of Hungary. The drawing of a frontier which would be ethnically fair is equally difficult. Throughout its colourful history, the area has changed hands many times and each change of ownership has brought new immigrants, many of whom have remained to farm the rich soils or to ply their trades as craftsmen and merchants. According to the Hungarian census of 1910 the largest single linguistic group was that of the Magyars (421,567), followed by the Serbs (381,000) and the Germans (301,035). The remaining 150,000 included Romanians, Czechs, Slovaks, Ruthenes, Russians and several other smaller groups. The geographical distribution of the various elements in the linguistic kaleidoscope defied any attempt to draw a frontier which would correspond to any principle of self-determination. Inevitably, therefore, the alternative principle of 'the spoils of the victors' was applied in the Treaty of Trianon which Hungary signed in June 1920. Although the Yugoslavs acquired a non-Slav population of three-quarters of a million, outnumbering the Serbs and Croats almost two to one, they were not satisfied. They refused to give up the coal-mining town of Pécs, which they had occupied in 1918. In August 1921, under pressure from their former allies, they withdrew under protest to the Trianon line. Two other small areas with Magyar-speaking populations were also transferred to the Yugoslavs: Prekomurje, lying between the river Mura and the Austro-Hungarian border, was attached to Slovenia; and Medjumurje, between the Drava and the Mura, came under Croatian control.

The Albanian frontier

Albania's fragile independence had hardly been established when the First World War broke out. The frontiers had been fixed in 1913 by a Conference of Ambassadors, one of whose objectives had been to prevent Serbia from obtaining an outlet to the Adriatic. The powers were not, however, concerned with the principle of self-determination and were content to leave Albanian populations totalling over 400,000 under Serbian rule in Kosovo, Metohija and western Macedonia, as well as others in Montenegro. In 1914 the country began to lose control of its own destiny. In October Greek forces moved into the southern provinces, and in December the

Italians, although still outside the war, occupied Vlöre (Valona) in the centre. In the summer of 1915 Serbian and Montenegrin troops advanced into the north. A few months later, after the defeat of the Serbs and the surrender of the Montenegrins, Austro-Hungarian forces replaced them and established an occupation zone, covering two-thirds of the country, although permitting a degree of local self-government. In 1916 the French landed in the south. The publication of the terms of the secret Treaty of London by the Bolsheviks in 1918 revealed that Italy had been promised a protectorate over the central area and that it was intended to give the southern provinces to the Greeks and the north to the Serbs. Italian plans were frustrated by the resistance of the Albanians, who objected to being 'sold like cattle in the markets of Europe'. In 1920 the Italians recognised Albanian independence and had to be content with a naval base on the island of Sazan (Saseno) controlling the entrance to the port of Vlöre. The occupation by Yugoslav troops of the Shkodër (Scutari) area in the north was not ended until 1921, when they were forced to accept the 1913 line and to forgo their ambitions to gain access to the sea at Shëngjin (San Giovanni). The details of the frontier demarcation in the Ohrid area were not settled until 1926, when the monastery of Sveti Naum was transfered to the Yugoslavs.

Other frontier settlements

The decisions of the Peace Conference regarding Yugoslavia's frontiers with Romania and Bulgaria were more easily settled in 1919, although in both cases the drawing of lines which favoured the strategic interests of the Yugoslavs left national minorities on the wrong side.

The Vidovdan constitution

Whilst these frontier problems were being settled with the neighbouring states, an even more important struggle was taking place within the country to decide upon the constitutional framework within which the kingdom was to be governed. It was at first necessary to set up a provisional government to administer the country until the new constitution was ready. A joint cabinet, composed of representatives of the Narodno Vijeće and the Serbian government, was established, and representatives of other groups were later added. In an attempt to give the new regime a semblance of representative government a Provisional Assembly was convened. It was made up of members of the Serbian Skupština and nominees of the

Narodno Vijeće and of the provincial assemblies of the various elements from Austria–Hungary which had been included in the new state, such as Bosnia–Hercegovina and the Vojvodina. In November 1920 this was replaced by an elected Constituent Assembly (Ustavotvorna Skupština) of 419 members, which functioned as a legislature whilst at the same time deciding on the new constitution. When the constitution was agreed, this body was converted into the National Assembly (Skupština) or parliament of the kingdom.

The largest single group in the Assembly were the Democrats, with 92 seats, followed closely by the Serbian Radicals, with 91. The Democrats, who were mainly Serbian, had a broader base than the Radicals, although they originated from a group who broke with the Radicals in 1919 to form a separate party. Their leader, Svetozar Pribičević, was an Orthodox Serb from Croatia, belonging to the people known as *prečani* (across the river, i.e. Serbs from the former Habsburg territories). The Democrats also drew support from centralist elements amongst non-Serbs, notably from some middle-class Croats and Slovenes. They were genuine believers in the Yugoslav idea, but also supported a unitary state with a strong central government. Unlike the Radicals, whose support was overwhelmingly in Serbia, the Democrats gained some votes in all areas, although mainly from *prečani* Serbs, especially in the former military frontier zones of Lika and Gorski Kotar, and from the Serbian minorities in Kosovo, Macedonia and Montenegro.

The third largest group, the communists, with 58 seats, also drew votes from all parts of the country and from all national groups. They were strongest in the towns and in the poorest regions of the south. In local elections, held shortly before the poll for the Constituent Assembly, they obtained majorities in several towns, including Belgrade, Zagreb and Skopje. They were also strongly supported by the tobacco workers in Macedonia and the railwaymen in all parts of the country. The communists received votes from peasants in the poorest regions, but where well-organised peasant parties existed they were unable to make much headway. This was particularly true in Croatia, where Radić's Peasant Party held the allegiance of the majority of the population. There were also several smaller peasant parties, the most important of which was the Serb Agrarian Party, which had the support of many Serbs in Bosnia–Hercegovina and Croatia. The Serb Agrarians and their allies were able to muster 39 seats in the Assembly.

Most of the other parties, except for the Social Democrats, made their appeal on sectional religious or national grounds, and could not hope to be regarded as being representative of the country as a whole. The Slovene Popular Party (also known as the Clericals) was a Roman Catholic, Slovene nationalist body, led by Monsignor Antun Korošec. They had 27 seats in the Assembly, all from Slovene constituencies. There were two Muslim parties, the largest (with 24 seats), known as the Muslim Organisation, based in Bosnia–Hercegovina; and the smaller Džemijet Party, with only 5 assembly members, representing the Albanian and Turkish communities of Macedonia and Kosovo. An extreme Croat nationalist party, known as the Party of Croat Rights, led by the militantly anti-Serb Dr Josip Frank, won 3 seats. The 'Frankists' later dropped out of parliamentary politics, and a section of them founded the extremist nationalist underground organisation the Ustaša, which organised the murder of King Alexander in 1934.

The Social Democrats, with 10 seats, were the survivors of a pre-war party founded in 1903 on the lines of the Austrian and German Social Democrat parties. They represented an implantation of western European labour policies into the alien soil of the Balkans. They had no trade union movement to nourish them, no industrial proletariat to vote for them. The more radical elements split off to join the Communists in 1919 and those who tried to maintain a democratic, non-communist labour movement were unable to influence events when an industrial working class eventually began to emerge.

The two largest parties in the Assembly, the Radicals and the Democrats, did not together command a majority of the 419 seats. Both were committed to a highly centralised system, although Pribičević and his Democrats were genuine supporters of the Yugoslav idea, their talk of equality among the three main national groups was seen by many – and with some justification – as a cloak for Serbian domination. Pašić and the Radicals wanted a Greater Serbia. They would not have found it so easy to get their way if the opposition had been more united and more skilled in parliamentary tactics.

The Serbs had a strong case to be the leading element in the kingdom. They had, for decades, been the standard bearers of the movement to emancipate the Slavs from Ottoman and Habsburg rule. By their victories in the Balkan wars and their sacrifices during the First World War they had paid with their own blood for the right to lead the Yugoslav people to freedom. They claimed to be the Piedmont of the Yugoslav *risorgimento*. The analogy with nineteenth-century Italy, although frequently made by both Serbs and the leaders of the Yugoslav Movement in Austria–Hungary, was not wholly accurate. Pašić was no Cavour. There was no

Yugoslav Garibaldi to fire the imagination of the nation's youth with his heroic deeds, and there was no counterpart to Mazzini, man of action and philosopher, whose advocacy of liberal nationalism had world-wide significance. In Italy, whatever the difference between north and south, there was one nation and one culture. In Yugoslavia there were several.

At a more mundane level, Serbia commanded the essential levers of power. There was no military force to rival the battle-hardened Serbian royal army. There was no apparatus of government comparable to that possessed by Serbia – an elected legislature, a civil service, a judiciary and a royal dynasty. The Serbs were also numerically the largest group. If the Macedonian Slavs and the Montenegrins were counted as Serbs – as they officially were – they could claim to constitute almost half of the inhabitants of the country. It was to be expected, therefore, that they would hold the key positions of power. The tragedy was that they took advantage of their position to ride roughshod over the rights of their fellow South Slavs.

They might not have been able to do this if the opposition had been more politically experienced and capable of forming a united front. The Croat Peasant Party boycotted the Assembly from the outset, and the other main anti-centralist groups – the smaller Croat parties, the Slovenes and the Social Democrats – withdrew from its deliberations early in 1921. The communists withdrew and were later banned. Pašić managed to win over the Muslims by making promises of favourable treatment for Bosnia over two issues which concerned them: the proposed land system and the drawing of provincial boundaries.

In the absence of 163 of the 419 members, the Assembly approved the centralist constitution proposed by the government, having previously rejected Croat and Slovene drafts which provided for a federal structure. The centralist formula was approved by 223 votes to 35, and the new constitution was promulgated on 28 June 1921 – Serbia's national day. The Vidovdan (St Vitus' Day) constitution lasted for eight years. Pašić had achieved a pyrrhic victory, which did nothing to heal the deep rift between the Serbs and their Slav cousins in Croatia and Slovenia. Even today, after almost forty years under a socialist regime, the effects of the Serbian victory still find an echo in contemporary political life. Fears of Serbian 'hegemonism' and of 'centralist tendencies' have played a part in stimulating countervailing pressures from other groups, notably the Croats and Albanians, which have led to serious civil unrest in the 1970s and 1980s.

The Vidovdan constitution was based on the same principles as the 1903 Serbian constitution. It was, in effect, the Serbian constitution adapted to the needs of the larger Yugoslav unit. The fact that it was promulgated on 28 June, the day on which Serbia's fate had been decided at Kosovo Polje in 1389 and in Sarajevo in 1918, served as a further reminder that the kingdom of Serbs, Croats and Slovenes was in reality Greater Serbia. Pašić and the centralists strenuously opposed the suggestion that the title should be the kingdom of Yugoslavia. Following the precedent of the Corfu Declaration, the fiction was perpetuated that there was a common Serb–Croat–Slovene language. The constitution also incorporated the principle enunciated in the Corfu Declaration that the new state would be 'a constitutional, democratic and parliamentary monarchy headed by the Karadjordjević dynasty'. The clauses guaranteeing equality among the nationalities, civic rights and freedom of religion and of political association might have been taken from any of the parliamentary democracies of western Europe. The '*loi écrite*' unfortunately often differs from the '*loi réelle*', and this proved to be the case with the Vidovdan constitution. The freedom it guaranteed proved to be almost as fictional as its linguistic fantasy about a single Yugoslav language.

The king was given far greater powers than is usual in constitutional monarchies. These included the right to summon the National Assembly, to appoint state officials and to negotiate treaties. The Council of Ministers was directly responsible to the king, who appointed the president of the Council (prime minister). The Assembly (Narodna Skupština) of 319 members, which was the only legislative chamber, met in Belgrade. At the time the only other unicameral legislatures in Europe were those of Finland and the Baltic republics. Like the Finnish Eduskunta, the Skupština used a committee system to act as a legislative filter, performing some of the functions usually carried out by second chambers. Like Finland also, election to the Skupština was by a system of proportional representation based on the Belgian model. But in Yugoslavia only males over thirty years of age could vote or hold office. Not all members of the Council of Ministers were elected. It was possible for non-political specialists to be given ministerial office. As all legislation had to be approved by both king and Skupština before it became law, there was supposed to be a balance between the two. They sat on opposite ends of a see-saw, but, as the king appointed the ministers and civil servants, the third participant in the game, the government, tended to lean towards the monarch rather than towards the parliament, and the balance tilted towards the executive.

In addition to the formal powers conferred by the constitution, the king had considerable influence because of the prestige of the dynasty. The

Karadjordjević family had been associated with the life struggle of the nation from the time of the first Serbian revolt against the Turks. The dynasty was older than the constitution, and the monarch provided a rallying point for the nation when the fragile political machinery began to disintegrate.

King Peter I, who came to the throne in 1903, had not played an active part in public life since 1914, when he conferred the title of prince regent on his twenty-six-year-old son, Alexander. Peter died a few days after the passing of the Vidovdan constitution, so that, for the whole of the short life of the Vidovdan regime, Alexander was the monarch. He was an intelligent and energetic man, who took an active part in the work of government. He expressed his opinions firmly and frequently influenced ministerial decisions, especially in foreign policy. On the issue of centralism versus federalism he was, of course, a centralist. He was first and foremost the head of the Serbian royal house, and was quite prepared to consider, during the crisis of 1928, the possibility of the secession of Croatia and Slovenia if this would preserve intact his Greater Serbian patrimony.

The local government system at its lowest level, the *opština* (commune), varied from place to place, according either to the practices of the former imperial power which had ruled before 1918 or to local traditions. Thus the Austrian municipal system remained in Ljubljana, and in parts of the Vojvodina the old Hungarian practices were followed. In some cases *opština* councils were elected; elsewhere they were appointed. What happened at the base of the pyramid was of little importance. The middle tier of *srezovi* (*srez* = district) and *oblasti* (*oblast* = province) was directly under the central government's control. The prefects (*župani*) of the provinces were civil servants, appointed by the king on the recommendation of the minister of the interior, who directly appointed the *načelnik* (sub-prefect) of each of the subordinate *srezovi*. The chain of command led directly back to Belgrade, and there was little room for local initiative or for the democratic involvement of the people in government.

The frustration which this authoritarian system engendered in the non-Serb population meant that when conditions became intolerable for them they had no outlet for their feelings except revolt.

Belgrade, at the centre of the decision-making process, became a hotbed of political intrigue, horse trading and corruption. Such a concentration of power within the hands of a relatively small clique of Serbs was a certain recipe for dissension in a society as culturally heterogeneous as that of the Yugoslav kingdom.

Politics during the first decade

The political life of the kingdom of Serbs, Croats and Slovenes (renamed Yugoslavia in 1929) can be divided into three periods. During the first decade an attempt was made to operate a parliamentary democracy on the lines which had evolved in western Europe during the nineteenth century. The attempt failed and was followed in 1929 by a royal dictatorship which came to an end in 1934 with the assassination of King Alexander. From 1934 until the German invasion of 1941, a Regency Council, headed by the king's cousin, Prince Paul, presided over a mock parliamentary system, which was overthrown by the *coup d'état* of March 1941, when Alexander's young son, Peter, was briefly installed on the throne. The whole system was then swept aside by the Axis invasion in April 1941.

The experiment in parliamentary democracy failed, as it did in all the other states of east-central Europe except Czechoslovakia, because the social conditions for its survival did not exist. Liberal parliamentary regimes are founded on the assumption that the majority of the population support the broad aims of the constitution. If a powerful minority does not accept the premises on which the system is based, either on class or national grounds, the parliamentary machinery cannot work. It depends for its success on the willingness of those who object to the policies of the government to accept the role of a loyal opposition, and of the government to change places with the opposition if it is defeated at the ballot box. From the outset these conditions were not fulfilled. The paper victory which Pašić won in the Constituent Assemby alienated large sections of the population. The Croats, who had been outmanoeuvred by the Serbian majority, were represented by the Croat Peasant Party, led by a fiery and mercurial demagogue, Stjepan Radić. The liberal-minded, middle-class Croats, like Trumbić, who had led the Yugoslav movement in the Habsburg lands up to 1918 were pushed to the sidelines and played little part in post-war politics. Radić was one of those radical peasant leaders who came to prominence in several of the eastern European states where the majority of the population lived off the land. Iuliu Maniu in Romania and Alexander Stambuliski in Bulgaria were cast in the same mould. Their appeal was based on demands for radical land reform – 'the land for those who till it' – and on an anti-town chauvinism which proclaimed the superiority of the simple values of rural life over those of the clique-ridden and corrupt town dwellers. They were particularly suspicious of such town-based institutions as banks, and of the machinery of law and politics.

Stambuliski, for example, even when premier, described his capital, Sofia, as 'a Sodom and Gomorrah, the total disappearance of which I should see without regret'. The special position of the Croats within the new Yugoslav state gave an additional dimension to Radić's platform – that of Croat nationalism. Whether his radicalism would have been tempered by the responsibilities of office was never put to the test, as he accepted office for only a few months in 1925–6. His murder in 1928 changed the whole political atmosphere and led to the institution of a royal dictatorship in which the normal interplay of party politics was suspended. His successor, Dr Vlatko Maček, was a middle-class intellectual who was far less radical than Radić.

Nikola Pašić, Radić's great opponent, was the spokesman of Serbian nationalism. He had started his political life as a radical peasant leader in the 1870s. In his early days he was much influenced by the ideas of Svetozar Marković, the pioneer of Balkan socialism. He was one of the founders of the Serbian Radical Party in 1881 and held office under Milan Obrenović, although the king suspected him of socialist and republican sympathies. After the murder of Alexander Obrenović in 1903 and the return of the Karadjordjević dynasty, Pašić became the dominant figure in Serbian political life, whether as foreign minister, prime minister or leader of the Radical Party. His prestige was greatly enhanced by Serbia's successes in the Balkan wars, and as prime minister on the outbreak of the First World War it was his destiny to lead the nation in its hour of crisis and to preside over its triumphal emergence as the leading element in the first South Slav state. In forty years of activity at the heart of Serbian political life he had developed from a typical Balkan peasant rebel into the father figure of his people and a statesman on the world stage. A British doctor who met him in 1915, during the height of the typhus epidemic, described him as a man of commanding presence who stood head and shoulders above his colleagues. 'We had an interview with the Prime Minister, M. Pasitch [*sic*], and knew at once that we had come in contact with a live man. With his fine eyes looking from his benevolent old face, he listened to our exposition of the case ... Once he grasped it, things began to move.'

There were many other facets to the character of this patriarchal figure, however. As his opponents in the tortuous corridors of power in Belgrade, and as the negotiators representing the Yugoslav Committee in Corfu, learned to their cost, he could be devious, crafty, ruthless and overbearing. The narrowness of his vision prevented him from breaking out of the prison of Serbian nationalism and using his undoubted talents to become the leader of a genuine Yugoslav state, instead of a Greater Serbia masquerading as the embodiment of South Slav unity. The measure of his failure is that within three years of his death, in 1926, the Vidovdan constitution was abolished and within fifteen years the state which he had helped to create had disappeared.

The leader of the Democratic Party, Svetozar Pribićević, was a *prečani* Serb who had been active in Austro-Hungarian politics as a member of the Croatian Sabor and as a representative of Croatia in the Hungarian parliament. He was a leader of the Serb Independent Party and edited the journal *Srbobran*. He and his three brothers, Milan, Adam and Valerian, worked within the Serbo-Croat coalition and were joint defendants in the notorious treason trials in Zagreb in 1908. Their Serbian nationalism was tempered by a genuine enthusiasm for the cause of Yugoslav unity. Svetozar at first rejected the narrow, authoritarian nationalism of Pašić, and in 1919 joined with a group of disaffected members of the National Party, led by Ljubomir Davidović, to form the broadly based, mainly Serbian, Democratic Party. Although Pribićević believed in a centralised constitution, he appeared far more willing to recognise the aspirations of the Croats, provided that they did not advocate separatism. Although in his Habsburg days he had worked closely with Supilo and other Croat leaders to further the Yugoslav cause, once the new kingdom was proclaimed he became identified with the Serbian centralists. As minister of the interior in the provisional government of Stojan Protić (December 1918 to July 1919) he authorised draconian measures to Serbianise the gendarmerie and the local administration in the former Habsburg lands. His political ally Milorad Drašković, who served as minister of the interior from August 1920 until his assassination in July 1921, was equally severe on both federalists and communists, and had Pribićević's enthusiastic support. As Pašić's chief ally in the Constituent Assembly, Pribićević was able to deliver the votes of his 92 Democrats, the largest single group amongst the 223 deputies who voted for the Vidovdan constitution. In 1924 he formed a minority group of Independent Democrats in protest against the more liberal views of the majority led by Davidović, who had shown a willingness to cooperate with the Croats. It is interesting to note that one of Pribićević's Independent Democrat associates was Dr Ivan Ribar. He presided over the debates in the Constituent Assembly in 1921 and survived long enough to become a Partisan and later chairman of the Presidium of the Federal Assembly under the 1946 constitution. In 1927 Pribićević abandoned his centralist views and formed an alliance with Radić and the Croats, and later became a resolute opponent of the Serbian-dominated royal dictatorship.

Politics under the Vidovdan constitution displayed the outward trappings of a parliamentary democracy, but none of the essential spirit of compromise which enables it to work. The divisions within the society were too deep to be resolved by the processes of parliamentary debate. Two major groups remained outside the framework of the constitution – the communists and the Croats – and other sections were too inarticulate and ill organised at that time to voice their grievances.

When the communists withdrew from the work of the Assembly they were already the subject of legal restrictions, introduced by the minister of the interior, Milorad Drašković, following a strike which they had organised in 1920 amongst miners and transport workers. The government issued an *obznana* (proclamation) which forbade communist activities at the grass roots, but it did not exclude communist deputies from the Assembly. On 2 August 1921, five weeks after the passing of the constitution, a young communist assassinated Drašković, and the party was then declared illegal under the State Security Act of 1921. It continued its activities underground, working through front organisations amongst trade unions and youth organisations, and it unsuccessfully contested the 1923 elections under the banner of the Independent Workers' Party, receiving a derisory 24,000 votes. Police harassment and internal quarrels amongst the leaders reduced the party to impotence. The faction-riddled Yugoslav Communist Party became a by-word in Comintern circles, where it was said that if you had two Yugoslavs, you would find three factions. Its fortunes revived after 1937, when Tito became secretary-general.

The Croat Peasant Party boycotted the Assembly until 1924, although they did contest the elections in 1923, gaining 70 of the 313 seats. Radić's decision to advise his followers to take their seats came after he had failed in an attempt to enlist the support of foreign sympathisers for a revision of the constitution. In London, Wickham Steed advised him to take part in the work of the Assembly. In Moscow he affiliated his party to the Comintern-inspired 'Green International' and appeared to favour Moscow's plan for the break-up of Yugoslavia. The Comintern conference of July 1924 proposed a federation of worker–peasant republics within the Balkans, which would include Bulgaria, Serbia and Macedonia, but Radić could not accept the term Balkan as applied to Croatia. To him, as to many Yugoslavs today, the term Balkan is not a neutral geographical designation. It contains emotive undertones, implying backwardness, squalor and ignorance. Radić saw Croatia as a central European country, with more in common with Austria, Hungary and Czechoslovakia than with the former Turkish territories south of the old Sava–Danube frontier. He told a Moscow audience, 'Croats are not part of the Balkans either geographically, politically or culturally.' On his return to Zagreb in the autumn of 1924, he hinted that he might accept the Vidovdan constitution and work for change from within. An opposition coalition of Democrats, Muslims and Slovenes forced Pašić out of office, and the king sent for Davidović. Radić and his Peasant Party deputies, whilst refusing office, agreed to use their votes to sustain this anti-centralist government. It lasted for only a hundred days. Radić's men may have given their votes to Davidović, but their unpredictable leader did his best to undermine the government's authority by a series of violent speeches, attacking the Karadjordjević dynasty, the army and the whole Serbian-dominated Vidovdan establishment. The result was the return to office of Pašić and Pribičević, who persuaded the king to dissolve parliament and to call new elections. These were held in February 1925 and produced a small majority for the Radical–Independent alliance, 163 seats in a house of 315 members. The Radicals increased their representation by 33 seats to 141. The Davidović Democrats, weakened by internal splits, fell from 51 to 37, and the Croat Peasants, Moslems and Slovenes all had a reduction in the number of their deputies. Radić was arrested on charges of sedition, and there were threats that his party would be banned. Whilst in prison he was able to receive visitors and to negotiate with both government and opposition leaders for a return to political life. There then occurred a political volte-face which demonstrated to many observers the unprincipled opportunism of Vidovdan politics. Radić emerged from custody to join a government headed by Pašić. This bizarre union of opposites lasted until March 1926, when Pašić was forced out of office as a result of a corruption scandal involving his son. One of the accusers was the minister of education, Stjepan Radić! Pašić, who had dominated the political life of the kingdom since 1918, and before that for more than twenty years under the Serbian crown, was a broken man. He died in December 1926 at the age of eighty-one. The Croat–Serb coalition having failed, and Pribičević having moved over to the opposition, the demoralised Radicals tried the only other possible combination – a coalition with Davidović's Democrats, Korošec's Slovene Populists and the Muslim Organisation of Mehmed Spaho. The opposition was formed by the Croat Peasants, Pribičević's Independent Democrats, the Serb Agrarians and a small group representing the Germans of Vojvodina.

The last elections held under the Vidovdan constitution took place in September 1927. The Radicals and the Croat Peasants both lost seats, whilst the Democrats recorded a dramatic leap from 37 to 63 and the other parties held their own. It seemed as if every possible line-up of parties had been tried, but there was still one more shuffling of the pack. Pribičević became a supporter of the anti-centralist bloc and joined forces with Radić, while the majority Democrats sided with the Radicals, now divided and unsure of themselves since the death of Pašić had removed their strong man. The king sent for the Radical Veljko Vukičević, who, having failed to persuade Radić to join him, put together a coalition of Democrats, Slovenes and Muslims, which had a paper majority of almost a hundred. In fact it was a weak and divided government facing a tough and determined opposition. The prime minister was a notoriously militant Serb nationalist who was in touch with some of those who advocated a resolution by force of the country's intractable political problems.

The Skupština degenerated into a bear garden. Insults and personal abuse were used in place of reasoned argument. When insults were thought to be insufficient, blows were exchanged. Finally recourse was had to the gun. On 20 June 1928, during a debate on government corruption, a Montenegrin Radical deputy, Puniša Račić, produced a revolver and shot Pavel and Stjepan Radić and three other opposition deputies. Pavel died immediately and his uncle Stjepan six weeks later. Račić was a leader of one of the Serbian Četnik organisations, extreme nationalist para-military groups who saw themelves as the successors to the Serbian patriots who fought the Turks. It was probably because of his Četnik connections that Račić escaped with a slight sentence. He met his end during the Second World War at the hands of the Partisans.

For the next few months the political fabric created in 1921 rapidly disintegrated. The Slovene leader Dr Korošec, who succeeded Vukičević in August, attempted to conduct the affairs of government, but the opposition deputies withdrew from the Skupština. An anti-parliament was established in Zagreb under the leadership of Radić's successor, Dr Vlatko Maček. Korošec was forced to resign in December 1928, and the king started talks with the opposition leaders to find out 'what the Croats want'. Maček wanted a truly federal state in which even the armed forces were federalised. The king decided to act to preserve the unity of his realm. On 6 January 1929 (the Orthodox Christmas Day) he announced that the Vidovdan constitution was abolished and with it the Skupština and the political parties. A temporary royal dictatorship was proclaimed. Yugoslavia's experiment in parliamentary democracy had ended in a fashion similar to that of Bulgaria, Romania, Poland and Greece.

Economic and social conditions, 1918–28

The conflict of interests between the inhabitants of Serbia and those of the former Habsburg lands which appeared during the constitutional and political struggles between 1918 and 1928 was equally sharp in the economic life of the country.

Industrial development in Slovenia and Croatia had begun in the nineteenth century, at a time when the Habsburg monarchy provided a central European market of some sixty million inhabitants. Suddenly these areas found themselves enclosed in a much less developed market of only twelve million. Serbia proper had also begun to industrialise in the nineteenth century, but the basis was different from that in the Habsburg lands. The state played a considerable role in Serbian industry. Railway construction – a vital necessity in a country without good roads – began with the construction of the Belgrade–Niš line in 1882, and was usually financed by foreign loans guaranteed by the state, but in 1888 the state took over all 480 km (300 miles) of railways then built, and subsequently most railway development was under state control. In 1920 an ambitious plan was prepared to modernise the existing track and to increase the network by 33 per cent by the construction of 3,000 km (1,900 miles) of new standard-gauge track. Most of this programme was completed.

The communications network which the Yugoslavs took over from the monarchy was naturally orientated according to the needs of the Habsburg economy. Slovenia's roads and railways were linked to Austria. The backbone of the system was the Südbahn, built between 1846 and 1857, to connect Vienna with Trieste via Maribor (Marburg) and Ljubljana (Laibach). This followed the line of an ancient routeway crossing the Julian karst via the Postojna Gate. Croatia's railway system gravitated towards Budapest, reflecting the historical links with Hungary. Communications across the Sava between the more developed areas of the Pannonian region and the underdeveloped interior were extremely poor. A narrow-gauge line, built for military purposes after the occupation of Bosnia–Hercegovina in 1878, linked Sarajevo with Brod on the main Zagreb–Belgrade line in 1884, and a connection to the coast at Metković was completed in 1890. In 1920 this was the only line from the interior lowlands to the Adriatic. Communications within the former Turkish territories of Kosovo and Macedonia were even more rudimentary. The only important line was the one which went south from Skopje to the Greek port of Salonika, forming part of the international route between Vienna and Istanbul.

Landlocked Serbia had been able to use Salonika with the consent of the Turks, but the Yugoslav state had a coastline of its own on the Adriatic. There was, however, no easy way of transporting goods from the main centres of population to the ports. The position was made more complicated by the Italian seizure of Fiume (Rijeka). At great cost a line was constructed to Sušak, a suburb of Fiume which remained outside Italian control. An arrangement with the Greeks made it possible for the Yugoslavs to enjoy the use of a free port at Salonika, but this facility was of limited value, as only the poorest and least developed areas lay within the effective hinterland of the Aegean port.

Before the Balkan wars, Serbia was a country of under three million inhabitants. As a result of the Balkan wars, another two million were added in Macedonia and Kosovo. These areas had not been assimilated into the economic or political system of Serbia before they were overrun by Bulgarians and Austro-Hungarian troops. In 1918 Serbia found itself at the centre of a state of twelve million inhabitants. This quadrupling of the market had a stimulating effect on the Serbian economy and provided a potential for expansion which the new regime was keen to exploit.

Thus, whilst Serbia's horizons had suddenly broadened, the inhabitants of the former Habsburg lands saw their opportunities contract. Serbia's interest was to build new industries behind protective tariff walls, while Croatia and Slovenia wanted to maintain the links which their already established industries had across the new international frontiers. Inevitably, Serbian interests prevailed, and a policy of economic autarky was followed. Between 1919 and 1922 the tariff rates current in pre-war Serbia were applied to the whole country, but after a financial crisis in 1922 tariffs were progressively raised. Average rates on the most important goods went up from 25 to 46 per cent between 1925 and 1931. The state intervened in many other ways to encourage the growth of industry. Direct state intervention was used in the opening up of copper, lead, zinc, silver and coal mines; mining concessions were granted to foreign firms; credits and subsidies were provided; foreign loans were raised under state guarantees. In retail distribution, the state maintained monopolies on tobacco and salt which went back to Turkish times. A state-owned trading company, Prizad, controlled two of the most important agricultural exports – grain and plums. A state-owned forestry company, Šipad, owned forests and wood-processing factories, and controlled 25 per cent of softwood exports.

The post-war economic boom which lasted until 1925 cannot be attributed directly to government initiative, although the drive to expand the railway network provided employment for thousands of unskilled workers and also stimulated the metalworking industries. In the aftermath of a world war there was an insatiable hunger for consumer goods. Hundreds of small firms sprang up to satisfy this demand. Textiles, footwear, food processing and furniture making were well established in Slovenia and Croatia. Government policy encouraged the development of these industries in areas such as Niš, Skopje and Sarajevo. Complaints that Slovene wages were being depressed by competition from low-wage areas in the south were ignored.

The exploitation of the rich reserves of non-ferrous metals, mainly in eastern Serbia and Kosovo, was left to foreign capital. In 1919 a French company acquired the Bor copper mine, and the British-owned Selection Trust worked the lead/zinc/silver mines of Kosovo. The lead and zinc were concentrated at a plant owned by Anglo-American Metals, and were then sent to Belgium via the Yugoslav free zone at Salonika. An international aluminium cartel allocated the bauxite mines of Dalmatia and Bosnia to a German concern, and Yugoslavia was prevented from manufacturing aluminium from its own raw materials. In addition to this direct use of foreign-owned capital, the government borrowed to finance the development of the railways, mortgaging the revenue from state monopolies to secure the loans.

The chaotic state of political life seemed to have little effect on economic development. The boom years 1918–25 were followed by a period of slower growth during the next five years, but steady progress continued until the effects of the world slump hit Yugoslavia in the early 1930s. There were, however, many financial scandals involving politicians. The tightly knit clique of Belgrade financiers and businessmen known as the *čaršija* had close connections with the political establishment and were able to manipulate politicians in order to further their own interests. The role of the state in economic life also provided opportunities for nepotism and corruption. The involvement of Pašić's son in a corruption scandal in 1926 was responsible for the prime minister's resignation.

Agriculture

Although progress was made in the development of industries, and although the proportion of the population dependent on agriculture declined from 78.9 per cent in 1921 to 75 per cent in 1941, the number of peasant farmers and their families actually increased by 28 per cent. The high birth rate in the rural areas, and especially in the poorest regions of the south, meant that rural overpopulation became more acute year by year. Rural population increased more slowly in the richer farming areas of Vojvodina and Croatia–Slavonia than in the poorer regions of Kosovo, Dalmatia, Bosnia and Macedonia.

Land reform

One of the first acts of the new regime in 1918 was to promise land reform. Even before the passing of the Vidovdan constitution the provisional government introduced decrees abolishing any vestiges of feudalism and promising, in the words of a royal Manifesto to the People issued in January 1919, that 'every Serb, Croat and Slovene should be the full owner of his land. In our free state there can and will be only free landowners.' The realisation of the slogan 'the land to those who till it' was a slow and often painful process. The legislative framework was not completed over the whole country until 1933 and the administrative provisions not until 1940.

Serbian land reform had been carried out before the First World War, and in 1918 Serbia proper was a land of small peasant proprietors. Ninety-five per cent of the area was occupied by farms of under 20 ha (50 acres).

Elsewhere the position varied considerably from place to place. In parts of Slovenia, Croatia and Vojvodina there were large estates owned by Volksdeutsche, Austrian and Hungarian landlords. In Kosovo and Macedonia there were the surviving remains of Turkish feudalism; in Bosnia there were still Muslim landlords owning large areas of land farmed by Christian peasants; and in Dalmatia the *colonate* system, which had been handed down from Roman times, reduced some peasants to a state of serfdom.

Interim decrees, issued in 1919, and later confirmed by legislation, dispossessed without compensation the ex-enemy Austrian, Hungarian and Turkish owners and redistributed the land to peasant proprietors. Priority was given to veterans and their families and to those who could show that they had worked for 'the liberation and unification of the Serbs, Croats and Slovenes'. The parcelling out of the land amongst 1.75 million peasant owners and their 2.8 million dependants may have been socially desirable, but it had adverse economic effects. In 1931 the average size of holding was under 6 ha (15 acres). Average yields of wheat between 1920 and 1924 were 11.1 quintals per hectare, compared with a pre-war average of 13 quintals. There was some recovery during the 1930s, but on the eve of the Second World War Yugoslavia was one of the poorest agrarian countries in Europe. Too many people tried to squeeze a living from underequipped, inefficiently farmed parcels of land. Measured by the standards of western Europe, there was a surplus population of 44.4 per cent engaged in agriculture. This average figure – obviously no more than an intelligent estimate – concealed enormous regional variations. Jozo Tomasevich has calculated that in Dalmatia the surplus was over 68 per cent, whereas in Vojvodina it was as low as 2.4 per cent.

Problems of the peasantry

The areas in which there was an export surplus of agricultural produce were mainly in the old Austro-Hungarian provinces covering Slovenia, Slavonia and Vojvodina. Here more than a quarter of the land was farmed in units of more than 20 ha (50 acres), and there were well-organised cooperatives for marketing produce and for supplying seed, breeding stock and implements. Some of the cooperatives were founded in pre-war times, but there were also many new ones established in the inter-war period. Gospodarska Sloga, a movement founded in 1935 by the Croat Peasant Party, had centres in 5,000 villages and did much to promote rural self-help. One of the greatest burdens which the peasants had to bear was that of indebtedness to unscrupulous money lenders. Most of the usurers were local shopkeepers, owners of rural industries such as corn and saw mills, and rich farmers (*kulaks*) who operated within the local economy. Others were city-dwelling parasites who descended on the villages like locusts. The poorest peasants were the easiest victims, as their holdings were too small to supply the basic necessities of life for the families who lived on them. They even had to borrow to buy food. This was often in the form of credit at the local shop, which was repaid in kind at harvest time, but at rates of exchange fixed by the shopkeepers. Interest charges of between 100 and 200 per cent per annum were not uncommon. In Bosnia, even commercial banks charged 50 per cent. The State Mortgage Bank was originally established to grant credits for the purchase of property and was intended to serve the need of both urban and rural dwellers. Although it did assist some of the more credit-worthy peasants to buy their farms, it could do little for the very poorest classes. Its funds were later diverted to finance general government expenditure. The Chartered (also known as Privileged) Agricultural Bank channelled most of its loans through the rural cooperatives, and rates of interest were usually kept at around 10 per cent. In Slovenia well-established cooperatives provided credits to farmers at single-figure rates of interest.

Agriculture in the national economy

Agricultural and forest products accounted for most of Yugoslavia's exports. Maize, wheat, tobacco and hemp were the chief export crops. Pigs and pigmeat and eggs were the chief livestock products exported. In the immediate post-war period there was an export market for foodstuffs throughout Europe, and, under the stimulus of an almost unlimited demand, farming soon recovered from the devastation and disruption of the war. The market-orientated producers of the northern lowlands were the most prosperous, whilst in the southern areas subsistence farming was the rule. There were exceptions, however. Cotton and tobacco were grown in Macedonia for export via Salonika and Kavalla on the Aegean, and in Dalmatia the products of the vineyards and olive groves were exported.

Following the great depression, there was a slight decline in the proportion of farm produce which was exported, and the contribution of agriculture to the national income fell from 45 per cent in 1923–5 to 42.9 per cent in 1938.

Foreign economic relations

Although the government's economic philosophy was, from the outset, based on a policy of autarky which had been inherited from pre-war Serbia, this did not mean that the country could escape from the necessity to involve foreign assistance. There was a great shortage of capital, skilled labour and technical knowledge. Much of this could only be obtained from abroad in the form of private capital, foreign state loans and the licensing of foreign firms to exploit the raw materials which Yugoslavia possessed. In the 1920s France, Britain and the USA were the chief suppliers of capital, but during the 1930s Germany's share increased at the expense of its former enemies, and on the outbreak of the Second World War Germany was the paramount foreign influence on the Yugoslav economy. Germany became Yugoslavia's principal trading partner in 1935, and retained this position until the outbreak of war. The *Anschlüss* of 1938 brought Austria into the German economic system, and the following year Czechoslovakia, another of Yugoslavia's major trading partners, came under German control. By this time the German stranglehold was complete. Trade with Germany accounted for 53 per cent of exports and 65 per cent of imports and, when trade with Germany's ally, Italy, was added, the figures were 67.8 per cent for exports and 70.3 per cent for imports. Germany's domination of the Yugoslav market was helped by international cartel agreements, which allocated to German industry a large share in the exploitation of Yugoslav raw materials and semi-finished products. Forty per cent of Germany's aluminium was produced from Yugoslav bauxite, and the German economy was heavily dependent on supplies of antimony, chrome, limestone and cement from Yugoslavia. The central European steel cartel (ZEG), which was formed in 1925, came under German control in 1938. The share of Yugoslav rolled steel products allocated under this agreement to Austria and Czechoslovakia accrued to Germany. In 1938 Reichsminister Funk drew up a trade agreement which the Yugoslavs were in no position to refuse. It provided that Germany would buy all Yugoslavia's exports of food and raw materials and in return would supply all the manufactured goods which Yugoslavia wished to buy.

Although Britain, France and the USA were still the major foreign investors in Yugoslav industry, especially in mining, transport and power supplies, their share of Yugoslav trade declined as Germany's influence increased.

The political consequences of these economic developments were reflected in the shift of Yugoslavia's position in relation to the Little Entente and the Rome–Berlin Axis.

8

The kingdom of Yugoslavia

The royal dictatorship

The apparent ease with which Alexander was able to overthrow the constitution can be attributed to a number of factors. The democratic experiment had obviously failed. The appalling scene of uproar in the Skupština, culminating in the murder of the Croat deputies, reflected the fact that the divisions within society were too deep to be resolved by the normal processes of parliamentary democracy. Even Dr Maček, Radić's successor, seemed to want the king to take power – 'There is no longer a constitution, but only the King and the people.'

Once he had decided to act, the king knew that he could rely on the army, the majority of whose senior officers were Serbs who were loyal to Alexander as head of the Karadjordjević dynasty rather than as king of the Serb, Croat and Slovene state. He invited General Petar Živković, commander of the Royal Guard and a close friend, to lead the new government. Živković chose a cabinet which included some former politicians, mainly Serbian, and a number of non-political specialists. The new regime immediately acted against the main opposition groups. Príbičević was arrested without trial in May and held in detention until August 1931, when the intervention of his friend President T. G. Masaryk secured his release and a safe passage to exile in Czechoslovakia. Some of the more extreme Croat nationalists fled abroad, including Ante Pavelić, the leader of the Ustaša. He was given asylum in Italy, where, under Mussolini's protection, he was able to plan acts of terrorism against the Yugoslav regime which culminated in the assassination of the king in 1934.

In the summer of 1929 thousands of alleged communists, Croat separatists and foreign spies were thrown into prison. The leadership of the Young Communist League (SKOJ) was rounded up after the police arrested a member who was distributing an illegal leaflet attacking the king. Under torture the prisoner divulged the names of the SKOJ committee for Serbia, and this led to the arrest and trial of the secretary, Alexander Ranković. In

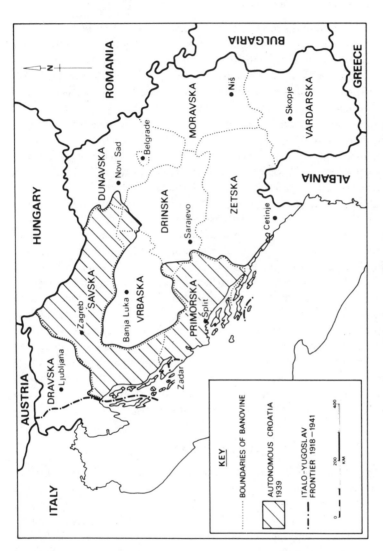

Map 3. The administrative boundaries of the kingdom of Yugoslavia, 1929–41.

the next few months many other communists, who later became leading members of the post-war regime, were brought before the Court for the Protection of the State and sentenced to terms of imprisonment. They included the Slovene leader, Edvard Kardelj, who was to become Tito's close friend and adviser. Tito himself and Moša Pijade, one of the founders of the Yugoslav Communist Party, were already in prison. Within the next few years almost every important party leader spent some time in prison, and many were tortured and ill treated by the police and prison guards.

In 1930 over twenty Croat leaders, including Dr Maček, were arrested on charges of inciting Croats to acts of terror. Maček himself was acquitted, but several others received prison sentences.

Alexander genuinely wanted Yugoslav unity, but he failed to see that this could not be imposed arbitrarily from above. It had to grow organically from below as people came to realise that the common interests which had brought them together in 1918 were more important than the historic differences which separated them. Above all, he did not realise that a Serbian-dominated government in Belgrade could not order the Croats, the Slovenes and the Muslims to forget their history and submerge their separate identities in a new kind of national unity under Serbian guidance. He could decree that the country's name should be changed to the kingdom of Yugoslavia; he could dissolve the Slovene and Croatian sporting and cultural clubs, the Sokols, and order young people to undergo compulsory physical education under a new, Serbian-led Sokol organisation; he could even create a new political party, the Yugoslav National Party; but he could not win the hearts of the non-Serbs by these measures.

The 1931 constitution

In 1931 Alexander introduced a new constitution, which did little more than provide a fig leaf of legitimacy to cover the crude reality of the royal dictatorship.

It provided for a National Assembly, elected for a four-year term by universal male suffrage, but not by secret ballot, and a Senate, half of whose members were to be appointed by the king and half by the local government assemblies. A new structure of local government was introduced. In an attempt to reduce separatist sentiments which were associated with the old historic provinces, the new units, known as *banovine*, were given geographical names, all but one taken from the rivers which flowed through them. The exception was Dalmatia, which became Primorska (the Littoral) Banovina. Belgrade and its environs became a prefecture, directly administered by the ministry of the interior. The only one of the nine *banovine* which corresponded to a national unit was Dravska Banovina, . which covered the Slovene homeland. Croatia was divided between Savska and Primorska, and Serbia among Dunavska, Moravska, Vardarska and the Belgrade prefecture. Macedonia was joined to southern Serbia to form Vardarska; Montenegro shared Zetska with Kosovo and parts of Bosnia and Hercegovina. The rest of Bosnia was split between Drinska and Vrbaska.

The governor, or ban, was directly responsible to the government in Belgrade for the administration of his *banovina*, and the *sreski načelniki*, who ran the subordinate *srezovi*, were under the direction of the ban. The lowest unit, the *opština* (commune), had an elected council, but it was responsible either to the ban or in some cases directly to the central government for its conduct. All the lines of power led back to Belgrade, and there the king exercised ultimate control.

An attempt was made to form a national political organisation which would appeal to supporters of the old parties, which had been banned in 1929. It was at first called the Yugoslav Peasant Radical Democratic Party but this grotesque and clumsy title was later changed to that of the Yugoslav National Party. Whatever its title, it was in reality the instrument of the Serbian ruling groups, headed by the king. It came as no surprise that in the first elections held under the new constitution, in November 1931, the government received an overwhelming majority. The electoral law required every party to show that it had registered supporters in every electoral district, and only parties presenting nation-wide lists were allowed to enter the election. The party with the largest number of votes was entitled to two-thirds of the seats. In fact, only one list was presented, as only the government could fulfil the conditions of the electoral law. There was a wholesale boycott of the elections in Croatia and Slovenia and a poll of under 65 per cent was recorded.

In 1932 Živković stood down in favour of a former Democrat, Vojislav Marinković, who had been foreign minister under Davidović in 1924 and Živković in 1930–1. The choice of an experienced politician from Vidovdan days was intended to signal the beginning of a process which would eventually lead to a more democratic regime. These hopes were dashed when Marinković resigned in June 1932, ostensibly on grounds of ill health, but in fact because he had incurred the mistrust of the more determined Serbian nationalists by his tentative proposals for liberalisation. He was replaced by Dr Milan Srškić, a hard-line Serb from Bosnia. An attempt to form a united opposition resulted in the issuing of a document known as the Zagreb Manifesto, in which the leaders of the Croats, Slovenes, Muslims and even some dissident Serbs called for democratisation of the regime and the granting of regional autonomy. The government's reaction was to order the internment of Maček, Korošec and Spaho. Maček was sentenced to three years in prison at a trial in Zagreb in April 1933 for criticising the regime when speaking to foreign journalists. The isolation of the government from large numbers of its citizens, even within Serbia, became increasingly apparent. Signs of dissent were met by severe repression. Political trials, arbitrary arrests and even the hiring of thugs to beat up its opponents were the weapons used by the government to enforce 'law and order'. Suspected communists in the army were sentenced to life imprisonment and even death. Terrorists from the far right, encouraged by the Italians, crossed from the Italian-held enclave of Zara, to add to the confusion. In 1933 a plot to murder the king was uncovered, and at the trial of the conspirators evidence was produced implicating Ustaša extremists living in Italy. The situation was made worse by the economic distress caused when the effects of the world depression began to strike Yugoslavia.

In October 1934 Alexander, who had always played an active part in foreign policy, set out on an official visit to France, where he hoped to enlist the support of the French in Yugoslavia's resistance to the threats from Italy, Hungary and Bulgaria. He never reached Paris. He had hardly set foot on French soil when a Bulgarian assassin, hired by the Ustaša leader, Pavelić, murdered both Alexander and the French foreign minister, Louis Barthou, who had received him on his arrival at Marseilles.

There was genuine grief in Yugoslavia when the news of the king's death was received. Although many of his opponents detested his methods, they recognised his sincerity, and above all they feared that his removal might cause an uncontrolled disintegration of the state which could only be to the advantage of Yugoslavia's enemies. In particular, the Slovenes and Croats feared Italy and had therefore supported Alexander's foreign policy, based on the Little Entente.

The king had provided for the continuity of the monarchist system in the event of his death while his heir, Peter, was still too young to take up the reins of power. In Yugoslavia at that time, kings attained their majority at the age of eighteen. Alexander's son was only eleven years old and was attending a private school in England. Sir Cecil Parrott, his tutor, records how he broke the news to the young boy and returned with him to Belgrade. As the car taking them from Peter's school in Surrey to the Yugoslav legation entered the suburbs of London, Parrott saw placards announcing the news of the king's murder. Until then the boy had merely been told that Alexander had suffered an accident in a car, but the tutor decided to tell the full story. Peter took the news calmly. There was little affection between the stern father and the immature boy, who did not realise the significance of what had happened.

The regency of Prince Paul

In his political testament Alexander nominated three regents to take his place until his son Peter came of age in September 1941. The first was his cousin, Prince Paul, who became known as the prince regent. The other two were Professor Radenko Stanković, a Serb who had served for a time as minister of education in 1932, and Ivan Perović, also a Serb, who had been ban of Primorska. Paul heartily disliked Stanković, and had never before met Perović. In fact, neither of the two co-regents played any significant role in the country's affairs. Paul reluctantly forced himself to assume the leading role, although he hated politics and later described his seven years in office as 'a dog's life'. He had two main objectives: in foreign policy to defend Yugoslavia's independence against the pressures of the Italians and Germans and their Hungarian and Bulgarian allies; in home affairs to liberalise the regime and to bring about a reconciliation between Serbs and Croats. The two objectives were linked, as the festering wound of Croat separatism provided an opportunity for the fascist regimes to undermine the Yugoslav kingdom by encouraging Croat extremists. A further opportunity for disruption existed in Macedonia, where Bulgarian ambitions to recover the San Stefano boundaries were often promoted by terrorist methods. As if to underline these twin dangers to the integrity of the state, it was discovered that the king's assassination had been plotted by the Croat extremist Pavelić and by Mihajlov, the Bulgarian head of IMRO (Internal Macedonian Revolutionary Organisation). The assassin had been trained in a Hungarian school for terrorists, and the Italian government, which had given a safe refuge to Pavelić and other Croat terrorists, was privy to the plot. The Italian ambassador in Paris was reported as saying to a French friend that assistance to Croat terrorists was one 'modality of the subterranean war which Italy was carrying on against Yugoslavia'.

Yugoslavia's attempt to persuade the League of Nations to condemn both Italy and Hungary for their complicity in the assassination was watered down, under pressure from Eden and Laval. The case against Italy was dropped altogether. Mussolini was too powerful to be called to account for his crime, and Hungary escaped with a rebuke.

When Paul became prince regent the government was headed by Nikola Uzunović, whose cabinet consisted almost entirely of Serbs. Shortly after the passing of the League of Nations resolution in December, the Uzunović government fell and the regents sent for Bogoljub Jevtić, the foreign minister who had presented the Yugoslav case in Geneva, to form a more broadly based government. Jevtić, however, failed to reconcile the conflicting interests of the hard-line Serbian hegemonists and the more liberal elements, who wanted a relaxation of the rigid centralism which had characterised the previous administration. Jevtić made a few conciliatory gestures to liberal sentiment, notably by releasing Maček and Professor Dragoljub Jovanović, the Serbian Agrarian Party leader, both of whom had been imprisoned during Alexander's reign. Jevtić decided to call for a general election, which was held in May 1935. Maček led an opposition bloc, which had the support of the Serbian Agrarians, the Democrats and the Muslims, as well as the Croat Peasants. Despite police repression, vote rigging and a ban on opposition meetings, the government was able to muster only 62 per cent of the votes cast. Because of the peculiarities of the electoral system the opposition's share of almost 40 per cent entitled them to only 67 seats (or 17 per cent of the 373 seats in the Skupština). The opposition refused to take their seats and shortly afterwards several ministers resigned, including the three Croat members of the cabinet as well as the minister of war, General Živković, and the minister of finance, Milan Stojadinović. In June, Stojadinović formed a new government which included the veteran Slovene Populist leader, Monsignor Korošec, and the leader of the Bosnian Muslims, Mehmed Spaho. Živković returned as minister of war, but most other members of the cabinet were either little-known Serbian politicians or non-political Croatian officials. The Croat opposition, under Maček, gave Stojadinović's administration a cautious welcome, and during the first few months of its life it appeared to be moving in the direction of conciliation and national unity. The premier was prepared to take up the issue of a concordat with the Vatican, which Alexander had suggested shortly before his death, although he incurred the anger of the more extreme Serbian nationalists. Their opposition appears to have been somewhat perverse, as all that Stojadinović was suggesting was an arrangement based on the concordat which had existed between the pre-war Serbian kingdom and the Vatican. Although Stojadinović signed the concordat on behalf of the Yugoslav government, its ratification was refused in 1937 by the Skupština after the Serbian Orthodox Church had threatened to excommunicate any Serb who voted for it.

The gesture proved abortive, but the fact that Stojadinović was prepared to make it was seen as a conciliatory move by the Croats. An equally encouraging sign was the amnesty which was granted to thousands of political prisoners, many of them Croats.

Stojadinović was one of the few Serbian politicians with a European reputation. He had studied economics in France, Germany and England, and was well known in European (especially British) banking and business circles. Sir Nevile Henderson, the British ambassador in Belgrade, was one of his enthusiastic supporters. He also had a good reputation in Serbian politics. As a comparatively young man employed as an official in the ministry of finance during the First World War, he had escaped to Corfu to join the government in exile there, reputedly bringing with him as much of the contents of the Treasury as he could carry in a small boat. He had served as minister of finance in three governments and had been a prominent figure in the Belgrade Stock Exchange.

When he first came to office he was thought to be a liberal. He convinced the prince regent that he genuinely believed in a parliamentary system on western lines and that he could effect a reconciliation with the Croats. His performance in office, however, fell far short of his promises. One of his first acts was to form a new government party, the Yugoslav Radical Union (Jugoslavenska Radjkalna Zajednica, or JRZ), which brought together the Serbian Radicals (apart from those who supported the ousted Jevtić), the Slovenes and the Muslims. It was a marriage of convenience, composed of office holders within his government, and dependent upon government patronage. Before it was a year old, it had forfeited the support of the majority of the old Serbian Radicals, and its ability to survive depended upon the government supporters whose jobs depended upon Stojadinović. It never developed any deep roots in the country at large. Nevertheless, Stojadinović survived as prime minister until February 1939, the longest continuous terms of office enjoyed by any Yugoslav premier since the passing of the Vidovdan constitution in 1921.

Stojadinović's foreign policy

The factors which determine the direction of a country's foreign policy depend to a large extent on forces outside the control of the government. This is particularly the case with the smaller countries like Yugoslavia, whose very existence as a nation state depended at this time on decisions taken by the major powers. As became evident in 1941, Yugoslavia was militarily weak and depended on foreign countries for the supply of all its major weaponry. The warship which took King Alexander to Marseilles in 1934, the destroyer *Dubrovnik*, was built in Britain. The planes which conveyed the king and his ministers from Nikšić to Athens in April 1941 were German Dorniers and Italian Savoia Marchettis. The economy was also heavily dependent upon foreigners, despite the policy of autarky which was followed in so far as this was possible. During the 1930s Germany became the predominant trading partner. By 1939 about 55 per cent of foreign trade was with Germany and a further 15 per cent with Italy.

Yugoslavia owed much to the Allied powers. There was a strong pro-French sentiment in Serbia, and Prince Paul's known pro-British feelings were shared by many of his subjects. Alexander's foreign policy had been based on the Little Entente. During the 1930s the Little Entente became less and less credible as a safeguard for the security of the states which belonged to it – Czechoslovakia, Yugoslavia and Romania. Its initial purpose was to prevent a Habsburg restoration and to restrain Hungary from violating the frontiers set by the treaty of Trianon, but it also envisaged economic and military cooperation to strengthen the ability of its members to resist the pressure of the 'revisionist' powers – Italy, Germany, Hungary and Bulgaria — who were working for the overthrow of the Versailles settlement. The *Anschlüss* of March 1938, followed by the Munich settlement and the dismemberment of Czechoslovakia during the next twelve months, effectively killed the Little Entente, and its two surviving members, Yugoslavia and Romania, formally buried it in February 1939. It had always been hoped that France would stand by the Little Entente in the event of a crisis. Alexander's last journey to Marseilles was in furtherance of this end. Daladier's role at Munich finally dispelled that illusion. When Stojadinović came to office in June 1935 it was obvious that Yugoslavia's security, particularly against the Italian threat, required a different arrangement. Italian reaction to the German-inspired murder of the Austrian chancellor, Dollfuss, in July 1934 indicated that there was as yet no accord between the dictators. Stojadinović, who was accused of being pro-German, began to look to Germany as a counterweight to Italy. Yugoslavia's support of the League of Nations' policy of sanctions against Italy after the invasion of Abyssinia in October 1935 gave Germany an opportunity to increase its economic penetration of Yugoslavia, as Italy had previously been a major trading partner.

It was possible to entertain the idea of playing Germany off against Italy until Italy joined the Anti-Comintern (Tripartite Pact) with Germany and Japan in November 1937. In the following spring, Mussolini accepted German occupation of Austria. The behaviour of Britain and France at

Munich in September 1938, when they agreed with Mussolini that Hitler should be allowed to detach the Sudetenland from Czechoslovakia, convinced many Yugoslavs that there was no hope of Anglo-French support. If Neville Chamberlain and many others in Britain could dismiss Czechoslovakia as 'a faraway country' and the Czechs and Slovaks as 'people of whom we know nothing', what help could Yugoslavia expect?

In 1937 Stojadinović, who, in addition to the premiership, retained the post of foreign minister, embarked on a round of diplomatic visits, taking in London, Paris and Rome. In early 1938 he went to Berlin, where he met Goering and Hitler. In Paris he made it plain to the French that Yugoslavia no longer placed any confidence in French assurances of support and he reaffirmed his rejection of a mutual assistance pact, which he regarded as a proposal to link Yugoslavia to the 'Paris–Moscow' bloc. In London he talked with Chamberlain and Eden, who nodded approval at his intention to improve relations with Italy. Despite the fact that Eden was within two months of resigning, ostensibly over Chamberlain's attitude towards Italy, the policy of Anglo-Italian friendship, which had been reaffirmed in the Anglo-Italian (Gentlemen's Agreement) Pact of January 1937, provided Stojadinović with a model for a Yugoslav–Italian pact. In Rome he was cordially received by Mussolini and his foreign secretary, Ciano. Ciano had a personal liking for Stojadinović, whom he described after meeting him in Belgrade in March 1937 as 'a fascist – if he is not one by open declaration, he is certainly one by virtue of his conception of authority, of the state and of life'. On that occasion the two 'fascists' had signed a treaty of friendship between Italy and Yugoslavia. In December the Yugoslav leader was greatly impressed by the Duce. He gave assurances that Yugoslavia would not take any further steps towards closer relations with Czechoslovakia or France and that an attempt would be made to improve relations with Italy's ally, Hungary. He had already signed a Pact of Eternal Friendship with the Bulgarians in March 1937, and a matching agreement with Hungary would complete Yugoslavia's shift from the Little Entente to the 'revisionist' side. However, the Czechoslovak crisis of 1938 and the activities of Hungarian irredentists prevented this. The pact with Hungary was signed in December 1940 by Stojadinović's successor. For good measure, he expressed approval of Italy's decision to leave the League of Nations and also told the Duce that he intended to organise Yugoslav youth on the lines of Mussolini's fascist youth movement. On his return to Yugoslavia, he introduced the fascist (Roman) salute and had himself styled Vodja (Leader). His supporters adopted a green-shirt uniform. When taxed by Prince Paul concerning these manifestations of dictatorship, he pretended that the title Vodja applied only to his position in the JRZ Party and that the salute was quite different from Mussolini's Roman Salute. Yet he had assured Mussolini of his intention to develop Yugoslavia on the basis of a one-party dictatorship.

His visit to Berlin in January 1938 was equally successful from the host's point of view. Stojadinović had a knack of telling people what he thought they wanted to hear, but in dealing with the dictators he really meant most of it. He was able to assure Hitler that Yugoslavia would no longer look at the world through 'French eyeglasses', and that he regarded the *Anschlüss* as a domestic affair of Germany and Austria.

The fall of Stojadinović

Although the government had an impressive paper majority, it rested on an insecure base. It depended upon the tactical support of the Slovenes and the Muslims, who might at any time leave office if they felt it in their interests to do so. Support for Stojadinović was crumbling in Serbia, where his pro-German policy and his dictatorial inclinations alienated many of his erstwhile supporters. The concordat crisis of 1937 gave the opposition in Serbia an opportunity to discredit Stojadinović in the eyes of the Serbian peasantry. In reality, the bill which was approved by the Skupština on 23 July 1937 was little more than a tidying-up operation, intended to extend to the whole country the provisions of the pre-1914 concordat between Serbia and the Vatican. The campaign against it was really directed against the government's foreign policy and against Stojadinović himself. It was seen by some of the Serbian opposition parties as a step towards an alliance with Italy. The Orthodox Church excommunicted the delegates who had voted for it; Stojadinović expelled those members of this party who did not vote for it. Jevtić, the leader of the Serbian opposition, made as much political capital out of the affair as he could and did not scruple to arouse feelings of the most primitive Serbian nationalism. He conveniently forgot that it was his government which had negotiated the original terms of the concordat three years earlier.

The Croats, Slovenes and Muslims appear not to have been greatly concerned by the furore over the concordat, which they regarded as an internal Serbian problem. Despite his majority in the Skupština, Stojadinović realised that he could not be certain of the bill passing the Senate and he therefore withdrew it. The concordat crisis was a symptom of widespread dissatisfaction with the government which permeated all levels of society. Stojadinović had come to office promising that he would tackle the Croat problem. The prince regent had at first believed him, but by the summer of 1937 Paul realised that his premier had no serious intention of reaching an understanding with the Croats. In a conversation with Terence Shone, the British ambassador, he confided that he wanted to dismiss Stojadinović but dared not because there seemed to be no alternative and also because he was unsure of the loyalty of the army if he took this step. Instead he took the responsibility for negotiations with Maček away from the premier and charged Dragiša Cvetković, the able and popular minister of social policy and public health, with the task of negotiating a *sporazum* (understanding) with the Croats. Stojadinović, who remained in charge of foreign affairs, then set out on his European tour. Whilst the premier was enjoying the hospitality of Hitler and Mussolini and assuring them of his devotion to the ideals of fascism, Paul, Maček and Cvetković were working hard to create the conditions necessary for national unity. They feared that the country would fall apart under the growing pressure of the Axis unless the Serbs and Croats could find a basis for living and working together.

Stojadinović was a man of little sensibility or tact, an opportunist who lacked political principle. He was convinced that the Munich agreement of September 1938, which showed up the weakness of France and Britain and the strength of Germany and Italy, confirmed his view that Yugoslavia's interests lay in friendship with the dictators. He appeared completely unaware of the feelings of the majority of his people, both concerning his foreign policy and concerning his own popularity. He called a general election for 18 December 1938 and was confronted by a broad opposition coalition, headed by Maček, with the support of Independent Democrats, the Serbian Agrarians and the National Radicals. Although the government won the election, the result was a moral victory for the opposition. More than 650,000 Serbs voted for Maček's coalition, a hopeful sign for the prospects of the proposed *sporazum*. Despite the absence of a secret ballot, the widespread vote rigging and illegal government pressure, 41 per cent of the electorate voted for the opposition. In the revealing letter to the regent, Stojadinović blamed Monsignor Korošec, the elderly Slovene minister of the interior, for the government's poor showing. He was, apparently, too liberal and had even allowed state employees to vote as they liked, instead of ordering them to vote for the government! Korošec was forced to resign and was replaced by Milan Aćimović, head of the Belgrade police force. Before the election Paul had entrusted Aćimović with a confidential investigation into Stojadinović's fascist activities. This indicated Paul's naivety, for Aćimović and Stojadinović were political allies, and the police chief simply went to the premier and told him of the investigation. Aćimović later appeared as minister of the interior in the puppet regime of General Nedić which was set up under the German occupation of Serbia.

Realising that the loss of Slovene support would weaken the government, Stojadinović persuaded Korošec to become president of the Senate, thinking that it would occupy him in a relatively harmless office. However, the premier had overlooked the fact that, in the event of a ministerial crisis, the president of the Senate advised the crown on the choice of a new ministerial team. Such a crisis occurred in early February – probably contrived by Paul. It arose first from an understanding which Stojadinović reached with Ciano concerning the partitioning of Albania between Yugoslavia and Italy. This was not reported to Paul, who found out about it by a chance allusion made by Ciano when the regent received him prior to his return home to Italy. Stojadinović made his position worse by refusing to disown a Serbian nationalist minister who made a violently anti-Croat speech in the Skupština. Paul, who had already decided that the premier must go, consulted Korošec, who persuaded five ministers to submit a collective resignation. They were the two Slovenes Krek and Snoj, the two Muslims Spaho and Kulenović, and the Serb Cvetković. Paul then called on Cvetković to form a new government. The fall of Stojadinović took the country by surprise and was seen in Rome and Berlin as a setback to the Italo-German plans for bringing Yugoslavia into alliance with the Axis. Stojadinović was interned by Paul in 1940, as it was feared that he might be intriguing with the Axis powers againt the Cvetković government. On the eve of the German attack, one of Paul's last acts before his abdication was to agree to the deportation of the former prime minister. With the agreement of the British and Greek governments, Stojadinović was sent to Athens and thence to exile on the island of Mauritius.

The *sporazum*

Paul chose Cvetković because he felt that he was the one person most likely to win the confidence of the Croats and to bring the negotiations with Maček to a successful conclusion. To allay the doubts of the Axis powers he chose as foreign minister the ambassador to Germany, Alexander Cincar-Marković, who was thought of as being pro-German.

With Stojadinović out of office, progress towards an agreement was rapid. Paul, conscious of the worsening international situation, saw that the question of national unity must be given priority and urged Maček and Cvetković to make haste. Agreement was reached on 20 August and was endorsed by the Skupština on 26 August. A new government was formed under Cvetković. Maček became vice-premier, Cincar-Marković remained foreign minister, and representatives of the parties which had formed the anti-Stojadinović coalition were also included. Maček's close collaborator, Ivan Šubašić, became ban (governor) of the newly established autonomous Croatian province, which covered most of the historic units of Croatia–Slavonia and Dalmatia, plus some of the Croatian-speaking areas of Vojvodina, Srem and Bosnia. The Croatian Sabor meeting in Zagreb was allowed to raise revenue and to administer certain aspects of internal policy, such as agriculture, forestry, welfare, education and domestic commerce. Foreign affairs, foreign trade, defence and security were amongst the matters reserved to the central government in Belgrade.

9

Yugoslavia and the Second World War

Between the signing of the *sporazum* on 20 August and its endorsement by the Skupština on 26 August 1939, Molotov and Ribbentrop concluded the Soviet–German Treaty of Non-Aggression (the so-called Nazi–Soviet Pact). Less than a fortnight later, on 1 September, the German invasion of Poland began. Paul at first imagined that he could keep out of the war until a suitable opportunity presented itself for Yugoslavia to join the Allied side. He believed that he could persuade the British and French to land at Salonika, with or without Greek and Italian consent, and that an Allied base on the Aegean would safeguard Yugoslavia's security and ensure the economic support necessary to break the German stranglehold on its economy. These hopes were based on the assumption that the Allies would have command of the Mediterranean and that the Italian fleet would be either neutralised or destroyed. A French military mission actually visited Belgrade and secret talks were opened with a view to coordinating plans. Hitler's successes in Norway and France in the spring of 1940 and Italy's declaration of war in June put an end to these pipe dreams. Yugoslavia was completely isolated and surrounded on all sides except the south by Axis-occupied countries or by regimes sympathetic to the enemy. Albania was under Italian control and was soon to become a base for the invasion of Greece. Austria was under Nazi occupation. Hungary, Romania and Bulgaria were moving towards the Axis.

The Yugoslav government had a realistic appreciation of the dangerous situation in which the country was placed. In June 1940 diplomatic relations with USSR were established, and on the eve of the German attack in April 1941 a Soviet–Yugoslav Treaty of Friendship and Non-Aggression was signed. Previous royal governments had refused to recognise the Soviet Union, and until 1939 they had even permitted an 'Imperial Russian Embassy' in Belgrade. Paul was reluctant to recognise the Soviet regime and urged his ministers to proceed with deliberate caution. As the Axis noose tightened he agreed to the opening of diplomatic relations and talks on trade. In return, the Soviet government made a half promise that it would oppose Italian designs on the Balkans. Like so many of the actions of the Yugoslavs during this period, the move came too late to be of any use. Paul hoped that the opening up of relations with the Soviets would signal a warning to the Axis that Yugoslavia would not be left completely alone if Italy moved into the Balkans. The agreement to exchange ambassadors was signed on 10 June, less than a week after the British withdrawal from Dunkirk and the collapse of the western front. On 6 April 1941, the day on which the Treaty of Friendship was signed, the German attack on Yugoslavia began. The ink was hardly dry on the document when Vyshinski told the Yugoslav ambassador in Moscow that the Soviet Union considered that Yugoslavia had ceased to exist. Paul was then in Greece, on the first stage of his journey into wartime exile in Kenya. In August he wrote from Kenya to his brother-in-law, the Duke of Kent, that people 'do not understand how much I hated my job . . . and that the last thing I wish is to have anything to do with Yugoslav politics! I was longing for Peter's majority to release me from a dog's existence, and I was at the end of my physical strength when the March events took place. I did my best for my country, according to my lights during nearly seven years, among the most eventful and difficult in the history of the world'.

He then describes how he tried 'to walk hand-in-hand' with Britain. He was forced to meet Hitler and to agree to Yugoslavia's adherence to the Tripartite Pact, as the Croats and Slovenes, as well as the war minister and the chief of the general staff, insisted on the Pact being signed. Paul believed that the short, disastrous campaign that followed the *coup d'état* proved that the country was unable to resist and that a large part of it did not desire to fight.

Peter was brought reluctantly to the throne by the *coup d'état* of 26/27 March, when the regency was overthrown by a group of air force officers led by Brigadier-General Bora Mirković and General Dušan Simović. There is some evidence that the British Special Operations Executive (SOE) had a hand in the planning of the *coup*. Hugh Dalton, the minister responsible for SOE, was anxious to claim credit, as he had been under pressure from Churchill to show results in the Balkans. There were other British intelligence units at work in Yugoslavia, and there has been some suggestion that the British air attaché in Belgrade also played a part. Prince Paul certainly blamed the British for his overthrow, but the evidence is not wholly convincing.

The versions which are accepted in Yugoslavia are coloured by the political interests of those who believe them. The communists, for example, claimed responsibility for organising the demonstration which occurred in Belgrade and in other cities when the news broke that Premier Dragiša Cvetković and his foreign minister, Alexander Cincar-Marković, had signed the Tripartite Pact in Vienna on 25 March. Tito's biographer, Vladimir Dedijer, wrote, 'The Central Committee of the Communist Party ... issued *on that very day* a proclamation, denouncing the betrayal in Vienna, while on the same evening powerful demonstrations broke out in Belgrade, Split, Kragujevac and several other places ... The wave of popular indignation swept the country with tremendous vigour.'

Tito, in his report to the Fifth Congress of the CPY in 1948, claimed that the party controlled the situation and was responsible for the demonstrations which brought about the overthrow of the government. The committee also claimed authorship of the slogans shouted by the demonstrators: 'Bolje rat nego pakt!' (Better war than pact) and 'Bolje grob nego rob! (Better the grave than slavery).

On 2 March the regents abdicated in favour of the frightened and ill-prepared Peter, who, despite the fact that he was six months short of his eighteenth birthday, was declared to be of age. He first learned of the *coup* when he heard a broadcast by a student, pretending to be the king, announcing that he had assumed full royal powers, had dismissed the regents, and had asked Simović to form a government. Paul had just left for Slovenia, and Peter refused to make any move until Paul returned. He had lunch with Paul's wife, Princess Olga. In her diary she wrote that the king 'was persuaded to drive round the various regiments, with Simović, to be seen. Paul returned at 7.30, and went straight to the War Ministry with the two other Regents, to resign. We were told that it was best all should leave for Greece ... poor little Peter tried to be brave and sensible, it was heartrending to leave him alone. As we parted he cried, and begged to go with us – the British radio broadcast several times we had fled to Germany'. Peter followed his uncle into exile less than a month later, but whereas Paul was placed under house arrest in Kenya, Peter eventually settled in London as head of the royal government in exile.

The Simović government was faced with an impossible situation. It was apparent that a popular, anti-Pact movement existed in Serbia, but it was not certain that the Croats, the Slovenes and the Bosnian Muslims were wholeheartedly committed to the same cause. Several Croats accepted the invitation to join the new government, including Dr Juraj Šutej, who had been finance minister in the Cvetković government. Maček hesitated for several days. He was under pressure from the Germans not to join, and to lie low in Croatia until the time came for him to head an independent

Croatia under German protection. Eventually, however, he acceded to Simović's request and joined the cabinet as vice-premier on 4 April, the same post which he had held under Cvetković. His joint vice-premier was the eminent Serbian historian Dr Slobodan Jovanović. The government fled to Užice, where Maček took the chair at a meeting at which a state of emergency was declared. Maček resigned and returned to Croatia. The government retreated first to Pale, near Sarajevo, then to Nikšić in Montenegro. The Germans and their Bulgarian, Hungarian and Roma-nian allies advanced into Croatia, Vojvodina and Macedonia. The Italians entered Slovenia and Dalmatia. The German–Bulgarian thrust took in the Greek as well as the Yugoslav parts of Macedonia. Skopje and Salonika were easily taken. Zagreb fell on 11 April, and the so-called Independent State of Croatia, under the Ustaša leader, Ante Pavelić, was proclaimed. Many Croat units surrendered without a struggle. A few even turned on the Serbs. To the Croats, the *coup d'état* of 27 March was a purely Serbian affair and they felt no allegiance to the Simović government. The frail structure of the *sporazum* collapsed at its first test and the occupying forces exploited the Serb–Croat division as they set about the task of dismember-ing the Yugoslav state.

Belgrade fell on 12 April, and two days later the king and the surviving members of his government were flown to Athens. There was no one left with the authority to sign the act of unconditional surrender which the Germans demanded. By a strange irony of history, the former foreign minister, Cincar-Marković, was tracked down to Pale, where he was hiding after escaping from the place of internment to which he had been consigned by the Simović government. He and General Radivoje Janković were taken to Belgrade in a German plane, where they signed the armistice agreement on 17 April. Royal Yugoslavia had ceased to exist, although its shadow lived on in exile in London.

Occupation, partition, resistance and revolution

Hitler had already decided on the destruction of the Yugoslav state and had promised pieces of territory to his allies. He had also settled on the creation of the Independent State of Croatia (Nezavisna Država Hrvatska, or NDH), although the final details were not worked out until after the military occupation was complete.

The largest unit was the NDH, with an area of over 98,000 sq km (37,840 sq miles) and a population of 6.3 million, about one-third of whom were Serbs and a further 750,000 Muslims. Within its borders were included most of the Croatian province established by the *sporazum* and most of historic Bosnia–Hercegovina. There were some former Croatian areas which were excluded, however. These included parts of central Dalmatia occupied by the Italians and the Magyar-speaking area of Medjumurje, which was annexed to Hungary; a number of Adriatic islands; and a corridor between Slovenia and the port of Rijeka (Fiume), which went to Italy. Italy also acquired half of Slovenia, including the city of Ljubljana (Lubiama), and the Kotor region of Montenegro. The rest of Slovenia (except for Prekomurje, which went to Hungary) came under German administration, the intention being to integrate these areas into the Reichsgäu Kärnten and Steiermark in neighbouring Austria, although this purpose was never fully realised. Vojvodina was divided between Hungary and Romania; Montenegro was occupied by Italy; and Kosovo and western Macedonia were attached to the Greater Albania which Italy created. The rest of Macedonia and part of south Serbia were taken by Bulgaria. What remained of Serbia – roughly the old kingdom before the gains of the Balkan wars – came under direct German military occupation, though in August 1941 a civilian administration was allowed to function, led by General Milan Nedić, who had served as war minister under both Stojadinović and Cvetković.

Superimposed on this pattern of administrative partition, the NDH was further divided into German and Italian spheres of influence, the dividing line being drawn so as to leave Zagreb, Jajce and Sarajevo inside the German zone. This division created some problems, both political and military, for the Axis partners. The German generals would have preferred an outright military occupation, but Ribbentrop and Hitler saw some advantage in allowing Mussolini's client, the Croat nationalist Ante Pavelić, to become the puppet Führer (Poglavnik) of the NDH. A series of agreements with Italy, signed in Rome in May 1941, created a *de facto* Italian protectorate over the new state, and considerably fettered the independence of the NDH. As the war progressed, German influence gradually replaced that of Italy, although there were no formal treaties comparable to those with Italy. German military, economic and political 'advisers' in Zagreb came to wield far greater authority than the Italians, and after the Italian collapse of 1943 their control was absolute. Nevertheless, the fiction was maintained that the NDH was an independent state with its own army, police and administrative apparatus.

Pavelić entered Zagreb on 15 April, from Italy, in company with a band of armed Ustaše. His aide, Colonel Slavko Kvaternik, had already, with German approval, proclaimed the establishment of the NDH in the

Poglavnik's name. In May, Pavelić agreed to his state becoming a kingdom, with the Duke of Spoleto, a member of the House of Savoy, as monarch, bearing the title Tomislav II – a symbol of the continuity of the NDH with the medieval Croatian kingdom of Tomislav I, whose reign began in AD 924. The duke never actually visited his kingdom, as Pavelić could not guarantee his safety. Pavelić probably saw himself playing the same role in Croatia as that which Mussolini had in relation to Tomislav's uncle, the King of Italy. The title of the NDH was, however, a misnomer. It was not independent; almost half of its inhabitants were not Croat; and its statehood was an illusion. Its economy was subordinated to the needs of the German war machine; its international status was not even recognised *de jure* by the Vatican; and its government could act only with the consent of the occupying powers.

Despite these limitations, Pavelić was able to wreak havoc on the Serbian population and to dishonour the name of Croatia by the appalling atrocities for which his regime became notorious. The regime declared that one of its chief objectives was to 'purify' Croatia of alien elements, especially the Serbs. The attitude to the Bosnian Muslims was ambivalent. Although there were cases of Ustaša atrocities against Muslims, there were also other incidents where Muslim gangs were encouraged by the authorities to massacre Serbs. In June 1941 the Croatian minister of education, Milan Budak, stated that the NDH was to be a state of two religions, Catholicism and Islam, and an art gallery in Zagreb was consecrated as a mosque. (It is now a Partisan museum.) Concerning the Serbs, they were to be dealt with in three ways: one-third to be exterminated, one-third to be deported, and the remainder converted to Roman Catholicism.

The process of extermination, which was later judged at Nuremburg to have amounted to genocide, started at once in the areas of Croatia where Serbs were concentrated. These included the old military frontier districts of Kordun and Bjelovar, where hundreds were slaughtered in Ustaša raids during June 1941. In the village of Glina all the male inhabitants were herded into the church, which was then burned down, the Ustaše waiting with guns to shoot any who tried to escape from the flames. The exact number of Serbs who were killed in the NDH is not known. Serbian estimates put it at 750,000; German, at 350,000.

Once the German invasion of the Soviet Union had begun, the *Wehrmacht* were anxious to avoid trouble in the Balkans. They were afraid that the violence of the Ustaša atrocities would provoke a reaction from the Serbs which might lead to a civil war, requiring the presence of German forces to prevent the disruption of the economy, which was expected to

provide essential supplies of food and war materials. They were also aware
that the scale of the Ustaša excesses was driving Serbs into the arms of the
resistance movement, including the communist-led Partisans. They had
hoped that their policy of divide and rule would so weaken and demoralise
the Yugoslavs that the task of pacifying them would be made easier. The
behaviour of the Ustaša, however, was becoming counter-productive. It
even shocked the SS, according to a German security police report of
February 1942:

The atrocities perpetrated by the *ustaša* units against the Orthodox in Croatian
territory must be regarded as the most important reason for the blazing up of
guerrilla activities. The *ustaša* units have carried out their atrocities not only
against Orthodox males of military age, but in particular in the most bestial
fashion, against unarmed old men, women and children . . . innumerable Orthodox
have fled to rump Serbia, and their reports have roused the Serbian population to
great indignation.

In October a German officer visited the Croat Peasant Party leader,
Vlatko Maček, who was held under house arrest on his family farm at
Kupinec between Zagreb and Karlovac. The visitor bore a request from the
German military authorities that Maček should replace Pavelić, as they felt
that the population would calm down if he were to assume control. Maček
refused, suggesting that perhaps the Germans themselves should take over
from the Ustaša. There was apparently a difference of opinion between the
army commander, General Glaise von Horstenau, and the Nazi
ambassador, Siegfried von Kasche. Horstenau was supposed to coordinate
the activities of the Croatian forces and to ensure the security of the railway
system. He had no fighting forces under his direct command at this time, as
the active German units in Croatia were under General Bader, who was
based in Serbia. Although both Horstenau and Kasche were early recruits
to the Nazi Party, the former being an Austrian officer who joined the
Nazis in the early 1930s, Kasche was more fanatical. It seems probable that
the attempt to persuade Maček to replace Pavelić came from Horstenau, as
Kasche was a great admirer of Pavelić. On Maček's refusal of the offer he
was transferred to the notorious concentration camp at Jasenovac on the
Croatian–Bosnian border.

The deportation of Serbs from Croatia to German-occupied Serbia
began in July 1941 under an agreement signed between the NDH and the
Germans. A State Directorate for Renewal (Državna Ravnateljstvo za
Ponovu) organised the rounding up of Serbs and their transportation to
camps to await deportation. The enthusiasm of the Ustaše for this work
ensured that, by September, the camps were overflowing with men, women

and children who were living in conditions of great deprivation and suffering. Inevitably, disease broke out amongst the wretched inmates and the Germans had to intervene to stop the traffic, but not before some 120,000 had been deported. The Serbian Orthodox clergy were a prime target for the deportation squads, and more than half of the 577 priests within the NDH were expelled before the Germans called a halt. The flow continued, however, as thousands of Serbs voluntarily abandoned their homes and fled across the border to escape the Ustaše. It has been estimated that over 300,000 had settled in Serbia by 1943.

The third method of 'purifying' Croatia – the conversion of Serbian Orthodox believers into Roman Catholics – has been the subject of much controversy, as has the whole relationship of the Catholic Church towards the NDH authorities. The different religious traditions of the Serbs and Croats constitute one of the most important cultural factors which separate the two peoples. Throughout history the Catholicism of the Croats and the Orthodoxy of the Serbs have been powerful buttresses in the development of the national consciousness of the two peoples. Pavelić's representative in the Vatican reported an interview with the papal secretary of state in February 1942. He was told, 'The Holy See has Croatia constantly in mind, since Croat is synonymous with Catholic, and the Holy See cannot imagine a Croat who is not a Catholic.' Many Roman Catholic priests had played an active part in the Croat nationalist movement. Some, like Archbishop Šarić of Sarajevo, actually became members of the Ustaša in the inter-war period. Others, like Archbishop Stepinac, of Zagreb, were supporters of the more moderate nationalist line of Dr Maček and the Croat Peasant Party. The clergy therefore welcomed the formation of the NDH, as they believed that it would provide a great opportunity for the Church to extend its influence. Stepinac lost no time in congratulating Pavelić when he arrived in Zagreb with two hundred armed Ustaše on 15 April 1941. The next day Stepinac visited Pavelić to welcome the new regime – even before the royal government to which he had sworn allegiance had surrendered to the invaders. He reported with approval Pavelić's view that the Orthodox Church 'is not a Church but a political organisation', and declared that Pavelić 'is a sincere Catholic' and that the Church would have freedom of action. On 28 April he issued a circular to the clergy in which he hailed the 'young Croat state' in language which is reminiscent of the most extreme forms of nationalism – even of fascism: 'The times are such that it is no longer the tongue which speaks, but the blood through its mysterious union with the earth in which we have glimpsed the light of God ... it is easy to discern the hand of God at work.'

Archbishop Šarić went even further, likening Pavelić to Christ, and appearing to justify the Ustaša atrocities when he wrote that 'it was stupid and unworthy of Christ's disciples to think that the struggle against evil could be waged in a noble way and with gloves on'.

Some of the most extreme nationalists from amongst the clergy came from the ranks of the Franciscans. Some served in the Ustaša government, and even on the staffs of concentration camps such as those at Gospić and Jasenovac. They were notorious for their cruelty towards Serbian prisoners and for their enthusiasm for forced conversions. Evelyn Waugh, the English Catholic writer, who served in the British forces attached to the Partisans in 1944, suggested that the Franciscans from Bosnia and Hercegovina were 'recruited from the least cultured part of the population ... and several wholly unworthy men were attracted to the Franciscan Order by the security and comparative ease which it offered. Many ... were sent to Italy for training. Their novitiate was in the neighbourhood of Pavelić's HQ at Siena, where ustaša agents made contact with them ... Sarajevo is credibly described as having been a centre of Franciscan *ustašism*.'

The issue of forcible conversion is one which excites violent passions. Apologists for Stepinac argue that many of the Orthodox Serbs, and even of the Jews, who were admitted to the Catholic Church were saved from death at the hands of the fanatics, and that by turning a blind eye to the breaches of canon law Stepinac and his bishops were acting from humanitarian motives. There was, for example, the case of a priest in Šarić's diocese who was sentenced to death because he counselled threatened Orthodox Serbs to become tactical Roman Catholics for the duration of the war in order to save their skins. 'Children,' he told them, 'you see that your mother [the Orthodox Church] cannot take care of you. Come to your aunt [the Catholic Church], and when your mother recovers, you can return to her.'

There is no doubt that many decent Roman Catholics, both clergy and laity, were revolted by the excesses of their compatriots. There were some, like the Bishop of Mostar, who felt that the atrocities were not only morally wrong but were likely to hold back the Catholic cause. He felt that a more intelligent policy would have enabled the Church to make converts amongst the Serbian 'schismatics' so that the Catholics might have become a majority in Bosnia–Hercegovina. He cited the case of a Muslim sub-prefect who boasted that seven hundred 'schismatics' were killed in one day at Ljubinje in south-eastern Hercegovina and that, on another occasion, a train collected six carloads of mothers, young girls and children from Mostar and Čapljina and took them to a place in the mountains where mothers and children were thrown alive from the cliff tops. The bishop reported these terrible happenings to Stepinac, who used the information in a letter to Pavelić in which he remonstrated with the Ustaša leader. There is no sign of any action having been taken to prevent a recurrence, but some respite for the hapless Serbs in Hercegovina came as a result of an appeal to Mussolini. The Italians moved back into Hercegovina, and later into other parts of the Dalmatian hinterland, with orders to prevent religious massacres.

Stepinac could not plead that he knew nothing of the inhumanity of the Ustaše nor of the close relations which existed between some of his priests and the murderers. Yet he continued to appear on public occasions with Pavelić and gave no indication that the Poglavnik was other than a faithful son of the Church. At the opening of the Sabor of the NDH in February 1942, he spoke of Pavelić's 'deep and lively sense of responsibility' and prayed that 'you, the leader of the NDH, may successfully help in the renewal and raising up of our beloved homeland on the eternal foundations of the Gospel of Christ's teaching'. He did, however, make private protests in letters to Pavelić, the strongest of these during the later period of the war when it was obvious that the Allies were winning and that the Poglavnik's days were numbered.

The Ustaša policy towards two smaller minorities – the Jews and the gypsies – was as savage as it was towards the Serbs. The Germans, of course, had no misgivings about encouraging their Croatian allies to exterminate members of either of these groups. There was no problem about a possible backlash from them, as even if they were provoked into resistance their numbers were too small to create any problems for the German military command.

The Ustaša militia was not the only armed force at the disposal of the NDH. It stood in the same relationship to the regular forces, known as Domobrani (Defenders of the Homeland), as did the SS to the Wehrmacht. The Ustaše, numbering some 28,500 at the time of the Italian collapse in September 1943, were committed Pavelić supporters, imbued with a fanatical hatred of Serbs and with a fervent Croat nationalism. When Maček, during his incarceration in Jasenovac, taxed one of his guards with the problem of reconciling his Catholic conscience with the monstrosity of his deeds, the officer replied: 'I am perfectly aware of what is in store for me. For my past, present and future deeds I shall burn in hell, but at least I shall burn for Croatia.'

The Domobrani, of whom there were over 90,000, included the gendarmerie and the regular forces of the NDH. They fought under Croatian command in operations in support of the Ustaša and at times also in local actions against the Serbian Četniks, but in major operations in which the Germans were involved, especially in the campaigns against the Partisans, the Domobrani came under direct German control. In addition, there were other Croatian forces which were enlisted directly by the Germans and Croatian volunteer units who fought with the Germans on the Russian front.

Serbia

German-occupied Serbia covered most of the territory of the old kingdom of Serbia before its enlargement during the Balkan wars, except for a large area in the south-east, which was allotted to Bulgarian-held Macedonia. A puppet administration was set up in May 1941, headed by a former chief of police of Belgrade, Milan Aćimović. This body was responsible for local administration and included several former members of the Stojadinović government. It operated under the military control of the German army. The insurgency which broke out in July 1941 in the Šumadija region south of Belgrade, in which both Serbian Četniks, under the command of a former officer in the Royal Army, Colonel Draža Mihailović, and communist-led Partisans, under Tito, could not be contained by the inadequately armed gendarmerie at the disposal of Aćimović. In an effort to win the support of the Serbian population and to strengthen the puppet regime's ability to quell the armed rising, the Germans called upon General Milan Nedić to form a government. The German forces in the Balkans were depleted by the demands of the armies on the Russian front. They wanted to find local leaders to police the Balkans for them. Nedić, who had served as minister of war under Stojadinović and Cvetković, and who had commanded the Yugoslav forces in Macedonia in 1941, was known to have pro-Axis leanings. The Germans did not entirely trust him, but they thought that his military experience, his authority in Serbian political life and his fierce anti-communism would at least ensure that he could be relied upon to contain the threat posed by the Partisans. Nedić saw himself in a similar light to Pétain, his contemporary in Vichy France. In August he formed a Government of National Salvation, which was promised German support for the equipping of an armed force of 17,000 men, which was known as the Serbian State Guard. Its personnel were drawn largely from men who had been under Nedić's command in pre-war days and from members of the gendarmerie. The Serbian counterpart to Pavelić was an extreme nationalist called Dimitrije Ljotić, who had served as a minister during the royal dictatorship. He formed a pro-fascist organisation, Zbor (Rally), which received payments from the Nazis.

Ljotić was allowed by the Germans to form a Serbian Volunteer Corps, which eventually numbered about 4,000 men. Other military formations which were permitted in Nedić's Serbia included a corps of White Russian émigrés and, for a time, a body of Četniks.

None of these units were at all reliable as fighting forces; they were mistrusted by the Germans and despised by many Serbs. When the Partisans began to take the initiative in Serbia the Germans were forced to commit an increasing number of their own troops to deal with them. In 1942, much to the embarrassment of Nedić, they brought in Bulgarian troops, further humiliating the Serbian people. Despite this, Nedić hung on until the Red Army entered Serbian territory in the autumn of 1944. He then fled to Austria, where the Americans imprisoned him, turning him over to the Yugoslavs for trial in February 1946. He never reached the courtroom, however, as he died when he fell from a window of the police headquarters, probably committing suicide.

Montenegro

In April 1941 Montenegro was occupied by the Italians, who announced in July that they had re-established the kingdom of Montenegro. An area in the south which had an Albanian population was detached from Montenegro and added to the Italian puppet state of Albania; otherwise the 'kingdom' covered the same territory as that over which Nikola I had reigned at the end of the Balkan wars. Some of Nikola's former ministers were persuaded to join a consultative council to assist the Italian civil commissioner in administering the country. A so-called National Assembly was convened in Nikola's old capital, Cetinje, and, prompted by its Italian masters, it duly passed a resolution 'linking the life and destinies of Montenegro with those of Italy'. The royalists wanted to offer the throne to Nikola's grandson, Prince Mihailo, but he had the prudence to decline. No other candidate was found.

The situation was transformed during the summer of 1941 by a rising of the Montenegrin people which began on the day after the proclamation of the new kingdom. Milovan Djilas, himself a Montenegrin, was sent by Tito with a mission to ensure that the popular rising should be brought under communist control. The aim was to appoint political commissars, who would forge a 'liaison with the people', in which there would be a fusion of nationalist and revolutionary forces in a broad resistance movement. A Provisional Supreme Command of the National Liberation Forces of Montenegro was established at Kotor on 18 July. Its leading figures, Djilas, Blažo Jovanović and the former royalist officer Arso Jovanović, were communists, but prominent non-communists were also included. There was also military collaboration among communist-led Partisans, Četniks and other nationalist groups. A joint British–Yugoslav military mission landed from a British submarine on the Montenegrin coast at Petrovac-na-Moru, on the night of 17/18 September, and was escorted by Partisans through Montenegro on its way to make contact with Mihailović in Serbia. It consisted of Captain (later Colonel) D. T. (Bill) Hudson, a South African mining engineer who had worked before the war in Serbia, and two Yugoslav air force officers with a radio operator. Unknown to Hudson, the Yugoslavs had been briefed by General Ilić, King Peter's minister of war, to confine their contacts to groups loyal to the royalist cause, whilst Hudson had orders from the Special Operations Executive to make contact with all groups, regardless of their affiliations, and to coordinate the forces of resistance against the enemy. Relations between the Partisans and royalists in Montenegro were, if not cordial, at least sufficiently cooperative to allow the mission to meet with representatives of both sides, and to be able to pass through Montenegro accompanied by Djilas and Arso Jovanović. Hudson later said that the Partisans were 'the only people who seemed organised in that part of the world . . . I formed a high opinion of them.' He met Tito at Užice in October and went on, under safe conduct from the Partisans, to join Mihailović at Ravna Gora on 25 October. By this time, however, the Italians had recovered from their initial surprise and were counterattacking with the help of Albanian troops. The heady days of July, when most of Montenegro was liberated from the Italians, had given way to a military débâcle, following which the Italians exacted a cruel revenge. The hastily formed alliance of revolutionaries and nationalists broke up in bitter recrimination. Tito accused Djilas of sectarian zeal and overconfidence. He suggested that the rising was inadequately prepared and that the wrong military tactics were used. 'Your basic error', he wrote to Djilas, 'is not a premature popular uprising, but your military strategy. Your frontal struggle forced you into a frontal withdrawal; it was pointless to expect that you would be able to put up strong resistance to a much stronger enemy . . . It was incorrect to call the National Liberation Struggle an anti-fascist revolution.' A dejected and chastened Djilas was recalled to Tito's headquarters in the Šumadija.

Once they had re-established control the Italians dropped the idea of an independent Montenegrin kingdom and appointed an Italian military governor, who had absolute powers throughout the areas which they controlled. As Partisan activity increased during 1942 and 1943 the occupation forces could only command the main towns. After the Italian surrender in September 1943 the Germans moved in and, although a puppet Montenegrin administration was set up, the country was virtually under direct German military rule. Meanwhile, large areas outside the towns were disputed by the Partisans and Četniks, who were conducting a civil war in which modern concepts like communism and nationalism were inextricably mixed with older concepts of clan warfare and family blood feuds.

Slovenia

The treatment of Slovenes varied according to the zone of occupation in which they found themselves. The northern areas annexed to Germany included the industrial centres of Jesenice, Kranj, Maribor and Celje. The German zone contained 75 per cent of the Slovene population and covered 65 per cent of the territory. The industries and their workers were harnessed to the German war machine. Thousands of Slovenes were deported to Germany and Austria to work in war factories. Many more fled to the Italian zone, where conditions were less rigorous. The Germans sought to deny the rights of the Slovenes to a separate national identity and subjected them to a brutal policy of Germanisation. The use of the Slovene language was banned in schools and children were punished if they used their mother tongue. The homes of those who had left for forced labour in the Reich, or who had fled, were handed over to German colonists.

Southern Slovenia, including the city of Ljubljana, was annexed to Italy as the province of Lubiama on 3 May 1941. A corridor linking the new province with the port of Fiume was added under a later boundary readjustment. The process of Italianisation was introduced gradually and without the brutality which characterised Mussolini's pre-war policy towards the Slovene population of Venezia Guilia. Unlike the Germans in the north, the Italians recognised the existence of a separate Slovene nationality, and the Slovene language was given official status alongside Italian. There were some Slovene collaborators from the pre-war Slovene People's Party, the right-wing clerical party which had been led for most of the inter-war period by Monsignor Korošec. Korošec died in 1940 and his successor, Fran Kulovec, who was a member of the Simovic–Maček government, was one of the first casualties of the German bombing of

Belgrade. Several other Slovene leaders, including Dr Miha Krek, had left with Simović and were supporters of the royal Yugoslav government in London. Of those who stayed behind, several were prepared to collaborate with the Italians. They were sustained in this intention by Bishop Rožman of Ljubljana and a section of the Church hierarchy and the lay members of Catholic Action. The most senior collaborationist was Dr Marko Natlačen, who had been ban of the Dravska *banovina* immediately before the occupation. He organised a Slovene Legion which was placed at the disposal of the Italians. He believed that it was necessary to collaborate with the Italians in order to maintain law and order and, like Nedić in Serbia and Pétain in France, saw himself as a patriot and a realist. He was, of course, bitterly anti-communist and was prepared to assist the Italians in the suppression of communist-led insurgency. The communists repaid him by assassinating him in October 1942. Another prominent collaborator was General Leo Rupnik, who became Mayor of Ljubljana in June 1942, and who played a prominent part in organising the last-ditch stand of the anti-communists in 1944, in collaboration with the forces of Mihailović, Nedić and Ljotić.

Although the Italians did not spurn the help of the Slovene collaborators, they ensured that the civil administration was firmly in Italian hands, and fascist administrators were drafted in to take over all senior posts. They worked under an Italian high commissioner, who appointed a Slovene consultative body from amongst the collaborators.

Rupnik organised a paramilitary unit known as the Bela Garda, which collaborated with the Italians until their surrender in 1943, and then with the Germans who succeeded them. There were other volunteer forces, mainly of an anti-communist character, which received the blessing of Bishop Rožman, and there were also Slovene Četniks. These groups were loosely attached to a political association formed mainly by members of the People's Party, known as the Slovene Alliance.

Apart from the capital city, the province was mainly rural in character, and contained hills and forests which provided excellent cover for guerrilla bands. Active resistance to the occupation began on 22 July 1941, but even before 3 May, when the province was formally annexed to Italy, preparations were in hand to build a broadly based anti-fascist front. The chief elements in the organisation, which came to be known as the Osvobodilna Fronta (Freedom Front), were the communists, led by Edvard Kardelj and Boris Kidrič, and left-wing members of the Sokol sporting clubs and the Christian Socialists. Some parish priests who rejected Rožman's collaborationist policy; many radically minded writers, artists and intellectuals; and some former army officers also took part in the movement. From the outset the Communist Party took a leading role, and by 1944 what had started out as a broad-based patriotic movement became a communist front organisation.

Macedonia and Kosovo

The partitioning of Macedonia between Bulgaria and Albania represented the fulfilment of long-cherished ambitions by Yugoslavia's two Balkan neighbours. The Bulgarian case was based on the claim that the Macedonian Slavs were really Bulgarians who had been placed under Serbian occupation following Bulgaria's defeat in the Second Balkan War, and that therefore the frontiers granted by the Treaty of San Stefano in 1878, and later rescinded under big-power pressures, were in accordance with the principles of ethnic justice. Bulgaria had achieved its aims during the First World War, and had been forced to relinquish them at Versailles. Bulgarian occupation of part of south-east Serbia was also based on an ethnic argument, as there were Bulgarian-speaking people in the area, although strategic considerations were also important.

The Albanian claims were based primarily on the ethnic argument that large parts of western Macedonia had a majority Albanian population.

Albania was already a puppet state of the Italians in 1941 and, with Mussolini's help, a Greater Albania was created which incorporated the neighbouring areas of Yugoslavia where there was an Albanian majority. This also included the Kosovo region and parts of Montenegro.

Četniks and Partisans

The word *četnik* has a venerable history in the Serbian nationalist movement. It literally means a member of a *četa*, or armed band, and came to have a special meaning as a band of guerrillas who fought against the Turks during the Ottoman occupation – the *hajdučka četnik*.

The movement came to have a more formal structure during the late nineteenth century, when it developed into an official Serbian volunteer force, officered by members of the Royal Serbian Army. It specialised in irregular warfare behind the enemy lines and played an active part in the Serbian victories during the Balkan wars. There was less fighting for the Četniks to do in royal Yugoslavia, but the organisation remained in existence as an extreme Serbian nationalist body, closely linked to the Serbian (and therefore the Yugoslav) military establishment. It operated not only in Serbia but also amongst Serbs in Croatia and Bosnia. The

Četniks combined some of the attributes of the British Legion and the Territorial Army, but with a far greater political content to their activities. At the beginning of the war the official Četnik leader was Kosta Pećanac, who had assumed his position in 1932 after a political struggle with rival political groups. A rival organisation, also using the Četnik name, had been dissolved by the king during the royal dictatorship. One of the issues which divided the two organisations had been Pećanac's policy of admitting new young members who had not served in the war. Pećanac turned the Četniks from a nationalist veterans' association, campaigning for servicemen's rights, into a militantly chauvinistic political organisation with over half a million members – virtually all of them, of course, of Serbian origin. Djilas told a Četnik officer who discussed the possible advantage of collaboration of Četnik and Partisan units in Montenegro that, although the Četniks had once been national liberation troops, they had been transformed into a chauvinistic organisation which terrorised the non-Serbian population. He also pointed out that Kosta Pećanac had issued a call to the Četniks to collaborate with the Germans. This was, in fact, true. Pećanac had put his forces at the disposal of the Germans after the surrender of the six specially formed Četnik battalions which had been recruited from the regular army in 1940.

The name Četnik, although tarnished by the intrigues and corruption of its leaders during the 1930s, still had an appeal to the Serbian peasantry. It is not surprising, therefore, that various people tried to appropriate it for their own ends. Nedić claimed it, as did the leaders of Serbian bands in Bosnia, Montenegro and Dalmatia. Some Četnik groups were openly collaborationist, others were fighting for purely local objectives, and some even worked with the Partisans. A German intelligence report summarised the position thus:

The *četnik* units are divided into three groups: those of Kosta Pećanac which support the Nedić government; those of General Novaković which lean towards the Communists; and the anti-Communist units of Staff-Colonel Mihailović. Mihailović is against Pećanać and Novaković. His supporters are mainly officers. His organisation is purely military. He rejects the Communists because he is of the opinion that the time has not yet come for a general uprising. He would like to organise the entire country and then to attack.

A British officer who met both Pećanac and Mihailović in 1941 spoke of 'the utter confusion, backbiting, antagonism and bloody hostility' which existed among the various Četnik groups. To the outside world, however, the man most associated with the name Četnik was Colonel Dragoljub-Draža Mihailović. Mihailović was a Serbian officer with a good record as a fighting soldier during the Balkan wars and the First World War. He had also served as a military attaché and as a member of the General Staff. Although attempts have been made to depict him as some kind of Serbian de Gaulle, he was in fact a man of limited political abilities. His narrow Serbian nationalism and his fanatical anti-communism made it difficult for him to see issues in an all-Yugoslav context. He was a standard bearer for Greater Serbia and for the House of Karadjordje, although events over which he had little control thrust him for a brief period onto the world stage.

At the time of the Yugoslav collapse Mihailović was serving in Bosnia, but he soon made his way to the wooded hills of Šumadija, establishing a base in the Ravna Gora district with a group of fellow officers from the defeated royal army. His aim was to build an underground movement which would be ready to take power and restore the monarchy when the fortunes of war turned against the Axis. Until that time came, he saw no point in provoking the Germans to savage reprisals against the civilian population by acts of sabotage or by isolated attacks on German troops. Mihailović followed the policy advocated by the government in exile and broadcast by the BBC. This advised the Yugoslavs to bear as calmly as possible their sufferings under the occupation and to refrain from armed resistance until the government gave the signal. This was also the view of the British government at that time. Despite this policy, Mihailović was forced into activity under pressure from some of his supporters. The presence of Tito's Partisans in the same area, who followed a totally different policy concerning sabotage and the ambushing of enemy troops, also induced Mihailović to sanction similar actions by his men. There were even joint Četnik–Partisan operations during the summer and autumn of 1941.

Mihailović eventually made contact with the government in exile, and in September a joint Yugoslav–British mission was sent out to talk with him. The British officer, Captain D. T. Hudson, who accompanied two Yugoslav government representatives, had talks with Djilas on his way through Montenegro, and then went on to talk with Tito at Užice and with Mihailović at Ravna Gora (see above, p. 184).

In October the British government, on advice from the Yugoslavs in London, decided to recognise Mihailović as the leader of the Yugoslav resistance movement, and ordered Hudson to stay with him. Mihailović's Četniks were credited with many of the acts of sabotage which were, in fact, carried out by Partisans. Despite the government's instructions to the contrary it was felt necessary to build up Mihailović's reputation as a guerrilla fighter and to understate the role of the Partisans. Mihailović was promoted to the rank of general and in January 1942 he was appointed minister of war in the London government.

The Partisans

The Yugoslav Communist Party operated illegally during most of the interwar period, having been outlawed in August 1921. Its numbers were depleted by police repression and by its own internal dissensions. Its leaders were caught up in the intrigues and faction fights which raged within the Comintern, and many of them were victims of Stalin's purges. Although it had some influence in the trade unions and youth organisations, its preoccupation with internal sectarian quarrels reduced its effectiveness as a credible political force, despite its good showing in the elections of 1920 (see above, p. 140). By 1932 its membership was down to a few hundred dedicated revolutionaries inside Yugoslavia, who were manipulated by a handful of leaders operating in Moscow, under the control of the Comintern. The severe measures taken under the royal dictatorship established on 6 January 1929 led to the arrest of many of the leaders who remained in Yugoslavia. The organisational secretary of the Central Committee, Djuro Djaković, was shot by the police in April; and shortly afterwards Pajo Marganović, secretary of the youth organisation, was also killed. Josip Broz, later known as Tito, who was a member of the Zagreb local committee, was sentenced to five years' imprisonment.

Josip Broz was born in 1892, in the village of Kumrovec, 60 km (37.5 miles) north-west of Zagreb on the Slovene–Croat border, the son of a Croat peasant and a Slovene mother. As a youth he was apprenticed to a locksmith in Sisak, and as a young man he travelled as a journeyman mechanic in Austria, Czechoslovakia and Germany. In 1910 he joined both the metal workers' union and the Social Democratic Party. During the First World War he enlisted in the Austro-Hungarian army, in which he rose rapidly to non-commissioned rank. He was taken prisoner by the Russians on the Carpathian front in the spring of 1915 and was taken to a prisoner-of-war camp in the Urals. He escaped in February 1917 at the time of the overthrow of the Tsar and was in St Petersburg in the summer, where he participated in the July demonstrations organised by the Bolsheviks against the Kerensky government. He was in Omsk when the Bolsheviks seized power in October, and he joined the Red Guards. When he returned to Yugoslavia in 1920 he immediately joined the newly formed Yugoslav Communist Party. During the next seven years he worked as a mechanic in various industrial centres in Croatia and Serbia, and was elected secretary of the Croatian metal workers' union. In July 1927 he was arrested and sentenced to two months in prison for his trade union activities. His upward progress through the hierarchy of the Communist Party began with his appointment as secretary of the Zagreb city committee in 1928. His five years in prison 1929–34 kept him out of the faction fighting which led to the liquidation by Stalin of the party secretary, Sima Marković, and his replacement by Milan Gorkić, who in his turn disappeared in the Moscow purges of 1935–8, along with the Hungarian leader Béla Kun and the majority of the Polish Central Committee.

On release from prison Broz was ordered to remain in his home village of Kumrovec, under police surveillance, but he soon resumed his clandestine revolutionary activities. It was at this time that he began to use the code name Tito, although in Comintern circles he was known as Comrade Walter. At a meeting of the Yugoslav Central Committee held in Vienna in August 1934, he was given the task of organising party conferences in Croatia and Slovenia. The Slovene conference was held in September in the summer palace of Bishop Rožman, at Medvode, a few miles outside Ljubljana! This audacious coup was achieved through the cooperation of the bishop's half-brother and the domestic staff of the palace, who were sympathetic to the party, and who enjoyed the opportunity given them to cock a snook at the absent bishop. The thirty delegates were wined and dined for two days in unaccustomed luxury at the expense of the unsuspecting prince of the Church. At the end of 1934 Tito was elected to the Central Committee, and was immediately sent to Moscow to report to the Comintern. He soon began work in the Balkan secretariat. Here he came to know the doomed Kun and those notable survivors of the purges the Bulgarian Georgi Dimitrov, the Italian Palmiro Togliatti and the wily Finn O. W. Kuusinen. Tito attributed his survival partly to his friendship with Dimitrov and partly to the fact that he kept a discreetly low profile.

At the Seventh Comintern Congress in July 1935, which launched the Popular Front, Tito had his first brief meeting with Stalin. After the Congress he travelled in and out of Yugoslavia and between Vienna, Paris and Moscow as a Comintern agent. One of his tasks was to organise from Paris the dispatch of volunteers to the International Brigade in Spain. The arrangements for Yugoslav contingents were organised at home by Milovan Djilas, a young Montenegrin intellectual who had joined the party in 1932 whilst a student in Belgrade. Several of the men who later became Partisan generals gained their battle experience in Spain. The most prominent were Koča Popović, son of a Serbian millionaire, who became chief of the General Staff; Peko Dapčević, the Montenegrin law student who was a member of the Supreme Command of the People's Liberation Army; and Ivan Gošnjak, the carpenter from Ogulin, who organised the Partisans in Croatia and became minister of defence after the war. These so-called Spaniards together with a few former officers in the royal army, like Captain Arso Jovanović, who was shot whilst attempting to defect to the Cominform in 1948, were invaluable to the Partisan movement in its early days, as they provided the military expertise and organising skills necessary to turn the inexperienced people's army into a disciplined fighting force.

Whilst he was in Paris in 1937 Tito learned that Gorkić had been deposed and that he had been appointed secretary-general of the party. During the four years that remained before the Axis invasion Tito built up the illegal Communist Party into a highly effective revolutionary avant-garde. Its numbers increased to 12,000 full members, with a further 30,000 in the youth movement, more than doubling its strength between 1937 and 1941. The new recruits included people from all walks of life and all national groups within Yugoslavia. Tito's personality, his drive and energy and, despite his experiences in Moscow during the purges, his unswerving loyalty to the policies of the Comintern, gave a sense of purpose and direction to the party. The faction fighting of the past fifteen years was forgotten. When the old regime disintegrated under the stress of war, the Communist Party was able to rise to the occasion and create a national movement which seized the leadership of the resistance movement and turned it into an instrument of social revolution. Although somewhat inhibited from public denunciation of Nazi Germany by the Hitler–Stalin pact of August 1939, which Stalin honoured until the German invasion of June 1941, the Yugoslav party made preparations for armed resistance against the Axis. But, as Tito later admitted, the Comintern continued to regard the war as a mutual showdown between the imperialists and kept on the sidelines until the invasion of the USSR in June 1941.

The party had, however, played a part in the demonstrations on 27 March against the signing of the Tripartite Pact by Cvetković and Cincar-Marković, and as the German tanks rolled into Zagreb on 10 April the Central Committee decided to urge the soldiers not to surrender but to take their weapons home and keep themselves in readiness for an armed rising. A proclamation in the Central Committee's name on 15 April declared that the communists were in the front rank of the popular struggle against the invader.

All inhibitions were removed when Hitler launched Operation Barbarossa against the Soviet Union on 22 June 1941. Tito, who was then in occupied Belgrade, received a message from the Comintern which called for all its member parties to rise in the defence of the Soviet Union. They were cautioned to 'take into consideration that at this stage your task is liberation from Fascist oppression and not Socialist revolution'.

The Yugoslav party's call to arms came on 4 July. This day is still celebrated as Dan Borca (Fighter's Day), and those who can claim that they responded are regarded as a privileged elite within the veterans' association. In fact, there had been sporadic acts of resistance before that day, both by communists and by Četniks.

Tito remained in Belgrade during the Montenegrin rising which began on 12 July. Throughout Serbia communist-organised sabotage caused some alarm to the German military command. In August it was admitted that German troops could only move about the country in armed convoys. The Germans recognised earlier than did the Allies that the communists were the prime movers, although by their skilful use of 'nationalist slogans' they were able to 'meet with a response' from wider sections of the population. In September a representative of the German Foreign Office reported that individual Četnik groups were now also taking up positions against the German occupation troops, often using 'nationalistically camouflaged communist slogans'.

In September the communist-led Partisans occupied the town of Užice in western Serbia and a large tract of adjoining territory in eastern Bosnia. Their conduct during their brief occupation of the town illustrates the difference in approach between the Četniks and the Partisans. The communists saw the fight against the invader as an essential part of a much broader revolutionary struggle to create a socialist Yugoslavia. The inhabitants of Užice found themselves citizens of the 'Užice republic'. The old local government administration was replaced by an elected 'People's Committee', schools were opened, the communist party newspaper *Borba* appeared three times a week, and People's Courts administered justice. Throughout the war, wherever the Partisans established a large enough area of liberated territory the inhabitants were given a foretaste of the socialist system which would eventually be established when the final victory was won. The structure of local government communes (*opštine*) which was adopted after the war was consciously based on the wartime People's Committees.

Užice was a great prize, as it contained a small-arms factory which was soon producing weapons for the Partisans. It was also discovered that banknotes and silver worth 56 million dinars (£280,000) had been left there by the royal government when it fled the country. This enabled the Užice republic to pay its way. It was not necessary for the highly disciplined Partisans to requisition supplies from the local peasants without paying for them, as was the case with the Četniks.

Tito entered the liberated area in mid September and on 19 September he met Mihailović, but these talks had no practical result. A second meeting on 27 October brought an agreement that the Partisans would supply rifles and ammunition from their factory in Užice in return for a share in any supplies dropped by the British to Mihailović. Unfortunately, Captain Hudson, who had joined Mihailović two days earlier, was not invited to the talks, so there is no independent witness to support Tito's claim that, in the interest of unifying the resistance movement, he was prepared to stand down in favour of the colonel and that Mihailović had declined the offer. Hudson was able to confirm, however, that the clashes which occurred a few days later between Partisans and Četniks were initiated by the latter. Mihailović was furious when he learned that Hudson's version, sent to SOE in Cairo, flatly contradicted the story which had been sent to the London government. Hudson had also advised that no more British arms should be sent to the Četniks.

The Germans could not tolerate a situation in which large parts of the territory they were supposed to be occupying were, in fact, denied to them. By October they had mustered sufficient forces, drawn both from their regular army units and from the 'army' of their puppet, Nedić, to start an offensive in the Šumadija. They hoped that their work would be made much easier if they could persuade Mihailović to attack the Partisans, and talks were held with the Četnik leader to that purpose. They also believed that they could cow the local population into submission by acts of barbarous cruelty against civilian hostages. Acting under a directive from Field-Marshal Keitel, an order was issued that one hundred Serbs would be shot for every German soldier who died at the hands of the 'bandits'. An incident in which a group of German soldiers had been killed in an ambush led to an appalling massacre in the town of Kragujevac. As insufficient adult males could be found to meet the required quota, the teachers were ordered to march the boys from their upper forms to the place of execution. One teacher is said to have cried out to the firing squad, 'Shoot me first, I have a lesson to teach!' An official German report states: 'The executions in Kragujevac occurred although there had been no attacks on members of the Wehrmacht in this city, because not enough hostages could be found elsewhere'. Estimates vary as to the total number of victims. German sources suggest that about 2,500 were killed in Kragujevac and over 1,700 in Kraljevo, but Yugoslav estimates vary from 5,000 to 7,000.

The effect of these atrocities on Mihailović was to persuade him that, if this was the price of resistance, it were better to remain inactive until the situation improved. He feared that slaughter on this scale would endanger the survival of the Serbian nation. Tito, on the other hand, saw the German terror squads as recruiting agents for the Partisans. Their actions would bring home to the population the futility of collaboration, whether passive or active, with those capable of such bestiality. In desperation, knowing that no one, innocent or guilty, was safe, many would see that armed resistance was the only choice available. The Partisans therefore increased their activity.

During November the Partisans made several attempts to persuade Mihailović to see their point of view, but he had already decided that the Partisans were a greater menace than the Germans. The last contact between the two commanders was in a phone call pleading for joint Partisan–Četnik action which Tito made on 28 November, at the height of the German offensive. Mihailović refused the request and ceased operations. Ironically, the British, misinformed by the exiles in London, credited Mihailović with the leadership of the resistance which the Germans encountered as they reconquered Užice in early December. As a result the Četniks continued to receive air drops of supplies from British planes, and Mihailović was regarded as a major war hero.

After abandoning Užice, the Partisans re-established their headquarters at Foča, a small town on the upper Drina in eastern Bosnia, within the Italian zone of occupation. Here they undertook a reorganisation of both the military and the political wings of the resistance movement. One important innovation was the establishment of the first Proletarian Brigade, the statute of which stated, 'The proletarian people's liberation shock brigades are the military shock formations of the peoples of Yugoslavia under the leadership of the Communist Party.' The brigade was formed on 21 December – Stalin's birthday. The Soviet leader did not receive his birthday gift with a good grace. He protested because of the explicit linking of the national liberation movement with the ultimate aim of establishing a communist state. He was afraid that this might upset the western allies. He also felt that it was an act of disobedience by the Yugoslavs, who had been told to play down the communist element in the resistance and to emphasise its broad anti-fascist and patriotic character. Apart from the openly declared communism of the Proletarian Brigades, they differed from other units in the People's Liberation Army in drawing their personnel from all regions of Yugoslavia and in being readily available for service in any part of the country. Most other units bore a purely local character, as their names often suggested (for example the

Ninth Dalmatian Division, the Fifth Montenegrin Brigade), and they tended to operate mainly in their own home areas.

At Foča regulations were agreed which 'laid down the basic principles for the setting up of a new people's government: responsibility of the people; election rights; unity of authority; self government'. The embryonic new government was at first known as the People's Liberation Committee.

During their three months' stay in Foča the Partisans entertained high hopes that the Soviet Union would send them supplies, but these never materialised. Moša Pijade spent thirty-seven nights in the bitter cold, waiting on a plateau on Mt Durmitor for Soviet planes which never came. Eventually a new enemy offensive was mounted against them at the end of March 1942. The combined force which was ranged against them included Italian, German, Ustaša and Četnik units. The Partisans now had five Proletarian Brigades, whose members were fit and well disciplined but woefully short of ammunition and food. They were forced to abandon Foča at the end of May, but they broke through the enemy's lines and trekked across Bosnia, sabotaging the railway from Sarajevo to the coast, where it crossed the Ivan Pass into Hercegovina. Then they turned north, capturing the old Bosnian capital of Bihać in September. During the long march they had been continually harassed by enemy forces and had suffered many casualties. The plight of the Partisan wounded was a particularly acute problem when the whole army was on the march. They had to be taken along, but without medical supplies and with inadequate transport and an acute shortage of doctors they could not be given proper attention. Many died on the way and others were slaughtered by the enemy.

The Partisans also picked up new recruits as they passed through Bosnia. Vladimir Dedijer, Tito's biographer, suggests that by the time they settled in Bihać the Liberation Army numbered 150,000 fighting troops.

AVNOJ (Anti-Fascist Council for the National Liberation of Yugoslavia)

An important political initiative was taken during the four months' stay in Bihać. This historic town, lying in the heart of Pavelić's NDH, became the venue for the first session of AVNOJ. This broadly based council was intended to be the political rallying point for all the resistance forces. Although it was under communist leadership, some effort was made to include prominent non-communists among the fifty-four delegates who attended. One such figure was Dr Ivan Ribar, who was Speaker of the Vidovdan Constituent Assembly and who was elected president of AVNOJ as a sign that the Council was not a purely communist body. In 1921 Ribar was riding in the same carriage as King Alexander when a communist, Baco Stejić, made an attempt at assassination. The two men later met as delegates to AVNOJ! Ribar opposed the royal dictatorship and moved further to the left during the 1930s. His two sons became active communists, and both were killed on active service with the Partisans. Dr Ribar never became a communist, although he held high office when the new regime was established after the war.

The decision to set up AVNOJ was not approved by Stalin and the Comintern. The Soviet policy was clearly enunciated in a telegram which Dimitrov, secretary-general of the Comintern, sent to Tito in March 1942:

At present the ... overriding priority is the defeat of the Fascist bandits ... Remember that the Soviet Union maintains relations based on treaties with the King and Government of Yugoslavia, and that an openly hostile attitude towards them would provoke new difficulties for the common war effort, and the relationship between the Soviet Union, Britain and America.

In August 1942 the royal legation in Moscow was raised to the status of an embassy. Thus, Tito's message in November that AVNOJ was to be 'a kind of government' provoked a sharp response warning him not to set up a rival administration to that of the king and not to raise the question of the future of the monarchy. Tito outwardly conformed, but for tactical reasons only, as he made plain in his address to the Bihać Assembly on 26 November. The resolutions passed by the Assembly included a call for national liberation, the equality of the Yugoslav peoples – mentioning specifically Serbs, Croats, Slovenes, Macedonians and Montenegrins – respect for private property and for private enterprise in industry and agriculture, and a promise of free elections after the war.

The year 1943 was a fateful one for the Partisans. It began with the opening of a German offensive – Operation Weiss – in January, which was intended to administer the *coup de grâce* both to the Partisans and to the Četniks. The Partisans had already decided to move south from Bihać and to attack the Četnik-held teritory in Hercegovina and Montenegro. They had come to regard the Četniks as their main enemy at this stage of the war. The Axis armies were beginning to suffer reverses on the Russian front and the Allies were advancing in North Africa. If an Allied landing were to occur in the Balkans it must not find Mihailović there to welcome them. The Germans also had good reason to want to see the end of the Četniks, and they profoundly mistrusted the Italians for their willingness to cooperate with the Četniks in local actions against the Partisans in Dalmatia and Montenegro. Thus, the German commander told his Italian opposite number that if any Četnik troops were found fighting with the Italians they would be attacked by the Germans. Tito told his troops, when they broke out of their encirclement in Bihać, to avoid unnecessary conflicts with the Germans and to concentrate their main thrust against the Četniks. There were even elements on each side who thought it possible to arrange some sort of accommodation which would allow the Partisans a free hand against the Četniks. Those on the German side who toyed with this idea included the German minister in Zagreb, Siegfried Kasche, who thought it would be to Germany's advantage to encourage the two Yugoslav groups to exhaust each other, whilst the German forces stood by until an opportunity arose for them to pick off the enfeebled remnants. This policy was rejected in Berlin, and tentative parleys between German and Partisan representatives in March 1943 were broken off after they had achieved a limited exchange of prisoners. One of those released by the Germans was Herta Has, the mother of Tito's second son, Alexander.

Operation Weiss – also known by the Partisans as the Fourth German Offensive – was conducted in three phases. The first was intended to encircle the Partisans in Bihać, but a break-through was effected in February, and by the end of March the Partisans had crossed the Neretva and had entered Četnik territory, inflicting heavy casualties on Mihailović's forces. The next phase of Operation Weiss was supposed to be an Italian offensive against the Četniks, but this never took place because the Italians had no stomach for it. The Partisans regrouped their forces in the Durmitor area on the Montenegrin–Bosnian border and waited for the next German offensive, which was launched on 15 May.

It is in the nature of partisan warfare that there is seldom a single focus of activity – no front line in the conventional military sense. Whilst the main body of Partisans were engaged in the long march from Bihać, other operations were taking place elsewhere. These activities included sabotage of communications in Croatia; the harassment of enemy forces in Slovenia; and pitched battles in Bosnia and Serbia in which Četniks, Ustaše, Italians and Germans were involved. In Bihać the Partisans claimed to muster 150,000 men organised in fighting units. The numbers fluctuated from time to time, but as the signs of Allied victory became increasingly hopeful, so there was a steady growth in numbers. Tito claimed that 80,000 new recruits were drawn into the movement during the summer and autumn of 1943.

The crossing of the Neretva and the successes of the Partisans against the

Četniks had international repercussions. For some time the BBC had been correctly attributing the major successes of the Yugoslav resistance to the Partisans, despite the protests of the royal Yugoslav government and of some elements in the British government. Eventually Churchill decided to take steps to find out the truth. On 28 May Captains William Deakin and William Stuart, joint heads of a six-man British military mission, landed by parachute on the wooded shores of the Black Lake at the foot of Mt Durmitor. Together with their radio operators, they joined Tito at his headquarters.

Deakin and Stuart arrived at a crucial time in the fortunes of the Partisans, for Operation Schwarz – the Fifth Offensive – had just started. The British mission retreated with the Partisans across the Bosnian border. During an enemy bombardment on 9 June, Captain Stuart was killed and both Tito and Deakin were wounded. The epic battle of Sutješka was the turning point in the fortunes of the Partisans. The river gorge was forced and 100,000 enemy troops were cheated of the prize which General Lüters, their commander, had thought to be in his grasp. On 10 June he announced 'the hour of the final liquidation of the Tito Army'. The 20,000 Partisans suffered appalling losses, including the slaughter of hundreds of their wounded, who had to be abandoned by their comrades. In all, over 7,000 men were killed during the Fifth Offensive, including several of the bravest guerrilla leaders, like Sava Kovačević, commander of the Fifth Montenegrin Brigade. Most of the political leaders, however, survived, including Tito, Ranković, Djilas, Koča Popović and Moša Pijade. There is no doubt that these men shared the dangers which faced their troops and proved to be as courageous as any of those who died fighting. It was by sheer good fortune that they all survived to form the core of the state and party leadership in the post-war period. Their powers of recovery from apparently overwhelming disasters were as miraculous to their friends as they were baffling and frustrating to their enemies. Within a few days of leaving behind the bloated corpses which littered the blood-soaked plateau of Tjentište, they were at Kladanj, in the heart of Bosnia. Once again they had snatched victory from the jaws of defeat.

In September there was a dramatic change in their fortunes. The surrender of the Italian forces enabled the Partisans to capture large stores of weapons and other supplies and to gain control of areas along the coast, including the port of Split, where they were able to commandeer several ships to add to the tiny Partisan navy which had just been formed. The Germans reoccupied Split on 26 September, but the ships were already on their way to Bari, with the first group of Partisan wounded to be treated in

British military hospitals in Italy. During the next few months, as the Allies strengthened their hold on the western shore of the Adriatic, it became possible for return cargoes of war material to be sent to Partisan-held islands off the Dalmatian coast – notably to Vis, where Tito later established his headquarters.

Some units of the Italian army surrendered to the Partisans, where they received gentler treatment than did those who were caught by their former allies the Germans. Sufficient numbers were found who were willing to fight with the Partisans to make it possible to form a Garibaldi Brigade.

In October the Partisan leaders were quick to seize the political initiative by starting preparations for a second session of AVNOJ, to be held in Jajce, the former seat of the Turkish governor or Bosnia. The comparative ease with which it was possible within a few weeks to assemble a meeting attended by 142 delegates from all parts of Yugoslavia indicates the extent of the recovery from near annihilation at Sutješka five months earlier. A sign that the growing strength of the movement was winning recognition in British government circles was the arrival, on 17 September, of a British military mission led by Brigadier Fitzroy Maclean. The Maclean mission had orders direct from Churchill to 'find out who is killing most Germans, and suggest means by which we could help them kill more'.

There had been indications for some time that the Partisans were the only effective fighting force against the Axis occupiers and their collaborators. When Maclean landed, ten days after the Italian surrender, there were, as well as the Deakin mission, British officers with the Partisans in Croatia and Slovenia. Little information had penetrated from these missions to enable the British government to form an overall picture of the situation in Yugoslavia. This was partly because of genuine difficulties of communication, but also, as Maclean has later confirmed, because of deliberate obstruction by elements in SOE in Cairo, who appeared to regard the Foreign Office as the real enemy, who 'must at all costs be outmanoeuvred and their knavish tricks frustrated'. Churchill had to some extent penetrated the fog and was determined to establish the full facts. Shortly after his arrival at Tito's headquarters in Jajce, Maclean received a first-hand account of the recent fighting from Deakin, which confirmed the impression of the Partisans which he had already begun to form. During the winter of 1943–4 there was a realignment of attitudes on the British side. SOE, both in Cairo and in London, abandoned their blind support of Mihailović, whilst the Foreign Office, which had previously been prodding SOE to establish contact with the Partisans, began to work for a reconciliation between the royal government and Tito. Eventually British policy settled first on persuading the king to drop Mihailović, and finally on backing Tito wholeheartedly against the king. Maclean's reports were a decisive factor in persuading Churchill that all aid should be given to the Partisans and that the British liaison officers with the Četniks should be withdrawn.

The second session of AVNOJ was held on 29 November, under the presidency of Dr Ribar. It declared itself to be 'the supreme legislative and executive body in Yugoslavia', and issued a declaration forbidding King Peter to set foot on Yugoslav soil until a vote had been taken to ascertain the wishes of the people. The Bihać resolution concerning the equality of the Yugoslav peoples and their right to democratic control over their future were reaffirmed. A National Committee was elected, to act as a 'temporary government', with Tito as prime minister and minister of war. Stalin was reported to have been furious at this show of independence on the part of Tito, as he was afraid that the western Allies, regarding the Yugoslav party as a tool of the Kremlin, would consider that the Soviet Union had broken its promises. In fact, the Soviets had given virtually no practical help to the Partisans and had little control over them. They were beginning to realise that Britain was far more interested in the effective prosecution of the war than in the future form of government of Yugoslavia.

The foundation of the provisional government

At the Teheran Conference which took place between 28 November and 1 December 1943, Churchill, Roosevelt and Stalin had agreed to support the Partisans as being the only effective Yugoslav resistance movement. On 23 February 1944 the first Soviet military mission arrived at Partisan head-quarters. By this time a shuttle service, sending Allied supplies across the Adriatic, was in full swing. The British decided to withdraw their mission to Mihailović a few days before the arrival of the Soviet mission to the Partisans.

There were still formidable military and political obstacles to overcome, but at the beginning of 1944 it was becoming increasingly obvious to all concerned that the Germans were losing the war and that the future government of Yugoslavia would be dominated by the communists.

Mihailović made a futile effort to capture the political initiative from Tito by calling a Congress at Ba on 25–8 January, which was attended by some three hundred members from all parts of Yugoslavia, though the overwhelming majority were Serbs. At Jajce, Tito's Congress had been attended by Captain Deakin as an observer on behalf of Britain. The St

Sava Congress, as Mihailović's meeting at Ba was called, had an American military observer present. The Congress was made physically possible because the Četniks had signed a cease-fire agreement with the Germans, thus removing the danger that the delegates might be harassed as they gathered for their meetings.

It was proposed that a federal Yugoslavia should be created after the war, with three semi-autonomous units – Serbia, Croatia and Slovenia – under the Karadjordjević dynasty. No recognition was given to the possibility of a separate Macedonian or Montenegrin unit, and no mention at all was made of the rights of the non-Slav peoples. In fact, a Greater Serbia was envisaged, which would suffer a truncated Croatia to exist. Slovenia might be allowed to expand at the expense of Italy. The Congress established a Yugoslav Democratic National Union and elected as its chairman Živko Topalović, a leader of the tiny pre-war Socialist Party. Other pre-war politicians who played a part were Adam Pribičević of the Independent Democratic Party and Mustafa Mulalić, a Muslim member of the Yugoslav National Party.

The Ba Congress had little effect either on the political situation in Yugoslavia or on the standing of the Četniks in the eyes of the British. Topalović went to Italy in May in company with the last British officers to be attached to the Četniks. He was joined there in August by Pribičević and some other leaders who were thought likely to have some influence with the Allies. Their arrival in Italy coincided with Tito's meeting with Churchill at Naples on 12 August. The Četniks had already lost the game. The appointment of Ivan Šubašić as prime minister of the royal government in exile was followed by the dropping of Mihailović as minister of war. It was only a matter of time before King Peter himself delivered the final blow to the Četniks. Under heavy pressure from Churchill he broadcast over the BBC on 12 September a speech drafted for him in which he called on all Yugoslav patriots to rally behind Tito, and declared that any who did not do so would be regarded as traitors.

The appointment of the Šubašić government on 1 June 1944 not only confirmed the end of British support for Mihailović, it was also the first step towards the removal of King Peter himself.

Even before his government was sworn in, Šubašić was taken in a British destroyer to meet Tito on Vis in order to reach an agreement concerning the conduct of the war and the outline of a political compromise which would ensure a smooth transition to peace. Šubašić accepted the resolutions of the Jajce Congress and agreed to the formation of a joint government, composed of members nominated by Tito's National Liberation Committee and representatives of the government in exile. It was agreed that the question of the monarchy should be decided after the war. Šubašić also promised to organise material and moral support for the Partisans.

During the winter of 1944–5 Šubašić, the king, Tito and the British government were involved in a complicated set of political manoeuvres which resulted in the formation of a three-man regency council, to which the king handed over his authority. The only act of the regency was to appoint a government in which Tito was prime minister and Šubašić foreign minister; there were also two other members of the exiled government who held non-departmental posts. All the other twenty-five members were either members of AVNOJ or known supporters of the Partisans. This government was sworn in on 7 March 1945.

Whilst these political arrangements were being worked out, the war continued to rage. In May 1944 the Germans launched their Seventh Offensive against the Partisans. This was the first occasion when the Partisans could rely on massive Allied air support from bases in Italy. The Germans almost captured Tito in a surprise parachute attack on his headquarters in the Bosnian town of Drvar. He escaped in an American plane piloted by a Russian, and landed in Bari, whence he was conveyed to Vis in a British destroyer. The Seventh Offensive was the last occasion on which German troops took a major initiative in the Balkans. From June 1944 until the final surrender, the Partisans, backed by an increasing weight of Allied support, gradually pushed the Germans back. In September the Red Army reached the Yugoslav–Romanian border. Tito was determined to meet Stalin and to discuss the situation before the Red Army entered the country. He therefore arranged to fly to Romania on 18 September in a DC 3, supplied to the Soviet Union under the US Lend–Lease programme. He then proceeded to Moscow, where an agreement was reached permitting the passage of Soviet troops through Yugoslav territory and securing Stalin's agreement that the Red Army would not interfere with the Yugoslav civil administration and would leave as soon as they had accomplished their military tasks. Tito's departure was concealed from the British on Vis, who spent several days looking for him and being fobbed off with excuses by the Partisans who were guarding his headquarters. The agreement with Stalin regarding the Red Army's entry into Yugoslavia was also kept secret. Eden learnt of it from Molotov three weeks later. In Churchill's words, 'Tito, having lived under our protection for three or four months at Vis, suddenly levanted, leaving no address.'

The Red Army entered Yugoslavia on 1 October, and on 20 October a joint Partisan–Red Army force entered Belgrade. The Soviet thrust was a two-pronged drive from Romania and Bulgaria. After the liberation of Belgrade the Red Army moved on into Hungary, leaving the Partisans and their western allies to deal with the remaining Germans in Croatia and Slovenia; the Ustaše in what remained of the NDH; and the Četniks in Serbia, Bosnia and Montenegro.

In the last stages of the war Mihailović vainly hoped that, just as the Red Army had entered Serbia from the east, the Allies might enter Slovenia and Istria from the west. He made a desperate effort to establish a presence in this area which would bring together the survivors of the Četniks, Ljotić's forces and General Rupnik's Slovene Home Guard. When it was apparent that this move had failed, most of the leaders fled to Austria or northern Italy, which was still in German hands. Some, like Nedić, were eventually returned by the Allies when they captured them. Others managed by various routes to reach safety in the United States and Latin America. Mihailović also made a bid to draw Maček into an anti-communist alliance, but the Croat leader refused and fled to Austria, whither also many of the Ustaša leaders and thousands of lesser collaborators made their way. Zagreb was the last major Yugoslav town to fall to the Partisans, on 9 May 1945, two days after they had entered Ljubljana.

The war may have officially ended with the German surrender on 7 May, but the killing in Yugoslavia did not end there. Thousands of Croats and Slovenes were rounded up by the British forces in southern Austria and were driven back to Yugoslavia, where many were shot out of hand by the victorious Partisans. Pockets of Četnik and Ustaša resistance continued throughout 1945, and there was a serious flare-up in Kosovo, where the Albanian-speaking population resisted the implementation of the Tito–Hoxha agreement, which acknowledged Yugoslav sovereignty over the area which had been added to the Italian puppet state in 1941. There were two areas where Partisan forces had crossed the pre-war frontier and entered areas of Italy and Austria, where there were Yugoslav minorities. This brought Tito into conflict with the Allies.

Trieste, the Julian region and Istria

In the winter of 1942–3 the Slovene resistance organisation, OF, began to organise guerrilla activities amongst Slovenes who had lived under Italian rule since the First World War. This national minority had been badly treated by the Italians and were easily roused by the prospect of reunification with their compatriots. A similar situation existed amongst the

Croats of Istria and Fiume (Rijeka). As the German retreat gathered momentum the main Partisan forces, advancing from Lika, reached the suburbs of Rijeka on 20 April 1945. By 27 April most of Istria had been liberated and the German garrisons in Rijeka and Trieste were surrounded. Whilst the Partisans were poised to take Trieste, New Zealand troops under General Sir Bernard Freyburg were advancing from the west.

There seems to have been no clear understanding between Tito and the Allies as to what would be the position in the Julian region when the enemy was driven out. The Yugoslavs expected to occupy the whole area, including Trieste, and already had large parts of it under their occupation in early 1945. The Italians hoped that they could retain the 1939 frontiers. The British were mainly interested in the immediate military situation and wanted the long-term frontier settlement to be decided at the peace conference. When Field-Marshal Alexander met Tito in Belgrade in February 1945 the question was becoming urgent, yet no clear agreement appears to have been reached. At that time a large part of the disputed areas was already under Partisan administration, and Tito assumed that the Allies would accept the *fait accompli*. The key issue was Trieste. Tito got the impression that Alexander was interested only in safeguarding his supply lines from Trieste northwards to Tarvisio and southern Austria. He offered the use of the Südbahn via Ljubljana. It appeared that the control of Trieste would rest with whoever got there first.

The Partisans arrived on 1 May and the New Zealanders on 2 May. A local agreement was reached on 6 May under which the British and New Zealand forces recognised the civil administration which the Yugoslavs had set up in return for the free use of the port facilities under the control of the western troops.

This situation lasted for forty days, until 12 June, when the Yugoslavs were persuaded to withdraw from the city after receiving an Anglo-American ultimatum. The so-called Morgan Line was established, which left Trieste, Gorizia and the port of Pula at the southern tip of Istria under Allied military control, with the right to use the connecting road through Istria. The rest of the area was left under Yugoslav occupation, pending a final settlement of the peace conference.

Carinthia

A similar situation arose in southern Austria, where the Partisans advanced across the pre-war frontier and occupied Slovene-speaking areas as far as Villach (Beljak) and Klagenfurt (Celovec). Again Tito backed down after

Table 2. *Yugoslavia's wartime losses*

Dead	1,700,000 (11% of the pre-war population)
Average age of dead	22 years
	Includes: 90,000 skilled workers
	40,000 'intellectuals'
Homeless people	3,500,000
Buildings	822,000 destroyed (289,000 peasant homesteads)
Ploughs and agricultural equipment	80% destroyed
Railway lines	50% destroyed
Locomotives	77% destroyed
Goods wagons	84% destroyed

Source: Figures taken from Denison Rusinow, *The Yugoslav Experiment, 1948–1974* (C. Hurst, London, 1977), p. 18, based on UNRRA and Yugoslav official sources.

receiving a visit from Alexander on 11 May, who told him that the Allies had decided to occupy and administer the areas at present held by the Partisans. Tito complied on 16 May, and at the same time withdrew his forces from the Tarvisio (Trbiž) area and the west bank of the Isonzo (Soča). This did not imply, however, that the Yugoslavs had given up their claims to the areas of Austria and Italy where there was a Slovene population, or even to the port of Trieste, which they could not claim on ethnic grounds, but for which a case based on economic need could be made out.

The cost of the war to Yugoslavia

It is impossible to compute accurately the human and material losses which Yugoslavia sustained between 1941 and 1945. It is thought that, of the 1.7 million dead, 1 million were killed in fratricidal struggle between the various groups of Yugoslavs rather than by the foreign enemies. Nor can an exact figure be given of those who either fled abroad or found themselves in other countries at the end of the war and who declined to return home.

The destruction of factories, farms and houses and the disruption of the lines of communication faced the new administration with formidable tasks. Table 2 attempts to summarise the scale of wartime losses.

10

The transition to socialism

The Tito–Šubašić government which came into existence in March 1945 was intended to be a caretaker administration, set up to govern the country during the difficult period of post-war reconstruction. It was, in reality, the National Liberation Committee plus three former ministers of the royal government in exile. A provisional Assembly of 318 members replaced AVNOJ in August 1945. It included 80 non-communists, some representing the pre-war political parties, but the overwhelming majority of members were supporters of the Communist Party and former participants in AVNOJ. In order not to disturb relations with the western Allies, a neutral title was used, which begged the question as to whether the new Yugoslavia was to be a republic or a monarchy. Elections to a Constituent Assembly were called in the name of Democratic Federative Yugoslavia (Demokratska Federativna Jugoslavija), and a single list of candidates who supported the newly formed People's Front was presented to the voters on 11 November.

Some of the pre-war politicians intended to contest the elections and an attempt was made to form a United Democratic coalition to oppose the People's Front list. Milan Grol, leader of the Democratic Party, resigned from the government on 18 August and joined forces with Miša Trifunović of the Radical Party, who had served as premier of the London government for a few weeks in 1943. Šutej and Šubašić resigned at the beginning of October and tried to form a Croat peasant group to collaborate with the Democrats, but they eventually gave up the unequal struggle against the all-powerful People's Front and advised their supporters to boycott the elections.

The elections on 11 November were held under a new electoral law which gave equal voting rights to men and women over the age of eighteen, and to ex-Partisans under that age. The franchise was withdrawn from a quarter of a million people who were alleged to have been collaborators.

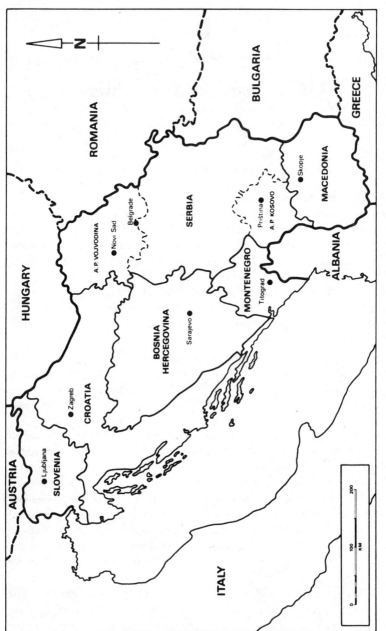

Map 4. The present-day administrative boundaries.

The People's Front received 90 per cent of the votes cast, and only 12 per cent of the eligible voters failed to turn out.

On 29 November the Constituent Assembly met and by acclamation approved the abolition of the monarchy and the establishment of the Federative People's Republic of Yugoslavia (Federativna Narodna Republika Jugoslavije, or F.N.R.J.). A new constitution was promulgated on 31 January 1946 and the Constituent Assembly became the first legislature of the FNRJ.

The 1946 constitution

The 1946 constitution was consciously modelled on the one introduced into the USSR by Stalin in 1936. Both included guarantees of civil liberty – all citizens are equal before the law; there can be no discrimination on grounds of ethnic origin, property status, level of education or religious belief; political and religious freedom are protected, including freedom of the press and of assembly; there are the rights of free speech and of political association. Articles concerning these matters might have been taken unchanged from any of the constitutions introduced into the western liberal democracies during the two centuries since Thomas Jefferson drafted the Declaration of Independence.

Of more specific interest to Yugoslavia was the framework of administration set up under the 1946 constitution. It established a federation of six republics, each given equal status. The boundaries of the republics corresponded more closely to the historic units which had originally come together in 1918 than had any of the administrative units established by the royal regime (see map 4). The largest unit, Serbia, contained three elements – Serbia proper, the autonomous province of Vojvodina and the autonomous region of Kosovo–Metohija. The justification for this division of Serbia was partly that it would dispel fears of a revival of the spectre of Serbian hegemonism which had cast a shadow over pre-war Yugoslavia. There were also ethnic reasons.

The autonomous status of Vojvodina gave recognition to the ethnic complexities of an area where, in addition to Serbs and Croats, there was a large Hungarian minority, as well as other non-Slav groups. The only important internal boundary change under the new federal structure was the transfer of the Srem region, between the Danube and the Sava, from Croatia to Vojvodina. Kosovo–Metohija was given separate treatment because of the existence of an Albanian-speaking population which made up two-thirds of the population.

Macedonia, which had been known as South Serbia since it was acquired by the Serbian kingdom in 1913, became a full republic, as did Montenegro.

The population of Bosnia–Hercegovina was divided into three main groups – Croats, Serbs and Muslims. The last named, most of whom spoke Serbian, were regarded as a distinct ethnic group. At various times in the past Croatia and Serbia had claimed the allegiance of the Bosnians. The creation of the republic of Bosnia–Hercegovina, approximately within the boundaries of the old Austro-Hungarian province, was intended to lay the ghosts of these past rivalries and also to give recognition of its ethnic diversity.

Thus, the lands which had been coveted by the Greater Serbian chauvinists were partitioned amongst six administrative units. This symbolic recognition of the rights of self-determination contrasted sharply with the plans which Mihailović and his friends had put forward at the Ba Congress a year earlier.

There is less need to comment on the formation of the two remaining republics, Slovenia and Croatia. Slovenia was enlarged by the acquisition of the Julian region from Italy and the small Slovene-speaking enclave of Prekomurje, which had been annexed to Hungary in 1941.

Slovenia became the most ethnically homogeneous of all the republics, with over 95 per cent of its people belonging to the Slovene national group. The Croatian republic covered the historic land of Croatia–Slavonia and Dalmatia, with the addition of Istria and Zara (Zadar) from Italy, and Medjumurje, which Hungary had taken in 1941. It was not quite the same area as that which had been allocated to Croatia by the *sporazum* of 1939, and it contained a 15 per cent minority of Serbs as well as smaller groups of Magyars, Italians and Slovenes. Nevertheless, 80 per cent of the inhabitants were Croats.

The delimitation of the boundaries of the new federal units may be criticised in detail on grounds of political and economic geography, but they represented a broad compromise which was accepted by the various national groups. They have now become so firmly established in the minds of the Yugoslav people that they are never seriously questioned.

The legal theory behind the federal structure is that the separate South Slav peoples voluntarily acceded to the FNRJ and have the right of self-determination. This resembles the situation in the USSR; as there, the possibility that any of them should exercise the right of secession is politically unthinkable.

The 1946 constitution, whilst guaranteeing private property rights, makes clear the socialist basis of the economy. The state-owned industries are described as being the mainstay of the national economy and all mineral wealth, power resources, means of communication and foreign trade are placed under state control. The state is charged with the responsibility for managing the economy within the framework of a central economic plan.

The legislature consisted of a Federal Assembly containing two elements: a Federal Council (Savezno Veće), elected by universal suffrage, and a Council of Nationalities (Veće Naroda), composed of equal numbers of representatives chosen by the Assemblies of the six republics and the two autonomous units. Day-to-day policy was determined by a Presidential Council (Prezidijum), elected from the Assembly. Its figurehead was Dr Ivan Ribar. Tito continued in office as prime minister.

The federal administration in Belgrade was responsible for defence, foreign policy, economic planning, the currency and banking system, communications, law and the maintenance of the social system. There was little left for the republics, although theoretically they had a degree of cultural autonomy. The right to use the national languages was perhaps the most important area left to the republican authorities. In practice the system was highly centralised and hierarchical. The subordinate organs of republican and local government, whilst supposedly responsible to their electors, 'the people', were in fact the agents of central government. The local government structure descended directly from the People's Committees which were created in the liberated areas during the war. They had continued to function during the period of the provisional administration and were easily absorbed into the new constitutional framework.

A study of the formal constitutional provisions does not convey the reality of Yugoslav society in the early post-war years. Just as the autonomy of the republics and communes were severely circumscribed by the centralised nature of the administrative hierarchy, so the structure of government was controlled by the Communist Party. The Yugoslav leaders later admitted that the close control which the party exercised over the whole governmental machine contained the seeds of a bureaucratic, centralised and fundamentally undemocratic system, in which orders flowed downwards from the Politburo to the lower strata of the party, whose members exercised day-to-day supervision over the organs of government. There was a close interlocking of party and state functions, symbolised at the summit by Tito's position as head of government, of the army and of the party.

This was a classic case of the dictatorship of the proletariat, as enunciated by Lenin and as practised by Stalin in the Soviet Union. There were, however, differences in theory, if less so in practice, between the Soviet and the Yugoslav systems. One such difference concerned the role of the People's Front and of the People's Army. Whereas in the other eastern European states which came under communist rule in 1945 Front organisations provided a route by which representatives of the pre-war bourgeois parties could participate in governments which were under communist control and could retain a shadow of their former identity, in Yugoslavia the pre-war parties had effectively disappeared before the elections of November 1945. The party set up the People's Front and never made any secret of the fact that it controlled the Front's activities and determined its policies.

The People's Army was Tito's Partisan army under a new name. It had played a political role from the outset and was, in a sense, the creator of the new Yugoslavia, drawing its support from the people and establishing People's Committees in the liberated areas as the forerunners of the socialist state. There was no intention of allowing it to become a copy of the Soviet Red Army – a professional national army of the conventional type. The differences in the Soviet and Yugoslav concepts of the role of the army in national life became apparent when Stalin rebuked Tito for forming proletarian brigades in 1942. The essence of these differences lies in the experiences of the Yugoslavs during the wartime battles between the Partisans and their enemies. The People's Army had grown from a mass resistance movement, and its revolutionary character could not be separated from its military functions. The autonomous nature of the Yugoslav resistance movement gave the Yugoslavs a self-confidence and pride which resisted Soviet attempts to bring them into conformity with the other People's Democracies, whose revolutions arrived ready-made in the supply columns of the Red Army. These differences of approach were concealed at the time, but broke the surface in 1948 during the dispute with the Cominform. Outwardly the Yugoslavs between 1945 and 1948 appeared to be the most apt pupils and loyal allies of the Soviet Union.

One of the first tasks of the new government, and one which would have faced any Yugoslav administration, was to establish its authority over the war-torn country in order to begin the task of post-war reconstruction. An advantage which the new Yugoslavia enjoyed from the outset, and which was not immediately accorded to several of its neighbours, was full diplomatic recognition by the international community. After the Allied governments had accepted the Tito–Šubašić government, Yugoslavia was able to become a founder member of the United Nations. During the first post-war winter the country's economic survival was greatly assisted by the UNRRA, which sent over $400 million worth of food, clothing and machinery. UNRRA help was particularly important in rebuilding the shattered railway system and in supplying engines and rolling stock to enable goods to be moved to the places where they were most needed.

The elimination of opposition

The consolidation of the regime's authority required the elimination of all forms of political opposition. The dismantling of the last traces of the pre-war political edifice was comparatively easy. A few politicians were absorbed into the system, but most were excluded, some imprisoned, some exiled and others simply ignored. One or two who were thought likely to be of some use during the transition period were allowed to play a part for a time and were then discarded. One such figure was the left-wing leader of the Agrarians, Professor Dragoljub Jovanović. He became secretary-general of the People's Front, but when he had served his purpose he was arrested in 1947, charged with espionage and sentenced to nine years' imprisonment.

The suppression of political resistance to the new regime was comparatively easy. Most of the Ustaša leaders who survived the war escaped abroad. For geographical reasons, it was more difficult for the Serbs to reach the United States or British-occupied territory in Austria or Italy, but many did so. Estimates of the numbers of Yugoslavs who either refused to return home from their workplaces in Germany or elsewhere, or who fled before the advancing Partisan and Red Army troops, suggest a figure of about half a million. In addition there were over 350,000 *Volksdeutsche*, mainly from Vojvodina, who escaped the vengeance which they knew would fall upon them because of their collaboration with the occupation regime.

The hard core of Četniks, with their leader Mihailović, were hunted down and captured in March 1946. A show trial was held in Belgrade, starting on 10 June and lasting for over a month. As well as Mihailović, several leading Četniks and Nedić supporters were also tried at the same time. Several of the accused were former ministers and officers in the services of the king and were tried *in absentia*. Of those who were within the jurisdiction of the court, Mihailović and seven others were executed. The Belgrade trial represented the tip of an iceberg. Below the surface thousands of former Četnik supporters were rounded up, interrogated and imprisoned.

In Croatia and Slovenia the leading collaborators escaped, but thousands of their followers who fled to Austria were returned by the British forces to face terrible retribution at the hands of the Partisans.

A serious situation arose in Kosovo in early 1945, where an armed revolt of Albanians occurred in protest against the agreement between Hoxha and Tito that the area should revert to Yugoslavia. Although the Partisans had collaborated closely with the Albanian resistance movement, and although some 50,000 Albanians had fought with the Yugoslavs, there was a strong Albanian nationalistic sentiment existing which wanted to maintain the Greater Albania which had been created in 1941. The 1945 revolt was suppressed by the Partisans, who were forced to commit 30,000 troops to Kosovo at a time when they were needed to pursue the retreating Germans.

The Catholic Church and the communists

A more difficult problem arose in Croatia because of the part played by some Roman Catholic leaders, both clerical and lay, in the political life of the NDH. The most sensitive issue was to decide how to deal with Archbishop Stepinac. He had welcomed the formation of NDH and had publicly supported Pavelić, although he had privately criticised some of the more extreme acts of the Ustaša. In the last few weeks before the collapse of the NDH he refused an offer by Pavelić to take over the leadership of a provisional government of Croatia but in April 1945 at a service of thanksgiving on the fourth anniversary of the NDH he praised Pavelić and bitterly attacked the communists. When the Partisans entered Zagreb on 8 May 1945 Stepinac refused to leave his post, although he gave permission for any of his priests to leave if they so wished. Very few joined the flood of Ustaše and other refugees pouring into Italy and Austria. This was in sharp contrast to the behaviour of Archbishop Šarić of Sarajevo and Bishops Garić of Banja Luka and Rožman of Ljubljana, who waited for no permission from the Vatican or any other Church authority before they abandoned their flocks. Stepinac was interned for his own protection on 17 May, but was released on 3 June after the trigger-happy Partisans had been brought under control and there was no danger to his life. He met Tito and the Croatian communist leader Bakarić on 4 June, and gained the impression that Tito would be prepared to accept him as the head of a national Catholic Church, freed from Vatican influence – although he later denied this.

In the first few months after the war many priests and nuns were ill treated and those who were accused of complicity in Ustaša atrocities were brought to summary justice. Over two hundred were executed. Stepinac protested to Bakarić and received an admission that some excesses had been committed. Stepinac also protested against the secularisation of education, the institution of civil marriage and the confiscation of Church lands under the Agrarian Reform Laws. Although his letters to Tito and Bakarić on these topics received civil replies, it was noted that his denunciation of the communists did not come well from a man who had co-operated with Pavelić. In September 1945 the archbishop issued a pastoral letter denouncing the authorities.

In September 1946 a trial of Ustaša members and sympathisers began in Zagreb. The accused included Pavelić's police chief, Erik Lisak; one of Stepinac's secretaries, Ivan Salić; and the Franciscan Provincial for Zagreb, Fra Martinčić. Evidence was produced which pointed to Stepinac's complicity in some of the crimes alleged against Salić and Martinčić, and Stepinac himself sat in the dock between Lisak and Salić; but he refused to recognise the court and remained silent. When the sentences were handed down, Stepinac received sixteen years at hard labour, Salić twelve years and Martinčić five years. Lisak was sentenced to death. In fact Stepinac did not serve the sentence as awarded by the court. He was imprisoned in conditions of reasonable comfort until 5 December 1951, when he was allowed to settle in the parish house of his home village, Krašić, where he lived under some restrictions until his death in 1960.

The trial of Stepinac marked the beginning of a period of strained relations between the Catholic Church and the state, especially in Croatia. The situation was not made much easier by the announcement by the Vatican on Yugoslav National Day, 29 November 1952, that Stepinac had been made a cardinal. This prompted the government to break off relations with the Vatican, but two years later an improvement began when both sides began to look for ways of promoting a *modus vivendi*. Tito admitted that there had been excesses on the government's side, and the Vatican, by appointing Monsignor Franjo Šeper as Archbishop-Coadjutor of Zagreb, tacitly admitted that Stepinac could no longer function as head of the see.

When Stepinac died on 10 February 1960 the authorities allowed his funeral to take place in Zagreb Cathedral and he was buried behind the altar. His grave has become a shrine for Croatian Catholics and, to some extent, a place of quiet pilgrimage for Croatian nationalists. Monsignor Šeper, who succeeded Stepinac as archbishop, was himself made a cardinal. He was able to achieve a great deal for the Church in Croatia by his more flexible approach, and during his term of office he saw the founding of the mass circulation Catholic newspaper *Glas Koncila* and the opening of a dialogue between the Catholic and Marxist philosophers. In the more relaxed atmosphere relations with the Vatican improved to the point where Tito was able to visit Pope Paul in 1971, a year after full diplomatic relations had been resumed.

The economy

Post-war reconstruction and the building of a socialist economy were tasks which were tackled simultaneously.

Agriculture

The provisional government introduced a Land Reform Law in August 1945. It was an attempt to implement the age-old promise of radical agrarian reformers from John Ball to Lenin – or, in Yugoslav terms, from Matija Gubec to Stjepan Radić – the land to those who till it. This has been included in the AVNOJ resolutions and made a strong appeal to the Yugoslav peasantry, who constituted almost 80 per cent of the population.

The 1945 law stated that the maximum agricultural holding to remain the property of the farmer cultivating it with his family should be established by provincial laws, with the proviso that it must not be under twenty or over thirty-five hectares of cultivated land. A land fund was established, to which were allocated all lands confiscated by the state. This included land abandoned by owners who had fled abroad – including 350,000 *Volksdeutsche* from the rich farming region of Vojvodina and Slavonia – and land previously owned by absentee landlords, foreigners, banks, religious houses and private companies. A total of 1,493,000 hectares of arable land and 79,000 hectares of forest was thus administered by the land fund. It was distributed as shown in table 3.

The reallocation of this land gave the new regime an opportunity to reward those peasants who had supported the Partisans, especially those who were landless or who came from the poorest farming areas in the limestone *polja* of Lika, Kordun, Banija and Gorski Kotor. Although these areas were in Croatia and Bosnia, a large proportion of the inhabitants were Serbs who were descended from the frontiersmen who had been induced to settle there in Habsburg times in order to strengthen the military frontier against the Turks. There was a long history of migration from these deprived areas to the richer lands of Pannonia. The 1945 land reform dramatically accelerated this process as, in all, 42,587 families were resettled under its provisions.

Table 3. *Distribution of the land fund*

Type of new owner	Area (ha)	% of total area
Individual peasants	797,400	50.7
State farms	287,700	18.3
State enterprises	39,700	2.5
Health and educational institutions	20,100	1.3
Nationalised forests	380,300	24.2
Agricultural cooperatives	47,000	3.0
Total	1,572,200	

Source: J. Tomasevich, 'The Collectivization of Agriculture in Yugoslavia', in Irwin T. Sanders, *Collectivization of Agriculture in Eastern Europe* (Lexington, Ky, 1958).

Many of those involved in this migration were receptive to the concept of collective or cooperative farming and were ready to accept the socialisation of agriculture. There was, however, resistance to the policy of forced deliveries (*otkup*) which the government introduced in 1945. The peasants were faced with a 'scissors crisis' similar to that which had faced Soviet peasants a generation earlier. They were expected to deliver their produce to the state agency at low fixed prices, but were compelled to buy manufactured goods at high prices. Failure to deliver quotas, often arbitrarily set by inexperienced officials, could lead to confiscation of their land. They reacted in the same way as had their Soviet counterparts in the 1920s, by passive non-cooperation and, on occasion, by physical resistance. In 1946 the policy was modified and a limited free market was permitted. Inducements were offered to those willing to join cooperatives. These included membership of social welfare schemes, which was not available to private peasants, and the issuing of coupons for the purchase of clothing at low prices.

At this stage no overt pressure was put on peasants to enter the socialist sector, as the government could not afford to alienate the mass of the population at a time when it was trying to establish its authority and to legitimise its power by introducing a new constitution. The collectivisation drive was to come later and proved to be a miserable failure (see pp. 224–5).

The first Five Year Plan

By the end of 1946, thanks to the strenuous efforts of the Yugoslav people and assisted by generous UNRRA aid, the worst of the wartime damage had been repaired. The railway bridges on the main lines, most of which had been blown up, were rebuilt, and traffic was moving freely. Factories and mines were reopened and production was rising. The national income was back to the level of 1938. The time had come to lay the economic foundation of socialism. The model was that of Stalin's Soviet Union. Boris Kidrič, the young Slovene dogmatist, had the responsibility of introducing the first Five Year Plan in 1947. He had boundless energy and a blind faith in the efficiency of the Stalinist blueprint for the rapid industrialisation of an underdeveloped peasant economy. In his speech to the Fifth Party Congress in July 1948, which took place less than a month after the expulsion of the Yugoslavs from the Cominform, he openly admitted his debt to Stalin. The targets set in the Plan were hopelessly over-optimistic and were based on an unreal assessment of the country's resources, especially of coal and oil. The emphasis was on the development of heavy industry, which was expected to be producing 552 per cent of the 1939 level at the end of the planning period. Consumer goods were to rise by only 274 per cent and agricultural output by 52 per cent.

The Plan was administered by a Federal Planning Commission which controlled the allocation of resources, and the Commission in its turn was closely supervised by the Communist Party. The totals for the whole period were subdivided into annual, quarterly, monthly and even daily quotas, and the overall national targets were broken down into the smallest detail, so that each republic, commune and factory knew what was expected of it. The annual plan weighed around 3,000 lb (1360 kg). A vast bureaucracy was created in order to process the returns which each enterprise and production unit were required to deliver to the central planners. This highly centralised and cumbersome machinery became clogged by masses of paper containing information which bore little resemblance to the realities of the situation.

The Plan was based on two false assumptions. The first was that a country the size of Yugoslavia, with its limited resources, could industrialise itself using methods which were thought appropriate to a continental area like the Soviet Union, covering one-sixth of the earth's surface. The other assumption was that a centralised planning system, which depended upon a vast information-gathering and accounting apparatus, could be operated in a country which lacked both the means of communication and the trained administration to carry it out.

Before the system could be tested properly the intervention of the economic blockade which the Cominform countries imposed in 1948 caused a major readjustment and led eventually to the abandonment of this type of planning.

Despite its many shortcomings, the Plan did achieve some of its objectives. The foundations of heavy industry were laid and it is probable that, without this basis, the rapid industrial growth of the 1950s could not have been accomplished. Industrial development, albeit at a heavy cost, was started in areas such as Macedonia, Kosovo, Montenegro and Bosnia, which had previously depended entirely on peasant agriculture.

Kidrič not only looked to Stalin for his planning model. He also assumed that Yugoslavia's current economic development would depend on trade with the Soviet bloc countries. In 1948 51.6 per cent of exports were sent to this area and 48.8 per cent of imports were derived from it. In 1949 these figures had dropped to 14 and 14.9 per cent respectively, and for the next four years they fell to zero. Yugoslavia was excluded from Comecon when that organisation was created in 1949, and the trade agreements which had been signed with individual eastern European countries were unilaterally abrogated, even in the cases where Yugoslavia had already fulfilled its side of the bargain. For example, machine tools from Czechoslovakia were never delivered, despite the fact that payment had been made in grain deliveries which Yugoslavia could ill afford to lose.

To add to Yugoslavia's difficulties there were severe droughts in 1950 and 1952 which caused near famine conditions. In both those years crop production fell to about two-thirds of the level of the 1930s.

The Cominform dispute

In 1943 the Soviet leaders decided that the Comintern should be disbanded. It was the international association of Communist parties and had its headquarters in Moscow. It had served its purpose and was thought to be an irritant in the smooth running of the wartime anti-fascist coalition. In the new situation which developed at the end of the war, with six eastern European states having communist-led governments, and with the Italian and French communists forming the largest political parties in their respective countries, it was considered appropriate to introduce a new form of international communist organisation. The Cominform (or Communist Information Bureau) was established in September 1947, with its headquarters in Belgrade. Its membership was limited to the USSR, the six ruling eastern European parties, and the French and Italians. Its functions were to coordinate the exchange of information and to establish a machinery of consultation among the member parties. It published a journal with the cumbersome title *For a Lasting Peace, for a People's Democracy*, in several languages. The Yugoslavs were members for nine months and the organisation was quietly disbanded in 1956.

If the Soviet leaders, who had pressed for the Cominform to be sited in Belgrade, felt that this would give them an opportunity to guide the policies of the Yugoslavs, they were soon disappointed. Although to the outside world Tito appeared to be second only to Stalin in the world communist hierarchy – and, judging by the rapturous reception which Tito had when he visited Prague and Warsaw in 1946, this was a view accepted in eastern Europe – serious strains were developing below the surface. The Yugoslavs had shown unwelcome signs of independence on several occasions during the war and had been rebuked by Stalin for these breaches of discipline. By 1947, however, it seemed that these lapses had been forgotten and the Yugoslavs appeared to be basking in the sunlight of Stalin's favour. He even encouraged Djilas to think of 'swallowing' Albania, and did not at first object to proposals for a Balkan federation, which had been discussed between Tito and the Bulgarian leader, Dimitrov.

During 1947 friction developed between the Yugoslavs and their Soviet allies in three sensitive areas: economic, military and foreign policies. The Soviet Union was not enthusiastic about the ambitious aims of the Five Year Plan, preferring Yugoslavia to buy the industrial goods it needed from the USSR in return for raw materials which it would supply to its more powerful partner. To the Yugoslavs this smacked of economic imperialism, although they did not say so at the time. The favoured instrument by which the Soviet Union brought the economies of eastern Europe under its control was the establishment of joint companies. Several of these had been started in Romania (the Sovrom companies) and other countries. The Yugoslavs did not like what they saw of these but reluctantly agreed to the formation of a joint company for commercial air transport (JUSTA) and another for river shipping on the Danube (JUSPAD). When they wound these companies up in 1949 they complained that the USSR had claimed the right to appoint the directors and had ignored the needs of the Yugoslav economy, although the agreed Soviet contribution to the capital and running expenses had never been paid.

Another source of friction concerned differences over the organisation of the Yugoslav People's Army (see above, p. 195) and the role of Soviet military advisers. In foreign policy the Yugoslavs supported the Soviet line on all important issues before the United Nations and, along with Bulgaria and Albania, gave active support to the communist guerrillas in Greece.

Their loyalty was not always rewarded. The Soviet Union did not back the Yugoslavs over their claims to Trieste and Slovene Carinthia. Tito began to suspect that a disreputable bargain had been struck between Churchill and Stalin at Yalta, at the expense of small countries like Yugoslavia. It was later revealed that such an agreement had indeed been reached, and that Yugoslavia was regarded as subject to a fifty–fifty arrangement regarding the spheres of influence of the two world powers. Concerning the Trieste dispute, Tito had declared as early as May 1945 that 'this Yugoslavia is not an object for barter and bargaining' and had received a note of protest from the Soviet ambassador.

The first public indication that there was Soviet–Yugoslav disagreement came obliquely in February 1948, when Dimitrov was compelled to withdraw his support for the proposed Balkan federation. Dimitrov had spoken of the scheme in a speech in Bucharest, implying that Romania might also be included in the federation. Tito was summoned to Moscow, but discovered a diplomatic illness, and sent two close associates, Vladimir Bakarić and Edvard Kardelj, to join Djilas, who was already there. Stalin and Molotov voiced their displeasure at the state of Yugoslav–Soviet relations, specifically mentioning the failure of the Yugoslavs to consult before sending troops into Albania at the request of Enver Hoxha, and complaining of the misinterpretation of the Balkan federation scheme by both Tito and Dimitrov.

During the next few months the scope of Soviet criticism widened and, in an exchange of letters between the leaders of the two parties, the whole basis of the Yugoslav Party's policy was held up to criticism. The issues raised included the role of the CPY in the People's Front, ideology, economic policy, the class struggle in the countryside, and the attitude of Yugoslav officials to Soviet advisers and diplomats. There were even bitter polemics about the achievements of the Partisans and the part played by the Red Army in the liberation of Yugoslavia. In May two leading communists were arrested in Belgrade – the Croat Andrija Hebrang, who had been chairman of the Federal Planning Commission, and Sreten Žujović, who was expelled from the Central Committee in 1946. Both were suspected of being Soviet agents. In June the Yugoslavs were summoned to a meeting of the Cominform, to be held in Bucharest to discuss 'the situation in the CPY'. The rift had, by this time, become so deep that the Yugoslavs refused to attend what they suspected might be a form of show trial. Tito felt that, if he went to the meeting breathing defiance, he might not be able to return home.

Although they must have suspected that the Bucharest meeting might result in their expulsion from the Cominform, the announcement on 28 June came as a shock to Tito and his associates. To the rest of the world it came as a bombshell. It was the first major setback to Soviet foreign policy since the end of the war and involved a fundamental re-examination of international relations by governments on both sides of the so-called Iron Curtain.

In Yugoslavia the call by the Cominform for 'healthy elements' within the CPY to replace their present leaders met with a poor response. One prominent ex-Partisan, the former chief of staff, General Arso Jovanović, was shot whilst attempting to flee to Romania on 13 August, and two other officers, General Branko Petričević and Colonel Vlada Dapčević, were arrested. Air force General Pero Popivoda was more successful. He commandeered a plane and flew across the frontier. The Yugoslav ambassador to Romania also defected, and a number of Yugoslavs studying in Moscow opted to stay in the Soviet Union. A large number of party members of lower status found it impossible to abandon the pro-Soviet attitudes which had been drilled into them during the previous decade, and many were imprisoned. In the autumn a prison camp was established in the desolate Goli Otok (Bare Island), which lies two miles offshore, overlooked by the towering cliffs of the Velebit mountains. During the next five years some 15,000 party members were 're-educated' on Goli Otok, most of them for alleged Cominform sympathies. At first the conditions were unbearably harsh, and there were circumstantial reports of brutal treatment. Protests by liberal-minded party members eventually resulted in an amelioration of the regime. The vigilance of Ranković's political police nipped in the bud any Soviet-inspired attempts to subvert the CPY, but there was never any serious likelihood that the leadership – referred to in the Cominform correspondence as 'the Tito clique' – would be overthrown. The majority of Yugoslavs, whether party members or not, stood by Tito. His wartime reputation as a Partisan leader and his obvious determination to stand up for Yugoslavia's rights in the face of Soviet pressure ensured his survival. No attempt was made to hide from the people the nature of the Soviet attack. As a visitor to Belgrade during the Fifth Party Congress, which opened on 21 July, I recall purchasing a copy of the Cominform journal containing an attack on Tito. Amused Yugoslav friends pointed to the bold type in which it was stated that Tito dare not allow this paper to be sold in Yugoslavia!

At the Fifth Congress Tito refuted the Cominform allegations but skilfully refrained from attacking Stalin. The psychological blunder which permitted the authors of the Cominform resolution to denigrate the achievements of the Partisans and to give sole credit to the Red Army for the liberation of Yugoslavia was used to great effect. The Yugoslavs knew that the statement of the Soviet general, Korneyev, that the Red Army did 'all in its power and beyond its power' to help the Yugoslavs was contrary to their experience, and that Djilas was right to complain about the excesses which the Red Army had perpetrated against Yugoslav civilians – rape, murder and looting – and that he was justified in comparing the excesses of the Russians with the correct demeanour of the British. Nevertheless, the impression was given that Stalin had been misled by false advisers and that, if only they could by bypassed, a reconciliation might be possible. Stalin's portrait still appeared alongside those of Marx, Engels, Lenin and Tito, the songs hailing Comrade Tito and Comrade Stalin were still sung, and the slogans shouted by the cheering delegates included 'Tito, Stalin, Stalin, Tito!'. The attitude gradually changed, the mood shifting from one which was more in sorrow than in anger to one of bitter hostility as the months passed and it became obvious that Stalin was the chief instigator of the anti-Yugoslav campaign. It took longer for the party to abandon its Stalinist economic programme and to re-examine the ideological basis of its policies.

The economic consequences of the Cominform dispute

Once the immediate political consequences of the dispute had been tackled so successfully at the Fifth Congress, it became necessary to examine the effect on the economy of the trauma of June 1948. The economic blockade dealt a cruel blow to the hopes of achieving the targets set out in the Five Year Plan. The sudden cessation of trade forced the Yugoslavs to seek trading partners in the west, but although this reorientation was eventually successful, it could not be achieved within a short time. Relations with the west were at a low ebb. The shooting down of a US plane which had strayed over Yugoslav territory had brought Yugoslav–American relations to a new low. The support which Yugoslavia was giving to the Greek communists under General Marcos (Markos Vafiadis) was in direct opposition to the Truman Doctrine of 1947. Relations between the Yugoslavs and the west had taken a further turn for the worse when a Tripartite Declaration by Britain, France and USA was published on 28 March 1948 which proposed the handing over of the Free Territory of Trieste, including the city itself, to Italy. This was an attempt to influence the voters in the Italian general election due on 18 April. It was bitterly opposed by Yugoslavia, which still laid claim to Trieste.

Although none of these contentious issues was resolved during 1948, the western powers quickly came to realise that it was in their interests to see that Yugoslavia survived and that help should be given to sustain it against Soviet pressure. Within less than a year after the Cominform resolution, both economic and military aid was sent, and for the next decade Yugoslavia's growing trade deficit was largely covered by western credits and other forms of aid.

At home, the disruption caused by the Cominform blockade forced the Yugoslavs to reschedule the timing of the Five Year Plan. In 1949 it was announced that it would run for an extra year, and many of the original targets were tacitly ignored. The planning methods were also relaxed and the economy was run on a looser rein. When the Plan officially ended in 1952, no attempt was made for several years to introduce another Five Year Plan. The second plan, launched in 1957, was based on very different premises. The introduction of workers' self-management in the early 1950s, and the accompanying decentralisation of economic decision-making, made it impossible to run the economy on the highly centralised Stalinist model.

Collectivisation of agriculture

Paradoxically, one of the reactions of the Yugoslav party to the Cominform attack on its agricultural policy was to introduce in 1949 a drive to collectivise agriculture. It seemed as if the Yugoslavs were trying to convince the world that the Cominform had been wrong in accusing them of being a 'party of kulaks'. The Five Year Plan had set a target for raising agricultural output by 52 per cent above 1939 levels, but it failed to provide either the investment or the economic incentives to enable the peasants to achieve this figure. They adopted, therefore, the Stalinist policy of collectivisation, believing that this would stimulate efficiency by creating larger farms and making mechanisation possible.

The land reform of 1945 increased the number of smallholdings by breaking up the larger and more prosperous farms of kulaks, especially those of the *Volksdeutsche* who had left Vojvodina and Slavonia. The newly settled colonists were unused to large-scale farming and to modern farm machinery. The first legislation in 1945 placed a maximum of 35 ha (85 acres) on individual holdings. This was later reduced to 10 ha of arable land. In fact, in 1948 the average size of a peasant holding was 5 ha.

The form of collective farm – known as a peasant work collective (*seljačka radna zadruga*) – varied from place to place. In some the peasant was rewarded solely in relation to the labour input of the family; in others some payment was made in proportion to the size of the plot which he handed over to collective working. In most cases the peasant could retain up to one hectare as a private plot. Any surplus from the private sector could be sold on the free market.

Various methods were used to induce peasants to join collectives. Although on the whole a carrot-and-stick approach was most commonly applied by offering or withholding certain welfare and taxation benefits, and by other forms of state patronage in the gift of the local government and party authorities, there were some examples of direct coercion. The attempt to apply uniform policies to the fertile arable lands of Vojvodina, the karstic plateaus of Dalmatia and the hill farms of the Slovene Alps indicated a reversion of bureaucratic methods which ignored the realities of the situation. The reaction of the peasants varied from sullen acceptance to cautious support, but there were few examples either of active sabotage or of wild enthusiasm.

When the collectivisation drive began, 94 per cent of the land was privately farmed. At the height of the campaign, in the autumn of 1950, 78 per cent still remained in private hands. In 1948 there had been 1,300 collectives, covering an area of 324,000 ha. In 1950 there were 6,600, occupying 1,840,000 ha. If one adds to the areas of state farms and those belonging to agricultural institutes and other public bodies, 2.5 million hectares were involved. The crippling drought of 1950 brought the drive to an end, although it was not until November 1951 that the party formally acknowledged a change in policy, and not until 1953, after a second drought in 1952, that peasants were given the legal right to leave the collectives. In practice, many left during 1951 and 1952, and over a fifth of the collectives were disbanded. As soon as the law was changed, the area under collective farming fell from 2.5 million ha in 1950 to 600,000 ha in 1953. By 1958 it had fallen to 216,000 ha. It became apparent to the pragmatic Tito that the country's food problems were not being solved by these policies. The promised irrigation and drainage works which would have ameliorated the situation had not been carried out because of lack of capital, the collectivisation drive had alienated many peasants, and there was no sign that it had increased efficiency. It were best to abandon the policy. The idea of socialised agriculture was not abandoned, but, as Tito made clear at the Sixth Congress of the CPY in Zagreb in November 1952, the new policy would be based on gradual, voluntary acceptance of membership of general agricultural cooperatives in which the peasants retained full ownership rights.

The end of the collectivisation drive marked the opening of a new chapter in Yugoslavia's post-war development. The phase of the 'dictatorship of the proletariat' – which meant in practice the dictatorship of the party acting in the name of the proletariat – was at an end.

11

The beginnings of self-management

When they recovered from the shock of the breach with the Soviet Union, the Yugoslav leaders began to examine why they had so misjudged Stalin and the Soviet system. They had themselves begun to build the new Yugoslavia in the image of the USSR. Would they also suffer from the bureaucratic degeneration which had transformed the first socialist state in the world into an oppressive form of state capitalism? To answer this question they began to examine the basic Marxist texts. Hitherto their Marxism had been filtered for them through the works of Stalin. Even the leading party intellectuals admitted that they had not recently studied the original works of Marx. Djilas, Kardelj and Kidrič began to talk about the free association of producers which Marx believed should take over the factories. They would provide a workers' answer to the bureaucratic distortions inherent in the *étatist* model. With a few exceptions, the Yugoslav communist leadership has never been strong on theory. They have been pragmatists and men of action rather than philosophers. They operate within a Marxist framework of reference, but often the theoretical justification for a particular course of action comes after the decisions have been taken on pragmatic grounds.

The decision to introduce workers' self-management on a nation-wide basis was taken in the spring of 1950. Before this time there had been advisory councils of workers in the state-owned factories. By June 1950 five hundred of these experimental workers' councils already existed. The decision to extend the system to all factories and to give the councils statutory powers was seen by its authors as a step towards a true workers' democracy, such as Marx envisaged when he wrote about the 'withering away of the state'. Tito did not accept the idea simply because it was a fulfilment of a Marxist dream. He did so because he saw that it suited Yugoslav conditions in 1950, by presenting to the workers a credible alternative to the Stalinism which had failed them in 1948.

In June 1950 Tito personally introduced before the Assembly a measure which was called the Basic Law on the Management of State Economic Enterprises by Working Collectives. At first, the changes wrought by the new law were more symbolic than real. The managers of state enterprises still retained wide powers to enforce industrial discipline and to hire and fire workers, and were accountable to the higher organs of the state for carrying out decisions handed down to them from above. The managing director was responsible for day-to-day decisions. The workers' council need be consulted only on broad policy questions, but the director, in practice, often decided into which category a particular decision fell.

In enterprises employing fewer than thirty workers, the whole workforce formed the working collective. In larger units a workers' council was elected to represent the workforce. In turn, the workers' council elected a managing board which was responsible, with the director, for the running of the firm. The director was initially appointed by a joint commission representing the workers' council and the People's Committee of the local commune. The workers' council could petition for the removal of a director who was considered unsatisfactory, but in practice this seldom happened.

It was expecting a great deal of Yugoslav workers, most of whom came from rural backgrounds and had never been employed in industry, to think them capable of taking decisions concerning the management of modern factories. In order to provide the necessary training, a nation-wide programme of adult education was launched, the main agency for its administration being the trade unions. The decision was taken to limit the term of office of members so that the councils would, over a period of time, involve the largest possible number of workers. This was to prevent the emergence of a professional class of workers' councillors who might lose touch with the grass-roots problems of their fellow workers. During the 1950s 700,000 people served on workers' councils. Considering that the total workforce in the pubic sector was only 2.3 million in 1953, rising to 2.6 million in 1961, it would seem that a very high proportion of those eligible served on workers' councils.

The area of responsiblity which was of greatest interest to the workers' council concerned the disposal of the income of the enterprise. At first there was a strictly circumscribed area in which the workers' council had powers to decide between the payment of personal incomes to its members and allocations to collective funds for social, recreational and welfare activities.

In 1953 the Skupština passed a constitutional law which amended the 1946 constitution, to take into account the development of self-management and also the reforms in local government which had occurred in 1952. These changes represented cautious steps on the road to decentralisation of decision making. The local government reforms gave a degree of autonomy to the People's Committees of the communes (*opštine*) and charged them with the responsibility for overseeing the economic, social and cultural life of the areas under their administration. The links between the *opštine* and the workers' councils were made more explicit. Local councils had a bicameral structure, with one house elected by universal adult suffrage and a Council of Producers elected from the workers' councils.

The constitutional law of 1953 introduced a similar structure at federal level, with a legislature, the Federal Assembly (Savezna Skupština), made up of two elements, a Federal Council (Savezna Veće), which incorporated the former Council of Nationalities, and the Producers' Council, indirectly elected by different groups of producers from assemblies of workers' council delegates. The supreme executive body, the Federal Executive Council (Savezno Isvršno Veće), was elected by the full Federal Assembly and was the effective government of the country. The first FEC to be elected consisted of thirty-eight members, thirty-six of whom were members of the Central Committee of the Communist Party. The post of president of the republic was created, and its first and only incumbent was Josip Broz Tito. (The post was abolished in 1980 following Tito's death.)

The constitutional changes were accompanied by changes in the two political organisations, the Communist Party and the People's Front. At its Sixth Congress in 1952 the party changed its name to that of the League of Communists (Savez Komunista Jugoslavije), and the People's Front followed a year later, becoming the Socialist Alliance of Working people of Yugoslavia (Socialistički Savez Radnog Naroda Jugoslavije). The changes of name symbolised a change in the concept of the role of communists in a self-managed society. The League of Communists (LCY) was intended to be the leading political force in the country, but, unlike the CPY in the early post-war period, it would no longer exercise day-to-day administrative control over all aspects of national life. Communists were expected to play an active part in all socio-political organisations, in the Socialist Alliance (SAWPY) and in the workers' councils, but they were to work through persuasion and the exercise of social pressure rather than by administrative fiat.

SAWPY was a corporate body, much larger than the LCY, which was made up of affiliated organisations such as the trade unions; the youth, student and women's organisations; and the prestigious war veterans' association, as well as the LCY. In 1961 SAWPY claimed 6.7 million members, whilst the LCY had only 1 million. Communists occupied the leading positions in SAWPY, and in some areas the two organisations shared premises and secretaries. SAWPY's role was to organise the masses and to nominate the lists of candidates for election to public office. It was theoretically possible for individuals who were not on the list to stand and occasionally unofficial candidates were successful, although this was a rare occurrence.

Although the grip of the communists was somewhat relaxed, they still represented the only organised political force in the country and could, where necessary, exercise complete control. Dissent was permitted within limits, but the limits were tightly drawn. The case of Milovan Djilas in 1954 showed that, even at the highest level, an elected member could be removed swiftly from office if he or she diverged too far from the party line. Djilas was returned as a deputy for a Montenegrin constituency with 98.8 per cent of the vote in the elections in December 1953, and was unanimously elected president of the Federal Assembly. In January 1954, because of a series of controversial articles which he wrote in the communist daily *Borba* and other journals, his mandate was withdrawn and he lost all his official positions.

The Seventh Congress of the LCY, held in Ljubljana from 22 to 26 April 1958, adopted a programme which offered a theoretical justification for the changes which had taken place during the previous decade. Whilst justifying the initial period of state centralism as a necessary stage in the building of a socialist society, the programme recognised the danger that 'bureaucratic étatist deformities' could become negative factors, leading to a betrayal of the revolution. It was argued that the alternative to state capitalism, bureaucracy and the cult of personality was to develop self-managing institutions through which the workers could exercise a direct democracy. This was the road to the free association of producers which Marx envisaged, which led eventually to the withering away of the state. This was what Lenin meant when, in October 1917, he drafted the decree on workers' control which recognised the right of workers to control all aspects of production and to oversee the administration of their factories.

The Ljubljana Congress was a direct repudiation of the course of development in the Soviet Union, and it was seen as such by the Soviet and other eastern European observers, who walked out of the meeting in protest. Only the ambassador of Gomulka's Poland remained to listen to the elaboration of the heresy of 'revisionism'.

Although the Yugoslav communists were willing to talk about the withering away of the state, and even to take practical steps to reduce the power of the central government, they were in no hurry to contemplate the withering away of the party. The LCY still believed in Lenin's concept of democratic centralism in the organisation of its own affairs, and still clung to the monopoly of political power which it enjoyed. One of the indictments levelled against Djilas in 1954 concerned his advocacy of a second socialist party in competition with the communists. It was made plain in 1954, and again at the Ljubljana Congress, that, however much the LCY might modify its role in society and liberalise its internal decision-making processes, there was no immediate prospect of its relinquishing its leading position.

The economy during the 1950s

The economic difficulties arising from the Cominform blockade and the bad harvests of 1950 and 1952 made economic planning, on the lines of the first Five Year Plan, impossible. During the early 1950s annual 'social plans' were operated, but these were pragmatic affairs conceived on an *ad hoc* basis. The state, through its control of investment, could still direct the economy in certain directions, but the realities of the situation prevented detailed planning and the achievement of predetermined targets. The overall objective of the goverment remained the same as during the 1947–51 Plan – rapid industrialisation – but new methods were evolved to reach this goal. When the second Five Year Plan (1957–61) was launched, workers' self-management was well established and there had been a considerable degree of administrative decentralisation. There was a two-way process of consultation in which enterprises, communes, districts and republics proposed targets in the light of their own assessment of their needs and possibilities. These were then coordinated by a Federal Planning Institute and amended in accordance with the national economic strategy. Eventually the Skupština debated the issue and passed the necessary legislation. The outline plan contained projections of demographic trends and stated the amount and allocation of investment, the overall increases expected in the output of various branches of industry and agriculture, and the anticipated rise in national income during the planning period. It also allocated investment to the less developed areas.

This form of indicative planning was in complete contrast to the detailed administrative planning of the 1947–51 Plan. Although the federal government retained control of foreign trade, the exchange rate, the monetary system and the investment banks, considerable initiative was left to the enterprises in cooperation with the communal and republican agencies.

During the five years before 1957 the Yugoslav economy had been growing at an average annual rate of 8.5 per cent, which suggests that the introduction of workers' councils had not acted as a brake on output. Industrial growth was even faster, at a rate of 12.6 per cent per year, but agriculture lagged behind at 5.9 per cent. The rate of growth during the second Five Year Plan exceeded the targets set, and the Plan was completed in only four years. The sustained growth in industrial output during the 1950s was faster than that achieved during the same period by any other country in the world, whether in socialist eastern Europe, capitalist western Europe or the Third World.

This period of rapid growth was, of course, from a very low starting point, and the apparently gratifying figures concealed certain underlying weaknesses. The volume of imports far exceeded the planned targets and led to a growing balance-of-trade deficit, which was financed by foreign loans. Throughout the period, export earnings averaged only 62 per cent of the cost of imports. Attempts to boost exports by the devaluation of the dinar had only a temporary effect and there were at this time no large earnings from tourism and other invisible exports, which came to play an important part in the balance of payments after the reforms of 1965.

The growth of the economy was achieved largely because of the artificial protective measures which shielded industries from the consequences of inefficiency and low productivity. The inevitable crisis arrived suddenly in 1961. The rate of growth was halved and imports soared out of control whilst exports remained at the same level as in 1960. The third Five Year Plan (1961–5) was abandoned before it had been in existence for a year and there was a reversion to one-year plans, while the planners went back to the drawing board to prepare a comprehensive series of reforms, based on the new-found principle of 'market socialism'.

The politics of the 1950s

The evolution of the system of self-management obviously involved serious debate within the LCY, the trade unions and the various socio-political and legislative bodies, and it was bound to lead to disagreements and differences of emphasis amongst those who participated in the discussion. There were some who felt that the process of decentralisation was proceeding too far and too fast and others who wanted to press forward even faster. They have been labelled by some western commentators as 'conservatives' and 'liberals', but the terms are misleading. The conservatives, for example, included advocates of an extension of the

Table 4. *The second Five Year Plan, 1957–61 (completed 1960)*

	Target (% growth)	Achievement (1960) (% growth)
National income	54.4	63.0
Industrial production	70.0	70.0
Agricultural production	41.2	59.8
Exports	75.4	76.7
Imports	41.9	70.5
Personal consumption	Between 34 and 40	45.8

Source: Social Plan for the Economic Development of Yugoslavia (Secretariat for Information, Belgrade, 1961), p. 47.

public sector in agriculture by the collectivisation of agriculture. Amongst the liberals were nationalists, whose attitude to the rights of national minorities within the boundaries of their particular republics was far from liberal. The national question cut across the conservative/liberal divide. Alexander Ranković, vice-president of the Federal Executive Council 1953–63, was considered to be both a conservative and a Serbian nationalist. Mika Tripalo, the president of the People's Youth 1955–62, and later secretary of the Croatian Party, was regarded as both a liberal and a Croat nationalist. These are but two examples of the difficulty of assigning labels to Yugoslav politicians. A further complication arises when one considers the attitudes of individuals on specific issues, as it soon becomes apparent that the same person votes 'conservative' on some questions and 'liberal' on others. Tito, for example, obviously approved of the changes which occurred at the Sixth Congress when the CPY became the League, but twenty years later he considered that the Sixth Congress marked the beginning of a decline in the influence of the communists in national life. It was, he said, conducted in 'a euphoria of liberalism', and he identified 'rotten liberalism' as a corrupting influence in the body politic.

One of the problems confronting the communist theoreticians in Yugoslavia during the 1950s was to define the role of the state in a self-managed society. There was no disagreement concerning the role of the state in protecting the socialist order against foreign enemies and internal subversion. Since the Cominform quarrel, the leaders had had to be vigilant on two fronts, and had been compelled to spend a large proportion of the national income on defence and internal security. This had implications for the prospects of the withering away of the state. As long as the enemy posed a threat, a strong state must exist to protect the system.

There was less agreement concerning the role of the state in the economy. How much of the state's economic functions should be transferred to workers' councils, to the People's Committees of communes and to the republics? Does decentralisation necessarily imply democratisation? At one extreme there were those who felt that the transfer of functions from the state to autonomous 'non-state' organs was all that was necessary. Opponents of this view considered that such a process might lead to anarchy and advocated a slower process of 'gradual and conscious permeation of the state apparatus by the masses'.

An issue of crucial importance in the management of the economy was the control of investment. In the structure of the early workers' councils, a very limited power was given to the workers to dispose of the income of an enterprise, but there was strict state control of investments. The main instrument of state control over investment was the banking system, and there was pressure to decentralise its functions and to give republics a greater control over their own regional banks. Republican autonomy did not, of course, mean a withering away of the state. But it could lead to the creation of six separate banking bureaucracies in place of the previous one. It was not until after the reforms of the 1960s that a serious effort was made to involve workers' councils in the control of investment.

Another problem concerned the role of trade unions in a system where workers theoretically managed their own factories. In the immediate post-war period, the unions were modelled on those of the Soviet Union. There were fourteen industrially based unions, financed mainly from state sources and employing 3,500 full-time officials. Their main purposes were to mobilise the workers in the interests of higher production, to enforce labour discipline, and to provide certain welfare benefits for their members. They were transmission belts for the passing on of instructions from state and party officials to the workers. Membership fees were very low and there were material advantages in the form of cheap travel, holidays and recreational facilities. The percentage of the workforce in the trade unions was, therefore, high.

With the introduction of workers' self-management the function of trade unions began to change. They saw their role as being protectors of the new system. Their disciplinary activities became less important and they developed broad educational activities, designed to explain to members how best to use the workers' councils. They also began to represent workers' interests at national level when, for example, legislation was being introduced on pensions, safety at work and industrial relations.

There has always been an ambiguous position regarding the attitude to strikes in Yugoslavia. Under the terms of the various constitutions, strikes are not forbidden, nor are they legal. They have occurred throughout the post-war period, but until the miners' strike at Trbovlje in Slovenia in 1958 their existence was never officially admitted. Since 1958 the reaction of the authorities has varied according to the circumstances. Before 1958 strikes were usually suppressed and their leaders disciplined as being trouble-makers. Tito was once reported as saying that, as the workers controlled the factories, they could not strike against themselves. However, there has been a growing acceptance that a 'work stoppage' can be a useful means of drawing attention to the failure of the official procedures for settling grievances. By focussing attention on weaknesses in the system they can lead to improvements. Most strikes are of short duration, seldom lasting for more than a day, and are spontaneous outbursts in response to purely local problems. The trade unions have never initiated strikes, and when they have occurred the main job of the officials has been to persuade the workers to go back to work.

The difficulty which many party officials experienced in implementing the policy of the Sixth Congress, concerning the new role of the League of Communists as an ideological guiding force rather than a bureaucratic administrative machine, is reflected in the erratic course of the political debates during the 1950s and subsequently. The authoritarian habits of mind developed in the early days were not really abandoned by many who had come to enjoy the exercise of power. Thus, periods of wide-ranging public debate, during which even the top leaders aired radical views about democracy, alternated with periods of relatively stricter control. Often the reversion to more severe conditions can be linked to some internal, or more often external, policy considerations. The key could frequently be found in the state of Yugoslavia's relations with the USSR. A study of the fortunes of Milovan Djilas between 1953 and 1966 illustrates these points.

The case of Milovan Djilas

The Yugoslav revolution devoured fewer of its children than did the revolutions of its eastern neighbours and the Soviet Union. After the removal of Cominformists in 1948 and 1949 there have been few trials of prominent communists for anti-party activities. Those who have been dropped from the leadership following political disagreements have usually been able to retire quietly into obscurity. This was not the case, however, with Milovan Djilas, the fiery Montenegrin, whose dismissal from public office in 1954 and subsequent resignation from party membership was followed by periods of imprisonment between 1956 and 1966. The action against him in 1954 was taken by the LCY Central Committee and was, officially, an internal party affair, although it did result in his loss of public office. In January 1955, however, he appeared before a Belgrade court, accused of a breach of Article 118 of the criminal code, which deals with activities calculated to damage abroad the vital interests of the country through hostile propaganda. Vladimir Dedijer, the only member of the Central Committee – apart from his ex-wife, Mitra – who attempted to defend him in 1954, found himself also in the dock on similar charges. Djilas' offence was that he gave an interview to the *New York Times* in which he criticised the LCY leadership for stifling the democratic elements within the party. He advocated the creation of a democratic socialist party which should be allowed to compete with the LCY. Only in this way, he thought, could real freedom of discussion be guaranteed. The alternative was a return to the bad old Stalinist policies. A memorandum incorporating these ideas, signed by Djilas and Dedijer, awaited Tito when he returned at the end of January 1955 from a long visit to India and Burma. By this time the court had pronounced its verdicts. Both defendants received suspended sentences – for Djilas eighteen months and for Dedijer six months. Dedijer remained within the terms of his probation and escaped imprisonment, but Djilas refused to keep silent. During 1956 he published several articles in western journals, some of which criticised Soviet policy on Poland and Hungary. These appeared at a time when relations between Yugoslavia and the USSR were in a delicate state, and the authorities were anxious that nothing should be done to worsen them. Djilas was arrested on 20 November and on 12 December was sentenced to three years' imprisonment. Between his first trial in 1955 and his imprisonment he had been working on the manuscript of *The New Class*, a book which examined contemporary communist society from a liberal Marxist standpoint. It concluded that a new ruling class had emerged which enjoyed all the privileges of the old capitalist elites but with none of the disadvantages involved in private ownership. The new class was able to wield power and to enjoy all the material advantages of the use of private property – cars, servants, villas, etc. – without having to pay for them. The book was published in America in 1957 and Djilas was immediately taken from prison to the local court in Sremska Mitrovia, where the jail was situated. Six years were added to his sentence.

He was conditionally released on 20 January 1961 after submitting a petition, written at the suggestion of an officer of the civilian security service, UDBA (Uprava Državne Bezbednosti), in which he promised to be of good behaviour and not to repeat the activities which had led to his imprisonment. He continued to write and publish abroad, however, and in 1962, following the announcement that a book with the title *Conversations with Stalin* was about to appear in New York, he was rearrested. This time the charge was that he had used classified material acquired during his period of government service. He was sentenced in May 1962 to a further five years, to which was added the unexpired three years and eight months from his previous sentence. On New Year's Eve 1966 he was unexpectedly freed under the terms of an amnesty granted by President Tito to several of the remaining political prisoners in Yugoslav jails. Since then he has lived in comparative freedom from official harassment, despite the publication of other books and articles abroad. In October 1968 he was able to travel to London, where he gave a television interview endorsing the Yugoslav government's support for Dubček's attempt to build 'socialism with a human face' in Czechoslovakia. He then went on to the USA and during 1969 visited Austria and Italy. The publication of *The Unperfect Society* in 1966 precipitated a further brush with the authorities, but on this occasion the only penalty he suffered was the withdrawal of his passport.

Foreign policy – the move towards non-alignment

The break with the Cominform did not immediately change Yugoslav foreign policy. Yugoslav delegates at the UN continued to vote with the Soviet bloc on all major issues, although it was accepted by mid 1949 that there was no hope of a reconciliation whilst Stalin lived. In June 1949 Soviet Foreign Minister Vyshinski told the Council of Foreign Ministers in Paris that the Soviet Union no longer supported Yugoslav claims to the Slovene-speaking areas of Carinthia. On 27 July Yugoslavia closed the Greek frontier and ceased to give aid to the Greek communists in their civil war with the Allied-backed royalist government. In September the Yugoslav foreign minister, Edvard Kardelj, officially raised in the General Assembly a complaint against Soviet harassment of Yugoslavia. In October Yugoslavia was elected to one of the non-permanent seats on the Security Council, despite the bitter hostility of the Soviet delegation.

The first major divergence from the Soviet line on a world issue unconnected with Yugoslavia's immediate interests came in September 1950 when Kardelj condemned North Korean aggression and promised Yugoslav support for the UN action in Korea.

In 1953 the Yugoslavs took the initiative in forming a Balkan Pact with two members of NATO – Greece and Turkey. This was an attempt to end

Yugoslavia's isolation in world affairs. It led to an increase in trade and cultural exchanges, and also to military consultations, but it ceased to have any importance when Greek–Turkish rivalries over Cyprus flared into open hostility during the late 1950s. By this time, also, Mr Khrushchev's visit to Yugoslavia in 1955 had started a process of *rapprochement* between Yugoslavia and the Soviet Union, which diminished Yugoslavia's fear of Soviet interference.

The development of close relations between Yugoslavia and the newly independent ex-colonial nations of the Third World began with the coordination of the policies of Yugoslavia, India and Egypt on the Korean issue at the United Nations in 1950 and 1951, when Yugoslavia was a member of the Security Council. Another Third World country with which Yugoslavia developed close relations at this time was Burma. Although they were geographically far apart, there were similarities in their political situations. Burma, under its socialist premier Aung San, was trying to carry out an independent socialist policy and was resisting pressure from its big eastern neighbour, Communist China. It was faced with internal problems arising from the cultural diversity of its people and had sought a federal solution to them.

During his visit to Burma in January 1955 Tito was referred to as the Aung San of Yugoslavia, and the compliment was returned to his host, who was described as the Tito of Burma. The visit to Burma was made during a break in Tito's visit to India, during which he endorsed the Panch Sila – the Five Principles of Peaceful Coexistence – which Nehru and Chou En-lai pronounced during the Chinese leader's visit to New Delhi in June 1954.

The non-aligned movement was given a major boost by the Bandung Conference of Afro-Asian Nations, held in April 1955. Although the Bandung Conference produced few tangible results, it did awaken the Yugoslavs to the idea that there was a community of interest between them and the growing number of newly independent nations. All wanted to steer clear of the power blocs which had developed in the world, and they did not want to be forced to choose between communism and capitalism.

Shortly after his return from his Asian tour Tito announced that a high-level Soviet delegation would visit Yugoslavia. Khrushchev, together with Marshal Bulganin, arrived in Belgrade in May 1955. Even before he had left the airport Khrushchev had read out a statement apologising for Soviet actions against Yugoslavia and blaming the recently liquidated police chief, Lavrenti Beria, for the break in relations. Tito had no objection to Khrushchev's proposals for normalising diplomatic relations, but he was more cautious about the re-establishment of close contacts between the communist parties of the two countries. Links between the parties were established in 1956 following Khrushchev's 'secret' speech to the Twentieth Congress of the CPSU in February 1956, in which he disowned Stalin. In 1957 Tito attended a conference of world communist parties in Moscow, but he held aloof from any suggestion that Yugoslavia would submit to any modification of its own road to socialism in order to meet criticisms from foreign communists.

The realisation that Yugoslavia's interests lay in developing closer relations with the non-aligned nations arose from the bitter experiences of the previous decade at the hands of the big powers. The cynical division of Europe into spheres of influence which Churchill and Stalin had agreed at Yalta, in which Yugoslavia was given a fifty–fifty status between east and west, was the first shock to Yugoslavia's hopes for an independent existence. The attempt of Stalin to overthrow Tito in 1948 served to confirm the Yugoslav's suspicions of big-power hegemonism. The solution to the problem of independence for small nations seemed to lie in non-alignment and collective self-help.

To further the policy, Tito embarked on a number of visits to Third World countries and, in his turn, acted as host to men like Nasser, Nehru, Nkrumah, Sukarno and Haile Selassie. From these exchanges there emerged the idea of a summit conference of the non-aligned nations. This took place in Belgrade in September 1961. Yugoslavia was the only European member amongst the fifty-one nations who were represented, but Tito's prestige ensured that he earned the title of 'Father of the Non-Aligned Movement'.

12

The 1960s – a decade of reform

In the early 1960s Yugoslavia was faced with the consequences of the unbalanced economic growth of the previous decade. The crisis in the overheated economy which caused the abandonment in 1962 of the third Five Year Plan compelled the planners to make a fundamental reassessment of the situation. A resolution of the LCY in 1962 pointed to the direction which the new course would take. It called for improvements in productivity to enable Yugoslavia to enter into free competition in world markets, and for the use of market forces as the yardstick with which to measure economic performance. The phrase 'entering the international division of labour' was used to describe this process. It implied the removal of the protective barriers behind which the spectacular growth of the 1950s had been achieved, and the withdrawal of the state from interference in the economy through subsidies, price fixing and cheap credit. At home, it was hoped that competition among autonomous worker-managed enterprises would act as a spur to greater efficiency and would shake out surplus labour, which was being hoarded because it was politically easier to keep semi-skilled and unskilled workers on the payroll in comparative idleness than to make them redundant.

The first steps towards 'market socialism' had been taken during a limited economic reform in 1961, but they were too piecemeal and uncoordinated to be successful. In fact, they made the position worse. The abolition of income controls led to inflationary wage payments. The liberalisation of foreign trade led to an increase in imports, but as Yugoslav industry was not able to secure a corresponding increase in export earnings, the balance-of-payments position worsened.

A fierce debate began amongst the economists and politicians, and Yugoslavia experienced one of those periods of wide-ranging, open discussion comparable to that which occurred during 1952–3 concerning the role of the LCY. This time the open season lasted longer and was terminated only in 1972, during the aftermath of nationalist demonstrations in Croatia in 1971. The issues raised went far beyond the original economic questions and eventually affected every aspect of political and social life. The changes which resulted have had a permanent influence upon Yugoslavia's subsequent development. In the economic debate the reformers had the advantage over those who feared that overemphasis on the role of the market would undermine the socialist basis of society. If market forces were to determine the production and distribution of goods and the allocation of labour, why should there not also be a free capital market? Although this question was raised in the early 1960s, it was not pursued to its logical conclusion at the time, but it resurfaced in 1971, when Stane Kavčič, the Slovene premier, suggested that private individuals should be allowed to invest in self-managed enterprises and to draw dividends based on the profits of the firm. The prospect of a class of 'socialist rentiers' was too much for the more orthodox Marxists and the proposal was dropped. The fact that it was publicly discussed indicates the openness of the debate.

The 1965 reforms

The first consequence of the discussions in the early 1960s was a reform of the banking system. During the 1950s there had been some decentralisation of investment decisions when republican and communal banks were established to administer investment funds originating mainly from federal government sources or from foreign loans. The principle of 'rentability' (*rentabilnost*) was applied to loans made for investment in new industries. The next step was to involve the enterprises more directly in investment decisions. Local banks were able to utilise funds provided by enterprises, and workers' councils were given a share in investment decisions. The liberalisation of the banking system was a necessary preliminary to a reform of the whole economic system.

In July 1965 the Federal Assembly introduced a package of over thirty new laws, which provided the legislative framework in which 'market socialism' was to operate. These laws abolished price controls over a wide range of goods and permitted price rises of up to 30 per cent on the limited number of basic foodstuffs and raw materials which remained subject to control. Export subsidies were withdrawn and import duties halved. Enterprises were allowed to deal directly with their trading partners abroad, but their allocation of foreign currency was determined by their export earnings. The quota of foreign currency left to an enterprise when the necessary amounts had been deposited in the National Bank could be freely used for its own investments, or could be deposited in a local bank to be borrowed by other enterprises, or could be used to pay for imports. The amounts compulsorily deposited with the National Bank were used to finance essential imports by the state or by enterprises which did not export. A proportion of these funds were used to assist the less developed areas.

The liberalisation of foreign trade was accompanied by a devaluation of the dinar by 70 per cent and by the introduction of a new, 'heavy' dinar, with a face value of one-hundredth of the old dinar. As the reforms represented a move towards a market economy, there was no difficulty in obtaining credits from the International Monetary Fund and western banks to cushion the shock. The IMF granted additional drawing rights of $80 million, and a consortium of western banks granted loans of $140 million.

The first effect of the reform on the individual consumer was a steep rise in the prices of food, clothing, rents and fuel. This was partly offset by reductions in personal taxes and social security contributions. There was also a tendency for workers' councils to vote for higher personal incomes to meet the rise in the cost of living.

Although the logic of the reform should have been to impose the iron discipline of the market, even if this meant an increase in unemployment and in the closure of factories, it was not possible, for social and economic reasons, to apply this principle with full rigour. As in other countries where the laws of the market were supposedly on a free rein, it was necessary for the government or the banks to come to the rescue of lame ducks. This was especially the case in the less developed areas where so-called political factories had been established in order to speed up the process of industrialisation.

This government intervention probably slowed down the growth in unemployment for a time, but, as table 5 shows, the numbers out of work increased rapidly after 1970. Between 1964 and 1970 the numbers increased by 40 per cent. During the next six years there was an increase of 230 per cent. The percentage of the workforce who were unemployed did not grow at the same rate, as there was a steady influx of new recruits from the rural areas. These were mainly people who had previously lived on privately owned farms and who were not counted as insured workers, or they were school leavers from the villages. Many of these filled vacancies in industrial occupations, replacing workers who had gone abroad. Others went directly to western Europe as temporary, unskilled 'guest workers'. The safety valve of temporary migration undoubtedly reduced the pressure on the labour market.

Table 5. *Employment and unemployment, 1962–82*

	1962	1964	1966	1968	1970	1972	1974	1976	1978	1980	1982
Total registered workforce (millions at year end)	3.4	3.7	3.6	3.66	3.95	4.31	4.6	4.9	5.4	5.8	6.1
Total seeking work (thousands at year end)	274	228	265	326	289	334	448.6	665	738	789	888
Percentage unemployed	8.2	6.3	7.4	9.0	8.1	7.7	9.7	13.5	13.6	13.75	14.5

Source: 1962–70: *Statistički godišnjak* (Belgrade, 1972), tables 104.2, 104.12.
1972–82: *Ibid.*, 1982, tables 105.13, 105.14, 204.1.

Two measures of liberalisation which had an important bearing on the economy, as well as on the social life of the country, were the relaxing of restrictions on the migration of Yugoslav workers who wished to work abroad and the encouragement of foreign tourists. The invisible exports arising from the remittances of Yugoslav workers in western Europe and from the foreign currency spent by tourists came to play an important part in the balance of payments (see table 6). By 1970 there were 400,000 Yugoslavs working in the Federal Republic of Germany alone, compared with only 10,000 in 1960. German tourists accounted for over 25 per cent of the five million visitors who entered Yugoslavia in 1970.

These developments drew Yugoslavia into closer dependence on the economies of western Europe. These links were further strengthened by the enactment, in 1967, of legislation which enabled private foreign investors to enter into partnership with Yugoslav enterprises. The foreign firm was allowed to invest up to 49 per cent of the capital in a joint enterprise and to repatriate its profits. The Germans were the first to take advantage of this opportunity, and by 1971 German capital represented 25 per cent of the $93.5 million which had been invested. In addition there were licensing agreements and marketing agreements which were entered into by Yugoslav firms, which increased the dependence of the economy on foreign partners. Yugoslavia's economic relations with the Soviet Union and its Comecon partners were on a different footing. Although trade with the east recovered rapidly during the late 1950s after the visit of

Table 6. *Net invisible earnings from tourism and remittances ($ millions)*

	1965	1966	1967	1968	1969	1970	1971
Remittances from workers abroad and private transfers	59	86	160	191	284	544	789
Net earnings from tourism	63	82	95	136	168	144	141
Total	122	168	255	327	452	688	930

Source: Organisation for Economic Cooperation and Development, *Economic Survey: Yugoslavia* (Paris, 1977), table M.

Khrushchev to Belgrade in 1955, it was conducted on a clearing basis, with a rough year-by-year balancing of exports and imports. Some credits were granted to finance the building of ships for Soviet customers in Yugoslav yards, and there were some partnership agreements with firms in Czechoslovakia and the DDR, but the involvement of Comecon countries was very small in relation to that of the west. When Yugoslavia was granted a special associate status with Comecon in 1964, its trade with that group amounted to less than one-quarter of the total, whilst that with OECD countries amounted to almost 60 per cent.

The Yugoslavs hoped that their sponsorship of the non-aligned movement would lead to an increase in economic ties with the Third World, but this did not happen to any great extent. In 1965 trade with the non-aligned countries amounted to 15 per cent, and there were a number of projects in Africa and Asia involving Yugoslav construction firms, which contained an element of foreign aid. In 1967 an agreement on the lowering of tariffs between India, Egypt and Yugoslavia was intended to form the basis of a closer economic association among the three countries, but the facts of political and economic geography ensured that it had little significance.

Political and social changes in the 1960s

The economic reform of 1965 involved the removal of barriers to the free movement of people and ideas as well as goods across the frontiers. This had profound effects on Yugoslav society. In no other country in eastern

Europe were the citizens able to travel as freely as the Yugoslavs, for both work and leisure, or to read western literature, buy foreign newspapers and exchange ideas with ordinary citizens of other countries. The relaxation may have been initiated from above, but it gathered a momentum of its own which was beyond the control of the authorities, had they wished to reverse it. As early as 1962 Tito told the Central Committee of the LCY that the process had gone too far and that freedom of expression in writing and speech should not go so far that it allowed the emergence of divisive national chauvinist polemics.

The 1963 constitution

The new constitution, introduced in 1963, provided a framework in which the movement for reform could expand. It also introduced further measures of decentralisation. It proclaimed the concept of a self-managed society, in which the rights enjoyed by workers in factories would be extended to those engaged in all forms of social activity – to the health and welfare services, education, and cultural and recreational activities. Workers' self-management was to become social self-management. The Federal Assembly was reorganised into five chambers. The Federal Chamber consisted of 190 delegates, most of whom were directly elected by universal suffrage, but it also included 70 who were nominated by the Assemblies of the republics and provinces (10 for each republic and 5 each for Kosovo and Vojvodina). The latter members could sit separately as a Chamber of Nationalities when certain constitutional matters affecting the relations among the republics were under discussion. Three of the remaining four chambers were indirectly elected to represent the interests of workers in different occupations. The Chamber of the Economy represented the public sector in industry and agriculture, and the others covered education and culture, social welfare and public health. The Organisational–Political Chamber represented the so-called socio-political organisations like the trade unions, SAWPY (Socialist Alliance of the Working People of Yugoslavia) and the LCY.

The Federal Executive Council, elected by the Assembly, had the responsibility of coordinating and supervising the federal administration and was, in effect, the government, its chairman being the prime minister.

The 1963 constitution also established a Council of the Federation (Savet Federacije), which had been dubbed the Yugoslav House of Lords. It had no executive or legislative functions and was purely advisory to the president. Its members were nominated by the president and were usually distinguished former ministers, ambassadors, party officials, soldiers, writers and artists.

The constitution introduced two important concepts into the federal and republican governmental machinery. It forbade the simultaneous holding, by any individual except Tito, of high office in both state and LCY organisations, and it introduced the principle of rotation, which limited the length of time for which a person could occupy a particular government post.

A constitutional court was created to safeguard 'socialist legality' and to prevent the arbitrary exercise of power.

The LCY and the Socialist Alliance were both referred to in the constitution. The LCY was assigned the role of guiding the political life of the country, of protecting the socialist system, and of initiating new ideas to extend it. SAWPY was given the responsibility of overseeing the elections to public bodies and of acting as a forum for the discussion of public issues.

The loosening of central control and the separation of the LCY from the state machine gave an opportunity for more effective assertion of local interests, particularly those of the republics in opposition to the centre. The differences of view tended to express themselves in terms of economic issues. In the more developed republics, Slovenia and Croatia, there was a feeling that the payments which they were forced to make to sustain the less developed areas were being squandered. Although the constitution reaffirmed the existence of a common Yugoslav economic and fiscal area (Article 28) and the right of free movement of goods and people throughout the whole territory, there developed a tendency for republican authorities to regard themselves as directors of autonomous economic units. Tito's warnings about the dangers of national exclusiveness became the constant theme of his speeches to audiences of LCY *aktivs*, republican Assemblies and meetings of workers and business organisations in all parts of Yugoslavia. His insistence on the need for 'brotherhood and unity' (*bratstvo–jedinstvo*) was enthusiastically applauded, but was largely ignored in practice.

The growing chorus of discontent from the republics came to a head in 1967, when the delegates from Bosnia–Hercegovina called an unprecedented meeting of the Chamber of Nationalities. Their immediate grievance was over the allocation of federal funds for economic development. The Slovenes also had problems of a different nature to discuss. The Slovene premier, Janko Smole, as an ex-officio member of the Federal

Executive Council, had introduced into the Slovene Assembly a federal proposal to reduce expenditure on social security. The Social Welfare and Health Chamber in Ljubljana overwhelmingly rejected the proposal, and Mr Smole offered to resign – a novel act for a minister in any communist country. A compromise was eventually reached, but the affair drew attention to the possible conflicts of loyalty which officials in Mr Smole's position might face when federal and republican interests diverged. At about the same time a furious row developed over the publication in Zagreb on 17 March of the 'Deklaracija', a statement signed by leading Croat intellectuals asserting the separate existence of a Croatian linguistic and literary tradition, and denying the validity of Serbo-Croat as a historic language. This was a gesture of defiance directed against the Serbs. The signatories included many members of the LCY, including Tito's friend the writer Miroslav Krleža, who was forced to resign from the Croatian Central Committee. There were also signs of discontent in Kosovo and Montenegro which were based on an assertion of national rights over those of the federation.

In an attempt to defuse these potentially explosive rumblings of revolt, a series of constitutional amendments were hastily prepared and rushed through the Federal Assembly on 18 April. The Chamber of Nationalities was given enhanced status and wider powers were given to the republics at the expense of the federation. The *ex officio* status of republic premiers in the FEC was also abolished.

These changes did not achieve the desired effect of damping down the fervour of the nationalists. Having won a small victory, they began to use it as a starting point for a further advance.

In 1971 twenty-three amendments to the 1963 constitution were passed by the Assembly. They provided for additional measures of devolution, not only from the federal to the republican governments but also within the republics to the organs of local government. Even more important were the measures of economic devolution which gave greater authority to the enterprises and enabled enterprises to exercise control over local banks in which they had deposited their funds. The economic clauses of the 1971 amendments represented an attempt to reinterpret the phrase in the 1963 constitution which referred to the 'right of working people to dispose of the fruits of their labour'. Amendment XXIII guaranteed the right of private employers to use their own means of production and to employ workers on a contractual basis, within the scope of agreements made with the trade unions.

At the level of the federal government, a twenty-two-member collective presidency was established, composed of three members elected by the republican assemblies and two from each of the autonomous provinces. The proposal for the formation of a collective presidency was taken at the suggestion of President Tito, who, in a speech in Zagreb on 21 October 1970, warned of the difficulties which would ensue if he died before arrangements had been made for the handing over of power to a successor. Tito was then seventy-eight years old and in apparent good health. The LCY had already instituted a collective Presidium a year earlier. The presidency elected annually one of its members to serve as its president, in accordance with a strict order of rotation which ensured that each republic and province had its turn. The title of President of the Republic was conferred on Tito for life, but the collective body gradually took more and more of the work from his shoulders. He continued to play an important role as head of state, and was free to concentrate on the two issues to which he devoted most of his remaining years – foreign policy and national unity.

The authors of the 1971 amendments may have thought that they had gone as far as possible along the road of decentralisation in order to satisfy the legitimate aspirations of the republics without turning the federation into a loose confederation of autonomous nations. They hoped that the nationalists would come to realise the truth of Benjamin Franklin's remark on signing the Declaration of Independence: 'We must, indeed, all hang together, or, most assuredly, we shall all hang separately.' Events in 1971 showed that this lesson had not been learned.

The LCY during the 1960s

The enthusiasm of the reformers permeated all aspects of political and economic life during the 1960s, but the old guard still had plenty of fighting spirit. One of the most formidable of the anti-reformers was Alexander Ranković, Vice-President of Yugoslavia, who was responsible both for the policy of the LCY cadres and for the running of UDBA, the secret political police. He was a Serb, and if not himself a Serbian nationalist, he had the support of this element. He was certainly a centralist, who opposed the devolution of power from the federal to the republican authorities, and, in the eyes of many Yugoslavs, centralisation of power in Belgrade meant Serbian hegemony. Ranković was a typical organisation man – an *apparatchik* – who was more interested in the retention of power than in the purpose for which the communists had taken power. He saw the liberalising tendencies of the reform movement as a threat to the power of the party, and probably genuinely feared that the polycentrism which was developing during the early 1960s presaged a disintegration of the system to which he had devoted his life. Even Tito had expressed doubts about the weakening of party discipline, although he came down firmly on the side of the reformers in his speech to the Eighth Congress in December 1964.

In early 1966 it was decided to investigate complaints against the activities of UDBA, especially in its harsh treatment of Albanians in the autonomous region of Kosovo–Metohija, or Kosmet. Kosmet was a part of Serbia, and the degree of autonomy which it enjoyed was considerably less than that of the autonomous province of Vojvodina. All key positions in the region were held by Serbs, although they constituted a minority of 23 per cent of the population. In particular, Serbs ran both the regular police force and Ranković's UDBA. The problem of collecting evidence against an organisation as powerful and ubiquitous as UDBA was solved by relying on the army intelligence service, which was mainly led by Croats. In the course of the investigation it was discovered that Ranković had authorised the surveillance of high party officials. Secret microphones were uncovered even in Tito's residence. A formal commission of enquiry was set up, under the chairmanship of the Macedonian LCY secretary, Krste Crvenkovski. Ranković sensed that he had lost the battle and offered to resign. His resignation was accepted at a special plenum of the Central Committee, held on 1 July at Tito's island retreat of Brioni. His expulsion from the Federal Assembly and from membership of the LCY followed a few weeks later, but he was not prosecuted and was allowed to retire on a state pension. He lived comfortably in his Belgrade home until his death in 1983 and, although he never attempted to engage in political activities, he was secretly regarded by Serbian nationalists as a defender of Serbian interests, especially in Kosovo. At his funeral in September 1983 thousands of Serbs turned out in silent tribute to his memory.

The fall of Ranković was followed by a reorganisation of both UDBA and the LCY and by a purge of Ranković supporters. Tito made it plain that UDBA was still necessary but that it should be made more accountable for its activities. He blamed both himself and the Central Committee for allowing UDBA to become a state within a state. The press gave a thorough airing to the revelations about the brutalities and the corruption which had flourished unchecked during Ranković's stewardship of UDBA.

The relaxation of the police repression in Kosmet gave an opportunity for pent-up feelings of frustration amongst the Albanians to come to the surface. In 1968 there were demonstrations both in Kosovo and in the Albanian-speaking areas of Macedonia. These were put down with a limited use of force, and the ringleaders, mostly young nationalist intellectuals, were given relatively light sentences by the courts. Political steps were taken to meet some of the more reasonable demands of the demonstrators. The region was renamed the Socialist Autonomous Province of Kosovo, giving it equal status with Vojvodina. It was allowed to choose as its flag the black eagle on a red background, which was the emblem of the Albanian republic. An Albanian university was founded in Priština to replace the faculties of Belgrade University, which had previously provided higher education in the town, and visiting professors of Albanian language and literature came from Tirana to develop an awareness of the national culture of the Albanian people.

The LCY held to its liberal course throughout the 1960s, and at its Ninth Congress in 1969 it revised its statutes in order to give its central-committee structure a confederal character, by adopting the 'ethnic key' principle. This ensured that in all important committees the representation from each of the republics was equal. Although Tito frequently spoke of the Leninist principle of 'democratic centralism', the real centres of authority within the LCY were in the republics and provinces. The members of the new Executive Bureau and of the collective presidency which replaced the old Central Committee saw themselves as the representatives of the interests of their home area, where their real power bases lay. In many areas membership of the LCY was purely nominal and the level of ideological commitment was low. The machinery of party control was becoming rusty through lack of use and the real focus of activity was in the economic and governmental organisations within the republics.

The LCY was no longer the sole centre of political power, as it had been in the previous two decades. The real political debate was taking place outside, in the press, in the universities and in the various philosophical journals which flourished in the more relaxed intellectual climate.

Praxis

One of the most important journals was *Praxis*. The founders of *Praxis* were members of the Yugoslav Philosophical Association, and were professors in the universities of Zagreb and Belgrade. Although they did not hold identical views on all philosophical questions, they represented a humanist view of Marxism which was in sharp contrast to the more dogmatic and authoritarian views of the orthodox party ideologists. They first came to public notice in 1960, when they engaged the orthodox Marxists in a debate at a meeting of the Philosophical Association, held in Bled. Between 1960 and 1968 they presented their ideas in meetings of the

Association and other academic bodies and in books and articles. In 1963 an international summer school was held on the island of Korčula, and for the next few years this became an annual event, providing a forum for discussion for philosophers and sociologists of various tendencies from America and western Europe. In 1964 the journal *Praxis* was founded and, through its international edition, rapidly established itself as a leading philosophical journal amongst western Marxists. The attitude of the authorities was critical, but they were prepared to tolerate it, and they did not try to suppress other journals of opinion which aired views fundamentally critical of the official party line. Matters came to a head in 1968, when students in Belgrade demonstrated in the streets, protesting against their poor living conditions and employment prospects. The Belgrade professors who were members of the *Praxis* group showed sympathy for the students and themselves protested against the severity of police measures against the demonstration. When some of the students widened their criticisms from the immediate material issues to a more general attack on the direction in which the country was being led, the authorities thought that they detected the corrupting influence of the *Praxis* group. There is no doubt that many of the student leaders accepted the views expressed in articles in *Praxis*, but there is no evidence that the group had a hand in organising the student protests. The student action was probably more influenced by the general ferment which swept through the European student movement in 1968 than by articles in *Praxis*. The professors did not attack the principles of self-management – in fact, they had played a part in advocating its extension – but they pointed out that the LCY, despite its professions of liberalism and democracy, still operated in an authoritarian way. They pressed for greater democracy and openness, both within the communist movement and within society at large.

Although Tito made a conciliatory broadcast, telling the students that he accepted many of their criticisms and offering to resign if he could not put things right, he lent his backing to a campaign to oust the eight Belgrade University professors from their posts. Those who were still members of the LCY were expelled, their publication funds began to dry up, and they were subjected to other forms of harassment. They fought back with great skill, supported by the students and many of their colleagues in the university as well as by an impressive lobby of world-famous philosophers and scholars. *Praxis* succumbed in 1975, but the international edition was revived in Britain in 1980, with the familiar 'Belgrade Eight' as contributors and members of the editorial board.

The experience of the *Praxis* group in successfully resisting pressure from the highest circles of the state and party hierarchy for over seven years illustrates the extent to which the area of individual freedom had widened since the Djilas case in the mid 1950s. They were able to use the procedures of self-management to protect themselves against arbitrary expulsion from the university, until the exasperated authorities were forced to change the rules in order to obtain their desired end. During most of the time the professors were free to accept invitations to lecture abroad and to attend international conferences. The *Praxis* story also illustrates the differences in approach among the different republics. The *Praxis* members in Zagreb were treated with far greater leniency than those in Belgrade and no attempt was made to force them out of the university. This may have been because the communists in Croatia had a far more serious problem to face, in tackling the nationalist elements within the League, than to waste their energies on a few dissident professors.

There was, however, one Croatian academic who found himself in trouble with the authorities during the 1960s. This was a young, non-Marxist lecturer from Zadar, Mihailo Mihajlov, who in 1965 published articles critical of the Soviet Union at a time when Yugoslav–Soviet relations were improving and the authorities were anxious not to upset them. Tito personally denounced the writer, who was dismissed from his post and put on trial. The court awarded the comparatively mild punishment of a five months' suspended sentence, but Mihajlov behaved like a latter-day Djilas in then writing articles for an American paper complaining about lack of freedom in Yugoslavia. He then went further and attempted to form an opposition political movement. In September 1966 he was again tried and sentenced to one year's imprisonment because of articles published by émigré Yugoslav papers. In 1967 his stay in prison was further extended when it was discovered that he had circulated émigré literature through the post. His case is, of course, completely different from that of the *Praxis* group, all of whom were Marxist and who were never accused of national chauvinism, links with émigré groups, or attempting to form a political opposition.

Foreign policy during the 1960s

The re-establishment of normal relations with the USSR following the visit of Khrushchev and Bulganin to Belgrade in 1955, and with China shortly afterwards, did not imply that Yugoslavia had any intention of joining the 'socialist camp'. The turn of events in Hungary in 1956 confirmed this decision, although Tito reluctantly gave his approval to the second Soviet invasion in November, following a secret consultation with Khrushchev at Brioni. He feared that Imre Nagy had lost control of the internal situation and that Soviet intervention was preferable to chaos and instability in a neighbouring state. He felt badly let down, however, when Nagy, who had been offered asylum, was tricked out of the Yugoslav embassy in Budapest and later shot. The bumpy course of Soviet–Yugoslav relations was a reminder of the traumas of 1948, and the Yugoslavs had no wish to repeat the experience. In 1960, in an attempt to prevent an open breach with the Chinese, who were bitterly attacking the 'Tito clique' in terms reminiscent of the Cominform resolution of 1948, the Soviet Communist Party joined in the denunciation of Yugoslav revisionism which was incorporated into the resolutions passed by the eighty-one parties attending the World Communist Conference in Moscow. All this convinced the Yugoslavs that they were right to pursue the path of independence and non-alignment.

The Belgrade summit conference of non-aligned nations in 1961 was a triumph for Tito's policy of steering a careful route between the two power blocs. Neither side dare offend him too much, lest they drive him into their opponents' arms. His popularity amongst the Third World countries, which his vigorous denunciations of the neo-colonialists greatly enhanced, also strengthened his position in dealing with the big powers. Neither could afford to alienate the champion of the Afro-Asian nations, over whose destinies both sides were struggling to gain control. Therefore both offered non-aligned Yugoslavia economic aid and diplomatic support. Yugoslavia had consistently campaigned for the establishment of UN agencies to assist the economic development of Third World countries, and was an active promoter of such organisations as SUNFED (Special UN Fund for Economic Development), UNIDO (UN Industrial Development Organisation) and UNCTAD (UN Conference on Trade and Development).

The non-aligned nations could not, however, provide the economic support which Yugoslavia needed. This had to come from trade and aid originating in either Comecon or the EEC. There were few political difficulties to hinder the growth of close economic ties with the west, but the course of Yugoslav relations with the east was never smooth. Although Khrushchev soon forgot about the attack on Tito's revisionism and happily allocated Yugoslavia a kind of associate membership of the socialist camp, the Soviet Union's behaviour towards its communist neighbours in eastern Europe caused considerable anxiety to the Yugoslavs. Tito made no secret of his admiration for Dubček in 1968 but he shared the alarm of his Romanian neighbour, Ceauşescu, that if the Czechoslovak leader did not act with great skill his country might be invaded as Hungary had been in 1956, and that Dubček might suffer the fate of Imre Nagy. Tito and Ceauşescu both went to Prague in August 1968, shortly before the Soviet troops moved in. A hastily convened meeting of the LCY Presidium strongly denounced the invasion. Czechoslovak tourists who were on holiday in Yugoslavia at the time of the Warsaw Pact invasion were treated with great warmth and friendship by their Yugoslav hosts, indicating that the leaders had the full backing of the people in their condemnation of the Soviet action. Ceauşescu refused to join the other Warsaw Pact countries which sent troops to support the Red Army. Both Tito and Ceauşescu feared that Romania might be next on the list of Soviet satellites to be disciplined, and this would bring the Red Army to the Yugoslav border. One result of this crisis was the establishment in Yugoslavia of an all-peoples defence organisation (Narodna Odbrana) which provided for the mobilisation of the whole adult population in the event of an invasion.

Relations with Yugoslavia's neighbours improved steadily during the 1960s, although there were problems with Albania and Bulgaria, and brief periods of tension with Italy, Greece and Austria.

13

Tito's last ten years

The decision to establish a collective presidency in 1971 was a prudent recognition, prompted by Tito himself, that the Tito era was entering its last phase. Yugoslavia's public life had been dominated for over a quarter of a century by the personality of Tito, and everyone was aware that problems would arise when he left the stage. There was no obvious successor who could command the same respect and loyalty of Yugoslavs in all republics. Men like the Slovene Edvard Kardelj or the Croat Vladimir Bakarić had lived in the shadow of Tito since the days when they had been Partisans; they were too closely associated with their own republics; and they were old and ailing. In the immediate post-war period it had seemed as if Djilas and Ranković were possible successors, but both had since left the LCY in disgrace. One of the problems which were beginning to emerge at this time, and one which has become increasingly insistent during the last ten years, is the absence of a post-war generation of leaders who have experience in public affairs and who will be able to replace the Partisan generation which has dominated Yugoslavia since the war. Many of the Partisans were comparatively young at the end of the war. Tito, one of the oldest – he was known to his comrades as 'Stari' (the Old Man) – was only fifty-six years old at the time of the Cominform dispute in 1948; Kardelj was thirty-eight, Bakarić thirty-six, and most of the other members of the Central Committee were under forty years old. They all had wartime records which entitled them to important positions in the political life of the new Yugoslavia, and they held onto these positions, blocking the chances of promotion for the generation immediately after them. The introduction of the principle of rotation of offices and the separation between state and party functions did not weaken the grip of the ex-Partisans. It simply meant that a larger number of them joined in the game of musical chairs, occupying a different seat each time the music stopped. In this game, however, instead of a chair being removed on each occasion, more chairs were added, thus ensuring that there were no losers.

The generation for whom the avenues of political advancement had been blocked by the veterans turned to the professions and to industry in Yugoslavia, or they joined the brain drain to western Europe and North America. Thus, although the decision to establish a collective leadership solved the immediate problem of finding a successor to Tito, it did not tackle the longer-term issue of providing the cadres to take over when advancing age inevitably thinned the ranks of the veterans.

The 1971 constitutional amendments had not been long on the statute book before it became apparent that the nationalists, especially in Croatia, were not appeased by the concessions granted to the republics. The immediate grievances of the Croats involved a mixture of cultural and economic factors, behind which lay centuries of Serb–Croat rivalry, in which religion, nationality, language and folk memories of real or imaginary historic wrongs were all interwoven. As the process of decentralisation gathered momentum during the 1960s, the Croats began to voice their complaints with increasing vigour.

It is usual for nationalist movements to be led by intellectuals and middle-class members of the liberal professions. The Croatian movement was no exception. Its first manifestation was the Deklaracija of 1967, in which Croat intellectuals repudiated the Novi Sad Agreement of 1954. This agreement between the writers' unions of the two republics accepted the policy of developing a common Serbo-Croat language. The reply of the Serbian writers to the Deklaracija was a document which, *inter alia*, demanded the right of the Serbian minority in Croatia to receive communications from the authorities written in the Cyrillic alphabet. This exchange of polemics was brought to a halt by the personal intervention of Tito, and the Croatian League of Communists expelled a score of intellectuals. During the next three years the Croats widened the scope of their attack, complaining of political, economic and cultural discrimination. Historians reassessed the pre-war relations between Serbs and Croats, emphasising the exploitation of Croatia by the Serb-dominated royalist regime. Economists drew attention to the disproportionate share of the federal budget which Croatia was forced to pay. An article in the journal *Kritika* in 1970 alleged that 45 per cent of the income of the capital, Zagreb, was drained away by the federation. Croat dissent expressed itself through cultural societies such as Matica Hrvatska, youth and student organisations, professional associations, and finally the League of Communists itself.

The three Croatian communist leaders most closely identified with the agitation were Mika Tripalo, one of the youngest of the ex-Partisans and a secretary of the Croatian League of Communists; Dr Savka Dabčević-Kučar, head of the Croatian government and a former economics lecturer at Zagreb University; and Dr Pero Pirker, a law graduate and former youth leader. Under their leadership the League of Communists in Croatia enjoyed an unprecedented popularity. Their championship of Croat interests on the question of the retention quotas for foreign currency (see above, pp. 241–2) and on the broader issues of the economic relations between the more developed northern republics and the developing south encouraged more extreme nationalists to demand independence for Croatia. Even Dr Dabčević-Kučar spoke of a 'socialist sovereign Croatia' and of 'a national state of the Croat nation' within the framework of a socialist Yugoslavia. There were many, both in Croatia and in the federal government, who regarded the professions of loyalty to socialist Yugoslavia as a tactical move, comparable to Monsignor Korošec's declarations of loyalty to the Habsburgs when he was, in fact, working for the dissolution of the Dual Monarchy (see p. 126 above). Matters came to a head in late November 1971, when students at Zagreb University went on strike. Street demonstrations followed, reaching a climax on 30 November, and the demands escalated from a claim for economic justice ('End the retention quotas!' and 'Stop the plunder of Croatia!' were two of the slogans emblazoned on the students' banners) to a call for the seating in the UN General Assembly of representatives of an independent Croatia.

There was a swift reaction from Tito and the LCY. For most of 1971 the president had been trying, by private persuasion and public warning, to bring the Croat leaders to a realisation of the dangers of the course on which they had embarked. In April he called a secret meeting at Brioni, attended by the Presidium of the LCY and a number of leading communists from the republics. A stern warning was then given to the Croat leaders, but, although they supported the final communiqué condemning nationalist excesses and divisions within the LCY, their subsequent actions showed that they were either unable or unwilling to check the nationalists. It seemed that they were prisoners of the Matica Hrvatska. They permitted the extremists to gain ascendancy in the student movement; they acquiesced in a purge of Yugoslav-minded officials; and they did nothing to discourage the harassment of Serbs in Croatia. At the federal level, Tripalo, as a member of the federal presidency, continued to press for the Croat economic demands and to defend the nationalists as being good socialists. In early November the veteran Croat communist Vladimir Bakarić, who was adept at keeping a low profile until he was able to throw his weight in on the winning side, became seriously alarmed at the extremism of the student leaders and of Matica Hrvatska and appealed to Tito to intervene.

After the street demonstrations in Zagreb, Tito made a nation-wide broadcast on 2 December in which he told the Croat communists that they had lost control of the situation. At a meeting of the Croatian Central Committee on 12 December, it was announced that Tripalo, Dabčević-Kučar and Pirker had resigned. Police and troops moved into Zagreb and arrested the student leaders. During the next few months there were over four hundred arrests; Matica Hrvatska was proscribed; and a wholesale purge of alleged nationalists affected all Croatian organisations – the trade unions, SAWPY, the veterans' associations and institutes of higher education.

It appeared that the students had overestimated their strength and had miscalculated the timing of their demonstrations. They had hoped to receive support from the workers, and particularly from Croatian workers who had been *Gastarbeiter* in West Germany, where Croat nationalist organisations were strong. Matica Hrvatska had established over thirty branches abroad, most of them in Germany, and there were close unofficial contacts with émigré organisations. Had the demonstrations taken place two or three weeks later, Zagreb would have been crowded with returning *Gastarbeiter*, visiting their relatives for the Christmas holiday, and they might have responded to the students' call to demonstrate. As in Belgrade in 1968, however, there was little public support from the workers, although many may have privately sympathised with the students.

The Croatian crisis raised many frightening possibilities, which convinced Tito and the leaders of the LCY of the need for a firm hand. It opened up the prospect of the disintegration of the federation and, in Tito's words, of 'shooting and civil war', and of foreign intervention. The outcome showed that the army stood behind Tito and that the LCY, despite its shortcomings, was still in command of the political situation.

The liberal policies of the previous decade had encouraged nationalists in other republics to become more vocal. In some cases, as in Slovenia, the discontent focussed on economic grievances, whereas in Serbia, Montenegro and Kosovo economic issues were less important than questions of cultural identity. Kosovo, the poorest area in Yugoslavia, did not press its claims for equality of status on purely economic grounds, although there was plenty of evidence to suggest that the gap in income per head between Kosovo and the northern republics had widened during the post-war period. Having won equal status with Vojvodina as an autonomous province within Serbia, the more extreme Albanian nationalists wanted to achieve full republican status. This was bitterly resisted by the Serbs and

Macedonians both on historic grounds and for reasons of practical politics. Once again, the fear was raised that any radical change in the federal framework would bring into question the whole basis of the Yugoslav state.

The decision to tighten discipline within the LCY and to suppress any manifestations of nationalism in the population at large was taken at meetings of the LCY Presidium held during December 1971 at Tito's hunting lodge near Karadjordjevo in the Banat.

Nationalism and 'rotten liberalism' were identified as being the chief enemies, and the record of the communist leadership in all republics was scrutinised in order to assess the extent to which these evils had penetrated into the fabric of the LCY. Throughout 1972 leading reformers who had been in the ascendant during the 1960s were removed from public life, and were often replaced by loyal veterans who had opposed the reforms. Inevitably, this meant the removal of many relatively young members of the post-war generation, including those who had been educated in the party high schools and new universities which had been established after the Second World War. These included the secretaries of the Serbian and Macedonian Leagues of Communists, Latinka Perović and Dr Slavko Milosavlevski, and the president of the League of Communists in Vojvodina, Mirko Čanadanović. Other well-known reformers to be dropped were Stane Kavčič, the Slovene premier; Krste Crvenkovski, the chief Macedonian representative on the federal presidency; and Marko Nikezić, a former foreign secretary and chairman of the Serbian League of Communists. In silent protest against the dismissal of Nikezić, Koča Popović, the wartime chief of Tito's General Staff, resigned from the federal presidency. These senior officials were allowed to retire quietly into obscurity. Some of them, who had held university posts, were able to return to academic life, but they were expected to maintain a low profile and to keep out of politics.

The leaders of the nationalist agitation, especially the Croat students, were treated more harshly. They were brought before the courts and sentenced to periods of imprisonment of up to four years. There were also trials in Serbia, Kosovo and other republics. The main targets were people accused of political crimes, but the net was spread wide enough to bring in those accused of economic crimes – like the two directors of the Agricultural Bank who were sentenced to twenty years' rigorous imprisonment for embezzling over £700,000; and the Mayor of Zagreb, who was accused of corruption.

In September 1972 Tito sent a letter to all branches of the LCY, in the name of the Executive Bureau. In it he analysed what had gone wrong and called for a return to the Leninist principle of democratic centralism. It was made plain that the LCY, as 'the connective tissue which binds socialist Yugoslavia together', could not be decentralised in the then foreseeable future. The LCY and the army were and are the two all-Yugoslav institutions which counteract the fissiparous tendencies which are inherent in the decentralisation of power to the republics, and which would endanger the unity of the country if they were allowed to develop unchecked.

There has been a tendency for western writers on Yugoslavia to characterise the deposed Croatian triumvirate of Tripalo, Dabčević-Kučar and Pirker as liberals, but in their handling of opposition to their policies within the LCY they showed themselves capable of manipulating the levers of power with as much determination as any of the so-called hard-liners. They also permitted the rise of a technocratic élite which often rode roughshod over the workers' rights of self-management in the factories. They were representatives of communism with a Croat face rather than with a more democratic and humane appearance. These tendencies were not absent in other republics, where large organisations in the fields of banking, foreign trade financing, air transport and tourism had developed into centres of economic and political power which were scarcely subject to democratic control. Two such organisations were INEX and GENEX, which established internal banks, enabling them to evade the normal banking laws. The so-called workers' amendments, which formed part of the 1971 constitutional changes, and which were intended to increase the scope of workers' self-management, had largely been ignored or bypassed.

The 1974 constitution (see diagram, p. 263)

In 1974 a new constitution was introduced which owed much to the concept of a self-managed socialist society which Edvard Kardelj had advocated in his theoretical writings. This constitution, which is still in force, replaced the 1963 constitution, as amended in 1967 and 1971, with a completely new set of legislative and executive institutions. It provided for a system of election based on delegations drawn from occupational and interest groups. The members of the delegations who sit in the various chambers of the Assemblies at federal, republican, provincial and communal level are subject to instant recall by the body which elects them. Tito and Kardelj considered this arrangement to be a guarantee that direct workers' democracy would prevail. In practice, it ensured that the LCY could keep a closer control of the legislatures than was possible under the

1963 constitution. In the late 1960s there had been a tendency for members of the Federal Assembly to behave in some way like representatives in the parliaments of liberal western democracies, but, as Tito put it when introducing the 1974 constitution. 'A determined break has been made with all the remnants of so-called representative democracy which suits the bourgeois class.'

The delegations are formed at local level from six groupings:

(1) *Workers in the social sector.* These delegations represent members of 'organisations of associated labour' and 'work units' (*delegacije zaposlenih u organizacija udruženog rada i radnih zajednica drustvenog sektora*). These are, in effect, the workers within self-managed enterprises, of whom there were then 4.3 million in 21,000 organisations.

(2) *Peasants and farm workers.* These represent 3.9 million active individual peasants.

(3) *Liberal professions.* These represent 300,000 doctors, dentists, lawyers, etc.

(4) *State and LCY officials and soldiers.* These delegations are formed from workers in the civil service and the socio-political organisations, and civilian employees of the armed forces as well as military personnel.

The four groups above send their delegates to the Chambers of Associated Labour (Veće Udruženog Rada) of both the communal and republican Assemblies.

(5) *Territorial constituencies.* Within each commune there are local units (*mestni zajendice*) of citizens resident in the area. The 500 communes contain approximately 10,000 such units. They send delegates to the Chambers of Local Communities within both the communal and republican Assemblies.

(6) *Socio-political organisations.* The delegations mentioned under 4 above include only the paid officials of the socio-political organisations. The rank-and-file members also have a separate voice through the delegates which they send to the socio-political chambers of both republican and communal Assemblies.

When the first set of elections was over in May 1974, Tito told the Tenth Congress that over 700,000 citizens, or one in twenty of all eligible voters, were serving on some kind of delegation. Delegates serve for terms of four years, and no one may serve on 'a delegation of the same-managing organisation or community for more than two consecutive terms' (Article 134). The electoral process is controlled by the Socialist Alliance or in some cases by the trade unions, except for delegations representing the army.

The Federal Assembly consists of two chambers, a Federal Chamber of 220 delegates elected by the Assemblies of the communes, and a Chamber of Republics and Provinces, composed of 88 delegates, elected by the republican and provincial Assemblies. One member from each republic or province is elected for a term of five years to the federal presidency, to which is added the president of the LCY, who sits *ex officio*. The collective presidency elects annually a president and vice-president. Until 1980 the office of President of the Republic also existed, but on the death of President Tito the post was abolished. The titular head of state is now the person elected for one year by the collective presidency, according to a strict rota, which ensures that each republic and province has its turn.

One of the significant new departures in the 1974 constitution was that, for the first time since the war, both the LCY and the army had their roles in the legislative machinery written into the fundamental law of the state. At the top level, the president of the LCY is *ex officio* a member of the federal presidency, and this situation is repeated in the republican and provincial presidencies, where the local LCY leaders have a similar *ex officio* status. The LCY officials have a place in the delegations to the chambers of Assemblies, and the rank-and-file members participate in the elections to the socio-political chambers. LCY members also have a strong voice in the election of the delegations by virtue of their leading position in the Socialist Alliance, as it is this body which draws up the lists of candidates for the elections.

The army's role in Yugoslav society has been greatly enhanced in recent years, both through the constitutional provision, which enables soldiers to elect delegates to the chambers of associated labour, and by the changes in the statutes of the LCY, which have increased the number of army officers in the governing bodies of the party. The coming together of the army and the LCY reflects a realisation, born of the experiences of 1971, that, in the event of a crisis threatening the stability of the country, these two centralising agencies, with an all-Yugoslav rather than a republican character, provide a strong defence against separatist tendencies.

The 1974 constitution is one of the longest and most complicated of such documents to be found anywhere in the world. It contains 406 articles and the text runs to over three hundred printed pages. It covers every conceivable aspect of social relations and spells out in detail the rights and duties of Yugoslav citizens in such matters as protection of the environment, family planning, national defence, freedom of movement and of the press, social insurance, education, minority rights, etc. It also outlines the rights,

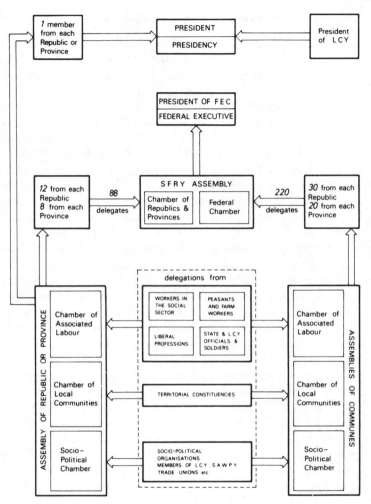

The constitution of 1974.

obligations and interrelations of a bewildering multitude of social and political organisations. In this respect the Yugoslav constitution is unique, and many of the terms used will be unfamiliar to non-Yugoslavs, for a new terminology has had to be invented in order to describe new concepts in social relations.

The Law on Associated Labour, 1976

Hardly had the Yugoslav public digested the complexities of the new constitution than they were confronted with yet another set of laws, this time regulating the system of self-management. The Law on Associated Labour (Zakon o Udruženom Radu) amounted to a mini-constitution, governing the economy. It attempts to codify the relations between the management and workers in enterprises (now called 'work organisations' or *radne organizacije*), and among the Basic Organisations of Associated Labour (BOALs; Osnovne Organizacije Udruženog Rada (OOURs)), other self-management organs and local and national government. The intention is that the state will gradually withdraw from intervention in the economy, leaving market forces to operate within a framework regulated by the decisions of the organisations of associated labour. Thus BOALs may make self-management agreements (*samoupravni sporazumi*) with their counterparts, regulating wages in an industry or establishing combines and other forms of industrial and commercial cooperation. Another form of agreement, the social compact (*društveno dogovor*), involves wider policy decisions concerning economic planning, investment and the provision of welfare and other facilities by means of 'communities of interest' (*interesne zajednice*). In these instances the BOAL becomes involved in economic and social policy in cooperation with agencies of local government.

Without going too far into the arcane terminology of self-management, it can be said that the effect of the 1976 Law was to decentralise economic decision making to the grass-roots organisations of associated labour, and to weaken the control of the federal government over economic planning and investment. Since then the federal authorities have often been forced to intervene in the economy, but they have usually done so clumsily and too late to achieve any useful objective. Having cast aside the fine-tuning controls which would enable them to make sophisticated adjustments, they have been forced to intervene in times of crisis with the blunt instruments of administrative regulation. Whenever they have been compelled to do so they have accompanied their actions with protestations that these were temporary emergency measures, and that the normal processes of self-management would be allowed to take over again when the crisis was over.

The Tenth Congress of the LCY, 1974

The Tenth Congress took place on 27–30 May 1974 in Belgrade. The revised statutes emphasised the principle of democratic centralism and strengthened the links between the LCY and the army. The new 166-member Central Committee included fifteen army officers, and delegates from the armed forces were prominent in other governing bodies. Tito, who was elected president of the LCY for life, stressed in his speech to the Congress the need for tighter discipline and a return to Leninist orthodoxy. The Congress took place three months after the promulgation of the new constitution, and much was said about the developments of self-management which it promised. Although there was no attempt made to reverse the process of economic decentralisation, there was a demand for the LCY to remain in the vanguard of the nation's political life and to resist decentralisation of its organisation. Since the early 1970s Yugoslavia has tried to reconcile the paradox inherent in the attempt to run a decentralised, market-orientated economy within the framework of a one-party state directed by a party which tries to implement a Leninist policy of democratic centralism. The tensions which arise in a multi-national federation from this dichotomy between economic and political objectives explain many of the crises which have arisen in recent years.

The economy in the 1970s

The reforms of the 1960s brought the Yugoslav economy into closer relationship with, and even a degree of dependence on, the market economies of western Europe. This meant that when the oil crisis of the early 1970s created havoc in the western economies Yugoslavia could not insulate itself from its effects.

The fifth Five Year Plan (1971–5) should have been launched at the beginning of the year, but it did not pass the Federal Assembly until November. The year 1971 saw the passing of the constitutional amendments which devolved as much political power to the republics as was felt to be consistent with the maintenance of the federation. The year ended with the Croatian crisis and the first steps towards a gradual political recentralisation. The Plan envisaged inter-republican economic co-operation on a voluntary basis, to strengthen the unity of the Yugoslav market and to avoid wasteful duplication of resources. It also expressed hopes for a greater degree of national consensus over the problem of raising the level of the more backward republics and so removing the economic basis for inter-republican rivalry.

Experience was to show that the time was not propitious for appeals to 'brotherhood and unity'. The Croats and Slovenes were not well disposed to the idea that their surpluses should be creamed off in order to provide funds for the assistance of the less developed, and they were not placated by the concessions made in 1972 and 1973 which partly met their demands for the raising of the retention quotas for foreign currency.

The 1971–5 Plan laid down general lines of social and economic development and set overall targets, but detailed planning was the responsibility of republican and communal institutions, working in close cooperation with the Organisations of Associated Labour. Although it achieved many of the targets set for it, there were serious shortcomings in the foreign trade sector, in the growth of output and in productivity. The failure of exports to grow in value by the expected 13 per cent was partly offset by the slower growth of imports. In the two years for foreign trade, 1972 and 1973, the value of exports rose respectively to 69.2 per cent and 63.2 per cent of the cost of imports, and the flow of invisible earnings from tourism and the remittances of workers abroad more than matched the trade gap, providing small surpluses in the balance of payments. This was an almost unprecedented outcome in the post-war years, and has only once been equalled since, in 1976.

The projected growth in the social product by an annual rate of 8 per cent contrasted with the actual achievement of 6.3 per cent, but agricultural output exceeded by 1.1 per cent its annual growth target of 3 per cent.

One of the major unsolved problems of the early 1970s was the failure of the system to find a reliable method for controlling inflation. For most of the period since the reforms of 1965 Yugoslavia has been at the top of the European inflation league, and the stabilisation programmes which governments have introduced from time to time appear to have had no effect on the situation. In November 1970 the federal premier, Mitija Ribičič, announced a six-month price freeze as a temporary measure until a comprehensive stabilisation programme could be worked out. At this time inflation was at an annual rate of 12.5 per cent. By March 1971 the rate had increased to 15.0 per cent and by 1975 it had reached 30 per cent. The failure of the price freeze was attributed to the deliberate evasion of regulations by the worker-run enterprises. One device used was to reclassify goods under different names and to enter them on the market as new goods not subject to price control. With the increased income from sales, workers' councils were able to vote themselves higher personal incomes, thus increasing the inflationary pressures. Other causes of inflation were uncontrolled government expenditure, the issuing of an ever increasing volume of currency, the sanctioning of investment programmes which were not backed by adequate resources, and the tendency for enterprises to run up large deficits. The general malaise can be summed up

Table 7. *Targets and achievements of 1971–5 Plan and targets of 1976–80 Plan (% increases in volume)*

	1971–5		1976–80
	Target	Outcome	Target
Private consumption	7.0	5.3	6.0
Gross fixed investment	7.0	7.1	8.0
Economic sectors	9.5	6.2	8.5
Non-economic sectors	9.5	8.4	7.5
Housing	—	8.5	8.0
Total domestic demand	—	5.7	6.5
Exports of goods and services	13.0[a]	7.3[a]	8.0
Imports of goods and services	11.0[a]	5.8[a]	4.5
Social product	8.0	6.3	7.0
Industrial output	9.5	8.1	8.0
Agricultural output	3.0	4.1	4.0
Social-sector employment	2.5	4.1	3.5
Productivity	6.0	2.4	4.0

[a] In terms of value.

Source: OECD, *Economic Survey*, May 1977, p. 26.

by the phrase 'lack of social discipline' – an attitude of irresponsibility which seemed to afflict all levels of Yugoslav society. These domestic causes were massively reinforced by world pressures, especially the rise in oil prices after 1973.

The sixth Five Year Plan, 1976–80

The Social Plan for 1976–80 employed the same methods of indicative planning that had been used in the previous five-year period, but, following the 1976 Law on Associated Labour, there was a greater emphasis on the machinery of self-management and particularly on the use of 'social compacts' and 'self-management agreements'.

The planners correctly identified the main problems facing the Yugoslav economy in the second half of the 1970s. Priority was given to the reform of the structure of industry; to the narrowing of regional inequalities; the improvement of labour productivity; the reduction of inflation, of unemployment, and of the balance-of-payments deficit.

The Plan fell short of its targets in almost every respect. This failure was in part caused by world factors outside Yugoslavia's control, but the situation was not helped by irresponsible behaviour on the part of the

Yugoslavs themselves. There was a mood of facile optimism which could be detected amongst decision makers at all levels concerning the prospects of recovery in the world economy. This led to a failure to take effective measures to curb inessential imports of consumer goods and to hold back on investments, especially in private house building, which was encouraged by interest rates well below the rate of inflation. There was a Micawber-like expectation that something would turn up at the eleventh hour to save the situation. To some extent this did happen, for the World Bank, the IMF and other western banks frequently came to the rescue with loans for specific purposes. By the end of 1976 the World Bank had loaned $1,500 million to Yugoslavia. In February 1977 a further two loans, of $56 million each, were approved, the first to support a programme of modernisation of agriculture in Serbia and Kosovo, and the second for highway construction in several republics. In June 1977 a further loan of $75 million was granted for a nation-wide agricultural programme, in which special consideration was to be given to the less developed republics. During 1979, World Bank and European Investment Bank loans of $40 million and $600 million respectively were given for highway construction.

It was perhaps appropriate that in October 1979 the annual meetings of the IMF and the World Bank were held in Belgrade. The Yugoslavs took the opportunity to plead with some of their creditors for a renegotiation of up to $600 million of the country's foreign debts. At the time it was stated that Yugoslavia's total indebtedness to western banks was between $11 billion and $13 billion, and debt servicing of these loans was estimated to be $1.8 billion in 1979, rising to $2.9 billion in 1981. Approximately 22 per cent of all foreign-currency earnings was needed to cover the servicing of these debts. In Belgrade in 1979 the bankers negotiated a rescheduling of Yugoslavia's debts to ease the burden of repayments, as it was obvious that unless this was done the development of the Yugoslav economy would suffer a serious setback.

In addition to World Bank loans, Yugoslavia has received aid from consortia of western banks, from foreign governments and from organisations such as the EEC and Comecon. Aid from Soviet and eastern European sources has been much less than that from the west, and has often been hedged round with restrictions imposed for both economic and political reasons which have limited its usefulness to the Yugoslav economy.

This international aid gave a temporary breathing space, but only stored up trouble for the future. In 1980, shortly after Tito's death, the dinar was devalued by 30 per cent, but this gave only a temporary boost to exports.

During the next few years the exchange rate of the dinar continued to fall, as inflation soared to around 50 per cent and unemployment grew to over one million.

As the western economies continued to grapple with their own problems, there was a tendency to look with increasing disfavour on Yugoslavia's persistent requests for help. The only way in which the Yugoslavs could make any progress in solving their own problems was by the imposition of a rigid discipline on their economy and by increasing their exports to the west, in order to pay for the imports needed to sustain their industrial growth. Despite agreements between the EEC and Yugoslavia in 1971 and 1980, which liberalised trade in some products, exports to the west continued to encounter difficulties. The share of trade with the Comecon countries continued to grow. In 1973 32 per cent of exports went to Comecon countries. By 1980 this had risen to 46 per cent. The share of exports which the EEC countries bought fell during the same period from 35.8 per cent to 26.3 per cent. The change in the source of imports was less dramatic. In 1973, 42.3 per cent of imports came from the EEC; this had fallen to 34.6 per cent by 1980. On the other hand, imports from the United States rose from 4.1 per cent to 6.7 per cent. Thus the hard-currency deficit continued to grow, and it was little consolation to note that trade in the non-convertible currencies of eastern Europe was in balance.

Regional economic inequalities

It has been the declared aim of all post-war Yugoslav governments to reduce the disparities in levels of economic development among the regions. These differences can be explained on historical grounds. The areas south of the Sava–Danube line were for centuries under Turkish rule, and their resources lay untouched; whilst in the northern areas, under Habsburg rule, economic development began in the nineteenth century. The problem of having in microcosm the North/South problem which faces the world at large – of having India and West Germany within the same country – cannot be solved simply by taking money from the relatively rich and giving it to the poor. In order to make investment effective, there must be a slow building up of the infrastructure of the south, and a realisation that the training of personnel at all levels from skilled engineers to clerks and office workers is a prerequisite of economic growth. The Yugoslavs have tried many methods in order to encourage the development of the poorer areas. At first they used administrative allocations, through the federal budget. Later a fund was established into which

Table 8. *Indices of national income per capita (Yugoslavia = 100)*

	1947	1962	1976	1978
Group 1 (above national average in 1947)				
Slovenia	175.3	198.5	201.7	195.3
Croatia	107.2	121.3	124.3	129.2
Vojvodina	108.8	103.4	116.6	123.6
Group 2 (below national average in 1947)				
Serbia proper	95.6	96.0	98.3	96.6
Bosnia–Hercegovina	82.9	72.7	64.2	66.2
Montenegro	70.8	66.3	70.3	67.7
Macedonia	62.0	57.1	68.1	66.2
Kosovo	52.6	34.0	32.2	26.8

Source: *Statistički godišnjak SFRJ*, 1955, 1967, 1978, 1980.

each republic contributed a fixed percentage of its gross national product. In 1966 this was fixed at 1.86 per cent, but it was later raised to 1.97 per cent and, at times, special amounts have been added to assist Kosovo, the least developed region. The criterion for determining whether a republic or province requires assistance is based on a calculation of national income per capita.

By this criterion the relative position has not improved since 1947, although the poorer areas have received massive investments, and there has been undoubted progress. The per capital figures reflect the differential rates of natural increase among the republics. Kosovo's birth rate, for example, at 30 per thousand is almost twice the national average. Also, account must be taken of the fact that investments in the less developed areas are not usually as cost-effective as those in the north.

The relative decline in the position of the poorer areas, measured in terms of national income per capita, is seen in table 8. This situation would be serious enough in a country with a culturally homogeneous population, but it becomes explosive in a multinational society like Yugoslavia, whose leaders have always maintained that a truly socialist society cannot exist as long as these great economic inequalities survive. Unfortunately, despite their best endeavours, the gap has widened steadily, and as the process of decentralisation has developed, the resistance of the richer republics to the demands of their poorer neighbours has stiffened. On both sides of the dividing line between rich and poor this situation has fuelled the fires of nationalism.

14

Yugoslavia after Tito

The death of the eighty-one-year old President Tito on 4 May 1980, after a long illness, was not unexpected, yet there was a deep sense of shock and genuine grief amongst the majority of Yugoslavs when they heard the news. Most Yugoslavs had known no other leader than this remarkable man, who had been at the head of both state and party for over thirty-five years. The impressive array of world leaders who attended his funeral was both a tribute to Tito's status as a world statesman and recognition of Yugoslavia's importance in the international community of nations. Thirty-three heads of state and sixteen heads of government took part in the ceremony. They included President Brezhnev, Chairman Hua Guofeng, Chancellor Helmut Schmidt, the Duke of Edinburgh and heads of state from Africa, Asia, eastern Europe and Scandinavia. The USA was represented by Vice-President Mondale and the president's mother; the absence of President Carter was made good a month later by a state visit undertaken immediately after the Venice summit meeting of western leaders.

The machinery for the succession worked smoothly, as the collective presidency had already been in effective operation for some months. Lazar Koliševski, the Macedonian who was in the chair at the time of Tito's death, acted as head of state until his one-year term expired on 15 May, and he was replaced in accordance with the predetermined rota by Cvijetin Mijatović, a Serb from Bosnia. Similarly, the leadership of the LCY passed on 4 May to Steven Doronjski, the representative of Vojvodina. On 20 October his turn came to make way for Lazar Mojsov of Macedonia. Since then the rotation of offices has followed the appointed course.

The difficulties which the new leadership has encountered since 1980 have not been related directly to the problem of replacing Tito, although there is no doubt that the lack of a single leader of Tito's stature has not made it easy to silence the voices of dissension.

There are two main areas of immediate difficulty – to some extent interconnected – the parlous state of the economy and the discontent of the

Albanians in Kosovo. Behind these immediate issues there are long-term problems concerning the future direction of political and economic life. A vigorous, and often acrimonious, debate which has covered the whole range of public affairs has raged in academic circles, in the columns of newspapers and amongst the leaders of the LCY. In no other country led by communists has there been such a free and open debate. Eventually, however, action must be taken, and so far there is no consensus as to what this should be. The government has reacted to the immediate stimuli of the moment, whether in dealing with the riots in Kosovo or in tackling the economic crisis. There is as yet no sign of an agreed long-term strategy.

The Kosovo riots

The Albanian-speaking population of Kosovo had been restive for some years before Tito's death, and various efforts had been made to placate them. In particular, the authorities in Belgrade appeared to believe that the nationalist agitation could be contained if sufficient money were provided for economic development. Unfortunately, the short-term palliatives stored up long-term troubles. The funds allocated to Kosovo were not always spent on economic development, in many cases because the infra-structure and trained personnel were not available to enable investment to be properly utilised. Instant prestige projects, which pandered to the growing middle class of Albanian nationalists, received funds which ought to have been used for the exploitation of Kosovo's mineral wealth or for the improvement of communications. The University of Priština became the centre of Albanian nationalism. Before 1968 it had been a dependency of Belgrade University, but one of the concessions made after the 1968 troubles was to allow it to become an independent Albanian-speaking university. In the late 1970s Priština University was turning on the labour market some 10,000 graduates a year. The only way in which many of them could be employed was in the inflated administrative machine and in the cultural institutions which had also been recipients of funds which ought to have been spent on projects of greater economic relevance. The expec-tations of these young people, many of them of peasant background, had been raised by the opportunity of university education. They would certainly reject any suggestion that they should undertake work which was not commensurate with their proper qualifications, and a return to family farms, from which higher education was supposed to have liberated them, was unthinkable.

As the general economic situation deteriorated, it was no longer possible for the federal authorities to buy off the discontent of the young graduates by providing them with jobs in the swollen bureaucracy. One in four of the employed workers was already engaged in administrative work and the system could absorb no more. An increasing number of graduates were faced with unemployment. A deep social and economic gulf developed between the minority who lived in relative affluence in well-paid administrative jobs and the underprivileged, who included the 50 per cent of the population who depended on peasant agriculture and the tens of thousands of unemployed urban youth.

Another aspect of the situation which created tension within Kosovo was the still relatively privileged position of the Serbian minority, whose proportion of the total population had fallen from 23.6 per cent in 1961 to 13.2 per cent in 1981. For historical reasons they still held a disproportionate share of the senior positions in the professions, especially in technology, medicine and law. The situation bore a resemblance to the position in many newly independent Third World countries, where posts requiring high technical qualifications were still held by expatriate Europeans, whilst the new universities became centres for the propagation of the national culture.

An important aspect of the curriculum in Priština University was the nurturing of Albanian culture in all its aspects – linguistic, literary, historical and artistic. Close links were established with Tirana University and students were exchanged. Militant Albanian nationalists harassed the minority of Serbian students, and in Serbian villages churches and graveyards were desecrated. These retaliatory actions represented an Albanian backlash after the years of Serbian domination before 1968. Although the leadership of the provincial League of Communists and the government tried to restrain the extremists, they followed in some respects the example set by the Croatian 'triumvirate' in 1971. They encouraged the cultural links with Tirana. When a standard Albanian language was developed, based mainly on the southern variant of Tosk, the Gheg-speaking Kosovars also accepted it as the official form of their language. In 1971 the president of the Kosovo League of Communists, the ex-Partisan Veli Deva, who was known for his anti-Tirana sentiments, was replaced by the thirty-five-year-old former youth leader Mahmut Bakali.

Whilst Tito was alive the situation was kept under control, although immediately after his death there were signs of unrest and a number of youth and student leaders were arrested. No publicity was given to these arrests until the accused were brought to trial in December and sentenced to long terms in prison.

The storm broke in March 1981, when students in the overcrowded university demonstrated against poor food and housing conditions in the student hostels, and against the declining job opportunities for graduates. The authorities at first appeared to be in control of the situation, but between 26 March and 3 April the disturbances spread, some workers were drawn in, and the demands of the demonstrators took on an openly nationalist character. Violence was shown to Serbs and Montenegrins living in the province. Demands were made for full republican status for Kosovo. More extreme elements demanded the inclusion of the Albanian-speaking areas of Macedonia in the proposed republic, and even the attachment of an enlarged Kosovo to the neighbouring state of Albania. There was some suspicion, never convincingly proved, that agents of Enver Hoxha were at work, promoting the cause of 'Greater Albania'.

The fear of a distintegration of the state probably explains the vigour with which the federal authorities acted. Violence between police and demonstrators resulted in eleven persons officially reported killed and a further fifty-seven seriously injured. Rumour, encouraged by an official news blackout, soon multiplied the casualty figures. Troops were sent in, martial law was declared, and the province was isolated from the rest of Yugoslavia. The university students were dispersed to their home villages, a curfew was ordered in Priština, and assemblies of more than five persons were banned.

When the immediate danger appeared to be over, a debate began in the Yugoslav press, and in government and LCY circles, to establish what had gone wrong. The provincial League of Communists was seen as the major culprit, although some saw the sinister hand of Tirana behind the troubles. Mahmut Bakali was sacked, and Veli Deva returned to his former post as president of the League of Communists. Another ex-Partisan, Ali Šukrija, became leader of the provincial government whilst retaining his position on the Presidium of the League of Communists. A wholesale purge of party and government officials, university lecturers and administrators followed. Those accused of participation in the riots were brought to trial and sentences of up to fifteen years were handed down. Similar trials took place in the Albanian areas of Macedonia.

At federal government level there was an attempt to seek a long-term answer to the problems of the province by promises of increased economic aid and assurances that future investments would be spent more wisely than had been the case in the past. A drive against corruption was launched, as it had been alleged that federal aid had been misappropriated. The population of Kosovo did not appear to have been placated by these promises. Although during the two years after the riots there was no public demonstration of discontent on the scale seen in 1981, there were signs of passive resistance and sullen non-cooperation. Throughout 1982 and 1983 trials of nationalists continued. The economic crisis of 1983 restricted the scope of assistance which might have been available, and other republics were in no mood to give further assistance to a rebellious province when they were being forced to impose cuts on their own people.

The economic crisis

The failure of the post-Tito leadership to alleviate the chronic economic malaise which they inherited – and, as many of them were in high office during Tito's last decade, for which they themselves are partly responsible – lies at the root of the political difficulties which have beset them during the first half of the 1980s.

The seventh Five Year Plan, 1981–5

The economic strategy which was formulated at the Eleventh Congress of LCY, held in June 1978, provided the framework in which the Plan was elaborated. It assumed that the basis of decision making would be the self-management system, and that the decentralisation of power to the republics and communes would continue. The LCY was assigned the role of watchdog in the interests of the whole working class and was expected to act as a coordinating force, helping to mitigate the 'self-managing pluralism' of the multitude of institutions, each pressing its own local or sectional interests, which functioned at all levels of society. The various bodies responsible for the economy took so long to work out reasonable compromises on a number of issues that the Plan was not presented to the Assembly until March 1981, three months after it should have been put into operation. One of the reasons for the delay was the difficulty in reaching a consensus regarding the measures needed to reduce regional economic inequalities.

The targets for economic growth were more modest than those for the 1976–80 Plan. The social product was expected to grow by 4.5 per cent annually, and investment by only 1.5 per cent. The least realistic targets were those for foreign trade. It was hoped that exports would grow at an annual rate of 8.5 per cent and that imports would rise at a rate of only 1 per cent. The aim was to reduce drastically the balance-of-payments deficit and, by greater efficiency in the use of domestic resources, especially of fuel and of mineral ores, to prepare the way for export-led growth during the second half of the 1980s. This hope depended upon a recovery in the world economy, which showed little sign of materialising in time to assist the Yugoslavs.

The hopes were soon dashed that, in an expanding world economy, Yugoslavia would be able to increase its exports to the western industrial nations and so pay off the debts which had been incurred during the earlier period of industrial expansion. In 1982 an austerity programme was launched, which involved direct state intervention in order to reduce inflation – then over 30 per cent – and to cut the balance-of-payments deficit. This involved foreign currency controls, import restrictions, petrol rationing, power cuts, acute shortages of some consumer goods, and a 20 per cent devaluation of the dinar. These measures achieved a limited success, but at the cost of a rise in unemployment to almost one million, or 18 per cent of the workforce. No progress was made towards the reduction of the regional gap. By 1983 the ratio between the income per capita in Kosovo, the poorest area, and Slovenia, the richest, had risen to 1 : 7.5.

Yugoslavia's foreign debts

In early 1983 the accumulated foreign debts, mainly to western banks and the IMF, had reached $20 billion, and interest repayments of $5 billion consumed 23 per cent of export earnings, or 8 per cent of GNP. Yugoslavia was compelled once again to ask for western help, but at this time the credit-worthiness of eastern European and developing countries was under question, following the economic difficulties experienced by countries such as Poland, Brazil and Mexico. The recipients of loans were required to satisfy much more stringent conditions than hitherto. The Yugoslavs were anxious to distance themselves from these near-defaulters and, although they really wanted a rescheduling of their debts, they went through considerable semantic contortions in order to avoid using the word. The western bankers, under some political pressure from their governments, were prepared to cooperate, provided the Yugoslavs adopted measures which convinced the creditors that they were serious about their austerity measures.

There was some justification in the Yugoslavs' claim that they had a good record in honouring their debts in the past. There was also a realisation amongst western governments that a collapse of the Yugoslav economy would have serious security implications for the stability of the Balkans.

One of the contributory causes to the crisis which the IMF officials identified was the lack of coordination among the economies of the republics. The decentralisation of the economy which had taken place since the reforms of 1965 had produced an attitude of near autarky amongst the republican leaders. Neither the LCY nor the government had succeeded in persuading the republics to operate as though there were a common Yugoslav market. There was wasteful duplication of resources – as, for example, in the steel industry, where each republic and province wanted its own heavy industry base, regardless of the economic justification. The existence of an iron and steel industry became, in fact, an expensive status symbol and a badge of national pride, which had little relevance to the rationality of federal economic planning. The lack of inter-republican cooperation was nowhere more apparent than in the sphere of banking and finance. Janko Smole, the chief foreign debt negotiator, accused the republican banks in Kosovo, Macedonia and Montenegro of irresponsibility in negotiating foreign loans without the full knowledge of the National Bank, and of asking for government help when they got into difficulties over repayments. There was some initial resistance to the IMF's demand that the federal authorities should accept responsibility for the operations of the regional commercial banks, but eventually a formula was accepted which satisfied the IMF, and agreement was reached in April.

The Soviet premier, Mr Tikhonov, visited Belgrade whilst the IMF package was being negotiated and offered an agreement guaranteeing a 20 per cent increase in Soviet aid deliveries, to be paid for by increased Yugoslav exports to the USSR. A few weeks later Hu Yaobang offered a $120 million Chinese loan and promised large orders for ships built in Yugoslav yards. The interest of the two communist powers in promoting closer economic ties with non-aligned Yugoslavia had obvious political overtones, as also did the western offers. The whole episode demonstrated the economic value to Yugoslavia of maintaining its policy of non-alignment.

Yugoslav foreign policy after Tito

During the last year of his life Tito was deeply involved in the Havana summit meeting of non-aligned nations, held under the chairmanship of Fidel Castro on 3–9 September 1979. Before the meeting the president made visits to a number of Middle Eastern and North African countries to enlist support for a toning down of the pro-Soviet emphasis which Castro wanted to introduce into the main conference resolution. In this endeavour he was partly successful.

Earlier in the year he had visited Moscow and had engaged in frank discussion with President Brezhnev concerning Soviet encouragement of the Bulgarians' refusal to recognise the existence of a separate Macedonian nationality. One of Tito's last acts of policy before he entered hospital on 5 January 1980 was to condemn the Soviet invasion of Afghanistan.

Tito was so closely identified with the policy of non-alignment that his departure from the political scene inevitably raised questions about the future course of Yugoslav foreign policy. There was no question of the abandonment of the basic principles of non-alignment which had served Yugoslavia so well during three decades. There was, however, a question of emphasis. In the 1960s there had been certain clear issues on which all the non-aligned countries could unite – anti-colonialism, opposition to the cold war and the arms race, and support for international aid to the Third World. On Middle Eastern questions, Egypt under Nasser had set the tone for a united anti-Israeli policy. During the 1970s, however, the international scene became more complicated. Newly independent nations in Africa and Asia quarrelled amongst themselves; the Chinese made an unsuccessful attempt, with Indonesian support, to convene an Afro-Asian conference on the lines of the 1955 Bandung meeting, as a rival to the non-aligned summit. Dissension reigned within the Arab world. President Gaddafi quarrelled with the Egyptians, who became increasingly isolated in the Arab world as President Sadat moved towards the 1979 peace treaty with Israel. Yugoslavia had to consider its economic interests, because Iraq and Libya were amongst its major suppliers of oil. It was prudent for it to take a more detached view of Middle Eastern affairs than had been the case during the Nasser era.

The 1975 Helsinki Conference, in which Tito played an active role, focussed the attention of the Yugoslavs on the importance of the neutral countries of Europe. They soon became involved in the so-called N & N group (Neutral and Non-Aligned) working for detente in Europe, and in 1977–8 the first review conference of the Helsinki agreement took place in Belgrade.

It is in Yugoslavia's interests to maintain good relations with its immediate neighbours and, on the whole, this policy was successful during the 1970s and early 1980s. The Trieste dispute with Italy was finally buried in 1975. The restoration of democracy in Greece, following the overthrow of the military junta in 1974, paved the way for an improvement in relations on the southern frontier. The building of a joint Romanian–Yugoslav hydro-electric and navigation scheme at the Iron Gate on the Danube was a symbol of the close relations which had developed between two communist-led nations who acted independently of the Soviet Union in their foreign policies. There were no serious problems with either Austria or Hungary.

The 'Macedonian Question' has frequently created tension in Yugoslavia's relations with Bulgaria, and it is usually assumed that the Bulgarians raise this issue at the prompting of the Soviet Union, but there is no reason to believe that the Bulgarians are not capable of acting independently on a matter about which they feel strongly. The refusal of the Bulgarians to accept the separate cultural identity of the Macedonians irritates the Yugoslavs, but it is not likely to be a major cause of trouble between the two countries. The Bulgarians officially accept the present frontiers and recognise that a Macedonian republic exists within Yugoslavia, even if their writers and historians appear to take some pleasure in opening up old wounds concerning the nationality of the leaders of the Ilinden Rising, the validity of the San Stefano frontiers, or the cultural history of medieval Macedonia. These problems are not a serious threat to the development of Yugoslav–Bulgarian trade or to cooperation between the two countries on political questions such as the proposal for a Balkan nuclear-free zone.

The more serious disputes with Albania involve both ideological questions concerning the nature of Yugoslav socialism and the explosive potential of Albanian irredentism in Kosovo. Despite these problems, practical cooperation in foreign trade does not seem to have been affected. In fact, trade with Albania increased more than tenfold between 1972 and 1981, and Yugoslavia agreed to the building of a railway across the frontier, from Titograd on the Belgrade–Bar line, to link the isolated Albanian rail system for the first time with the railways of the rest of Europe.

Yugoslavia began to place the emphasis in foreign policy increasingly on its relations with its Mediterranean and Balkan neighbours. This did not imply an abandonment of non-alignment. The schemes for a Balkan nuclear-free zone and for other forms of international cooperation implied a realisation that non-alignment could be applied usefully nearer to home.

The great debate

The long illness and subsequent death of Tito had a traumatic effect on Yugoslav politics. To many Yugoslavs, mourning the loss of their leader and worrying about the future without Tito, it seemed that to engage in political argument was disrespectful to the memory of the dead leader. There was a closing of ranks as people rallied round their new leaders.

Membership of the LCY went up dramatically during 1980, rising from 1.8 million to 2.05 million. Many young people joined during the months of the final illness, as if to honour the dying Tito.

The Kosovo riots of 1981 broke the spell which had given the new collective leadership a welcome breathing space during its first year of office. Once the dam had been breached, a flood of criticism, comment and argument swept through the country. It soon became apparent that the LCY leadership was itself divided, with regard to both the attitude which should be adopted to this unprecedented outbreak of polemics and the long-term objectives towards which they should be aiming.

There were some, remembering Tito's intervention in 1971 after the Croatian troubles, who called for 'a new Karadjordjevo'. The demand for a 'firm hand' came most insistently from the veterans' associations, who yearned for the old certainties of the pioneer days, when Tito had been in absolute command and always knew the correct answers to any problem. There were others, whose views were openly stated at a meeting of historians in Zagreb in October 1983, who called for a demystification of the Tito image. They called for a more objective assessment of the wartime period, and even of the last years of the Yugoslav kingdom. The relevance of these historical enquiries to the political situation in 1983 became explicit when the Belgrade Institute for Social Studies published a book, *Party Pluralism or Monism (Stranački pluralizam ili monizam)*, by two university professors, Vojislav Kostunica and Kosta Čavoski. The book examined the social movements and the political system between 1944 and 1949. The authors argued that, at the end of the war, the Communist Party had the choice of building socialism through parliamentary means or by the imposition of 'monism', following the Soviet model of the 'dictatorship of the proletariat'. The People's Front, which could have been the vehicle for developing a genuine socialist democracy, was used instead as an instrument for the suppression of democracy. The authors saw in the self-management system elements of economic and social pluralism which could be expanded to embrace the political system. They quoted Kardelj's phrase 'the pluralism of self-management interests' in order to give an air of orthodoxy to their views.

Their advocacy of a multi-party system and their plea for greater political freedom contained echoes of the Djilas heresy of the early 1950s. The fact that such a book could be published, and that the ideas in it could be publicly discussed, indicates the extent to which the area of free debate had widened since the death of Tito. In 1973 one of the authors, Professor Čavoski, had been sentenced to five months' imprisonment for writing that the judicial system did not guarantee basic human freedoms. In 1983 he and others were freely able to publish trenchant criticisms of the system, to attack the incompetence of the party leadership and to advocate new political initiatives, without incurring the penalties which would certainly have descended upon them a few years earlier. It is interesting to note that the institute under whose auspices the book was published was created specifically in order to accommodate the *Praxis* group of Belgrade professors, who had previously been driven out of their university posts because of their non-conformist views (see above, pp. 250–2).

The counter-arguments to these libertarian views were put by officials of the LCY, who demanded ideological and political unity in order to ensure the success of the stabilisation programme, and by army spokesmen, who feared that public order might be endangered if too much freedom were permitted. With the Kosovo riots of 1981 in mind, and with manifestations of nationalism appearing in other republics, this concern is understandable. The 'firm hand' party looked to the events in Croatia in 1971 to give justification for their views. The liberals looked a few years further back, to the Ranković affair of 1966, to illustrate the dangers of overcentralisation and police repression.

The arrest of twenty-eight alleged dissidents in April 1984, at a flat in Belgrade, where they were attending a meeting addressed by Milovan Djilas, appeared to have been ordered to give notice that the authorities were keeping a vigilant eye on the non-conformists. The release, during the next three days, of all those arrested, including the only two against whom charges of engaging in hostile propaganda were laid, suggested that the action was in the nature of a warning rather than the start of a campaign of repression. Except for Djilas himself and his brother, Akim, most of those involved were young intellectuals who had been involved in the student demonstrations of 1968. The affair took on a more serious character when Radomir Radović, a thirty-three-year-old electrical technician and trade union activist, was found dead in unexplained circumstances two weeks after his release from detention. The government, obviously concerned about Yugoslavia's international standing in the eyes of the western powers, on whose economic support it relied, at first prudently refrained from comment.

In the absence of Tito there was no clear answer from above to the problems posed by the turbulent academics. In July a young Bosnian lecturer, Vojislav Šešelj, was sentenced in Sarajevo to eight years for 'endangering the social order' by his writings. The savagery of this sentence was denounced by Mitja Ribičič, the veteran Slovene member of the LCY

Presidium; and a Montenegrin member of the Federal Council resigned his seat in protest. Nevertheless, six of the Belgrade group were rearrested in August and were bitterly attacked by the president, Veselin Djuranović. A fierce public controversy raged over the propriety of his prejudgement of the issue before the trial. It seemed that the authorities were not sure where the line was to be drawn between permitted critical debate within the context of the existing political system and an open challenge to the foundations of their power.

The collective presidency which came into office on 15 May 1984 appeared to bring new blood into the highest level of state authority, as all but one of the previous incumbents retired on the expiry of their five-year terms of office. On closer examination of the list, however, it is apparent that the 'new' men all have long records in the service of the state and party. Most had been Partisans who joined the party during or even before the war. They had all been involved in the decision-making processes during the Tito era, and shared responsibility for the policies which led to the deepening economic crisis which faced the country in 1984. The senior member, sixty-eight-year-old Serbian General Nikola Ljubičić, was minister of defence from 1967 to 1981, and he also served a term on the LCY Presidium. The youngest, fifty-six-year-old Branko Mikulić, who represented Bosnia–Hercegovina, had started his political career in the immediate post-war period as an organiser of the communist youth movement in Bosnia, and had later represented his republic on the LCY Presidium, as well as holding senior positions in both state and party organisations in Bosnia–Hercegovina. The man chosen to head the new body during its first year was Veselin Djuranović, Tito's last prime minister. The average age of the new presidency fell from sixty-eight to sixty-one, but it still represented the thinking of the Partisan generation. It did not seem likely that these men would bring new ideas to bear on the problems of the 1980s.

At the same time as the new presidency took office there was a government reshuffle. Two of these changes were made necessary by the promotion of former ministers Lazar Mojsov (foreign affairs) and Stane Dolanc (interior) into the ranks of the presidency. Others retired because of illness or advancing age.

Two prominent Slovene economists, Zvone Dragan, who had been a vice-premier, and Janko Smole, the negotiator of the IMF loans, were dropped. There was a new foreign minister, Raif Dizdarević, and a new minister of the interior, the reputedly liberal-minded Montenegrin Dobroslav Čulafić. Mrs Planinc was re-elected for a further two-year term as prime minister. Mrs Planinc came to national prominence, during the

Croatian troubles of 1971, when she rallied the Croatian LCY to the side of Tito and helped to oust the rebellious 'nationalists' who supported Tripalo, Pirker and Dr Dabčević-Kučar (see above, pp. 256–8). Although she had a reputation as the 'iron lady' of Croatia, Mrs Planinc has shown in office a down-to-earth pragmatism and a flexibility, especially in the handling of economic problems, which have little to do with ideology. On her re-election in May 1984 she made the routine declaration that the political system must remain unchanged, and that socialist self-management was inviolable. She particularly stressed the need to maintain the federal framework in the face of centralising tendencies. She has shown herself to be fully aware of the need to present an image of 'responsibility' and financial orthodoxy if the western bankers who have supported the Yugoslav economy in the past are prepared to continue that support. Thus, on her visit to London in November 1983 she tried to impress an audience of City bankers by giving detailed statistics to show that, during her premiership, the living standards of the Yugoslav people had fallen by 10 per cent per year, and that the austerity programme would be maintained – an unusual attitude for a socialist politician. She has warned her own people that, unless the stabilisation programme succeeds, 'a new system' of economic and political management might be necessary. If those who control the polycentric machinery of economic decision making – and especially the semi-autonomous and often nationalist-minded republican bodies – cannot be persuaded to coordinate their policies on a voluntary basis, there was, she believed, a serious danger of economic collapse.

Mrs Planinc is the only woman in the highest stratum of state policy making. There has never been a woman member of the federal presidency, and there is only a token representation of women in the LCY Presidium. This is a reflection of the subordinate position of women in Yugoslav society. Although there is legal equality between the sexes, and women were treated as equals in the resistance movement, it has proved impossible to reverse within a few generations the inherited traditions of past centuries. Although women have made considerable headway in the professions, especially in medicine and in academic life, amongst the mass of working people and in the rural areas the lot of women has changed little. Their position is worst in the Muslim areas and in the least developed republics of the south. Those who do go out to work, even in the big cities, are usually in the lower-paid jobs and they are expected to run the households when they return home. The small group of women in senior positions in public life, like Mrs Planinc, are exceptional. Most of their sisters appear to accept their subordinate role, and the women's liberation movement, which has swept through the middle classes of western Europe and North America, has in the main made little impact in Yugoslavia.

Conclusion

Since the Second World War the people of Yugoslavia have been governed under the same political system and within the same frontiers for forty years. In the life of a nation this is a short span of time, but in the history of the South Slavs and their non-Slav compatriots it represents the longest period during which a Yugoslav state has survived. Inevitably, the question of the durability of the present regime arises. The chronic economic crisis which has developed since the mid 1970s is not the cause of the present turbulence in Yugoslav society, but it is the catalyst which has stimulated the forces which make for dissension, and whose roots lie deep in history.

The death of President Tito in 1980 removed a figure of world stature whose influence was a force for unity. The collective leadership which replaced him appears to have neither the will nor the power to control the situation. On the other hand, it could be argued that Tito's influence, especially in his later years, prevented the search for new solutions to old problems. Whilst he was alive the range of permitted options was limited by his perception of a socialist society, led by a Leninist type of Communist Party. It was not possible to contemplate a radical readjustment in the framework of the edifice which had been erected in the first post-war decade. This was particularly true of the relations among the republics and provinces within the federation. Changes in the status of Kosovo, for example, could not be contemplated lest they provoked a re-examination of the position first of Macedonia, with its large Albanian minority, and then of the other federal units. Even the changing of the name of the province from that of the Autonomous Region of Kosovo to the Autonomous Province of Kosovo was accomplished only after serious disturbances. The attempt of the Croats to change their status in 1971 provoked a national crisis.

The same resistance to radical change can be seen in the attitude to the role of the LCY in Yugoslav political life. Although the change of name in 1952 was intended to herald a separation of the party from the state machine (and in the 1960s the separation seemed to have occurred), when the risk of disintegration appeared in 1971 it was the LCY and the army which stepped in to restore the equilibrium.

Similarly with the economy – although decision making became decentralised and central planning a pious platitude rather than a rational system of ordering economic affairs, when matters got out of hand the central government intervened with administrative measures which, by its own admission, were contrary to the principles of self-management. Ironically, the tightening of central control over the banking system was forced through on the insistence of that pillar of capitalist orthodoxy, the IMF.

There are, however, many positive factors in the balance sheet. Yugoslavia has made much progress economically, socially, culturally and politically during the post-war period. The people may be restless and difficult to govern, but they are vital, energetic, resourceful and optimistic. Yugoslavia has progressed during forty years from a poor peasant country, which emerged from the war crippled by appalling material and human losses, into the middle rank of the industrial nations of the world. Looking at some of the other eastern European nations, like Poland and Romania, its people are, on the whole, more prosperous and freer than in many of the post-war people's democracies.

The attitude of the major world powers to non-aligned Yugoslavia is also a factor which encourages hope. It is not in the interests of either east or west to allow the strategically important area which Yugoslavia occupies to become a focus of conflict, as so often happened in the past. The best way to ensure that this will not occur again is to maintain an economically stable and strong non-aligned Yugoslavia.

The external factors making for the survival of Yugoslavia must be balanced by a will for unity amongst the Yugoslav peoples themselves. Experience during the post-war period suggests that this lesson has been learned. Although centrifugal forces do exist and are sometimes given greater impetus by the activities of émigré groups, some of whom appear to want to fight again the battles of the revolutionary war, the mass of the people, and especially the post-war generation, will want their leaders to pull them back from the abyss. The wide-ranging and open debate about the future which came to the surface in the 1980s is a necessary preliminary to the working out of a consensus, which will, I believe, provide a new point of departure for the creation of a more democratic but still socialist Yugoslavia. If the present leaders do not recognise this, and if they attempt to silence debate by the imposition of a 'firm hand', possibly with the cooperation of the army, they may worsen the situation. Their behaviour since 1981 suggests that the balance has tilted against those who want to turn back the clock. My own inclinations are towards optimism and hope for the future.

Bibliography

(Books in languages other than English are cited only where they are of special interest or where no English equivalent is available.)

The Yugoslav Bibliographic Institute (Jugoslovenski Bibliografski Institut) has issued, since 1950, a fortnightly list of books and pamphlets published in Yugoslavia (*Bibliografija Jugoslavije*), and has also produced a twenty-one-volume retrospective bibliography covering the period 1945–67 (*Jugoslovenska retrospektivna bibliografska gradja*).

For the English-speaking student there are several excellent bibliographies, published in Britain and the USA, which are readily available and which include works in English, Serbo-Croat and other European languages. Special mention should be made of M. B. Petrovich's *Yugoslavia: a bibliographic guide* (Washington, D.C., 1974) and J. J. Horton's volume *Yugoslavia* in the World Bibliographic Series (Oxford, 1977). A more recent publication is Rusko Matulić, *Bibliography of Sources on Yugoslavia* (Palo Alto, Calif., 1981).

Other useful sources, but alas becoming dated, are P. L. Horecky (ed.), *Southeastern Europe: a guide to basic publications* (Chicago, 1970) and J. M. Halpern's *Bibliography of English Language Sources on Yugoslavia* (Amherst, Mass., 1969).

There are a number of valuable specialist bibliographies, including, J. Tadić (ed.), *Ten Years of Yugoslav Historiography, 1945–1955* (Belgrade, 1955), B. Hunter, *Soviet–Yugoslav Relations 1948–1972* (London, 1976) and F. W. Carter, *A Bibliography of the Geography of Yugoslavia* (King's College, London, 1965).

Each of the Yugoslav republics has its own bibliographical publications, e.g. for Slovenia, *Slovenska bibliografija* (Ljubljana, 1948 – (annual)); for Macedonia, *Makedonska bibliografija* (Skopje, 1950– (annual)); and for Montenegro, *Bibliografski vjesnik* (Cetinje, 1972 –). Two bibliographies concerned with Macedonia which are of particular interest are H. Andonov-Poljanski's *British Bibliography on Macedonia* (Skopje, 1966), which lists over 4,000 items on Macedonia which have appeared in British books, periodicals and newspapers, and G. M. Terry's *A Bibliography of Macedonian Studies* (Nottingham, 1975), which lists over 1,600 items in English, Macedonian and other languages.

The abstracting service ABSEES contains a section on Yugoslavia in each of its quarterly issues. It is mainly concerned with items from periodicals and newspapers, and deals with the social sciences, but it also gives summaries of books. It was published in book form by Glasgow University from its foundation in 1971 until 1976, when it was transferred to microfiche, and has been published since 1977 by Oxford Microform.

General works in English

During the post-war period many general books on Yugoslavia have been published in Britain and the USA which cover geographical, historical and current political and economic topics. A pre-war book in this genre was John Buchan (ed.), *Yugoslavia* (London, 1923). The indispensable three-volume Naval Intelligence Division handbook (often known as the Admiralty handbook) is an excellent source of background material on physical and economic geography, the history of the Yugoslav peoples up to 1939, and the commercial, social and cultural life of the people in the kingdom of Yugoslavia (*Yugoslavia*, 3 vols., Naval Intelligence Division, London, 1944 – previously classified, but now freely available in libraries and secondhand bookshops).

The first of the post-war general works was Robert Kerner (ed.), *Yugoslavia* (Berkeley, 1949), and this was followed by Muriel Heppell and Fred Singleton's *Yugoslavia* (London, 1961), A. W. Palmer's *Yugoslavia* (Oxford, 1964), Phyllis Auty's *Yugoslavia* (London, 1965) and Stevan Pavlowitch's *Yugoslavia* (London, 1971).

Stephen Clissold's *Short History of Yugoslavia from Early Times to 1966* (Cambridge, 1968), of which the present volume is a successor, is based on the historical chapters of the Admiralty handbook, with an additional section by Phyllis Auty covering the wartime and post-war periods to 1966.

1. The lands of the South Slavs

Volume I of the Admiralty handbook is a useful starting point for a study of the geography of Yugoslavia. A handy topographical atlas with a hundred-page index of place names is P. Mardešić and Z. Dugački (eds.), *Geografski atlas Jugoslavije* (Zagreb, 1961), which contains thirty-seven general maps on a scale of 1:500,000 and many specialist maps on a smaller scale.

There are a number of works in English dealing with the geographical background to the formation of the first Yugoslav state, and in particular with the drawing of its frontiers. A. E. Moodie's study *The Italo-Yugoslav Boundary* (London, 1945) gives a detailed survey of the problems of frontier demarcation in the Julian region. Jovan Cvijić, the father of Serbian geographers, ably argues the Yugoslav case in *La frontière septentrionale des yougoslaves* (Paris, 1918), and the Slovene point of view is presented in F. Seidl's *La future frontière politique entre la Yougoslavie et l'Italie: étude géologique et géographique* (Ljubljana, 1919). An objective review of the geographical background to the Macedonian Question is presented in H. R. Wilkinson's *Maps and Politics: a review of the ethnographic cartography of Macedonia* (Liverpool, 1951).

The administrative geography of socialist Yugoslavia and the problems of regional diversity are covered in J. C. Fisher's interesting *Yugoslavia, a Multinational State: regional difference and administrative response* (San Francisco, 1966). F. E. I. Hamilton's *Yugoslavia: patterns of economic activity* is a standard work on the economic geography of the early post-war period, and Antun Melik's *Yugoslavia's Natural Resources* (Ljubljana, 1950) offers a straightforward account of the country's resource base as known at the beginning of the post-war industrialisation drive.

The best survey in English of the historical geography of Yugoslavia is to be found in F. W. Carter (ed.), *An Historical Geography of the Balkans*, although it is far from comprehensive in its coverage.

2. The early Slav settlers

Edward Gibbon's *Decline and Fall of the Roman Empire* (6 vols., London, 1954) is a work of literature rather than a reliable historical guide, but there is still much of value in it to the cautious historian. A translation of Constantine Porphyrogenitus' *De administrando imperio* by R. J. H. Jenkins from Gy. Moravcsik's edition (Budapest, 1949) is another classic source which must be used with caution, as it was written over a century after the period it describes.

A standard work which places the South Slavs in the wider context of their relations with the other Slav-speaking peoples is Francis Dvornik's *The Slavs in European History and Civilization* (New Brunswick, N.J., 1975) and is more reliable than Roger Portal's *The Slavs* (London, 1969). Prince Dmitri Obolensky's *The Bogomils: a study in Balkan neo-Manichaeism* (Cambridge, 1948, reprinted Twickenham, 1972) is still the standard English text on both the theological and historical importance of the Bogomil heresy, but the non-specialist reader may find the approach of O. Bihalji-Merin and A. Benac in *The Bogomils* (London, 1962) more interesting, as it concentrates on their archaeological legacies and is illustrated by an excellent set of photographs.

3. The early Slav kingdoms

A. Vlasto's *The Entry of the Slavs into Christendom: an introduction to the mediaeval history of the Slavs* (Cambridge, 1970) covers a wide field and admirably fulfils the objective of providing a readable introduction to the subject. G. Ostrogorsky's *History of the Byzantine State*, translated by J. M. Hussey (Oxford, 1956), presents the fruits of a lifetime of study by a distinguished Yugoslav scholar, and is a work of reference for many aspects of the medieval history of the Balkans and particularly for the relationships between the early Slav kingdoms and the Byzantine empire. Further enlightenment on this period can be found in D. Obolensky, *The Byzantine Inheritance of Eastern Europe* (London, 1982).

4. The South Slavs under foreign rule

The Ottoman occupation

General surveys of the role of the Ottomans in the Balkans are to be found in P. H. Coles, *The Ottoman Impact on Europe* (London, 1968) and L. S. Stavrianos, *The Balkans since 1453* (New York, 1958). An outstanding work of scholarship covering the five centuries before 1804 is P. Sugar, *South Eastern Europe under Ottoman Rule, 1354–1804* (Seattle and London, 1977). The diplomatic history of the relations between the Turks and the European powers in D. M. Vaughan's *Europe and the Turk: the pattern of alliances* (Liverpool, 1960) contains useful material on the Balkans, although its scope extends to much wider issues.

A recent American work which brings new insights into the economic development of the Balkans under Ottoman rule is Bruce McGowan's *Economic Life in Ottoman Europe* (Cambridge, 1981).

Slovenes, Croats and Serbs under Habsburg rule (pre-nineteenth-century)

Books in English on the early Habsburg period are not readily available. There is a one-volume *History of Yugoslavia* (New York and London 1974) by Vladimir Dedijer, I. Božić, S. Ćirković and M. Ekmečić which has a brief account of Slovenia and Croatia before 1526. Clissold's *Short History of Yugoslavia* also has chapters on Slovenia, Croatia and Vojvodina under Habsburg rule. The relevant chapters in Zvane Črnja's *Cultural History of Croatia* (Zagreb, 1962) can also be recommended. A comprehensive survey of the history of Dubrovnik is provided by F. W. Carter in *Dubrovnic (Ragusa): a classic city state* (London and New York, 1972).

The military frontier zone established by the Habsburgs in the sixteenth century is the subject of two works by Gunther E. Rothenburg: *The Austrian Military Border in Croatia, 1522–1747* (Urbana, 1960) and *The Military Border in Croatia, 1740–1881: a study of an imperial institution* (Chicago, 1966).

5. The development of independence

Michael E. B. Petrovich's two-volume *History of Serbia, 1804–1918* (New York, 1976) provides an excellent account of the development of the Serbian nation, from the Karadjordje revolt of 1804 to the formation of the first Yugoslav state. The Karadjordje and Obrenović revolts are dealt with in Leopold von Ranke's classic, *The History of Servia and the Servian Revolution*, originally published in 1829 and translated into English by Mrs A. Kerr (London, 1874).

There are several fascinating works concerning the colourful characters who helped to further the course of Serbian independence. *The Life and Times of Vuk Stefanović Karadžić* by Sir Duncan Wilson (Cambridge, 1979) assesses the importance of the father of the modern Serbian language and its literature in the context of the Serbian renaissance of the early nineteenth century. Vuk's predecessor, Dimitrije (Dositej) Obradović, is able to speak for himself in G. R. Noyes' translation of *The Life and Adventures of Dimitrije Obradović* (Berkeley, 1953). Life in Serbia during the Karadjordje revolt is vividly recounted by one of the men at the centre of events in L. F. Edwards' edition of *The Memoirs of Prota Matija Nenadović* (Oxford, 1969). The standard work on Miloš Obrenović by Vladimir Stojančević (*Miloš Obrenović i njegova doba* (Belgrade, 1966)) has not been translated into English.

Other biographical works of interest are M. Djilas, *Njegoš – Poet, prince, bishop* (New York, 1966), which depicts the situation in Montenegro during the early nineteenth century, and W. D. McClellan's *Svetozar Marković and the Origins of Balkan Socialism* (Princeton, 1964), which provides a background to Serbian politics during the stormy reigns of Michael and Milan Obrenović.

There is a wealth of specialist studies on the diplomatic background to the struggles of the Balkan peoples for independence. S. K. Pavlowitch's *Anglo-Russian Rivalry in Serbia, 1837–1839* (Paris and The Hague, 1961) is a scholarly monograph on the background to the pressures exerted on Miloš Obrenović during the last years of his first reign.

There are many studies which are concerned with the relations between the European powers and the nascent Balkan nations in the period immediately before and after the Congress of Berlin, the most notable of which are B. H. Sumner's *Russia and the Balkans, 1870–1880* (London, 1962), Charles Jelavich's *Tsarist Russia and Balkan Nationalism: Russian influence in the internal affairs of Bulgaria and Serbia, 1879–1886* (Berkeley, 1968) and M. D. Stojanović's *The Great Powers and the Balkans, 1875–1878* (Cambridge, 1968).

The nationalities problem as seen by a noted Slovene historian is given in Fran Zwitter's *Nacionalni problemi v Habsburski Monarhiji* (Ljubljana, 1962).

The Bosnian crisis of 1908 is covered in Bernadotte E. Schmitt, *The Annexation of Bosnia, 1908–1909* (New York, 1970) and in Wayne Vucinich's *Serbia between East and West: the events of 1903–1908* (Stanford, Calif., 1954). H. N. Brailsford's first-hand impressions of life in Macedonia at the time of the Ilinden rising are vividly recounted in his *Macedonia: its races and its future* (London, 1906), and is complemented by Leon Trotsky's eyewitness reports of the situation in Macedonia and South Serbia in *The Balkan Wars, 1912–13: the war correspondence of Leon Trotsky* (New York, 1980).

R. W. Seton-Watson's classic *The Southern Slav Question and the Habsburg Monarchy* (London, 1911) is written by the leading western European champion of the South Slav cause. It should be read in conjunction with *R. W. Seton-Watson i Jugoslaveni* (Zagreb and London, 1976), which contains Seton-Watson's correspondence with leading figures in the Yugoslav movement before 1918 (vol. I) and of politicians, diplomats and scholars in the Yugoslav kingdom between the two wars (vol. II).

Two excellent volumes in the monumental series *A History of East Central Europe* published by the University of Washington (Seattle and London) are Charles and Barbara Jelavich, *The Establishment of the Balkan National States, 1804–1920* (vol. VIII, 1977) and Robert A. Kann and Zdenek David, *The Peoples of the Eastern Habsburg Lands* (vol. VI, 1984). Barbara Jelavich's two-volume *History of the Balkans* (Cambridge, 1983) is an indispensable guide to the eighteenth, nineteenth and twentieth centuries.

The situation in Bosnia–Hercegovina under Habsburg rule is admirably dealt with in two outstanding works. Peter F. Sugar's *The Industrialization of Bosnia–Hercegovina, 1878–1918* (Seattle, 1963) concentrates on economic developments, whilst relations between the Habsburg and Muslim authorities is the theme of Robert Donia's *Islam under the Double Eagle, 1878–1914* (New York, 1981).

6. The First World War

Vladimir Dedijer's *The Road to Sarajevo* (London, 1967) gives the accepted Yugoslav version of the events which led to the assassination in 1914, whilst Joachim Remak in *Sarajevo* (London, 1959) presents the same events from a point of view more sympathetic to the Habsburgs. Luigi Albertini's *Origins of the War of 1914* (3 vols. Oxford, 1967) traces the diplomatic history of Europe between 1878 and 1918 in great detail, and has useful chapters on the relations among Serbia, Montenegro and Austria–Hungary. A. J. P. Taylor's *Struggle for Mastery in Europe, 1848–1918* (Oxford, 1954), although mainly concerned with the events which led to war, has a final chapter which gives a concise account of 'The Diplomacy of War, 1914–18'.

The military history of the war in the Balkans is dealt with in C. R. M. F. Cruttwell, *A History of the Great War, 1914–1918* (Oxford, 1934) and Sir John Edmonds, *A Short History of the First World War* (Cambridge, 1951). The Salonika campaign is the subject of Alan Palmer's *The Gardeners of Salonika: an account of the campaign in Macedonia 1915–1918* (London, 1965), and the appalling plight of the Serbian sick and wounded in the winter of 1914–15 is depicted in *My Balkan Log* (London, 1922) by a Scottish surgeon, J. Johnston Abraham, who tended the casualties sent down to Skopje from the Kolubara front.

The activities of the South Slav Committee during the First World War are recorded in the *Southern Slav Bulletin*, published in London and Paris between 1915 and 1919 and available in the British Library and the Bodleian. There are also a number of pamphlets issued under the title The South Slav Library which present the Yugoslav case.

7 and 8. The kingdom of Serbs, Croats and Slovenes and the kingdom of Yugoslavia

The diplomatic manoeuvres amongst the Allied powers concerning the establishment of the Yugoslav state and the delimitation of its frontiers are the topic of Ivo J. Lederer's *Yugoslavia at the Paris Peace Conference* (New Haven, 1963), and the internal and external problems of the new state are discussed in *The Creation of Yugoslavia, 1914–1918*, edited by Dimitrije Djordjević (Santa Barbara and Oxford, 1980). Of particular interest in the last-named work is John R. Lampe's essay, 'Unifying the Yugoslav Economy, 1918–1921: misery and early misunderstanding'.

There are few objective works in English on the history of the Yugoslav state between the wars. One that can be recommended, despite its pro-Serbian orientation, is Alex N. Dragnich, *The First Yugoslavia* (Stanford, Calif., 1983). Another scholarly study of the early days of the kingdom of Serbs, Croats and Slovenes, and of the ideological antecedents of the men who created the Vidovdan constitution, is *The National Question in Yugoslavia: origins, history, politics*, by Ivo Banac (Ithaca and London, 1984). Useful material is to be found in several general works such as the Admiralty handbook, vol. II, Pavlowitch's *Yugoslavia*, and the volume in the United Nations series edited by R. J. Kerner, *Yugoslavia* (Berkeley, 1949). Jozo Tomasevich's *Peasants, Politics and Economic Change* (Stanford, 1955) is excellent on the rural economy of the kingdom of Yugoslavia. Vera St Erlich, *Family in Transition: a study of 300 Yugoslav villages* (Princeton, 1977) presents a colourful picture of everyday life and customs in rural areas during the inter-war period. Ruth Trouton's *Peasant Renaissance in Yugoslavia, 1900–1950* is a valuable work of social history which examines the role of education amongst the peasants. Rudolf Bićanić describes in great detail the life of the peasantry in the hinterland of the Dalmatian coast, in his *Kako živi narod* (Zagreb, 1936 and 1939). An English translation of the essential parts of this work is also available: *How the People Live: life in the passive regions* (Amherst, Mass., 1981). Rebecca West's *Black Lamb and Grey Falcon* is a two-volume account of a journey through Yugoslavia in the 1930s by an acute observer of the political scene. There is a brief survey of the inter-war economy in F. Singleton and B. Carter, *The Economy of Yugoslavia* (London and New York, 1982).

Several biographical and autobiographical works on and by leading politicians of the inter-war period are available in English. They should be used with caution as the authors are mainly concerned with explaining and defending their particular national and political viewpoints. In this category are the memoirs of the Croat Peasant Party leader, Vlatko Maček, *In the Struggle for Freedom* (University Park, Pa. and London, 1957), and Alex N. Dragnich's *Serbia, Nikola Pašić and Yugoslavia*, which paints the patriarchal figure of the Serbian and Yugoslav premier in a most favourable light. Two books which give a personal account of inter-war Yugoslavia from a Slovene standpoint are *The Native's Return* (New York, 1934) and *My Native Land* (New York and London, 1943), by the anti-royalist exile Louis Adamič. Milan Stojadinovic's apologia, *Ni rat, ni pakt*, was first published in Buenos Aires in 1963 and reprinted in Rijeka in 1970. J. B. Hoptner's *Yugoslavia in Crisis, 1934–1941* (New York, 1962) deals with the tragic drift to war during the 1930s, and D. N. Ristić, in *Yugoslavia's Revolution of 1941* (University Park, Pa., 1962), gives an account of the *coup d'état* of 1941 by a committed participant in the event. King Peter II's memoirs, *A King's Heritage* (London, 1955) was probably not written by the king, and the ghost writer's accuracy is dubious. *Paul of Yugoslavia: Britain's maligned friend* (London, 1980) is a sympathetic account by Neil Balfour and Sally Mackay of the regent and his family, which is based on family papers, but shows little understanding of the wider political context. An interesting glimpse of life in the royal household is given in Sir Cecil Parrott's autobiographical work, *Tightrope* (London, 1975). Stephen Graham's *Alexander of Jugoslavia: strong man of the Balkans* is mainly concerned with the assassination of the king in 1934, but it also gives a rather romanticised account of his life.

The fullest treatment in English of the early history of the CPY is by Ivan Avakumović, *History of the Communist Party of Yugoslavia*, vol. I (Aberdeen, 1964). Unfortunately this takes the story only as far as 1941; the projected vol. II has not yet appeared.

9. Yugoslavia and the Second World War

Two histories of the war in Yugoslavia which, if not official histories, have the seal of approval of the government, are Pero Morača and V. Kučan, *The War and Revolution of the Peoples of Yugoslavia* (Belgrade, 1962) and D. Plenča, *Yugoslavia in the Second World War* (Belgrade, 1967). Ilija Jukić, *The Fall of Yugoslavia* (New York, 1974) presents the war from a pro-Mihailović point of view, as might be expected from a former minister in the royal government in exile. Konstantin Fotić, *The War We Lost – Yugoslavia's tragedy and the failure of the west* (New York, 1948) takes a similar line. A well-researched book by a former US diplomat which is sympathetic to Mihailović is Walter R. Roberts, *Tito, Mihailo-vić and the Allies, 1941–1945* (New Brunswick, N.J., 1973).

A scholarly assessment of the Četniks, which also gives a well-balanced picture of the confused situation in Yugoslavia during the war, is Jozo Tomasevich, *The Chetniks* (Stanford, Calif., 1975). A work of more limited scope, and displaying greater sympathy for the Četniks, is Matteo J. Milazzo, *The Chetnik Movement and the Yugoslav Resistance* (Baltimore and London, 1975).

Eyewitness accounts by Allied liaison officers and Yugoslav fighters provide abundant material on the Partisans, and rather less on the Četniks. The first to appear were Basil Davidson's *Partisan Picture* (London, 1946), which is enthusiastically pro-Tito; and Jasper Rootham's *Miss-Fire: the chronicle of a British mission to Mihailovich, 1943–1944* (London, 1946). These were followed by Stephen Clissold's *Whirlwind: the story of Marshal Tito's rise to power* (London, 1949) and Fitzroy Maclean's *Eastern Approaches* (London, 1950). Maclean's predecessor with the first British mission to Tito, F. W. D. Deakin, describes his adventures with the Partisans in *The Embattled Mountain* (London, 1971).

Yugoslav accounts include Vladimir Dedijer's *With Tito through the War: Partisan diary 1941–1944* (London, 1951) and the more intensely personal *Wartime* (London and New York, 1977), by the controversial Milovan Djilas.

Several members of SOE and of British military missions to Yugoslavia are contributors to *British Policy towards Wartime Resistance in Yugoslavia and Greece* (London, 1975), edited by Phyllis Auty and Richard Clogg.

The arguments over the establishment of the new frontier with Italy at the end of the war gave rise to a spate of memoranda and pamphlets putting the Yugoslav case for the inclusion of Trieste in the new Yugoslavia. Although A. E. Moodie's *The Italo-Yugoslav Boundary: a study in political geography* (London, 1945) is concerned with the delimitation of the post-First World War boundary, it provides an invaluable background of geographical and historical data against which the post-1945 problems may be better understood. Yugoslav official publications on the Julian region and Trieste include: *Memorandum of the Government of the Democratic Federative Yugoslavia Concerning the Question of the Julian March* (Belgrade, 1945) and *Memorandum of the Government of the Federative People's Republic of Yugoslavia on the Economic Problem of Trieste* (Belgrade, 1946), with an *Annex on Natural Ties Linking the Julian March and Trieste with Yugoslavia*. A survey of the whole problem of Trieste and the Julian region is given in Jean-Baptiste Duroselle, *Le conflit de Trieste 1943–1954* (Brussels, 1966).

10. The transition to socialism

The establishment of the new regime is sympathetically treated by several British authors in works published in the first few post-war years. These include some which deal with all the people's democracies of eastern Europe, such as Hugh Seton-Watson's *East Europe Revolution* (London, 1956); R. R. Betts (ed.), *Central and S.E. Europe, 1945–48* (London, 1950), which includes a chapter on Yugoslavia by Phyllis Auty; and Doreen Warriner's *Revolution in Eastern Europe* (London, 1950). E. P. Thompson's *The Railway: an adventure in construction* (London, 1948) captures the élan of the international youth brigades which went to Yugoslavia to build roads and railways in the first years after the war.

The dispute between the Yugoslav Communist Party and the Cominform produced a flood of polemics, the most bitter attacks coming from communist writers who had been fervent admirers of Tito until the excommunication of June 1948. Typical of these is James Klugman, *From Trotsky to Tito* (London, 1950).

The best scholarly account, which includes reprints of all the relevant documents and covers relations between the USSR and Yugoslavia both before and after 1948, is *Yugoslavia and the Soviet Union, 1939–1973: a documentary survey* (London, 1975), edited by Stephen Clissold. Clissold's 112-page introduction to the documents is a masterly survey of the topic.

The political background to the period is covered in *The Transformation of*

Communist Ideology: the Yugoslav case, 1945–1953 (Cambridge, Mass. and London, 1972), by A. Ross Johnson.

The economy during the period of the first Five Year Plan, 1947–51, is dealt with in a number of official publications, for example V. Begović, *Two and a Half Years of the First Five Year Plan* (New York, 1949), and in the general books on the Yugoslav economy which are referred to in the following section.

11, 12, 13 and 14. The Tito era and beyond

As most of the books covering the period after the introduction of self-management do not readily conform to the divisions of the book's chapters, the bibliography covering the last four chapters is arranged under one heading, and an additional section on Yugoslav literature is added.

One of the best general accounts of the Yugoslav system from 1945 to 1960, which includes an assessment of the self-management system and of the non-alignment policy, is G. W. Hoffman and F. W. Neal, *Yugoslavia and the New Communism* (New York, 1962). A macro-economic study of the post-war Yugoslav economy by a critical insider is R. Bićanić's posthumous *Economic Policy in Socialist Yugoslavia* (Cambridge, 1973), which includes a postscript by Marjan Hanžeković on the 1965 economic reforms. Another Yugoslav writer who is even more critical than Bićanić, although from a different standpoint, is Branko Horvat, in *The Yugoslav Economic System* (White Plains, N.Y., 1976). A recent work which deals with the economy up to the death of Tito is Singleton and Carter, *The Economy of Yugoslavia.*

Works which focus on the self-management system *per se* include the ILO report *Workers' Management in Yugoslavia* (Geneva, 1962), which is generally sympathetic to the system; Jan Vanek's *The Economics of Workers' Management* (London, 1972), which is enthusiastically favourable; and Ljubo Sirc's *The Yugoslav Economy under Self-Management* (London, 1979), which is sharply hostile. A semi-official account of the system which discusses some of the problems facing the self-managers is Milojko Drulović's *Self-Management on Trial* (Nottingham, 1978).

General works which cover various aspects of the economic, social or political scene during the post-war period include Dennison Rusinow, *The Yugoslav Experiment, 1948–1974* (London, 1977), Sir Duncan Wilson, *Tito's Yugoslavia* (Cambridge, 1979), Fred Singleton, *Twentieth Century Yugoslavia* (Basingstoke, 1976) and Duško Doder, *The Yugoslavs* (London, 1978). Sharon Zukin's *Beyond Marx and Tito: theory and practice in Yugoslav socialism* (Cambridge, 1975) includes interesting case studies of the reactions of Yugoslavs from different social backgrounds to the policies of post-war Yugoslavia. A general overview of the processes of political decision making, covering the period from the reforms of the mid sixties to the post-Tito period, can be found in Steven L. Burg, *Conflict and Cohesion in Socialist Yugoslavia: political decision making since 1966* (Princeton, 1983).

The policy of non-alignment is examined in Lars Nord, *Nonalignment and Socialism: Yugoslav foreign policy in theory and practice* (Stockholm, 1973) and Alvin Z. Rubinstein, *Yugoslavia and the Nonaligned World* (Princeton, 1970).

A thorough treatment of the constitutional framework of the federation is contained in F. W. Hondius, *The Yugoslav Community of Nations* (The Hague, 1968). It takes the story up to the 1963 constitution.

The texts of the various constitutions have been published in English by the Secretariat for Information, Belgrade. A handy reference book which contains extracts from the constitutions and from the laws relating to self-management is Blagoje Bošković and David Dašić, *Socialist Self-Management in Yugoslavia, 1950–1980* (Belgrade, 1980). A theoretical justification for the system by one of its authors is Edvard Kardelj, *Democracy and Socialism* (London, 1978).

The political background to the reform period is the subject of April Carter's *Democratic Reform in Yugoslavia: the changing role of the Party, 1964–1977* (London, 1982). The stormy career of Milovan Djilas is analysed in *Djilas: the progress of a revolutionary* (London, 1983), by Stephen Clissold. Djilas' own works are available in English. The most interesting are *Land without Justice* (London, 1958), *Conversations with Stalin* (London, 1962), *The Unperfect Society* (London, 1969) and *Wartime*. His personal account of his relations with Tito, *Druzenje s Titom*, has appeared in an English version, *Tito – the story from inside* (London, 1981).

The debate stimulated by the *Praxis* group of Marxist humanists can be followed in *Marxist Humanism and 'Praxis'* (New York, 1978), edited by Gerson S. Sher, which reproduces articles by ten members of the group. Mihailo Marković's *From Affluence to 'Praxis'* (Ann Arbor, 1974) applies the *Praxis* critique to contemporary social problems. S. Stojanović's *Between Ideals and Reality* (New York, 1973) is a clear and concise statement of socialist humanism. A history of the *Praxis* group is given in *Yugoslavia: the rise and fall of socialist humanism* (Nottingham, 1975) by Robert S. Cohen and Mihailo Marković.

Tito's life is the subject of several official and adulatory works, originally published in Yugoslavia but later translated and published in Britain or the USA – for example Vilko Vinterhalter, *In the Path of Tito* (Tunbridge Wells, 1972). The speeches and writings of Tito, many of which contain autobiographical material, are available in English: For example *Tito: Selected Military Works* (Belgrade, 1966) and *Non-Alignment* (Belgrade, 1979). *Tito: a biography* (Harmondsworth, 1974), by Phyllis Auty, is still the standard work in English, although we may have to wait some time before a complete assessment of his life is available. Emile Guilovaty's *Tito* (Paris, 1979) draws on Phyllis Auty, Fitzroy Maclean and others, but puts the author's own interpretation on the life and character of Tito.

Relations between the religious communities and the state are examined critically by Stella Alexander in *Church and State in Yugoslavia* (Cambridge, 1979), which deals only with the two main Christian traditions since 1945. The official view is put in Todo Kurtović, *Church and Religion in the Socialist Self-Managed Society* (Belgrade, 1980).

The explosive question of relations among the national groups is the theme of Paul Shoup's *Communism and the Yugoslav National Question* (London, 1971) and Paul Lendvai's *Eagles in Cobwebs: nationalism and communism in the Balkans* (London, 1970). The economic aspects of the tensions among the nationalities is the subject of F. Singleton's *Regional Economic Inequalities* (Bradford University, 1979). The political implications are elaborated in Slobodan Stanković's *Titos Erbe: Die Hypothek der alten Richtungskämpfe ideologischer und nationaler Fraktionen* (Munich, 1981).

The position of the Albanian community in Yugoslavia has produced, in addition to some well-publicised riots, several articles in English and one short but well-informed monograph, Patrick F. R. Artisien's *Friends or Foes: Yugoslav–Albanian relations over the last 40 years* (Bradford University, 1980). The troubles to come in 1981 are foreshadowed in Dennison Rusinow's *The Other Albania: Kosovo 1979* (American Universities Field Staff Reports, 1980). The only full-length book to appear is Jens Reuter's *Die Albaner in Jugoslawien* (Munich, 1982).

The position of the Turkish-speaking minority is dealt with in C. N. O. Bartlett's brief but competent *The Turkish Minority in Yugoslavia* (Bradford University, 1980).

Anticipating Tito's death, Gavriel D. Ra'anen wrote *Yugoslavia after Tito: scenarios and implications* (Boulder, Colo., 1977) three years before the event. It was one of the first of several speculative works. Slobodan Stanković is on firmer ground in his *The End of the Tito Era: Yugoslavia's dilemmas* (Stanford, Calif., 1981). A scholarly assessment of the whole period from the break with the Cominform to the last year of Tito's life is *Jugoslawien am Ende der Ära Tito* (2 vols., Munich, 1983–4), edited by K.-D. Grothüsen, O. N. Haberl and W. Höpken, which is a collection of papers originally produced for an academic conference in Hamburg in June 1979.

Yugoslav literature

Throughout this book I have tried to introduce the cultural achievements of the South Slav peoples, in the knowledge that I was walking through a minefield. Until 1918 there was no Yugoslavia. The attempt to build a Yugoslav state implied a common Yugoslav culture, but few Yugoslavs accept that such a culture exists. Ivo Andrić, the Nobel Prize winner for literature in 1961, is claimed as a Serb. Miroslav Krleža is a Croat, Djilas is a Montenegrin, Alojž Gradnik a Slovene, Blaže Koneski a Macedonian, etc., etc. In this sense there is no such thing as Yugoslav literature. I can only refer the readers who are interested in the rich heritage of South Slav literature to the following reference books and let them sort out the question for themselves: *The Multinational Literature of Yugoslavia* edited by Albert B. Lord (*Review of National Literature*, vol. v, no. 1 (Spring 1974)); *Yugoslav Literature in English*, edited by Vasa D. Mihailovich and Mateja Matejić (Cambridge, Mass., 1976); and *Contemporary Yugoslav Literature: a sociopolitical approach* (Urbana, 1972) by Sveta Lukić.

Original works translated into English include the anthology of Slovene poetry *The Parnassus of a Small Nation* (London, 1957) and several of the works of Davičo, Andrić, Ćosić, Bulatović, Krleža and other twentieth-century writers.

Early writers who have been translated into English include the Slovenes Ivan Cankar and France Prešeren; the Croats Ivo Vojnović and Stanko Vraz; the Montenegrin Petar Petrović-Njegoš, author of the epic poem *The Mountain Wreath*; and the Macedonian Grigor Prličev, who, although he originally wrote his epic *The Sirdar* in Greek for a traditional poetry prize in Athens in 1980, is regarded as the father of modern Macedonian literature. A useful anthology of prose and poetry which includes translated excerpts from Yugoslav writers from 1800 to 1970 is *Introduction to Yugoslav Literature* (New York, 1973), edited by B.

Mikasinovich, D. Milivojević and V. Mihailovich. It begins with extracts from Dositej Obradović and Vuk Karadžić, and ends with modern Macedonian poetry. Ante Kadić's *Contemporary Serbian Literature* (The Hague, 1964) and his *From Croatian Renaissance to Yugoslav Socialism* (The Hague, 1969); *Yugoslav Popular Ballads* (Cambridge, 1932), by Dragutin Subotić; Antun Barac's *History of Yugoslav Literature* (Belgrade, 1955); and Svetozar Koljević's *The Epic in the Making* (Oxford, 1980) are also recommended for those wishing to explore further.

Index

Abdülaziz, sultan, 36, 102
Abdülhamid I, sultan, 76
Abdülhamid II (the Damned), sultan, 36, 102, 103
Abrahams, Dr Johnston, 121
Aćimović, Milan, 169–70, 182
Adrianople, Treaty of (1829), 86
Adriatic Question, 136
Adriatic Sea, 5, 6, 58
Aegean Sea, 8
Aerenthal, Lexa von, Count Alois, 109, 110
Agram (Zagreb) treason trials, 109
Agram, 51, 52 (see also Zagreb)
agriculture in inter-war period, 153–6
Akkerman, Convention of, 85
Alaric the Goth, 14
Albania, 2, 3, 15, 29, 123, 220–1; relations with Yugoslavia, 272–3
Albanians, 131, 139, 183, 214
Albanian–Yugoslav frontier, 138–9
Alboin, 14
Albrecht II, Holy Roman Emperor, 22, 49
Alexander, Field-Marshal Harold, 205
Alexander, King, murder of, 158, 162, 166 (see also Karadjordjević dynasty)
Alexander I, tsar, 78, 81
Alexander the Great, 33
Alföld, 1
Alpine region, 2
Andrássy, Count Gyula, 101, 102
Anglo-American Metals, 153
Ankara, battle of (1402), 27
Anschluss (1938), 166
Anti-Comintern (Tripartite) Pact, 166
Apis (Colonel Dragutin Dimitrijević), 98, 116, 117
Aquileia, 2, 15
Aquileia, patriarchate of, 28
Arsenije (Arsen) III, Patriarch of Peć, 45, 87

Associated Labour, Law on (1976), 264, 267
Athos, Mount, 18, 25
Attila the Hun, 14
Ausgleich (1867), 105, 106
Austria, 14, 15, 22, 80, 81
Austro-Hungarian monarchy, 23; collapse of, 129–30
Avars, 13, 14, 15, 16
AVNOJ (Anti-Fascist Council for the National Liberation of Yugoslavia), 196ff, 203

Bach, Alexander, 106
Ba (St Sava) Congress (1944), 201–2
Bakali, Mahmut, 273
Bakar, 5
Bakarić, Vladimir, 214–15, 221, 255, 257
Balkan federation, 148
Balkan Pact (1953), 237–8
Balkan wars (1912–13), 47, 112, 152
Balsa III, ruler of Zeta, 30
Banat, 11
Banija, 50, 216
banks, agricultural, 155
Bari, 12, 199–200
Basil (Bulgaroctonus), Byzantine emperor, 18, 31, 33
Bayezid I, sultan, 26, 27, 46
Bekir Pasha, Vizier of Bosnia, 78
Bela Garda, 186
Belgrade, 1, 8, 13, 27, 40, 79, 83, 122, 124, 130, 131, 160–1; fall of, 175
Belgrade, Metropolitan of, 82
Belgrade, pashalik of, 75, 76, 81
Belgrade, Treaty of (1739), 72
Belgrade–Bar railway, 279
Benedictine monks, 17
Berchtold, Count, 113, 119
Beria, Lavrenti, 238
Berlin, Congress of (1878), 23, 103

298